Reading STREET

Program Authors

Peter Afflerbach
Camille Blachowicz
Candy Dawson Boyd
Elena Izquierdo
Connie Juel
Edward Kame'enui
Donald Leu
Jeanne R. Paratore

P. David Pearson
Sam Sebesta
Deborah Simmons
Alfred Tatum
Sharon Vaughn
Susan Watts Taffe
Karen Kring Wixson

PEARSON

Glenview, Illinois • Boston, Massachusetts
Chandler, Arizona • Upper Saddle River, New Jersey

We dedicate Reading Street to
Peter Jovanovich.

His wisdom, courage,
and passion for education
are an inspiration to us all.

Accelerated Reader®

PEARSON

ISBN-13: 978-0-328-46991-8
ISBN-10: 0-328-46991-2
2 3 4 5 6 7 8 9 10 V064 14 13 12 11 10
CC1

Any Path, Any Pace

"Welcome to
Reading Street!
Bienvenidos too."

PEARSON

PEARSON SCOTT FORESMAN

Find Your Place on Reading Street!

Who said so?

Program Authors

Peter Afflerbach, Ph.D.
Professor
Department of Curriculum and
Instruction
University of Maryland at
College Park

**Camille L. Z. Blachowicz,
Ph.D.**
Professor of Education
National-Louis University

Candy Dawson Boyd, Ph.D.
Professor
School of Education
Saint Mary's College of California

Elena Izquierdo, Ph.D.
Associate Professor
University of Texas at El Paso

Connie Juel, Ph.D.
Professor of Education
School of Education
Stanford University

Edward J. Kame'enui, Ph.D.
*Dean-Knight Professor of
Education and Director*
Institute for the Development of
Educational Achievement and
the Center on Teaching and Learning
College of Education
University of Oregon

Donald J. Leu, Ph.D.
*John and Maria Neag Endowed
Chair in Literacy and Technology
Director, The New Literacies
Research Lab*
University of Connecticut

Jeanne R. Paratore, Ed.D.
Associate Professor of Education
Department of Literacy and
Language Development
Boston University

P. David Pearson, Ph.D.
Professor and Dean
Graduate School of Education
University of California, Berkeley

Sam L. Sebesta, Ed.D.
Professor Emeritus
College of Education
University of Washington, Seattle

Deborah Simmons, Ph.D
Professor
College of Education and
Human Development
Texas A&M University

Alfred W. Tatum, Ph.D.
*Associate Professor and Director
of the UIC Reading Clinic*
University of Illinois at Chicago

Sharon Vaughn, Ph.D.
*H. E. Hartfelder/Southland
Corporation Regents Professor
Director, Meadows Center for
Preventing Educational Risk*
University of Texas

Susan Watts Taffe, Ph.D.
Associate Professor in Literacy
Division of Teacher Education
University of Cincinnati

Karen Kring Wixson, Ph.D.
Professor of Education
University of Michigan

Consulting Authors

Jeff Anderson, M.Ed.
Author and Consultant
San Antonio, Texas

Jim Cummins, Ph.D.
Professor
Department of Curriculum,
Teaching and Learning
University of Toronto

Lily Wong Fillmore, Ph.D.
Professor Emerita
Graduate School of Education
University of California, Berkeley

Georgia Earnest García, Ph.D.
Professor
Language and Literacy Division
Department of Curriculum
and Instruction
University of Illinois at
Urbana-Champaign

George A. González, Ph.D.
Professor (Retired)
School of Education
University of Texas-Pan American,
Edinburg

Valerie Ooka Pang, Ph.D.
Professor
School of Teacher Education
San Diego State University

Sally M. Reis, Ph.D.
*Board of Trustees Distinguished
Professor*
Department of Educational
Psychology
University of Connecticut

Jon Scieszka, M.F.A.
*Children's Book Author
Founder of GUYS READ
Named First National Ambassador
for Young People's Literature 2008*

Grant Wiggins, Ed.D.
Educational Consultant
Authentic Education
Concept Development

Lee Wright, M.Ed.
Pearland, Texas

Practitioners, and Authors.

Consultant

Sharroky Hollie, Ph.D.
Assistant Professor
California State University
Dominguez Hills, CA

Teacher Reviewers

Dr. Bettyann Brugger
Educational Support Coordinator–
Reading Office
Milwaukee Public Schools
Milwaukee, WI

Kathleen Burke
K–12 Reading Coordinator
Peoria Public Schools, Peoria, IL

Darci Burns, M.S.Ed.
University of Oregon

Bridget Cantrell
District Intervention Specialist
Blackburn Elementary School
Independence, MO

Tahira DuPree Chase,
M.A., M.S.Ed.
Administrator of Elementary
English Language Arts
Mount Vernon City School District
Mount Vernon, NY

Michele Conner
Director, Elementary Education
Aiken County School District
Aiken, SC

Georgia Coulombe
K–6 Regional Trainer/
Literacy Specialist
Regional Center for Training and
Learning (RCTL), Reno, NV

Kelly Dalmas
Third Grade Teacher
Avery's Creek Elementary, Arden, NC

Seely Dillard
First Grade Teacher
Laurel Hill Primary School
Mt. Pleasant, SC

Jodi Dodds-Kinner
Director of Elementary Reading
Chicago Public Schools, Chicago, IL

Dr. Ann Wild Evenson
District Instructional Coach
Osseo Area Schools, Maple Grove, MN

Stephanie Fascitelli
Principal
Apache Elementary, Albuquerque
Public Schools, Albuquerque, NM

Alice Franklin
Elementary Coordinator, Language
Arts & Reading
Spokane Public Schools, Spokane, WA

Laureen Fromberg
Assistant Principal
PS100 Queens, NY

Kimberly Gibson
First Grade Teacher
Edgar B. Davis Community School
Brockton, MA

Kristen Gray
Lead Teacher
A.T. Allen Elementary School
Concord, NC

Mary Ellen Hazen
State Pre-K Teacher
Rockford Public Schools #205
Rockford, IL

Patrick M. Johnson
Elementary Instructional Director
Seattle Public Schools, Seattle, WA

Theresa Jaramillo Jones
Principal
Highland Elementary School
Las Cruces, NM

Sophie Kowzun
Program Supervisor, Reading/
Language Arts, PreK–5
Montgomery County Public Schools
Rockville, MD

David W. Matthews
Sixth Grade Teacher
Easton Area Middle School
Easton, PA

Ana Nuncio
Editor and Independent Publisher
Salem, MA

Joseph Peila
Principal
Chappell Elementary School
Chicago, IL

Ivana Reimer
Literacy Coordinator
PS100 Queens, NY

Sally Riley
Curriculum Coordinator
Rochester Public Schools
Rochester, NH

Dyan M. Smiley
Independent Educational Consultant

Michael J. Swiatowiec
Lead Literacy Teacher
Graham Elementary School
Chicago, IL

Dr. Helen Taylor
Director of English Education
Portsmouth City Public Schools
Portsmouth, VA

Carol Thompson
Teaching and Learning Coach
Independence School District
Independence, MO

Erinn Zeitlin
Kindergarten Teacher
Carderock Springs Elementary School
Bethesda, MD

Any Path, Any Pace

UNIT 6

Putting It Together

In this Teacher's Edition Unit 6, Volume 1

Table of Contents..vi–xiii
Unit 6 Skills Overview ....xiv–xv
Unit 6 Monitor Progress ....xvi–xvii
Assessment and Grouping..............................xviii–xix
Unit 6 Concept Launch .... xx–xxi
Flexible Pacing Plans.. xxii

WEEK 1 • Building with Dad

Informational Fiction...7–106

Differentiated Instruction SI OL A ELL ....DI•1–DI•17

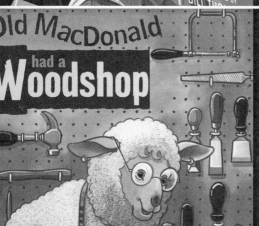

WEEK 2 • Old MacDonald had a Woodshop Animal Fantasy

Old MacDonald had a Woodshop Animal Fantasy.................................107–204

Differentiated Instruction SI OL A ELL ....DI•18–DI•34

WEEK 3 • Building Beavers

Expository Nonfiction...205–304

Differentiated Instruction SI OL A ELL ....DI•35–DI•51

Customize Literacy..CL•1–CL•31

In the **First Stop** on Reading Street

- **Dear Kindergarten Teacher**

- **Research into Practice on Reading Street**

- **Guide to Reading Street**

- **Assessment on Reading Street**

- **Differentiated Instruction on Reading Street**

- **ELL on Reading Street**

- **Customize Literacy on Reading Street**

- **21ˢᵗ Century Skills on Reading Street**

- **Teacher Resources for Kindergarten**

- **Index**

 GO Digital!

See It!

- **Big Question Video**

- **Concept Talk Video**

- **Envision It! Animations**

- **Sing With Me Animations**

Hear It!

- **Sing With Me Animations**

- **eReaders**

- **Grammar Jammer**

- **Leveled Reader Database**

Do It!

- **Story Sort**

- **Letter Tile Drag and Drop**

All Together Now

Table of Contents..vi–xiii
Unit 1 Skills Overview ....xiv–xv
Unit 1 Monitor Progress ....xvi–xvii
Assessment and Grouping ....xviii–xix
Unit 1 Concept Launch .... xx–xxi
Flexible Pacing Plans xxii

Volume 1

WEEK 1 • **The Little School Bus**
Animal Fantasy 7–108

Differentiated Instruction SI OL A ELL ....DI•1–DI•17

WEEK 2 • **We Are So Proud!** Realistic Fiction...........109–204

Differentiated Instruction SI OL A ELL ....DI•18–DI•34

WEEK 3 • **Plaidypus Lost** Realistic Fiction 205–310

Differentiated Instruction SI OL A ELL ....DI•35–DI•51

Volume 2

WEEK 4 • **Miss Bindergarten Takes a Field Trip with Kindergarten** Animal Fantasy 311–416

Differentiated Instruction SI OL A ELL ....DI•52–DI•68

WEEK 5 • **Smash! Crash!** Fantasy 417–518

Differentiated Instruction SI OL A ELL ....DI•69–DI•85

WEEK 6 • **Dig Dig Digging** Nonfiction...........................519–615

Differentiated Instruction SI OL A ELL ....DI•86–DI•102

Customize Literacy..CL•1–CL•31

UNIT 2

Look at Us!

Table of Contents.. vi–xiii
Unit 2 Skills Overview .... xiv–xv
Unit 2 Monitor Progress .... xvi–xvii
Assessment and Grouping .... xviii–xix
Unit 2 Concept Launch .... xx–xxi
Flexible Pacing Plans xxii

Volume 1

WEEK 1 • Flowers Nonfiction 7–104

Differentiated Instruction SI OL A ELL .... DI•1–DI•17

WEEK 2 • Nature Spy Nonfiction 105–204

Differentiated Instruction SI OL A ELL .... DI•18–DI•34

WEEK 3 • Animal Babies in Grasslands
Nonfiction 205–304

Differentiated Instruction SI OL A ELL .... DI•35–DI•51

Volume 2

WEEK 4 • Bear Snores On Animal Fantasy 305–406

Differentiated Instruction SI OL A ELL .... DI•52–DI•68

WEEK 5 • A Bed for the Winter Nonfiction 407–506

Differentiated Instruction SI OL A ELL .... DI•69–DI•85

WEEK 6 • Jack and the Beanstalk Fairy Tale 507–603

Differentiated Instruction SI OL A ELL .... DI•86–DI•102

Customize Literacy .... CL•1–CL•31

ix

UNIT 3

Changes All Around Us

Table of Contents.. vi–xiii
Unit 3 Skills Overview ....xiv–xv
Unit 3 Monitor Progress ....xvi–xvii
Assessment and Grouping ....xviii–xix
Unit 3 Concept Launch .... xx–xxi
Flexible Pacing Plans xxii

Volume 1

WEEK 1 • **Little Panda** Nonfiction 7–106

Differentiated Instruction SI OL A ELL .... DI•1–DI•17

WEEK 2 • **Little Quack** Animal Fantasy.............................107–206

Differentiated Instruction SI OL A ELL .... DI•18–DI•34

WEEK 3 • **George Washington Visits**

Historical Fiction..207–304

Differentiated Instruction SI OL A ELL .... DI•35–DI•51

Volume 2

WEEK 4 • **Farfallina and Marcel**

Animal Fantasy 305–404

Differentiated Instruction SI OL A ELL .... DI•52–DI•68

WEEK 5 • **Then and Now** Nonfiction.............................405–502

Differentiated Instruction SI OL A ELL .... DI•69–DI•85

WEEK 6 • **The Lion and the Mouse**

Classic Fable 503–599

Differentiated Instruction SI OL A ELL .... DI•86–DI•102

Customize Literacy...CL•1–CL•31

UNIT 4

Let's Go Exploring

Table of Contents.. vi–xiii
Unit 4 Skills Overview .... xiv–xv
Unit 4 Monitor Progress .... xvi–xvii
Assessment and Grouping .... xviii–xix
Unit 4 Concept Launch .... xx–xxi
Flexible Pacing Plans xxii

Volume 1

WEEK 1 • Rooster's Off to See the World
Animal Fantasy 7–102

Differentiated Instruction **SI** **OL** **A** **ELL** .... DI•1–DI•17

WEEK 2 • My Lucky Day Animal Fantasy 103–204

Differentiated Instruction **SI** **OL** **A** **ELL** .... DI•18–DI•34

WEEK 3 • One Little Mouse Animal Fantasy 205–304

Differentiated Instruction **SI** **OL** **A** **ELL** .... DI•35–DI•51

Volume 2

WEEK 4 • Goldilocks and the Three Bears
Classic Fairy Tale 305–406

Differentiated Instruction **SI** **OL** **A** **ELL** .... DI•52–DI•68

WEEK 5 • If You Could Go to Antarctica
Nonfiction 407–502

Differentiated Instruction **SI** **OL** **A** **ELL** .... DI•69–DI•85

WEEK 6 • Abuela Fantasy 503–605

Differentiated Instruction **SI** **OL** **A** **ELL** .... DI•86–DI•102

Customize Literacy .... CL•1–CL•31

UNIT 5

Going Places

Table of Contents...vi–xiii
Unit 5 Skills Overview ....xiv–xv
Unit 5 Monitor Progress ....xvi–xvii
Assessment and Grouping .... xviii–xix
Unit 5 Concept Launch .... xx–xxi
Flexible Pacing Plans xxii

Volume 1

WEEK 1 • Max Takes the Train Animal Fantasy.........7–104

Differentiated Instruction SI OL A ELL ....DI•1–DI•17

WEEK 2 • Mayday! Mayday! Nonfiction.................105–210

Differentiated Instruction SI OL A ELL ....DI•18–DI•34

WEEK 3 • Trucks Roll! Rhyming Nonfiction.......................211–310

Differentiated Instruction SI OL A ELL ....DI•35–DI•51

Volume 2

WEEK 4 • The Little Engine That Could
Classic Fantasy 311–414

Differentiated Instruction SI OL A ELL ....DI•52–DI•68

WEEK 5 • On the Move! Nonfiction 415–512

Differentiated Instruction SI OL A ELL ....DI•69–DI•85

WEEK 6 • This Is the Way We Go to School Informational Fiction...513–615

Differentiated Instruction SI OL A ELL ....DI•86–DI•102

Customize Literacy...CL•1–CL•31

Putting It Together

Key
SI Strategic Intervention
OL On-Level
A Advanced
ELL ELL

Table of Contents...vi–xiii
Unit 6 Skills Overview ....xiv–xv
Unit 6 Monitor Progress...xvi–xvii
Assessment and Grouping...xviii–xix
Unit 6 Concept Launch ....xx–xxi
Flexible Pacing Plans..xxii

Volume 1

WEEK 1 • Building with Dad Informational Fiction........7–106

Differentiated Instruction SI OL A ELL ....DI•1–DI•17

WEEK 2 • Old MacDonald had a Woodshop
Animal Fantasy...107–204

Differentiated Instruction SI OL A ELL ....DI•18–DI•34

WEEK 3 • Building Beavers Expository Nonfiction......205–304

Differentiated Instruction SI OL A ELL ....DI•35–DI•51

Volume 2

WEEK 4 • Alistair and Kip's Great Adventure Animal Fantasy..305–406

Differentiated Instruction SI OL A ELL ....DI•52–DI•68

WEEK 5 • The House That Tony Lives In
Informational Fiction...407–502

Differentiated Instruction SI OL A ELL ....DI•69–DI•85

WEEK 6 • Ants and Their Nests
Expository Nonfiction..503–599

Differentiated Instruction SI OL A ELL ....DI•86–DI•102

Customize Literacy...CL•1–CL•31

Skills Overview

Key	
T	Tested
🎯	Target Skill

Building with Dad
Informational Text pp. 59–73

Old MacDonald had a Woodshop
Animal Fantasy pp. 160–171

Get Ready to Read

	WEEK 1	WEEK 2
Question of the Week	How is a school built?	What tools do you need to build things?
Amazing Words	groundbreaking, trenches, foundation, welding, waterproof, gleaming	saw, drill, hammer, screwdriver, file, chisel
Phonemic Awareness	**T** 🎯 /a/ **T** 🎯 /i/	**T** 🎯 /o/
Phonics	**T** 🎯 /a/ Spelled *Aa* **T** 🎯 /i/ Spelled *Ii* **Review** /y/ Spelled *Yy*; /kw/ Spelled *qu*	**T** 🎯 /o/ Spelled *Oo* **Review** /a/ Spelled *Aa*; /i/ Spelled *Ii*
High-Frequency Words	**T** *here, do, little, with, what*	**T** *where, is, go, that, come*

Read and Comprehend

	WEEK 1	WEEK 2
Comprehension	🎯 **Skill** Compare and Contrast **Review** Draw Conclusions	**T** 🎯 **Skill** Character **Review** Plot

Language Arts

	WEEK 1	WEEK 2
Writing	List	Song
Conventions	Pronouns *I* and *me*	Prepositional Phrases
Vocabulary	Compound Words	Location Words
Speaking/Listening	Recite Language	Discuss Fact and Opinion

The Big Question

What are different ways of building?

WEEK 3	WEEK 4	WEEK 5	WEEK 6

Building Beavers Expository Nonfiction pp. 257–271	**Alistair and Kip's Great Adventure** Animal Fantasy pp. 358–373	**The House That Tony Lives In** Informational Fiction pp. 459–469	**Ants and Their Nests** Expository Nonfiction pp. 556–567
How do beavers build their homes?	What can friends build together?	Who helps to build a house?	How do ants build their nests?
beaver, lodge, paddle, river, stream, lake	*gathered, distant, drifting, voyage, island, aboard*	*architect, electricians, plumbers, painters, landscapers, movers*	*colony, underground, chambers, silk, twigs, pebbles*
T /e/	**T** /u/	**T** Initial, Medial, and Final Sounds	**T** Initial, Medial, and Final Sounds
T /e/ Spelled *Ee* **Review** Short Vowels	**T** /u/ Spelled *Uu* **Review** /e/ Spelled *Ee*	**T** Decode Words **Review** Decode Words	**T** Decode Words **Review** Decode Words
T *the, was, to, like, from*	**T** *for, of, my, we, yellow*	**T** *have, they, four, two, blue*	**T** *you, said, see, look, three*
T **Skill** Main Idea **Review** Cause and Effect	**T** **Skill** Plot **Review** Draw Conclusions	**T** **Skill** Setting **Review** Realism and Fantasy	**Skill** Draw Conclusions **Review** Compare and Contrast
Rhyme	Rhyme	Poem	Writing Process: Report
Telling Sentences	Questions	Exclamations	Complete Sentences
Words for Actions	Location Words	Words for Feelings	Words for Bugs
Interpret Information	Discuss Literary Elements: Character	Oral Presentations: Book Report	Discuss Literary Elements: Setting

UNIT **6**

Monitor Progress
Make Data-Driven Decisions

Data Management
- Assess
- Diagnose
- Prescribe
- Disaggregate

Classroom Management
- Monitor Progress
- Group
- Differentiate Instruction
- Inform Parents

Don't Wait Until Friday!

SUCCESS PREDICTOR	WEEK 1	WEEK 2	WEEK 3	WEEK 4
Phonemic Awareness *(Phonemic Awareness)*	T /a/ T /i/	T /o/	T /e/	T /u/
Phonics *(Sound-Spelling)*	T /a/ Spelled *Aa* T /i/ Spelled *Ii*	T /o/ Spelled *Oo*	T /e/ Spelled *Ee*	T /u/ Spelled *Uu*
High-Frequency Words *(Word Reading)*	T here T do T little T with T what	T where T is T go T that T come	T the T was T to T like T from	T for T of T my T we T yellow
Oral Vocabulary/ Concept Development (assessed informally)	groundbreaking trenches foundation welding waterproof gleaming	saw drill hammer screwdriver file chisel	beaver lodge paddle river stream lake	gathered distant drifting voyage island aboard
Comprehension *(Retelling)*	T **Skill** Compare and Contrast **Strategies** Preview and Predict; Retell	T **Skill** Character **Strategies** Preview and Predict; Retell	T **Skill** Main Idea **Strategies** Preview and Predict; Retell	T **Skill** Plot **Strategies** Preview and Predict; Retell

WEEK 5	WEEK 6
T Initial, Medial, and Final Sounds	**T** Initial, Medial, and Final Sounds
T Decode Words	**T** Decode Words
T have **T** they **T** four **T** two **T** blue	**T** you **T** said **T** see **T** look **T** three
architect electricians plumbers painters landscapers movers	colony underground chambers silk twigs pebbles
T **Skill** Setting **Strategies** Preview and Predict; Retell	**T** **Skill** Draw Conclusions **Strategies** Preview and Predict; Retell

GO Digital!

See It!

- **Big Question Video**
- **Concept Talk Video**
- **Envision It! Animations**
- **Sing with Me Animations**

Hear It!

- **Sing with Me Animations**
- **eReaders**
- **Grammar Jammer**
- **Leveled Reader Database**

Do It!

- **Story Sort**
- **Letter Tile Drag and Drop**

Assessment and Grouping
for Data-Driven Instruction

4-Step Plan for Assessment
1 Diagnose and Differentiate
2 Monitor Progress
3 Assess and Regroup
4 Summative Assessment

STEP 1 Diagnose and Differentiate

Baseline Group Tests

Diagnose

To make initial grouping decisions, use the Baseline Group Test, the Texas Primary Reading Inventory (TPRI), or another initial placement test. Depending on students' ability levels, you may have more than one of each group.

Differentiate

If... student performance is **SI** **then...** use the regular instruction and the daily **Strategic Intervention** small group lessons.

If... student performance is **OL** **then...** use the regular instruction and the daily **On-Level** small group lessons.

If... student performance is **A** **then...** use the regular instruction and the daily **Advanced** learners small group lessons.

Small Group Time

SI Strategic Intervention

- Daily small group lessons provide more intensive instruction, more scaffolding, more practice, and more opportunities to respond.
- Reteach lessons in the *First Stop* provide more instruction of target skills.
- Leveled readers, decodable readers, and other weekly texts build background and provide practice for target skills and vocabulary.

OL On-Level

- Explicit instructional routines teach core skills and strategies.
- Daily On-Level lessons provide more practice and more opportunities to respond.
- Independent activities provide practice for core skills.
- Student Readers and Get Set, Roll! Readers provide additional reading and practice for core skills and vocabulary.

A Advanced

- Daily Advanced lessons provide instruction for accelerated learning.
- Independent Leveled Readers provide additional reading tied to lesson concepts and skills.

Additional Differentiated Learning Options

Reading Street Response to Intervention Kit
- Focused intervention lessons on the five critical areas of reading: phonemic awareness, phonics, vocabulary, comprehension, and fluency

My Sidewalks on Reading Street
- Early Reading Intervention

Don't Wait Until Friday

Use these tools during lesson teaching to **monitor student progress.**

- **Skill and Strategy** instruction during reading

- **Don't Wait Until Friday** boxes to check letter and sound fluency, word reading, retelling, and oral vocabulary

- **Weekly Assessment** on Day 5 to check phonics, high-frequency words, and comprehension

- **Reader's and Writer's Notebook** pages at point of use

Weekly Phonics and High-Frequency Words Assessment

Weekly Comprehension Assessment

STEP **3** Assess and Regroup

Use these tools during lesson teaching to **assess and regroup.**

- **Weekly Assessments** Record results of weekly assessments for phonics and high-frequency words to track student progress.

- **Unit Benchmark Assessment** Administer this assessment to check progress of unit skills.

- **Regroup** We recommend the first regrouping to be at the end of Unit 2. Use weekly assessment information and Unit Benchmark Assessment performance to inform regrouping decisions. Then regroup at the end of each subsequent unit.

Unit 1 Reading Chart in First Stop

Group

Baseline Group Test → Regroup Units 1 and 2 → Regroup Unit 3 → Regroup Unit 4 → Regroup Unit 5 → **End of Year**

| Unit 1 Weeks 1–6 | Unit 2 Weeks 7–12 | Unit 3 Weeks 13–18 | Unit 4 Weeks 19–24 | Unit 5 Weeks 25–30 | Unit 6 Weeks 31–36 |

Outside assessments, such as DRA, TPRI, and DIBELS, may recommend regrouping at other times during the year.

STEP **4** Summative Assessment

Use these tools after lesson teaching to **assess students.**

- **Unit Benchmark Assessments** Use to measure a student's mastery of unit skills.

- **End-of-Year Benchmark Assessment** Use to measure a student's mastery of program skills covered in all six units.

Unit and End-of-Year Benchmark Assessment

Concept Launch

Putting It Together

Reading Street Online
www.ReadingStreet.com
• Big Question Video
• Envision It! Animations
• Story Sort

What are different ways of building?

UNIT 6

Small Group Time
Flexible Pacing Plans

Small Group Time

Sometimes you have holidays, programs, assemblies, or other interruptions to the school week. This plan can help you make Small Group Time decisions if you have less time during the week.

Key
- **SI** Strategic Intervention
- **OL** On-Level
- **A** Advanced
- **ELL** ELL

5 Day Plan

DAY 1
- Phonemic Awareness
- Phonics
- Reading Practice

DAY 2
- Phonemic Awareness
- Phonics
- Reading Practice

DAY 3
- Phonemic Awareness/ Phonics
- Leveled Reader

DAY 4
- Phonemic Awareness
- Reading Practice

DAY 5
- Phonics
- Reading Practice

4 Day Plan

DAY 1
- Phonemic Awareness
- Phonics
- Reading Practice

DAY 2
- Phonemic Awareness
- Phonics
- Reading Practice

DAY 3
- Phonemic Awareness/ Phonics
- Leveled Reader

DAY 4
- Phonemic Awareness
- Reading Practice

3 Day Plan

DAY 1
- Phonemic Awareness
- Phonics
- Reading Practice

DAY 2
- Phonemic Awareness/ Phonics
- Leveled Reader

DAY 3
- Phonemic Awareness
- Reading Practice

ELL

5 Day Plan

DAY 1
- Frontload Concept
- Phonemic Awareness/ Phonics
- Comprehension

DAY 2
- Comprehension
- Vocabulary

DAY 3
- Phonemic Awareness/ Phonics
- Conventions

DAY 4
- Phonemic Awareness/ Phonics
- Concepts and Oral Language

DAY 5
- Language Workshop
- Writing

4 Day Plan

DAY 1
- Frontload Concept
- Phonemic Awareness/ Phonics
- Comprehension

DAY 2
- Comprehension
- Vocabulary

DAY 3
- Phonemic Awareness/ Phonics
- Conventions

DAY 4
- Language Workshop
- Writing

3 Day Plan

DAY 1
- Frontload Concept
- Phonemic Awareness/ Phonics
- Comprehension

DAY 2
- Phonemic Awareness/ Phonics
- Conventions

DAY 3
- Language Workshop
- Writing

Common Core Standards
Weekly Planning Guide

Selection: Building with Dad
Genre: Informational Fiction

Alignment of the Common Core Standards with This Week's Skills and Strategies

This Week's Common Core Standards for English Language Arts	Instructional Summary
Reading Standards for Informational Text	
Informational Text 1. With prompting and support, ask and answer questions about key details in a text.	This week's lesson focuses on the skill **compare and contrast.** It explains that comparing is telling how two things are alike and contrasting is telling how two things are different. The lesson instruction for **predict** and **set a purpose** helps children look at the selection to predict what the selection might be about and to set a purpose to help them understand what they read.
Informational Text 2. With prompting and support, identify the main topic and retell key details of a text.	
Informational Text 3. With prompting and support, describe the connection between two individuals, events, ideas, or pieces of information in a text.	
Foundational Skills Standards	
Foundational Skills 2.e. Add or substitute individual sounds (phonemes) in simple, one-syllable words to make new words.	The lesson includes work with **blending** phonemes to make words. This week, children will use /a/ and /i/ sounds as well as reviewing /y/ and /kw/. Children will also apply blending skills as well as other **word analysis** skills to decode words.
Foundational Skills 3.b. Associate the long and short sounds with the common spellings (graphemes) for the five major vowels.	
Writing Standards	
Writing 2. Use a combination of drawing, dictating, and writing to compose informative/explanatory texts in which they name what they are writing about and supply some information about the topic.	Writing activities include sharing **ideas** about things that make us special. Group activities for writing include a **response** to the literature, a **list,** and writing about how to make a classroom garden. The wrap-up activities ask children to tell about their favorite book or song in this week's lesson and to write a **poem.**
Writing 6. With guidance and support from adults, explore a variety of digital tools to produce and publish writing, including in collaboration with peers.	
Speaking and Listening Standards	
Speaking/Listening 1.a. Follow agreed-upon rules for discussions (e.g., listening to others and taking turns speaking about the topics and texts under discussion).	In the **listening** and **speaking** activities, children practice reciting language or saying things from memory. Children recite the Pledge of Allegiance and simple poems and rhymes.
Language Standards	
Language 1. Demonstrate command of the conventions of standard English grammar and usage when writing or speaking.	Children work with the **pronouns** *I* and *me* and learn that the pronoun *I* is used as the subject of a sentence while the pronoun *me* is used after an action verb. The lesson also teaches children about word meaning as they read the selections in the lesson.
Language 5. With guidance and support from adults, explore word relationships and nuances in word meanings.	
Language 6. Use words and phrases acquired through conversations, reading and being read to, and responding to texts.	

Additional Support for a Common Core Standard This Week

Use the following instruction to supplement the teaching of one of this week's Common Core Standards.

Common Core Standard: Language 1.
Write this sentence frame: _____ *got a book.* Say this sentence: *Bob got a book.* Ask children to tell what word you used to finish the sentence. Repeat with this sentence: *I got a book.* Point out to children that the pronoun *I* can be used to take the place of a name.

• Write this sentence frame: _____ *went to school*. Have children write the sentence with their name and then write the sentence using the word *I*. Have volunteers read their sentences and tell which word *I* replaces.

• Continue the procedure with the sentence frame: *The book is for _____*. Read the sentence using a child's name and then have the child replace the name with the word *me* to complete the sentence frame.

• Have children continue creating other sentences with the pronouns *I* and *me.*

ISBN-13: 978-0-328-64361-5   ISBN-10: 0-328-64361-0

You Are Here: Week 1

Building with Dad

Question of the Week
How is a school built?

As children answer this unit's Big Question and this week's Question of the Week, they will address:

Reading 2. Determine central ideas or themes of a text and analyze their development; summarize the key supporting details and ideas. **(Also Reading 1.)**

Concept Talk Guide children as they discuss questions such as:

- What is cement used for?
- What kinds of machines are used to build the school?

As children answer this week's Concept Talk questions, they will address:

Speaking/Listening 1. Prepare for and participate effectively in a range of conversations and collaborations with diverse partners, building on others' ideas and expressing their own clearly and persuasively.

Writing Have them write or dictate a list of things from *Building with Dad* they want to learn more about.

As children write this week, they will address:

Writing 2. Write informative/explanatory texts to examine and convey complex ideas and information clearly and accurately through the effective selection, organization, and analysis of content.

Listening and Speaking On page 29, children learn to recite language.

As children do so, they address:

Speaking/Listening 1. Prepare for and participate effectively in a range of conversations and collaborations with diverse partners, building on others' ideas and expressing their own clearly and persuasively.

Grade K • Unit 6 • Week 1
Building with Dad

Unit 6

THE BIG Q **What are different ways of building?**

Common Core Standards and Concept Development

- Introduce and explore this unit's weekly concepts through rich, structured conversations
- Develop complex content knowledge and vocabulary
- Expand on a single concept with engaging literature and nonfiction
- Build better readers in all content areas

Get Ready For Grade 1
Align instruction to **Common Core Anchor Standards**

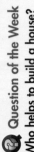

Week 6

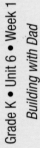

Ants and Their Nests

Question of the Week
How do ants build their nests?

Concept Talk Guide children as they discuss questions such as:

- Where do birds build their homes?
- Why do many animals build their homes in the ground?

Writing Reread and discuss what you wrote about how a bird builds a nest, underlining key words in your draft. Have children write or dictate the group draft or copy the underlined key words on p. 474 in *Reader's and Writer's Notebook*.

Week 5

The House That Tony Lives In

Question of the Week
Who helps to build a house?

Concept Talk Guide children as they discuss questions such as:

- What happened to this builder? How did the builder solve the problem?

Writing Have children turn to p. 458 of *Reader's and Writer's Notebook*. Have them copy a line from the poem about the house.

Week 4

Alistair and Kip's Great Adventure!

Question of the Week
What can friends build together?

Concept Talk Guide children as they discuss questions such as:

- What would you and your friends build using the large box? Would it be real or make-believe?

Writing Have children turn to p. 446 of *Reader's and Writer's Notebook*. Have them copy the poem about Alistair and Kip's trip and then draw a picture to go with it.

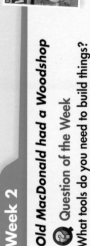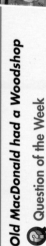

Week 3

Building Beavers

Question of the Week
How do beavers build their homes?

Concept Talk Guide children as they discuss questions such as:

- What new information did you learn about beavers?

Writing Have children turn to p. 434 of *Reader's and Writer's Notebook*. Have them copy the rhyme about beavers and draw a picture of the beaver.

Week 2

Old MacDonald had a Woodshop

Question of the Week
What tools do you need to build things?

Concept Talk Guide children as they discuss questions such as:

- What kind of sounds do these tools make?

Writing Have children turn to p. 422 of *Reader's and Writer's Notebook*. Have them complete the song "Old MacDonald" by copying an animal word from the list and then illustrating that animal. Sing the song with children, featuring each child's picture for a verse.

This Week's ELL Overview

ELL Handbook

- Maximize Literacy and Cognitive Engagement
- Research Into Practice
- Full Weekly Support for Every Selection

  ### Building with Dad
  - Routines to Support Instruction

- Transfer Activities
- Professional Development

Daily Leveled ELL Notes

ELL notes appear throughout this week's instruction and ELL Support is on the DI pages of your Teacher's Edition. The following is a sample of an ELL note from this week.

English Language Learners

Beginning Picture Support Point to details in the pictures on pp. 12–13 of *My Skills Buddy* as you say their corresponding words. To clarify understanding, have children point to the images as you say the words.

Intermediate Frontload Decodable Story 31 On the board, draw a large dog and label it *Kip.* Draw a small dog and label it *Sam.* Display p. 3 of Decodable Story 31 and say: If Kip can do it, Sam can do it. Kip can. Will Sam? Explain that this structure is used throughout the story. Helping children understand the basic language structure will help them comprehend the meaning of the story.

Advanced High-Frequency Words After the Team Talk activity, have children continue to work in pairs to check understanding. Have one child read one of the sentences aloud while another child makes a simple drawing to illustrate the sentences.

Advanced High Build Survival Vocabulary Use the Compare and Contrast picture to help children understand the expression "rain or shine." Point to the cloud and sun and say: Sometimes people will send you an invitation for a party or other event that says "rain or shine." That means the event will happen no matter what the weather is like, whether it is raining or the sun is shining.

ELL by Strand

The ELL lessons on this week's Support for English Language Learners pages are organized by strand. They offer additional scaffolding for the core curriculum. Leveled support notes on these pages address the different proficiency levels in your class. See pages DI•12–DI•17.

ELL Guy
Dr. Jim Cummins

The Three Pillars of ELL Instruction

ELL Strands	Activate Prior Knowledge	Access Content	Extend Language
Vocabulary p. DI•14	Frontload Vocabulary	Provide Scaffolding	Practice
Reading Comprehension p. DI•14	Provide Scaffolding	Set the Scene	Frontload Vocabulary
Phonics, Spelling, and Word Analysis pp. DI•12, DI•15–DI•16	Frontload Words with Initial /a/ and /i/	Isolate Medial /a/ and /i/	Review /y/ and /kw/
Listening Comprehension p. DI•13	Prepare for the Read Aloud	First Listening	Second Listening
Conventions and Writing pp. DI•15, DI•17	Provide Scaffolding/ Introduce and Model	Practice	Leveled Practice Activities/ Leveled Writing Activities
Concept Development p. DI•12	Read the Concept Literacy Reader	Read the Concept Literacy Reader	Develop Oral Language

This Week's Practice Stations Overview

Six Weekly Practice Stations with Leveled Activities can be found at the beginning of each week of instruction. For this week's Practice Stations, see pp. 14–15.

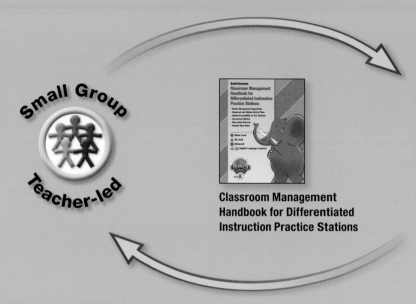

Practice Stations

Classroom Management Handbook for Differentiated Instruction Practice Stations

Small Group Teacher-led

Daily Leveled Center Activities

 Below   Advanced

 On-Level   E L L

Practice Stations Flip Charts

	 **Listen Up**	 **Word Work**	 **Words to Know**	 **Let's Write**	 **Read for Meaning**	 **Let's Make Art**
Objectives	• Identify beginning, middle, and ending sounds of words.	• Identify and build words.	• Identify and use action words.	• Write a how-to report.	• Draw a conclusion about a selection.	• Make a collage.
Materials	• *Listen Up* Flip Chart Activity 31 • Picture Cards • paper, pencils, crayons	• *Word Work* Flip Chart Activity 31 • Alphabet Cards • Picture Cards • Letter Tiles	• *Words to Know* Flip Chart Activity 31 • Find pictures (or take quick digital photos and print out) for action words: *ride, jump, skip, hop, climb* • Teacher-made Word Cards: *ride, jump, skip, hop, climb* • paper, pencils, crayons	• *Let's Write* Flip Chart Activity 31 • Teacher-made Writing Steps Poster: 1) Plan 2) Write 3) Revise 4) Edit 5) Share • books about different games • crayons, paper, pencil	• *Read for Meaning* Flip Chart Activity 31 • Trade Book *This Is the Way We Go to School* • paper, pencils, crayons	• *Let's Make Art* Flip Chart Activity 31 • Trade Book *This Is the Way We Go to School* • construction paper • art tissue • fabric scraps • safety scissors • glue

This Week on Reading Street!

 Question of the Week

How is a school built?

Daily Plan

 Don't Wait Until Friday

Whole Group

- ◉ /a/ Spelled *Aa*
- ◉ /i/ Spelled *Ii*
- ◉ Compare and Contrast
- • Vocabulary

MONITOR PROGRESS	Success Predictor			
Day 1 Check Phonemic Awareness	Day 2 Check Sound Spelling/ Retelling	Day 3 Check Word Reading	Day 4 Check Phonemic Awareness	Day 5 Check Oral Vocabulary

Small Group

Teacher-Led

- • Reading Support
- • Skill Support
- • Fluency Practice

Practice Stations

Independent Activities

Customize Literacy More support for a Balanced Literacy approach, see CL•1–CL•31.

Whole Group

- • Writing
- • Conventions: Pronouns *I* and *me*
- • Listening and Speaking

Assessment

- • Day 5 Assessment for Phonics
- • Day 5 Assessment for Comprehension

 You Are Here! Unit 6 Week 1

This Week's Reading Selections

Big Book
Genre: **Informational Fiction**

Decodable Reader 31

Leveled Readers

Get Set, Roll! Reader 31

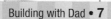

Resources on Reading Street!

	Build Concepts	Phonemic Awareness and Phonics	Vocabulary
Whole Group	Talk With Me/ Sing With Me	 Student Edition pp. 12–13 Student Edition p. 16	Student Edition p. 17 Student Edition p. 28
Go Digital	• Concept Talk Video • Sing with Me Animations	• eReaders	
Small Group and Independent Practice	 Practice Station Flip Chart — Leveled Readers	Practice Station Flip Chart Decodable Reader 31 Leveled Readers Get Set, Roll! Reader 31	Practice Station Flip Chart — Student Edition p. 17
Go Digital	• eReaders	• eReaders • Letter Tile Drag and Drop	
Customize Literacy	• Leveled Readers	• Decodable Reader	• High-Frequency Word Cards
Go Digital	• Concept Talk Video • Big Question Video • eReaders	• eReaders	• Sing with Me Animations

How is a school built?

Comprehension

Student Edition
pp. 14–15

Big Book

- Envision It! Animations

Practice Station
Flip Chart

Leveled
Readers

Get Set, Roll!
Reader 31

- Envision It! Animations
- eReaders

- Leveled Readers

- Envision It! Animations
- eReaders

Fluency

Decodable
Reader 31

Kdg. Student
Reader K.6.1

Get Set, Roll!
Reader 31

- eReaders

Practice Station
Flip Chart

Leveled Readers

- eReaders

- Leveled Readers

- eReaders

Conventions and Writing

Reader's and
Writer's Notebook

- Grammar Jammer

Practice Station
Flip Chart

Reader's and
Writer's Notebook

- Grammar Jammer

- *Reader's and Writer's Notebook*

- Grammar Jammer

You Are Here! Unit 6 Week 1

My 5-Day Planner for Reading Street!

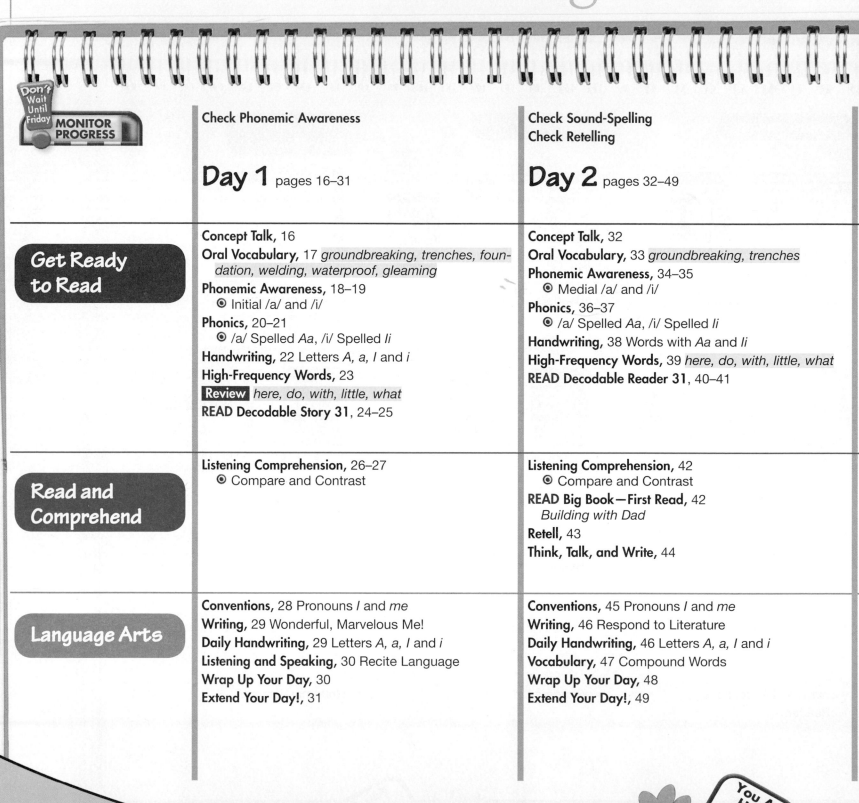

Don't Wait Until Friday
MONITOR PROGRESS

	Check Phonemic Awareness **Day 1** pages 16–31	Check Sound-Spelling Check Retelling **Day 2** pages 32–49
Get Ready to Read	**Concept Talk,** 16 **Oral Vocabulary,** 17 *groundbreaking, trenches, foundation, welding, waterproof, gleaming* **Phonemic Awareness,** 18–19 ◉ Initial /a/ and /i/ **Phonics,** 20–21 ◉ /a/ Spelled *Aa,* /i/ Spelled *Ii* **Handwriting,** 22 Letters *A, a, I* and *i* **High-Frequency Words,** 23 Review *here, do, with, little, what* **READ Decodable Story 31,** 24–25	**Concept Talk,** 32 **Oral Vocabulary,** 33 *groundbreaking, trenches* **Phonemic Awareness,** 34–35 ◉ Medial /a/ and /i/ **Phonics,** 36–37 ◉ /a/ Spelled *Aa,* /i/ Spelled *Ii* **Handwriting,** 38 Words with *Aa* and *Ii* **High-Frequency Words,** 39 *here, do, with, little, what* **READ Decodable Reader 31,** 40–41
Read and Comprehend	**Listening Comprehension,** 26–27 ◉ Compare and Contrast	**Listening Comprehension,** 42 ◉ Compare and Contrast **READ Big Book—First Read,** 42 *Building with Dad* **Retell,** 43 **Think, Talk, and Write,** 44
Language Arts	**Conventions,** 28 Pronouns *I* and *me* **Writing,** 29 Wonderful, Marvelous Me! **Daily Handwriting,** 29 Letters *A, a, I* and *i* **Listening and Speaking,** 30 Recite Language **Wrap Up Your Day,** 30 **Extend Your Day!,** 31	**Conventions,** 45 Pronouns *I* and *me* **Writing,** 46 Respond to Literature **Daily Handwriting,** 46 Letters *A, a, I* and *i* **Vocabulary,** 47 Compound Words **Wrap Up Your Day,** 48 **Extend Your Day!,** 49

You Are Here! Unit 6 Week 1

Question of the Week

How is a school built?

Check Word Reading	Check Phonemic Awareness	Check Oral Vocabulary
Day 3 pages 50–79	**Day 4** pages 80–91	**Day 5** pages 92–105
Concept Talk, 50 **Oral Vocabulary,** 51 *foundation, welding* **Phonemic Awareness,** 52–53 ◉ Medial /a/ and /i/ **Phonics,** 54–55 ◉ /a/ Spelled *Aa,* /i/ Spelled *Ii* **READ Kindergarten Student Reader K.6.1,** 56–57	**Concept Talk,** 80 **Oral Vocabulary,** 81 *waterproof, gleaming* <u>Review</u> **Phonemic Awareness,** 82 /y/ and /kw/ <u>Review</u> **Phonics,** 83 /y/ Spelled *Yy,* /kw/ Spelled *qu* **Spelling,** 84 ◉ /a/ Spelled *Aa,* /i/ Spelled *Ii* **READ Get Set, Roll! Reader 31,** 85	**Concept Wrap Up,** 92 **Oral Vocabulary,** 93 *groundbreaking, trenches, foundation, welding, waterproof, gleaming* <u>Review</u> **Phonemic Awareness,** 94 ◉ /a/ and /i/ <u>Review</u> **Phonics,** 95 ◉ /a/ Spelled *Aa,* /i/ Spelled *Ii* **Assessment,** 96–97 Monitor Progress
Comprehension, 58 ◉ Compare and Contrast **READ Big Book—Second Read,** 59–73 *Building with Dad*	**Comprehension,** 86 ◉ Compare and Contrast <u>Review</u> Draw Conclusions **READ Big Book—Third Read,** 87 *Building with Dad*	**Let's Practice It!,** 98–99 Expository Text **Assessment,** 100–101 Monitor Progress
Conventions, 74 Verbs **Writing,** 75 Genre: List **Daily Handwriting,** 75 Letters *A, a, I* and *i* **Listening and Speaking,** 76–77 Recite Language **Wrap Up Your Day,** 78 **Extend Your Day!,** 79	**Conventions,** 88 Pronouns *I* and *me* **Writing,** 89 Extend the Concept **Daily Handwriting,** 89 Letters *A, a, I* and *i* **Vocabulary,** 90 Compound Words **Wrap Up Your Day,** 90 **Extend Your Day!,** 91	<u>Review</u> **Conventions,** 102 Pronouns *I* and *me* **Writing,** 103 This Week We… **Daily Handwriting,** 103 Letters *A, a, I* and *i* **Wrap Up Your Week!,** 104 ⊗ How is a school built? **Extend Your Day!,** 105

Grouping Options for Differentiated Instruction
Turn the page for the small group time lesson plan.

Week 1

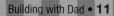

Planning Small Group Time on Reading Street!

SMALL GROUP TIME RESOURCES

DAY 1

Look for this Small Group Time box each day to help meet the individual needs of all your children. Differentiated instruction lessons appear on the DI pages at the end of each week.

Teacher-Led

SI Strategic Intervention	**OL** On-Level	**A** Advanced
Teacher-Led • Phonemic Awareness and Phonics **Reread** Decodable Story	**Teacher-Led** • Phonemic Awareness and Phonics **Reread** Decodable Story	**Teacher-Led** • Phonemic Awareness and Phonics **Reread** Decodable Story for Fluency

ELL Place English language learners in the groups that correspond to their reading abilities in English.

Practice Stations	**Independent Activities**
• Listen Up • Word Work	• Read Independently • *Reader's and Writer's Notebook* • Concept Talk Video

ELL Poster 31

Day 1

SI Strategic Intervention	**Phonemic Awareness and Phonics,** DI•1 **Reread** Decodable Story 31, DI•1	
OL On-Level	**Phonemic Awareness and Phonics,** DI•6 **Reread** Decodable Story 31, DI•6	
A Advanced	**Phonemic Awareness and Phonics,** DI•9 **Reread** Decodable Story 31 for Fluency, DI•9	
ELL English Language Learners	DI•12–DI•13 Frontload Concept Phonemic Awareness and Phonics Comprehension Skill	

Reading Street Response
to Intervention Kit

Reading Street Leveled
Practice Stations Kit

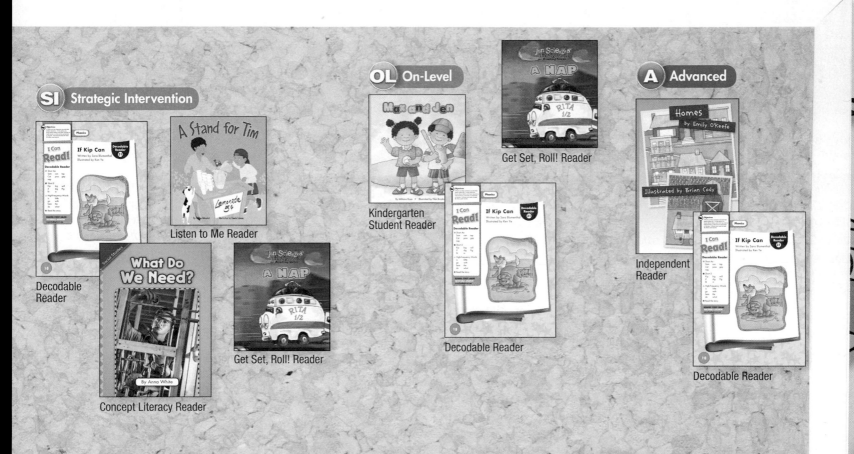

SI Strategic Intervention

OL On-Level

A Advanced

Listen to Me Reader

Decodable
Reader

What Do
We Need?
By Anna White

Concept Literacy Reader

Get Set, Roll! Reader

Kindergarten
Student Reader

Decodable Reader

Get Set, Roll! Reader

Independent
Reader

Decodable Reader

Week 1

Small Group Weekly Plan

Day 2	Day 3	Day 4	Day 5
Phonemic Awareness and Phonics, DI•2	**Phonemic Awareness and Phonics,** DI•3	**Phonemic Awareness and Phonics,** DI•4	**Phonics Review,** DI•5
Reread Decodable Reader 31, DI•2	**Read** Concept Literacy Reader K.6.1, DI•3	**Read** Get Set, Roll! Reader 31, DI•4	**Read** Listen to Me Reader K.6.1, DI•5
Phonemic Awareness and Phonics, DI•6	**Phonemic Awareness and Phonics,** DI•7	**Review Phonics and High-Frequency Words**	**Phonics Review,** DI•8
Reread Decodable Reader 31, DI•6	**Read** Kindergarten Student Reader K.6.1, DI•7	**Read** Get Set, Roll! Reader 31, DI•8	**Reread** Leveled Books, DI•8
Phonics and Spelling, DI•9	**Read** Independent Reader K.6.1 or Kindergarten Student Reader K.6.1, DI•10	**Read** Get Set, Roll! Reader 31 or **Reread** Kindergarten Student Reader K.6.1, DI•11	**Fluency and Comprehension,** DI•11
Reread Decodable Reader 31 for Fluency, DI•9			**Reread** Independent Reader K.6.1 for Fluency, DI•11
DI•14	DI•15	DI•16	DI•17
Comprehension Skill	Review Phonemic Awareness and Phonics	Review Phonemic Awareness and Phonics	Language Workshop
Frontload Vocabulary	Scaffold Conventions	Revisit Concepts and Oral Language	Writing

Practice Stations for Everyone on Reading Street!

Listen Up!
Beginning, middle, and ending sounds

Objectives
• Identify beginning, middle, and ending sounds of words.

Materials
• *Listen Up!* Flip Chart Activity 31
• Picture Cards: *ant, bed, can, cap, cat, desk, doll, egg, fan, hen, inch, jet, mop, net, ox, pig, red, six, ten, top, van, web*
• paper, pencils, crayons

Differentiated Activities

⬤ Choose a Picture Card. Say the sound you hear at the beginning. Find another Picture Card that has the same sound at the beginning. Find a Picture Card that has the same middle sound. Find a Picture Card that has the same ending sound.

▲ Choose a Picture Card. Say the sound you hear at the beginning. Say the sound you hear in the middle. Say the sound you hear at the end. Find other Picture Cards that have the same sounds.

■ Choose a Picture Card. Say the sound you hear at the beginning. Say the sound you hear in the middle. Say the sound you hear at the end. Sort the other Picture Cards into groups that have the same sounds.

Word Work
Sound-spellings

Objectives
• Identify and build words.

Materials
• *Word Work* Flip Chart Activity 31
• Alphabet Cards
• Picture Cards
• Letter Tiles

Differentiated Activities

⬤ Find the Alphabet Cards for the letters *Yy, Ww, Xx, Uu*. Find Picture Cards with the sounds /y/, /w/, /ks/, or /u/ at the beginning, middle, or end. Sort the Picture Cards into groups with the sounds /y/, /w/, /ks/, /u/.

▲ Find the Alphabet Cards for the letters *Yy, Ww, Xx, Uu*. Find Picture Cards with the sounds /y/, /w/, /ks/, or /u/ at the beginning, middle, or end. Choose an Alphabet Card. Use the Letter Tiles to build words that have the same sound at the beginning, middle, or end.

■ Find the Alphabet Cards for the letters *Yy, Ww, Xx, Uu*. Find Picture Cards with the sounds /y/, /w/, /ks/, or /u/ at the beginning, middle, or end. Use the Letter Tiles to build other words that have the same sounds at the beginning, middle, or end.

Technology
• Letter Tile Drag and Drop

Words To Know
Action words

Objectives
• Identify and use action words.

Materials
• *Words to Know* Flip Chart Activity 31
• Find pictures (or take quick digital photos and print out) for action words: *ride, jump, skip, hop, climb*
• Teacher-made word cards: *ride, jump, skip, hop, climb*
• paper, pencils, crayons

Differentiated Activities

⬤ Choose the picture cards that show the actions, *ride, jump, skip, hop,* and *climb*. Say the name for each picture.

▲ Match the picture cards and word cards that show the action words, *ride, jump, skip, hop,* and *climb*.

■ Match the picture cards and word cards that show *ride, jump, skip, hop,* and *climb*. Write a sentence tells about a time you ride, jump, skip, hop, or climb. Underline the action word that you use.

You Are Here! Unit 6 Week 1

Use this week's materials from the Reading Street Leveled Practice Stations Kit to organize this week's stations.

Key

● Below-Level Activities

▲ On-Level Activities

■ Advanced Activities

Practice Station Flip Chart

Let's Write!
How-to report

Objectives
• Write a how-to report.

Materials
• *Let's Write!* Flip Chart Activity 31
• Teacher-made writing steps poster:
  1) Plan 2) Write 3) Revise 4) Edit
  5) Share
• books about different games
• crayons, paper, pencil

Differentiated Activities

Direct all children to look at the Writing Steps poster.

● Look at the books that tell about games. Think about a game you like to play. Write sentences or draw pictures that tell how to play the game.

▲ What is your favorite game? What do you need to play the game? How many people can play? Write three sentences that tell how to play your favorite game.

■ What is your favorite game? What do you need to play the game? How many people can play? What are the rules? Write a how-to report that tells others how to play the game.

Read For Meaning
Draw conclusions

Objectives
• Draw a conclusion about a selection.

Materials
• *Read for Meaning* Flip Chart Activity 31
• Trade Book *This Is the Way We Go to School*
• paper, pencils, crayons

Differentiated Activities

To **draw a conclusion** we think about what we read and what we already know.

● Look at the selection. Choose a picture. What does this picture tell you? What do you already know about the picture? Draw a picture or write a sentence that tells what you know about where this child lives.

▲ Read the title. Look at the illustrations of the selection. Think about what you read. What did you already know? Draw a conclusion by writing a sentence that tells what you know about where this child lives.

■ Read the title. Look at the illustrations of the selection. Think about what you read. What did you already know? Draw a conclusion by writing about what you know about where this child lives.

Let's Make Art!

Objectives
• Make a collage.

Materials
• *Let's Make Art!* Flip Chart Activity 31
• Trade Book *This Is the Way We Go to School*
• construction paper
• art tissue
• fabric scraps
• safety scissors
• glue

Differentiated Activities

● Look at your story. Find pictures that show ways children go to school. Look at the shapes, colors, and lines. Use the art supplies to make a collage that shows different ways children around the world go to school.

▲ Look at your story. Find pictures that show ways children go to school. Make a collage that shows different ways children around the world go to school. Think about ways to use shape, color, and line as you create your collage.

■ Look at your story. Find pictures that show ways children go to school. Make a collage that shows different ways children around the world go to school. Think about ways to use shape, color, and line. Use a variety of textures as you create your collage.

My Weekly Work Plan

Objectives
• Share information and ideas about the concept.

Today at a Glance

Oral Vocabulary
groundbreaking, trenches, foundation, welding, waterproof, gleaming

Phonemic Awareness
◉ Initial /a/ and /i/

Phonics
◉ /a/ Spelled *Aa*
◉ /i/ Spelled *Ii*

Handwriting
A, a, I, and *i*

High-Frequency Words
here, do, little, with, what

Comprehension
◉ Compare and Contrast

Conventions
Verbs That Add -*s*

Writing
Wonderful, Marvelous Me!

Listening and Speaking
Recite Language

TRUCKTOWN on Reading Street

Start your engines! Display p. 10 of *Truckery Rhymes.*

• Read aloud "This Is the Way" and track the print.

• Reread the rhyme and have children chime in as they wish.

• Ask children to identify words that repeat. (*scoop, dump, smooth, dirt*)

Truckery Rhymes

Concept Talk

Question of the Week

How is a school built?

Introduce the concept

To build concepts and to focus children's attention, tell them that this week they will talk, sing, read, and write about **building a school.** Track each word as you read the question of the week.

Play the CD that features the process of a new school being built. What is cement used for? What kinds of machines are used to build the school?

🔘 Background Building Audio

ROUTINE   Activate Prior Knowledge   Team Talk

1 **Think** Have children think for a minute about what they know about the steps to build a school.

2 **Pair** Have pairs of children discuss the question of the week. Remind them to take turns speaking. Have children use complete sentences in their discussions about building.

3 **Share** Call on a few children to share their ideas with the group. Guide discussion and encourage elaboration with prompts such as: What kinds of workers help build a school?

Routines Flip Chart

Anchored Talk

Develop oral language

Display Talk with Me Chart 31A. This week we will talk about how a new school is built. The chart shows some words from the story that tell about this process. What do you see in this picture? Why is the foundation an important part of a building? Continue with the other pictures.

We are going to learn six new Amazing Words this week. Listen as I say each word: *groundbreaking, trenches, foundation, welding, waterproof, gleaming.* Have children say each word as you point to the picture.

Display Sing with Me Chart 31B. Today we are going to sing a song called "This Is the Way We Build Our School." Listen for the Amazing Words *groundbreaking, trenches, foundation, welding, waterproof,* and *gleaming.* Have children tell what is happening in the picture. Sing the first verse of the song to the tune of "Here We Go 'Round the Mulberry Bush." Then have children sing the first verse with you. Repeat the routine with the second verse.

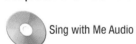 Sing with Me Audio

Talk with Me/Sing with Me Chart 31A

Talk with Me/Sing with Me Chart 31B

ELL **Preteach Concepts** Use the Day 1 instruction on ELL Poster 31 to assess and build background knowledge, develop concepts, and build oral vocabulary.

 Poster 31

Amazing Words

groundbreaking	trenches
foundation	welding
waterproof	gleaming

Writing on Demand

Develop Writing Fluency
Ask children to write about what they know about building. Have them write for two minutes. Children should write as much as they can. Tell them to try to do their best writing. You may want to discuss what children wrote during writing conferences.

ELL

English Language Learners
Build Background English learners will benefit from additional visual support to understand words in the song. As you sing, point to the *foundation* in the art to scaffold meaning.

ELL Support Additional ELL support and modified instruction is provided in the *ELL Handbook* and in the ELL Support lessons on pp. DI•12–17.

My Skills Buddy, pp. 12–13

Phonemic Awareness
🎯 Initial /a/ and /i/

Picture Card

Picture Card

Teach Display the *apple* Picture Card. *Apple* begins with /a/ /a/ /a/, *apple*. What sound does *apple* begin with? Continue with the *ant* and *astronaut* Picture Cards. Repeat the routine for /i/ using the *igloo, inch,* and *insect* Picture Cards.

Model Have children look at the picture on pp. 12–13 of *My Skills Buddy.* I see *animal* balloons. What sound do you hear at the beginning of *animal?* The first sound in *animal* is /a/. What other things do you see that begin with /a/? Repeat with /i/ and *iguana.*

Guide practice As children name example words from the picture, guide them in stating the beginning sound. Discuss with children some bulleted items on p. 12 of *My Skills Buddy.* Save the other bulleted items for discussion on Day 2.

Corrective feedback If... children have difficulty naming words that begin with /a/ or /i/, then... say the word again, stretching the beginning sound.

Discriminate sounds

Hold up the *apple* Picture Card. I am going to say two words. One word will begin with /a/, like *apple.* I want you to tell me which word begins like *apple.* I will do the first one: *attic, otter. Attic* begins with /a/, like *apple.* Continue with the following pairs of words: *elephant, alphabet; ask, up; octopus, animal; Eddie, Agnes.* Then repeat the routine for /i/ using the the *igloo* Picture Card and these word pairs: *itch, odd; Ellen, Isabel; insect, under; infant, olive; umbrella, iguana.*

Corrective feedback

If... children cannot discriminate initial /a/ or /i/, **then...** have them practice saying *apple* and *igloo.*

Sounds for consonants and blends

Review the sounds for consonants and blends. Display the *clock* Picture Card. What is this? (clock) What sound does the word *clock* begin with? (/kl/) Have children identify more initial sounds using the *blue, five, grapes, lemon, spoon, train,* and *wagon* Picture Cards. Then repeat the routine with the *bed, dog, lamp, moon, nest, soap,* and *tent* Picture Cards, asking children to identify the final sounds.

MONITOR PROGRESS ⟳ Check Phonemic Awareness   Words with Initial /a/ and /i/

Say the following words: *aster, into, Albert, Italy, ignore, alley, amber, impress, ill, add.* Have children tell whether each word begins with /a/ or /i/.

If... children cannot discriminate /a/ or /i/,

then... use the small-group Strategic Intervention lesson, p. DI•1, to reteach /a/ and /i/.

Day 1	Day 2	Day 3	Day 4	Day 5
Check Phonemic Awareness	Check Sound-Spelling/ Retelling	Check Word Reading	Check Phonemic Awareness	Check Oral Vocabulary

Success Predictor

Differentiated Instruction

SI **Strategic Intervention**

Support Phonemic Awareness If children have difficulty pronouncing /a/, model how to form /a/ by showing the front part of the tongue low in your mouth and your lips unrounded. If children have difficulty pronouncing /i/, remind them that their mouths are open and slightly up.

English Language Learners

Picture Support Point to details in the pictures on pp. 12–13 of *My Skills Buddy* as you say their corresponding words. To clarify understanding, have children point to the images as you say the words.

Phonics — Teach/Model
/a/ Spelled *Aa* and /i/ Spelled *Ii*

Teach

Display the *Aa* Alphabet Card. Point to the *astronaut* on the Alphabet Card. *Astronaut* begins with /a/. Say the word with me, *astronaut*. Write *astronaut* on the board and point to the *a*. *Astronaut* begins with /a/ spelled *a*. Now point to the letters *Aa* on the card. The sound we learned for this letter is /a/. The names of these letters are uppercase *A* and lowercase *a*. What is the sound we learned for this letter? What are the names of these letters? Repeat the routine with the *Ii* Alphabet Card.

Alphabet Card

Model

Write this sentence on the board: *Tim hit the bag with the bat.* Point to the *i* in *Tim.* When I see this letter, I might think of the sound /i/. This word is /t/ /i/ /m/, *Tim.* Repeat with the other /i/ words *hit* and *in*. I know that when I see an *i* the sound might be /i/. Point to the *a* in *bag.* When I see this letter, I might think of the sound /a/. This word is /b/ /a/ /g/, *bag.* Repeat with the other /a/ word *bat.* I know that when I see an *a* the sound might be /a/. Let's read the sentence. Point to each word as children say it.

Alphabet Card

Guide practice

Display Phonics Songs and Rhymes Chart 31. Teach children the song "Here Comes King Vip's Big Ship," sung to the tune of "Little Sally Saucer." Play the CD or sing the song several times. When children are familiar with the song, have them sing along with you. Then have them help you find and point to any words that begin with /a/ or /i/. *Into* begins with /i/ /i/ /i/. That sound is spelled *i*. Other words are *it, as, is,* and *in*.

Phonics Songs and Rhymes Chart 31

 Phonics Songs and Rhymes Audio

On their own

Write *Aa* and *Ii* as headings on chart paper. Have children think of as many words as they can that begin with one of those letters and tell you under which pair of letters to write each word they say.

 Phonics Songs and Rhymes Audio

Blend Words

Review To review sound-spellings, use the Alphabet Cards *Bb, Cc, Dd, Gg, Kk, Nn, Pp, Rr, Tt,* and *Vv* and the *bat, cap, dog, goat, kite, nut, pig, rock, ten,* and *van* Picture Cards. Then use this routine for sound-by-sound blending to have children blend new words.

ROUTINE — Sound-by-Sound Blending

1 **Connect** Write the letter *a*. What is the sound we learned for this letter? The sound is /a/. Say it with me: /a/ /a/ /a/. When you see this letter in a word, what sound will you say?

2 **Model** Write *had* on the board.

- Touch under the letter *h*: What is the sound for this letter? Say it with me: /h/ /h/ /h/. Repeat the routine touching under *a* and *d*.

- Let's blend the sounds together. Listen as I blend the sounds: /h/ /a/ /d/. Say it with me: /h/ /a/ /d/, *had*. Now say it without me.

- Listen as I use *had* in a sentence: *Sue had a new pen.* Say the sentence with me. Then have children use *had* in their own sentences.

3 **Guide Practice** Continue the routine established in step 2 with the words below:

| bag | big | can | kit | rag | zip | trip | Vin |

Children should successfully read these words before reading Decodable Story 31 on p. 403 of *Reader's and Writer's Notebook*.

Corrective Feedback If children have trouble reading a word, model blending the sounds to read the word. Then have children say it with you.

Routines Flip Chart

Differentiated Instruction

A **Advanced**

Connect Sound-Spelling Read these words aloud: *alphabet, inch, am, at, into, insect.* Have children listen to the beginning sound of each word and trace the letter on their hand that spells /a/ or /i/.

Teacher Tip

If children are having difficulty blending sounds, write the letters *a, b, d, i, m, p,* and *t* on cards. Give cards to children and have three of them stand in front of the class in a sequence that forms a word. Tell each child to pronounce the sound on his or her card. Then have the rest of the class blend the word.

Handwriting

Teach	Remind children of the rule for writing words that begin with /a/. Words that begin with /a/ are written with either an uppercase *A* or a lowercase *a*. Which letter is uppercase *A*? Which letter is lowercase *a*? Repeat with /i/.
Model uppercase *A* and *I*	Write *Andy* on the board. Point to the uppercase *A*. This is the name Andy. We use an uppercase letter to begin sentences and for the first letter in a name. Watch as I trace the uppercase *A* with my finger. Follow the stroke instructions pictured below. Repeat the uppercase *I* and the word *Isabel*.
Guide practice	Have children write uppercase *A* in the air. Use your finger to make an uppercase *A* in the air. Now write it on your hand. Repeat the routine with uppercase *I*.
Model lowercase *a* and *i*	Write *ant* on the board. Point to the lowercase *a*. This is the word *ant*. This is a lowercase *a*. Watch as I trace a lowercase *a* with my finger. Write another lowercase *a* on the board following the stroke instructions. Again, have children write *a* in the air and on their hands. Repeat with lowercase *i* and the word *inch*.
Guide practice	Have children use their Write-On Boards to write a row of uppercase *A* and *I* and a row of lowercase *a* and *i*.

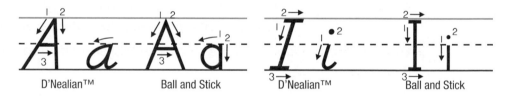

D'Nealian™   Ball and Stick   D'Nealian™   Ball and Stick

More practice	Use *Reader's and Writer's Notebook,* pp. 401, 402, for additional practice with *a* and *i*.

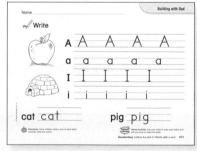

Reader's and Writer's Notebook, p. 401

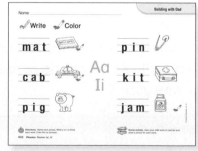

Reader's and Writer's Notebook, p. 402

High-Frequency Words

Teach

Use the routine below to review high-frequency words *here, do, little, with,* and *what.*

Routines Flip Chart

ROUTINE **Nondecodable Words**

1 **Say and Spell** Some words we must learn by remembering the letters rather than saying the sounds. We will say and spell the words to help learn them. **Write** *here* **on the board. This is the word** *here.* **It has four letters. The letters in** *here* **are** *h, e, r, e.* **Have children say and spell the word, first with you and then without you.**

2 **Demonstrate Meaning** I can use the word *here* in lots of sentences. Here is one sentence: *Here is my favorite hat.* Now you use the word in a sentence.

Repeat the routine with the words *do, little, with,* and *what.*

Academic Vocabulary

Write the following on the board:

compare	contrast
prediction	pronoun
author	illustrator
realistic fiction	compound word
list	expository text

Point to the list. This week we are going to learn these important words. They are tools for learning. As we work this week, you will hear them many times. Read the words. Preteach the Academic Vocabulary at point-of-use by providing a child-friendly description, explanation, or example that clarifies the meaning of each term. Then ask children to restate the meaning of the Academic Vocabulary in their own words.

Differentiated Instruction

A **Advanced**

Build Background Have children create rebus sentences using the high-frequency words *little* and *go.*

English Language Learners
Physical Response Scaffold meanings of the words *little* and *go* by pantomiming the words and having children guess the words.

Decodable Story 31
/a/ Spelled *Aa*, /i/ Spelled *Ii*, and High-Frequency Words

Review

Review the previously taught high-frequency words by having children read each word as you point to it on the Word Wall.

a	the	is	he	one	little	go

Read Decodable Story 31

Display Decodable Story 31. Today we will read a story about a boy named Vin who is packing a bag for a trip. Point to the title of the story. What is the title of this story? *Vin and the Bag* is the title of the story. Which word in the title has /a/? (*Bag*) Which word in the title has /i/? (*Vin*) We will read other short *a* and *i* words in this story. Have children read Decodable Story 31 on pp. 403–404 in *Reader's and Writer's Notebook*.

Reader's and Writer's Notebook, pp. 403–404

Use the routine for reading decodable books to read Decodable Story 31.

ROUTINE Reading Decodable Books

1. **Read Silently** Have children whisper read the story page by page as you listen in.

2. **Model Fluent Reading** Have children finger point as you read a page. Then have children reread the page without you.

3. **Read Chorally** Have children finger point as they chorally read the page. Continue reading page by page, repeating steps 1 and 2.

4. **Read Individually** Have children take turns reading aloud a page.

5. **Reread and Monitor Progress** As you listen to individual children reread, monitor progress and provide support.

6. **Reread with a Partner** Have children reread the story page by page with a partner.

Routines Flip Chart

Small Group Time

DAY 1 Break into small groups after reading the Decodable Story and before the comprehension lesson.

Teacher-Led

SI Strategic Intervention	**OL On-Level**	**A Advanced**
Teacher-Led Page DI•1 • Phonemic Awareness and Phonics • **Reread** Decodable Story 31	**Teacher-Led** Page DI•6 • Phonemic Awareness and Phonics • **Reread** Decodable Story 31	**Teacher-Led** Page DI•9 • Phonemic Awareness and Phonics • **Reread** Decodable Story 31 for Fluency

 Place English language learners in the groups that correspond to their reading abilities in English.

Practice Stations
• Visit the Listen Up! Station
• Visit the Word Work Station

Independent Activities
• Read independently
• Concept Talk Video
• *Reader's and Writer's Notebook*

Differentiated Instruction

SI Strategic Intervention

Letter Recognition Write one of the previously taught high-frequency words on the board. Read the word with children. Have a child find an example of the word in the story. Have the child compare the word in the story to the word on the board letter by letter.

English Language Learners Frontload Decodable Story 31 Display p. 2 of Decodable Story 31 and say: *He got one big can. He got one little net.* These are telling sentences. They tell what Vin will pack. Look at the sentences on p. 3. They follow the same pattern. Helping children understand the basic language structure will help them comprehend the meaning of the story.

Objectives
◎ Teach compare and contrast.

Skills Trace
◉ **Compare and Contrast**
Introduce U2W1D1; U3W1D1;
U5W3D1; U6W1D1
Practice U2W1D2; U2W1D3;
U2W1D4; U3W1D2; U3W1D3;
U3W1D4; U5W3D2; U5W3D3;
U5W3D4; U6W1D2; U6W1D3;
U6W1D4
Reteach/Review U2W1D5;
U2W3D4; U3W1D5; U3W3D4;
U4W1D4; U5W3D5; U3W5D4;
U6W1D5; U6W6D4

KEY:
U=Unit   W=Week   D=Day

My Skills Buddy, pp. 14–15

Listening Comprehension
Compare and Contrast

Introduce

Envision It!

When we **compare**, we tell how things are alike. *Alike* means how things are the same. When we **contrast**, we tell how things are different. *Different* means how things are not the same. Good readers compare and contrast things as they read. They look for how these things are alike and different. This helps them understand what they read.

Have children turn to pp. 14–15 in *My Skills Buddy*.

• What is the boy looking at? (two bicycles)

• Compare and contrast the two bicycles. How are they alike and different? (They both have handlebars, pedals, and a seat. One has training wheels, but the other does not.)

Model

Today I will read aloud a story about a doghouse and a big house. Read **"A House for Freckles"** and model how to compare and contrast.

Think Aloud

This story tells about a girl and her dad building a doghouse. They plan, measure, and cut the boards for the doghouse just right so the pieces will fit together. That is one way the doghouse and the people's house are the same: The boards for the big house were planned, measured, and cut just right too. The doghouse doesn't have windows, but the big house does. That is one way the two houses are different.

Guide practice

After reading, have children compare and contrast Freckles's doghouse with Marie's house.

- In what other ways are the houses alike? (They have the same style and color. They have walls, doors, and roofs.)
- In what other ways are the houses different? (Marie's house is big. It has pipes and wires. Freckles's house is small. It has no pipes or wires.)

More practice

Display *The Little Engine That Could.* Page through the story. Help children compare and contrast the train engines. How are the four engines alike? (All are train engines.) How are they different? (One is shiny and new, one is big and strong, one is rusty and old, and one is little and blue.)

Connect to everyday life

Think about you and a friend. Are you and your friend exactly the same? Of course not, but the two of you are alike in some ways. That's why you are friends. Tell me how you and your friend are alike. Then tell me how you and your friend are different.

Differentiated Instruction

 Strategic Intervention

Build Background Show children a pencil and a crayon. Help them recognize how they are alike and different. Write their suggestions on the board in a T-chart.

Academic Vocabulary

compare to point out how things are alike

contrast to point out how things are different

E L L

English Language Learners
Oral Comprehension To prepare English learners for the Read Aloud, use the modified Read Aloud in the ELL Support lesson p. DI•13.

 Read Aloud

A House for Freckles

Marie and her dad are building a doghouse for Freckles. Marie wants the doghouse to look like their big house. They plan, measure, and cut the boards just right. That way, the pieces will fit together tightly. Freckles does not need a leaky house!

They nail boards down for a floor. They nail boards up and then crosswise to form the walls. They leave a space for the door, of course. Dad says Freckles does not need windows. A dog will not need pipes or wires, either. The roof goes on last.

Marie paints the doghouse with paint left over from the big house. Dad nails leftover shingles on Freckles's roof. Home at last, Freckles. How do you like it?

Objectives
- Identify and use pronouns *I* and *me*.
- Write or dictate about special qualities.

Conventions
Pronouns *I* and *me*

Teach pronouns *I* and *me*

Remind children of what they learned about pronouns. Pronouns are words that can take the place of nouns. When I tell about myself, I use the pronouns *I* or *me* instead of using my name.

Model

Listen to these sentences:

[your name] reads a book.
I read a book.

Instead of using my name in the sentence, I use the pronoun *I*.

Please give the book to [your name].
Please give the book to me.

Instead of using my name in the sentence, I use the pronoun *me*.

Guide practice

Write the following sentence frames on the board and read them one at a time to children. Have children insert their name in the sentence and say it aloud. Then have them reread the sentence, substituting the pronoun *I* or *me* for their names. When children use *I* or *me*, write the word on the blank line. Point to the pronoun as you reread the completed sentences.

- [name] played a game. (*I* played a game.)
- [name] jumped rope. (*I* jumped rope.)

- Throw the ball to [name]. (Throw the ball to *me*.)
- Mom called [name]. (Mom called *me*.)

Team Talk Pair children and have them take turns telling about a fun activity they share with their family using the pronouns *I* and *me*. Remind them to use complete sentences. Have them draw a picture of the activity and write a sentence about it using *I* or *me*.

Daily Fix-It

Use the Daily Fix-It for more conventions practice.

Writing
Wonderful, Marvelous Me!
I Am Special Because…

Introduce

Talk with children about how everyone is special. Everyone in this room is special. There are many wonderful, marvelous things about each of us. We are special because of who we are on the inside, what we can do, even how we look. Someone may be special because he or she can draw well. Someone else may be special because he or she has two dogs. Encourage children to share their thoughts and ideas about things that make us special.

Model

Today we're going to write about how each of us is special. I'm going to close my eyes and think about something that makes me special. One thing I do that makes me special is that I can remember many things. I remember birthdays, math problems, and words to my favorite songs. Write *birthdays, math,* and *songs* on the board. Another thing that makes me special is that I have been skiing. I had to take a special trip to get to a place that has snow and mountains. Draw a picture of a snow-covered mountain and write *snow* and *ski* underneath.

Guide practice

Encourage children to help you name other things that make you special. Write down their ideas and draw pictures when appropriate.

Independent writing

Now you're going to share something about you. Close your eyes and think about wonderful, marvelous you. What is something that makes you special? Remember, there are so many things about you that are special, but today pick just one. Have children write or dictate their ideas and then illustrate them.

Daily Handwriting

Write *Annie, an, Italy,* and *ice* on the board. Review correct letter formation of uppercase *A* and *I* and lowercase *a* and *i.*

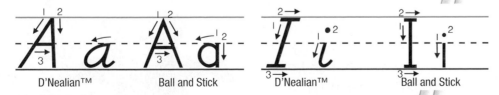

D'Nealian™ Ball and Stick D'Nealian™ Ball and Stick

Have children write *Annie, an, Italy,* and *ice* on their Write-On Boards. Remind them to use proper left-to-right and top-to-bottom progression and proper spacing between letters when writing *A, a, I,* and *i.*

 Write Guy
Jeff Anderson

Writers Write!

Children writers succeed in classrooms where they write. Children need to read every day and to write every day. Teachers do not need to read and assess everything that children write.

Academic Vocabulary

pronoun word that can take the place of a noun or nouns

Daily Fix-It

it is ten past six
I̲t is ten past six.̲

This week's practice sentences appear on Teacher Resources DVD-ROM.

Writing Routine

Day 1 Wonderful, Marvelous Me!

Day 2 Respond to Literature

Day 3 Genre Writing

Day 4 Extend the Concept

Day 5 This Week We…

Objectives
- Practice reciting language.
- Share information clearly and loudly.

Listening and Speaking
Recite Language

Teach

Have children recall what they do every morning when they put their hand over their heart and look at the flag. When we say the Pledge of Allegiance, we are reciting language. When we recite things, we say them from memory. I must speak loudly and clearly so everyone can hear me and understand me. I must also wait my turn to speak.

Model

Listen as I recite the Pledge of Allegiance. Recite the entire Pledge of Allegiance, speaking slowly and clearly. Ask children to help you recite it a second time.

Guide practice

Who wants to try reciting the Pledge of Allegiance? Assure children that they need recite only as much as they can and that they are not expected to be able to recite the entire pledge. Refer children to the Rules for Speaking on p. 2 of *Reader's and Writer's Notebook.* Remind children to speak loudly and clearly.

Reader's and Writer's Notebook, p. 2

Wrap Up Your Day

✔ **Phonemic Awareness** I am going to say some words. Clap if a word has /a/ and stomp if the word has /i/. Listen carefully: *class, chick, sack, fill, gas, camp, rib, twig.*

✔ **Conventions** Have children say a sentence about something they do. Have children say another sentence that uses the word *me.*

✔ **Homework Idea** Send home the Family Times Newsletter on Let's Practice It! TR DVD•61–62.

Preview DAY 2

Tomorrow we will read a selection about how a new school is built.

Science
Homes for People and Animals

Materials: chart paper, Venn diagram or Graphic Organizer 28, markers

Use a Venn Diagram to Compare and Contrast Have children think about homes for people and homes for animals. Draw a Venn diagram on chart paper and label the circles *People's Homes* and *Animals' Homes.* Have children tell you about the homes that people and animals make for themselves, such as what the homes are made of, what they look like, and what they are used for. As children offer ideas, ask whether each idea is true only for an animal's home, only for a person's home, or for both kinds of homes. Write children's ideas in the appropriate parts of the diagram. Then demonstrate how the diagram can be used to compare and contrast the two topics.

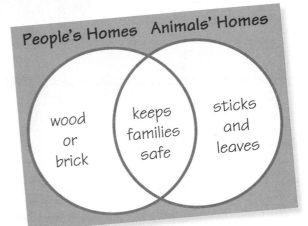

People's Homes   Animals' Homes

wood or brick | keeps families safe | sticks and leaves

Listening and Speaking
Recite a Rhyme

Learn to Recite a Nursery Rhyme Remind children that when we recite things, we say them from memory. Demonstrate by reciting a nursery rhyme, such as "Humpty Dumpty."

Let children join in if they can. Remind them to face their audience and to speak slowly and clearly. Remind listeners to sit quietly and pay attention to the speaker.

Go through the rhyme, saying each line and having children repeat it several times, until everyone can recite "Humpty Dumpty" together.

Phonemic Awareness
Name the Sounds

Materials: *box, five, fox; black, block, flag; doll, map, mop; pig, web, wig; nest, van, vest* Picture Cards

Match Initial, Medial, Final Sounds Hold up the *box, five*, and *fox* Picture Cards. Have children say the picture names with you. Then have them name the words that have the same beginning sound (*five, fox*) and identify the sound (/f/). Repeat the routine for medial and final sounds with the remaining Picture Cards.

Objectives
- Discuss the concepts to develop oral language.
- Build oral vocabulary.

Today at a Glance

Oral Vocabulary
groundbreaking, trenches

Phonemic Awareness
◉ Medial /a/ and /i/

Phonics
◉ /a/ Spelled *Aa*
◉ /i/ Spelled *Ii*

Handwriting
Words with *Aa* and *Ii*

Comprehension
◉ Compare and Contrast

Conventions
Pronouns *I* and *me*

Writing
Respond to Literature

Vocabulary
Compound Words

TRUCKTOWN on Reading Street

Start your engines! Display p. 10 of *Truckery Rhymes.* Point to "This Is the Way." Which trucks are in this rhyme? Let's read the rhyme together. Now have a child point to the rhyming words as the class reads the rhyme again. Give additional children the opportunity to say the rhyme aloud and track the print.

Truckery Rhymes

Concept Talk

 Question of the Week

How is a school built?

Build concepts

Write the question of the week on the board and track the print as you read it to children. Ask them to answer the question in complete sentences. Display Sing with Me Chart 31B. Tell children they are going to sing the song about building a new school.

 Sing with Me Audio

Listen for Amazing Words

Listen for the Amazing Words *groundbreaking* and *trenches* in the song. Read the title and have children describe what is happening in the picture. Sing the song several times to the tune of "Here We Go 'Round the Mulberry Bush." Tell children to sing along with you. Have them stand in a circle, hold hands, and swing their arms up high when they say the Amazing Word *groundbreaking* or *trenches*.

This Is the Way We Build Our School

This is the way we build our school,
    build our school, build our school;
This is the way we build our school
    so gleaming bright and new!
Groundbreaking day makes us jump
    for joy, jump for joy, jump for joy;
Groundbreaking day makes us jump
    for joy for our school gleaming and new!
Cement will make the foundation strong,
    foundation strong, foundation strong;
Cement will make the foundation strong
    for our school gleaming and new!

Talk with Me/Sing with Me Chart 31B

ELL Reinforce Vocabulary Use the Day 2 instruction on ELL Poster 31 to reinforce the meanings of high-frequency words.

 ELL Poster 31

Oral Vocabulary
Amazing Words

Amazing Words

Teach Amazing Words

Amazing Words — Oral Vocabulary Routine

1 Introduce the Word *Groundbreaking* work must be done before construction can begin. What's our new Amazing Word for getting the ground ready so building can begin? Say it with me: *groundbreaking*.

2 Demonstrate Provide examples to show meaning. *Groundbreaking work is done before building begins.* What things do you think are part of *groundbreaking* work?

Repeat steps 1 and 2.

Introduce the Word Trenches are long, narrow ditches. Pipes for a building are laid in *trenches* in the ground. What's our new Amazing Word for long, narrow ditches in the ground? Say it with me: *trenches*.

Demonstrate *Trenches are dug on a construction site.* Where else might *trenches* be dug?

3 Apply Have children use *groundbreaking* and *trenches* to describe two of the steps in constructing a building.

Routines Flip Chart

Use Amazing Words

To reinforce the concept and the Amazing Words, have children supply the appropriate Amazing Word for each sentence.

The first step in building is doing the _____ work. (groundbreaking)

A backhoe digs _____ for pipes. (trenches)

Amazing Words

groundbreaking	trenches
foundation	welding
waterproof	gleaming

Differentiated Instruction

SI Strategic Intervention

Sentence Production If children have difficulty completing the sentences, say the sentence with each Amazing Word. Have children repeat the sentence and tell you which word is the correct Amazing Word.

English Language Learners
Visual Support Scaffold understanding of today's Amazing Words, *groundbreaking* and *trenches,* by pointing to the pictures in *Building with Dad*.

Objectives
- ◎ Practice medial /a/ and /i/.
- • Review sounds for consonants and blends.

Phonemic Awareness
🔊 Medial /a/ and /i/

Isolate medial /a/
Display the *cap* Picture Card. This is a *cap*. Listen as I say the sounds in *cap:* /k/ /a/ /p/. What is this picture? What sound do you hear in the middle of *cap?* Continue the routine with the *cat, van,* and *pan* Picture Cards.

Isolate medial /i/
Display the *pig* Picture Card. This is a *pig*. Listen as I say the sounds in *pig:* /p/ /i/ /g/. What is this picture? What sound do you hear in the middle of *pig?* Continue with the *wig* Picture Card.

Continue with the *six* and *hat* Picture Cards.

Guide practice
Have children look at the picture on *My Skills Buddy* pp. 12–13. Remember that we saw things that begin with /a/ or /i/. Let's look for things with the middle sounds /a/ or /i/. What things do you see that have the same middle sound as *cap?* What things have the same middle sound as *pig?* Discuss with children those bulleted items on p. 12 not discussed on Day 1.

Corrective feedback
If... children cannot discriminate medial /a/ or /i/, **then...** have them enunciate /a/ or /i/ as they segment short *a* or *i* words.

Listen as I segment a word: /b/ /i/ /t/. Say the sounds with me: /b/ /i/ /t/. What sound do you hear in the middle? I hear /i/ in the middle. Continue with the following words: *fan, pin, jam, tip, pat.*

Picture Card

Picture Card

My Skills Buddy, pp. 12–13

On their own Display Phonics Songs and Rhymes Chart 31. Remind children of the song, "Here Comes King Vip's Big Ship," sung to the tune of "Little Sally Saucer." Have them sing the song with you several times. This time I want you to clap when you hear /a/ or /i/ in the middle of a word. Read the title aloud. I hear /i/ in the middle of four words in the title. Which words have /i/ in the middle? (*King, Vip's, Big, Ship*) Continue with the lines of the song.

Here Comes King Vip's Big Ship

Here comes King Vip's big ship,
Into it we all zip.
Quick! Grab my hand!
This band is grand!
Flip as you dance;
Now mix with the band.
The king's jazz band is
Best in the land!

Phonics Songs and Rhymes Chart 31

Review **Initial consonants and blends** I am going to say some words, and I want you to tell me the beginning sound in each word. Listen carefully: *cap* (/k/), *gap* (/g/), *lap* (/l/), *map* (/m/), *nap* (/n/), *rap* (/r/), *sap* (/s/), *tap* (/t/), *clap* (/kl/), *flap* (/fl/), *slap* (/sl/), *snap* (/sn/), *trap* (/tr/). What do you notice about these words? (They rhyme because their middle and ending sounds are the same.)

Final consonants and blends I am going to say some more words. This time I want you to tell me the ending sound in each word. Listen carefully: *mad* (/d/), *Mag* (/g/), *man* (/n/), *map* (/p/), *mat* (/t/), *Max* (/ks/), *mask* (/sk/), *mast* (/st/). Do these words rhyme? (no) Why not? (They have the same middle sound, but they do not have the same ending sound.)

ELL

English Language Learners
Language Transfer Final consonant blends do not exist in Spanish, so Spanish speakers may omit one of the sounds in a final consonant blend or add an ending vowel sound. Provide extra practice with hearing and pronouncing words with final consonant blends.

ELL Support For additional support for language transfer, see Linguistic Contrastive Analysis in the *ELL Handbook*.

Objectives
◎ Practice /a/ spelled *Aa*.
◎ Practice /i/ spelled *Ii*.
• Blend words.

Check Sound-Spelling
SUCCESS PREDICTOR

Phonics—Teach/Model
🔊 /a/ Spelled *Aa* and /i/ Spelled *Ii*

Alphabet Card

Review
/a/ *Aa*
and /i/ *Ii*

Point to the *igloo* on the *Ii* Alphabet Card. What is this? What sound does *igloo* begin with? *Igloo* begins with /i/. Write *igloo* on the board and point to the letter *i*. The letter for /i/ is *i*. What letter does *igloo* begin with? Repeat the routine to review /a/*Aa* using the *Aa* Alphabet Card.

Model

Display the *pig* Picture Card. What is this? Say the sounds in *pig* with me: /p/ /i/ /g/, *pig*. Where do you hear /i/ in *pig*? I hear /i/ in the middle. Do you? Write *pig* on the board. Point to each letter as you say the sounds, /p/ /i/ /g/, *pig*. Repeat the routine to review /a/ *Aa* using the *cap* Picture Card.

Alphabet Card

Guide
practice

Envision It!

Have children open *My Skills Buddy* to p. 16. Demonstrate using the blending arrows on *My Skills Buddy*, p. 16, as you model blending the first word. Put your finger on the red arrow below the *d*. Say the sound that *d* stands for: /d/. Continue with the letters *i* and *g*. Now I run my finger along the blue arrow as I blend the letters quickly to read *dig*. Repeat with the word *ill*. Point out how when *w* is added to *ill* it makes a new word: *will.* Have children work with a partner to blend the rest of the words on the page.

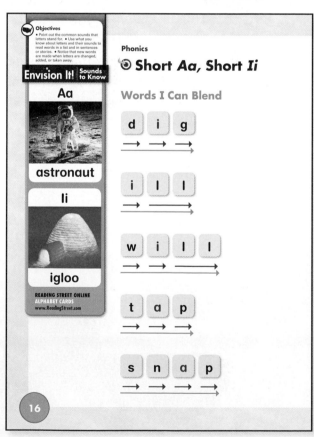

My Skills Buddy, p. 16

Blend Use the following routine to blend *a* and *i* words.

 ROUTINE ## Sound-by-Sound Blending

1 Connect Write the letter *i*. What is the sound we learned for this letter? The sound is /i/. Say it with me: /i/ /i/ /i/. When you see this letter in a word, what sound will you say?

2 Model Write the word *dig* on the board.

- Point to *d* and ask: What is the sound for this letter? Say it with me: /d/ /d/ /d/. Repeat the routine for *i* and *g*.

- Let's blend the sounds together. Listen as I blend the sounds: /d/ /i/ /g/. Say it with me: /d/ /i/ /g/, *dig*. Now say it without me.

- Listen as I use *dig* in a sentence: *I can dig in the dirt*. Say it with me. Have children use *dig* in a sentence.

3 Guide Practice Continue the routine established in step 2 with these words:

| if | will | tap | pass | fit | gap | nap |

Have children successfully read all of the words before reading Decodable Reader 31 on p. 18 of *My Skills Buddy*.

Corrective Feedback Model blending the sounds to read the word. Then have children say it with you.

Routines Flip Chart

 Don't Wait Until Friday

MONITOR PROGRESS  Check Sound-Spelling /a/ Spelled *Aa* and /i/ Spelled *Ii*

Have children write *Aa* on one card and *Ii* on another card. I will say some words. When you hear a word with /a/, hold up your *Aa* card. When you hear a word with /i/, hold up your *Ii* card. Listen: *crib, glad, lift, king, land, skip, cast, wilt, plan, limp, brag*.

If... children cannot discriminate /a/ or /i/ words,

then... use the small-group Strategic Intervention lesson, p. DI•2 to reteach /a/ and /i/.

Continue to monitor children's progress using other instructional opportunities during the week so that children can be successful with the Day 5 Assessment.

Day 1	Day 2	Day 3	Day 4	Day 5
Check Phonemic Awareness	**Check Sound-Spelling/ Retelling**	Check Word Reading	Check Phonemic Awareness	Check Oral Vocabulary

Differentiated Instruction

 SI Strategic Intervention

Letter-Sound Connection
Display the *Aa* and *Ii* Alphabet Cards. Tell children to name the sound and the letter, and say words that have that sound.

A Advanced

Sound Blending Display the *Aa, Pp,* and *Ss* Alphabet Cards and model blending the word *sap*. Have children substitute the *Ii* Alphabet Card to blend the word *sip*.

ELL

English Language Learners
Support Phonics After blending the words on *My Skills Buddy,* p. 16, help children employ English spelling rules for double *l*. Remind them that some words with final /l/ are spelled with *ll*. Then have them spell the words *ill, will,* and *full* on their Write-On Boards.

Objectives
- Write *A, a, I,* and *i.*
- Read high-frequency words.
- Write high-frequency words.

Handwriting
Write Words with *Aa* and *Ii*

Review

Write *Alex* on the board. This is the name *Alex*. I use an uppercase *A* for the first letter in *Alex*'s name. Watch me make an uppercase *A*. Write another uppercase *A* on the board using the strokes indicated in the model. Repeat the routine with *Izzy* and uppercase *I*.

Write *cat* on the board. This is the word *cat*. There is a lowercase *a* in the middle of the word. Watch me make a lowercase *a*. Write another lowercase *a* on the board using the proper strokes. Repeat the routine with *jig* and lowercase *i*.

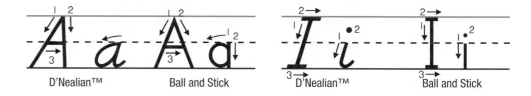

D'Nealian™   Ball and Stick   D'Nealian™   Ball and Stick

Guide practice

Have children use their Write-On Boards to make a row of uppercase *A* and *I* and a row of lowercase *a* and *i*. Circulate around the room, assisting children when necessary. Have children then write the following words: *Abby, Iggy, pan, fit, dab, mix*.

High-Frequency Words

Model reading

Have children turn to p. 17 of *My Skills Buddy*. Read the high-frequency words *here, do, little, with,* and *what* together. Then have children point to each word and read it themselves. Read the sentences on *My Skills Buddy* page together to read the high-frequency words in context.

Team Talk Pair children and have them take turns reading each of the sentences aloud.

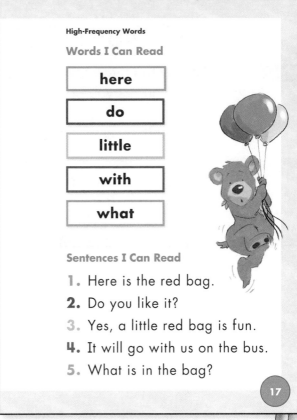

High-Frequency Words

Words I Can Read

here

do

little

with

what

Sentences I Can Read

1. Here is the red bag.
2. Do you like it?
3. Yes, a little red bag is fun.
4. It will go with us on the bus.
5. What is in the bag?

17

My Skills Buddy, p. 17

On their own

Use *Reader's and Writer's Notebook,* p. 405, for additional practice with this week's high-frequency words.

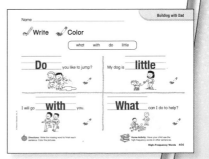

Reader's and Writer's Notebook, p. 405

Differentiated Instruction

 Advanced

High-Frequency Words in Context Have children write their own sentences using the high-frequency words.

English Language Learners

High-Frequency Words After the Team Talk activity, have children continue to work in pairs to check understanding. Have one child read one of the sentences aloud while another child makes a simple drawing to illustrate the sentences.

Decodable Reader 31
/a/ Spelled *Aa* and /i/ Spelled *Ii* and High-Frequency Words

Review

Review the previously taught high-frequency words. Have children read each word as you point to it on the Word Wall.

is	little	go	with	here	the	do	what

Have children turn to Decodable Reader 31, *If Kip Can,* on p. 18 of *My Skills Buddy*. Today we will read a story about a big dog named Kip and a little dog named Sam. **Point to the title of the story.** What is the title of this story? (*If Kip Can*) Which word in the title has /a/? (*Can*) Which words in the title have /i/? (*If, Kip*) What do you see in the picture on the cover? What do you think this story will be about? **Point to the name of the author.** The author's name is Sara Blumenthal. What does the author of a book do? **Point to the name of the illustrator.** The illustrator's name is Ken Ye. What does the illustrator of a book do?

Use the routine for reading decodable books to read Decodable Reader 31.

My Skills Buddy, 18–25

ROUTINE Reading Decodable Books

 Read Silently Have children whisper read the book page by page as you listen in.

2 **Model Fluent Reading** Have children finger point as you read a page. Then have children reread the book without you.

3 **Read Chorally** Have children finger point as they chorally read the page. Continue reading page by page, repeating steps 1 and 2.

4 **Read Individually** Have children take turns reading aloud a page.

5 **Reread and Monitor Progress** As you listen to individual children reread, monitor progress and provide support.

6 **Reread with a Partner** Have children reread the book page by page with a partner.

Routines Flip Chart

Differentiated Instruction

SI Strategic Intervention

Recognize Sounds Before children read *If Kip Can,* review /a/ with the *ant* and *bat* Picture Cards and /i/ with the *inch* and *pig* Picture Cards.

Academic Vocabulary

author a person who writes books or stories

illustrator a person who draws pictures for books or stories

Small Group Time

DAY 2 Break into small groups after reading the Decodable Reader and before the comprehension lesson.

Teacher-Led

SI Strategic Intervention	**OL** On-Level	**A** Advanced
Teacher-Led Page DI•2	**Teacher-Led** Page DI•6	**Teacher-Led** Page DI•9
• Phonemic Awareness and Phonics	• Phonemic Awareness and Phonics	• Phonics and Spelling
• **Reread** Decodable Reader 31	• **Reread** Decodable Reader 31	• **Reread** Decodable Reader 31 for Fluency

 E L L Place English language learners in the groups that correspond to their reading abilities in English.

Practice Stations
• Visit the Word Work Station
• Visit the Words to Know Station

Independent Activities
• Read independently
• Background Building Audio
• *Reader's and Writer's Notebook*

Objectives
- ◎ Practice compare and contrast.
- • Preview and predict.
- • Retell a story.

Check Retelling
SUCCESS PREDICTOR

Listening Comprehension
◎ Compare and Contrast

Review

Envision It!

Have children turn to p. 14 of *My Skills Buddy.* When we tell how things are alike, we **compare.** When we tell how things are different, we **contrast.** Good readers compare and contrast when they read because it helps them understand the story.

My Skills Buddy, pp. 14–15

First Read—Big Book
Building with Dad

Triple Day Read!

Concepts of print

Display the cover of *Building with Dad.* Point to the title of the book. The title of this book is *Building with Dad.* Point to the author's name. The author of this book is Carol Nevius. Point to the illustrator's name. The illustrator of this book is Bill Thomson. Have children tell how this book is different from most books they read. (You have to turn the book because it opens from the bottom, not the right side.)

Preview and predict

Think Aloud

What do you see on the cover? I see a boy wearing a hard hat. What do you think this story will be about?

Use illustrations

Take children on a walk through the book. As we walk through the book, tell me what you see. Point out the unusual arrangement of pictures.

Introduce genre

Realistic fiction tells about imaginary characters and events that seem real. We will read about a boy who helps build his new school.

Set purpose

Remind children of the question of the week: *How is a school built?* Have children listen as you read to see how a new school is built.

Model

Read *Building with Dad* with expression for enjoyment.

DAY 2 Read for enjoyment

DAY 3 Reread using Develop Vocabulary notes

DAY 4 Reread using Guide Comprehension notes

Retell

Check retelling

 Envision It!

Have children turn to p. 26 of *My Skills Buddy.* Walk through the retelling boxes as children retell the story *Building with Dad.* Let's retell what happens in the first box—the beginning of the story. The bulldozer helps start the ground-breaking work. Let's retell what happens in the next box. Continue with the rest of the boxes. After children retell the story as a group, have them draw a picture to retell a favorite part of the story. Have them write or dictate a word or sentence to go with each picture.

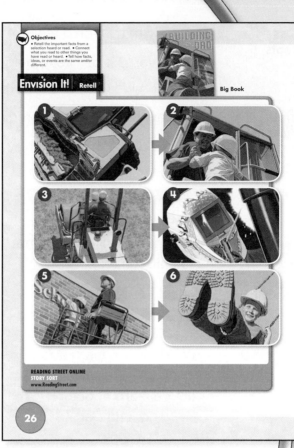

My Skills Buddy, p. 26

Top-Score Response A top-score response describes events in sequence with details.

 **MONITOR PROGRESS** **Check Retelling**

If... children have difficulty retelling the story,

then... go through the selection one page at a time, and ask children to tell what happens in their own words.

Day 1	Day 2	Day 3	Day 4	Day 5
Check Phonemic Awareness	Check Sound-Spelling/ Retelling	Check Word Reading	Check Phonemic Awareness	Check Oral Vocabulary

Academic Vocabulary

realistic fiction a story about imaginary characters and events that seem as if they could be real

retell telling a story in one's own words

Retelling Plan

☑ **This week assess Advanced students.**

☐ **Week 2** Assess On-Level students.

☐ **Week 3** Assess Strategic Intervention students.

☐ **Week 4** Assess Advanced students.

☐ **Week 5** Assess On-Level students.

☐ **Week 6** Assess Strategic Intervention students.

ELL

English Language Learners
Professional Development
Activate Prior Knowledge
Dr. Jim Cummins from the University of Toronto writes, "It is important to activate students' prior knowledge because students may not realize what they know about a particular topic or issue. Their knowledge may not facilitate learning unless that knowledge is brought to consciousness." Before reading *Building with Dad,* activate children's prior knowledge by having them brainstorm and discuss the parts of a building and how workers might build those parts.

Retelling

Success Predictor

Objectives
◎ Practice compare and contrast.
• Confirm predictions.
• Practice pronouns for *I* and *me*.

Think, Talk, and Write

Discuss concepts

Imagine what it would feel like to be one of the workers in the story.

• What would it be like to help build a building? Why?

• How would you feel when the building was finished? Why?

Confirm predictions

Have children recall their predictions before you read *Building with Dad*.

• What did you think the story would be about?

• Was your prediction correct?

Have children turn to p. 27 of *My Skills Buddy*. Read the questions and directives and have children respond.

Text to self

1. Think about *Dig Dig Digging*. How is this story like *Dig Dig Digging*? What did we learn about in *Dig Dig Digging*? What do we learn about in *Building with Dad*?

◎ **Compare and contrast**

2. How are a steamroller and a cement mixer alike? How are they different? Let's make a chart to show how they are alike and different. Make a Venn diagram and label the circles *steamroller* and *cement mixer*. (A steamroller flattens the road. A cement mixer mixes and dumps out cement for the road. They both have wheels. They are both trucks used to build roads.)

Look back and write

3. Let's look back at our story and write about it. We read about how a new school is built and what machines help. Let's listen for what a cement mixer does. Read pp. 16–17 of *Building with Dad*. Now let's write our ideas. Discuss with children what the cement mixer does and what part of the building it helps build. Record children's responses on chart paper. (Possible responses: Cement mixers make gray glop. They help make the foundation of the building. The gray glop dries hard.)

Think, Talk, and Write

1. Think about *Dig, Dig, Digging*. How is *Building with Dad* like *Dig, Dig, Digging*?

Text to Text

2. How are a steamroller and a cement mixer alike? How are they different?

◎ Compare and Contrast

3. Look back and write.

27

My Skills Buddy, p. 27

Conventions
Pronouns *I* and *me*

Review

Remind children that this week they are learning about the pronouns, *I* and *me.* Pronouns are words that can take the place of nouns. When you talk about yourself, you replace your name with the pronouns *I* or *me.* Write *I* and *me* on the board. Point to each word as you read it.

Guide practice

When I talk about myself, I use the pronouns *I* or *me*, instead of my name. Read and write these sentences:

> **[name] saw my friend at the park.**
> **_____ saw my friend at the park.**
>
> **Dad took [name] to the store.**
> **Dad took _____ to the store.**

Have each child say his or her name to complete the first sentence. Then tell the child to use the correct pronoun to replace his or her name in the second sentence. Write the pronoun on the blank line. After each child says the sentences, echo read the sentences with children pointing to the pronouns as you say them.

On their own

Use the *Reader's and Writer's Notebook,* p. 406, for more practice with pronouns.

Daily Fix-It

Use the Daily Fix-It for more conventions practice.

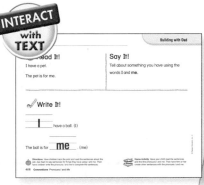

Reader's and Writer's Notebook, p. 406

Differentiated Instruction

 Strategic Intervention

Support Discussion Show children *Dig Dig Digging* to help them recall what the selection is about. Have them use the pictures in both *Dig Dig Digging* and *Building with Dad* to see how the two books are alike and different.

Academic Vocabulary

prediction a statement that tells what will happen next based on known information

Daily Fix-It

do you live in the city
<u>D</u>o you live in the city<u>?</u>

This week's practice sentences appear on Teacher Resources DVD-ROM.

Objectives
- Write or dictate sentences about machines that help build.
- Identify compound words.

Writing
Respond to Literature

Discuss concept

Discuss *Building with Dad.* Have children briefly describe what each machine does.

Model

In *Building with Dad,* the first picture of a machine is a bulldozer. The bull-dozer helps with the groundbreaking. I am going to write this sentence that tells about the picture:

> **The bulldozer gets the ground ready.**

Guide practice

Have children look at the pictures and help you write more sentences about machines.

> **The dump truck carries dirt and rocks.**
> **The grader smoothes the ground.**

Independent writing

Have children draw a picture of a machine they read about in *Building with Dad*. Then have them write or dictate a sentence about it.

Daily Handwriting

Write *Ann, flag, Ike,* and *slim* on the board. Review correct letter formation of uppercase *A* and *I* and lowercase *a* and *i.*

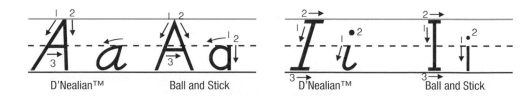

D'Nealian™   Ball and Stick   D'Nealian™   Ball and Stick

Have children write *Ann, flag, Ike,* and *slim* on their Write-On Boards. Remind them to use proper left-to-right and top-to-bottom progression when writing *A, a, I,* and *i.*

Vocabulary
Compound Words

Model

Have children turn to p. 28 of *My Skills Buddy.* Use the first Vocabulary bullet on the page to guide the discussion. Direct them to the picture of the children playing. These children play. Direct them to the picture of the grassy area. This is the ground. If we put the words *play* and *ground* together, we make a new word: *playground. Playground* is a compound word made up of two shorter words, *play* and *ground.* The meaning of the compound word *playground* is a combination of the meanings of the words *play* and *ground.* Repeat the routine with the words *classroom* and *bookshelf.*

My Skills Buddy, p. 28

Guide practice

Write the words *playground, classroom,* and *bookshelf* on the board. Point to each word as you read it.

playground	classroom	bookshelf

Let's practice our new words. What two short words can we use to make a compound word that means a shelf for books? Have children look at the pictures on p. 28 of *My Skills Buddy.* Point to the pictures of the book and the shelf. We can put the two short words *book* and *shelf* together to make the compound word *bookshelf.* Repeat the routine with the word *classroom.*

On their own

Have children choose two smaller words to make a compound word. Have them draw a picture of the compound word and share it with the class. Then have them tell what two shorter words make the compound word.

Differentiated Instruction

SI Strategic Intervention

Visual Support Show children pictures of playground equipment such as slides, swings, chin-up bars, trapeze rings, and see-saws.

Academic Vocabulary

compound word a word made up of two shorter words

English Language Learners
Build Background Read the following list and have children identify things they do in the classroom, on the playground, or both: *read, jump, color, play games, climb, paint, hop, write.*

Objectives
- Review skills learned and practiced today.
- Use pronouns *I* and *me* in sentences.

Wrap Up Your Day

✔ **Concept Talk** Today we read a story about a boy watching his new school being built. What is the first machine the boy watches?

✔ **Phonemic Awareness** I am going to say a sentence. Clap your hands when you hear an /a/ word. Snap your fingers when you hear an /i/ word: *Adam can fit in the bag. Izzy will stand at the sink.*

✔ **Vocabulary Skill** Today we talked about compound words. What is a compound word? What are the two shorter words in *classroom?*

✔ **Homework Idea** Have children say sentences with the pronoun *I* or *me.*

Preview DAY 3

Tomorrow we will reread the story about the building of a new school.

Science
Two Dogs

Materials: Decodable Book 31, chart paper, markers

Compare and Contrast Kip and Sam Display Decodable Book 31, *If Kip Can.* Help children recall the story of the two dogs, Kip and Sam. Draw a Venn diagram on chart paper. Label the left circle *Kip* and the right circle *Sam.* Have children think about what Kip and Sam look like and what they do in the story. If necessary, prompt with questions about similarities and differences, such as these:

- What kind of animal are they?
- Are both Kip and Sam big or little?

- Which dog digs here?
- Do both dogs tap Cat?
- Which dog passes Pig?

Remind children that the ways Kip and Sam are alike go in the center section and the ways they are different go in the circles. Let children tell you where to write their ideas on the Venn diagram. Then check the diagram together.

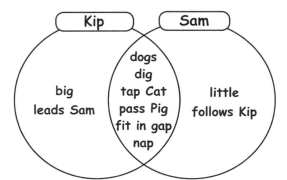

Conventions
Pronouns *I* and *me*

Write *I* or *me* Write these sentence frames on the board: ____ *sing lots of songs. Pam hit the ball to* ____. *The dog ran by* ____. ____ *like to read books.* Read the sentence frames with children. Tell them to choose a sentence frame and complete it by writing the pronoun *I* or *me.* Remind children to say the sentence using both of the pronouns to see which pronoun makes sense. Then have children tell you which pronoun fits in each sentence. Write the pronoun in the sentence frame and read the completed sentence.

Phonics
Word Bingo

Materials: bingo cards; counters; *ant, bat, can, cap, cat, fan, hat, jam, man, map, pan, pig, six, van, wig,* and *yak* Picture Cards

Play Bingo with /a/ and /i/ Words Make bingo cards by writing the name of each Picture Card in the squares of a 4 x 4 grid. Provide each child with a bingo card and 16 counters. Mix the Picture Cards and place them face down. Display the cards one at a time and say the name of the picture. Children look for the word on their card and place a counter on it. Remind them to say "Bingo!" when they have four counters in a row.

Objectives

- Share information and ideas about the concept.
- Build oral vocabulary.

Today at a Glance

Oral Vocabulary
foundation, welding

Phonemic Awareness
⊙ Medial /a/ and /i/

Phonics
⊙ /a/ Spelled *Aa*
⊙ /i/ Spelled *Ii*

Comprehension
⊙ Compare and Contrast

Conventions
Pronouns *I* and *me*

Writing
List

Listening and Speaking
Recite Language

TRUCKTOWN on Reading Street

Start your engines! Display p. 10 of *Truckery Rhymes.*

Do you know the rhyme "Here We Go 'Round the Mulberry Bush?" Recite it first, and then have children repeat it with you:

> Here we go 'round the mulberry bush,
> The mulberry bush, the mulberry bush.
> Here we go 'round the mulberry bush,
> So early in the morning.

Truckery Rhymes

Concept Talk

 Question of the Week
How is a school built?

Write the question of the week on the board. Read it as you track the print. Talk with children about the steps to build a school. Remind children to respond in complete sentences and to take turns speaking.

Listen for Amazing Words

Let's Sing Display Sing with Me Chart 31B. Tell children they are going to sing the song about building a new school. Today we are going to listen for the Amazing Words *foundation* and *welding.* Read the title and have children tell about the picture. Sing the song several times to the tune of "Here We Go 'Round the Mulberry Bush." Have children sing along with you, clapping their hands twice when they say the Amazing Word *foundation* or *welding.*

Talk with Me/Sing with Me Chart 31B

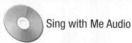 Sing with Me Audio

Oral Vocabulary
Amazing Words

Amazing Words

Amazing Words Oral Vocabulary Routine

Teach Amazing Words

① **Introduce the Word** The *foundation* of a building is the base, or the part on which all the other parts of a building are placed. What's our new Amazing Word for the base, or part on which other parts rest for support? Say it with me: *foundation.*

② **Demonstrate** Provide examples to show meaning. *The new school's foundation is made of cement and rocks that dry hard.* Why does the school need a hard *foundation?*

Repeat steps 1 and 2.

Introduce the Word *Welding* means heating the ends of two pieces of metal until they melt and flow together to make one piece of metal. *Welding* the ends of two pipes together keeps the pipes from leaking. What's our new Amazing Word for joining two pieces of metal to make one piece? Say it with me: *welding.*

Demonstrate *A person who is welding uses a very hot flame.* Why should someone who is *welding* wear heavy gloves and safety goggles?

③ **Apply** Have children use *foundation* and *welding* to describe two more steps in constructing a building.

Routines Flip Chart

Amazing Words

ground breaking trenches
foundation welding
waterproof gleaming

Differentiated Instruction

SI Strategic Intervention

Visual Support Have children use the pictures on the Talk with Me Chart to help them complete the sentences with the Amazing Words.

A Advanced

Access Content Have children find pictures of *foundation* and *welding* in *Building with Dad.*

Use Amazing Words

To reinforce the concept and the Amazing Words, have children supply the appropriate Amazing Word for each sentence.

The cement mixer pours concrete for the _____. (foundation)

The worker is busy _____ pipes. (welding)

ELL **Expand Vocabulary**
Use the Day 3 instruction on ELL Poster 31 to help children expand vocabulary.

ELL Poster 31

Building with Dad • **51**

Objectives
- ◎ Isolate medial /a/.
- ◎ Isolate medial /i/.
- • Discriminate sounds.

Phonemic Awareness
🎯 Medial /a/ and /i/

Picture Card

Picture Card

Review

Initial /a/ and /i/ Display the *ant* Picture Card. Listen as I say this word: *ant.* What is the first sound in *ant?* Say it with me: /a/ /a/ /a/, *ant.* Repeat the routine with *inch.*

Isolate medial /a/

Display the *man* Picture Card. Listen as I say this word: *man.* Listen to the sounds in *man:* /m/ /a/ /n/. Do you hear /a/ in *man?* (yes) Where do you hear /a/ in *man?* (in the middle)

Isolate medial /i/

Display the *six* Picture Card. This is *six.* Listen to the sounds in *six:* /s/ /i/ /ks/. Do you hear /i/ in *six?* (yes) Where do you hear /i/ in *six?* (in the middle)

Discriminate sounds

Listen to the middle sound in *hat. Hat* has /a/ in the middle. Now listen to these two words: *rib, bag.* Which word has the same middle sound as *hat?* Does *rib* have /a/ in the middle? (no) Does *bag* have /a/ in the middle? (yes) *Hat* and *bag* have /a/ in the middle. Continue the routine with these pairs of words: *camp, skit; hint, grass; twig, tack; ran, sit.*

On their own

Display the *can, mask, pig,* and *brick* Picture Cards. Have children draw pictures of two objects that have the same middle sound. Have them write the letter that spells the middle sound.

Substitute sounds	Listen carefully as I say a word: *trip.* Say the sounds with me: /tr/ /i/ /p/, *trip.* I can make a new word by changing the middle sound in *trip.* I will change the middle sound to /a/. Listen carefully as I say the sounds in the new word: /tr/ /a/ /p/. Say the sounds with me: /tr/ /a/ /p/. What is the new word? The new word is *trap.* Continue practice with the following pairs of words: *bag, big; clip, clap; ham, him; pick, pack; tan, tin.*

Corrective feedback	**If...** children do not grasp the concept of substituting sounds in words, **then...** provide practice using pairs of words with only two sounds: *an, in; at, it; as, is.*

Identify initial and final sounds	Listen to this word: *tap.* Think about the sounds in the word. What is the beginning sound in *tap?* (/t/) What is the ending sound in *tap?* (/p/) Continue with the following words: *swim, band, lid, class, blink, grab, fist, sat, win.*

Differentiated Instruction

 Strategic Intervention

Support Phonemic Awareness
Have children identify which of the following word pairs rhyme: *bag, rag; sap, sip; lamp, damp; hint, mint; hand, band; slim, trim.*

 Advanced

Support Phonemic Awareness
Say the following words and have children replace the middle sound in each word with /a/: *bug (bag), sock (sack), pen (pan), hem (ham).* Then have children change the middle sound in each word to /i/: *bag (big), sack (sick), pan (pin), ham (him).*

Teacher Tip

Use sound discrimination activities that focus on words with medial /a/ and /i/ to check on children's ability to discriminate sounds in the medial position.

Objectives
◎ Practice /a/ spelled *Aa*.
◎ Practice /i/ spelled *Ii*.
• Substitute phonemes.
• Read /a/ and /i/ words.
• Read high-frequency words.

Check Word Reading
SUCCESS PREDICTOR

Phonics—Teach/Model
/a/ Spelled *Aa*, /i/ Spelled *Ii*

Review **/a/Aa and /i/Ii** Display the *Aa* Alphabet Card and point to the *astronaut*. What sound do you hear at the beginning of *astronaut*? What letter spells that sound? Point to the letters *Aa*. What is the sound for this letter? What are the names of these letters? Repeat with the Ii Alphabet Card.

Alphabet Card

Review **Letter Names and Sounds** Use Alphabet Cards to review the following letter names and sounds: *Cc, Dd, Ff, Gg, Kk, Nn, Ss, Tt.*

Blend sounds Write *six* on the board. Point to each letter as you say the sound: /s/ /i/ /ks/. When I blend these sounds together, I make the word *six.* Say the sounds with me: /s/ /i/ /ks/. Now blend the sounds with me as I point to the letters: /s/ /i/ /ks/, *six.* Continue the routine with the following words: *and, kid, at, gift, Dad, it, cat.*

Alphabet Card

More practice Use *Reader's and Writer's Notebook,* p. 407, for additional practice with /a/ and /i/.

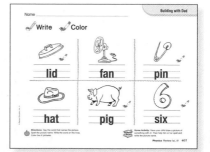

Reader's and Writer's Notebook, p. 407

Review **Sound-Spelling** Display the *Bb* Alphabet Card. *What sound do you hear at the beginning of baby? What letter spells that sound?* Yes, the letter *b* spells /b/. Review the sound-spellings for the other consonants. Then review the sound-spellings for initial and final consonant blends such as *tr, gl, nd,* and *mp.*

Review **High-Frequency Words** Write *here* on the board. *This is the word here. What is this word?* Continue the routine with *do, little, with,* and *what.*

Bb English

baby

Alphabet Card

 Don't Wait Until Friday

MONITOR PROGRESS Check Word Reading   High-Frequency Words

Write *are, they, do, little, what, look, see, have,* and *is* on the board. Have children take turns reading the words.

Practice reading these words from Kindergarten Student Reader K.6.1, *Max and Jen.*

Max	Jen	six	big	kids	zip	run	can
red	Mom	gift	box	cat	Tag	soft	and

If... children cannot read the high-frequency words,
then... write the words on cards for them to practice at home.

If... children cannot blend sounds to read the words,
then... provide practice blending the words in chunks, /m/ *-ax.*

If... children can successfully blend sounds to read the words,
then... have them read Kindergarten Student Reader K.6.1, *Max and Jen.*

Day 1	**Day 2**	**Day 3**	**Day 4**	**Day 5**
Check Phonemic Awareness	Check Sound-Spelling/ Retelling	Check Word Reading	Check Phonemic Awareness	Check Oral Vocabulary

Success Predictor

Differentiated Instruction

 SI **Strategic Intervention**

Blend Words Tell children that AlphaBuddy only likes to say whole words. *I will say a word in parts. Tell me what word AlphaBuddy will say.* Say the following words in parts: *crib, duck, leaf, sun, block, glad, trip.* Tell children to blend the parts and then say the word. Have AlphaBuddy provide corrective feedback if necessary.

A **Advanced**

Sound Identification Show children a page from *Max and Jen. I will say a name of something in the picture, but I will not say the beginning sound. If I see a boy, I will say* oy. *You will add the beginning sound and say* boy. *Then name the letter that spells that sound.* Repeat the routine with final sounds.

Word Reading

Success Predictor

Objectives
• Read /a/ and /i/ words.
• Read high-frequency words.

Kindergarten Student Reader K.6.1
/a/ Spelled *Aa* and /i/ Spelled *Ii* and High-Frequency Words

Review

High-Frequency Words Review the previously taught high-frequency words. Have children read each word as you point to it on the Word Wall.

are	they	like	to	have	a	is
what	the	for	you	look	see	little

Read Kindergarten Student Reader K.6.1

Display Kindergarten Student Reader K.6.1. Today we are going to read a new book. Point to the title of the story. The title of this book is *Max and Jen. Jen* and *Max* are names for people. What do you see on the cover? Who do you think these children are? What do you think the book will be about? Let's look for /a/ and /i/ words as we read the book.

ROUTINE **Reading Decodable Books**

Small Group

1) **Read Silently** Have children whisper read the book page by page as you listen in.

2) **Model Fluent Reading** Have children finger point as you read a page. Then have children reread the page without you.

3) **Read Chorally** Have children finger point as they chorally read the page. Continue reading page by page, repeating steps 1 and 2.

4) **Read Individually** Have children take turns reading aloud a page.

5) **Reread and Monitor Progress** As you listen to individual children reread, monitor progress and provide support.

6) **Reread with a Partner** Have children reread the book page by page with a partner.

Routines Flip Chart

Jen and Max are six.
They are big kids.

Kindergarten Student Reader K.6.1

Jen can zip.
Max can run.
They like to zip and run.

Mom and Dad have a box.
It is a big red box.
It is a gift.

What is in the box, Mom?
It is a gift for you and Max.

Jen and Max look at the box.
They look in the big red box.

Look! Jen and Max see a cat.
It is Tag, the little cat.

Tag is little and soft.
Jen and Max like Tag.
Tag likes Jen and Max.

Small Group Time

DAY 3 Break into small groups to read the Kindergarten Student Reader before the comprehension lesson.

 Teacher-Led

SI Strategic Intervention	**OL** On-Level	**A** Advanced
Teacher-Led Page DI•3 • Phonemic Awareness and Phonics • **Read** Concept Literacy Reader K.6.1 or Kindergarten Student Reader K.6.1	**Teacher-Led** Page DI•7 • Phonemic Awareness and Phonics • **Read** Kindergarten Student Reader K.6.1	**Teacher-Led** Page DI•10 • **Read** Independent Reader K.6.1 or Kindergarten Student Reader K.6.1

ELL Place English language learners in the groups that correspond to their reading abilities in English.

Practice Stations
• Visit the Words to Know Station
• Visit the Let's Write! Station

Independent Activities
• Read independently
• Audio Text of Big Book
• *Reader's and Writer's Notebook*

Differentiated Instruction

 **Strategic Intervention**

High-Frequency Words Have children read a Kindergarten Student Reader from a previous week with a partner to practice reading high-frequency words.

Teacher Tip

Review the high-frequency words on each page before reading Kindergarten Student Reader K.6.1.

Objectives

- Recall and retell a story.
- Practice compare and contrast.
- Develop and use vocabulary.
- Develop and use comprehension skills.

Comprehension

Retell the story

Have children turn to p. 26 of *My Skills Buddy* and use the retelling boxes to retell the story *Building with Dad*.

Envision It!

 Think Aloud Direct children to the first retell box. This is a bulldozer. How does it help build a school? Tell me the steps to build a new school.

Continue reviewing the retelling boxes and having children retell the story.

My Skills Buddy, p. 26

Review

Compare and Contrast Display illustration in *Building with Dad*. Let's compare and contrast things in the story.

- Compare the bulldozer on pp. 6–7 and the dump truck on pp. 8–9. How are they alike? (They are both machines. They are both big and yellow. They are both used at the construction site.)

- Contrast the bulldozer on pp. 6–7 and the dump truck on pp. 8–9. How are they different? (The bulldozer pushes dirt. It has treads. The dump truck brings in and dumps rocks, or fill. It has tires.)

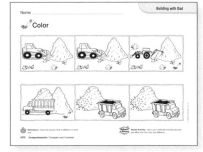

More practice

Use *Reader's and Writer's Notebook,* p. 408, for additional practice with compare and contrast.

Reader's and Writer's Notebook, p. 408

Second Read—Big Book
Building with Dad

Reread *Building with Dad*. Follow the Day 3 arrow beginning on p. 59, and use the Develop Vocabulary notes to prompt conversations about the story.

Have children use the Amazing Words *groundbreaking, trenches, foundation, welding, waterproof,* and *gleaming* to talk about the story.

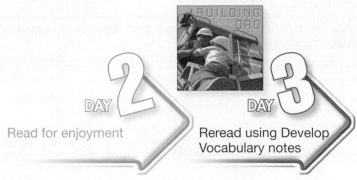

DAY 2 — Read for enjoyment

DAY 3 — Reread using Develop Vocabulary notes

DAY 4 — Reread using Guide Comprehension notes

Develop Vocabulary

DAY 3

***Wh-* question**
What is happening in the picture? (A boy is riding on his dad's shoulders.)

* A boy is riding on his dad's shoulders.
  Where are the boy and his dad?

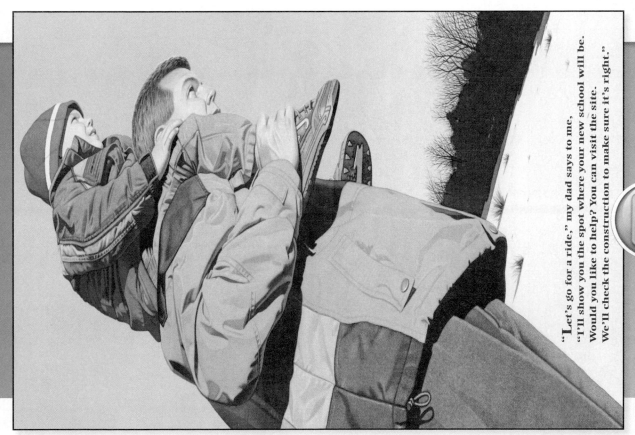

"Let's go for a ride," my dad says to me,
"I'll show you the spot where your new school will be.
Would you like to help? You can visit the site.
We'll check the construction to make sure it's right."

Big Book, pp. 4–5

Guide Comprehension

DAY 4

***Wh-* question**
What will be built at the construction site?
(The boy's new school will be built there.)

Develop Vocabulary, continued

DAY 3

Recall

What machine is this? (a bulldozer)

- This machine is a bulldozer. What does a bulldozer do?

Expand Vocabulary diesels

We wait till the groundbreaking work has begun. Watch bulldozers ROAR. Pushing dirt, diesels run.

Big Book, pp. 6–7

Guide Comprehension, continued

DAY 4

Inferential

Why are bulldozers the first machines to do work at a construction site? (Bulldozers push away dirt, trees, and rocks to get the ground ready for construction.)

Distancing

What is this dump truck dumping at the construction site? (rocks)

- This dump truck is dumping rocks, or fill, at the construction site. What else can a dump truck carry and dump?

Develop Vocabulary spill

Big Book, pp. 8–9

Compare and Contrast

How are the bulldozer and the dump truck alike? (They are both machines. They are both used in construction work.) How are they different? (The bulldozer pushes dirt. It has treads. The dump truck carries and dumps rocks. It has tires.)

Develop Vocabulary, continued

Recall

What does the backhoe do? (It digs trenches.)

- The backhoe digs trenches. What are the trenches for?

DAY 3

I help Dad's mechanic. We count all her wrenches, and watch as the backhoe digs long pipeline trenches.

Big Book, pp. 10–11

Guide Comprehension, continued

DAY 4

Compare and Contrast

How are the backhoe and the bulldozer alike? (They are both machines. They are both used in construction work.) How are they different? (The backhoe digs trenches. The bulldozer pushes dirt.)

Distancing

What is the boy doing? (He is climbing up into a huge machine.)

- The boy is climbing up into an earthmover. Why is he wearing a hard hat and work boots?

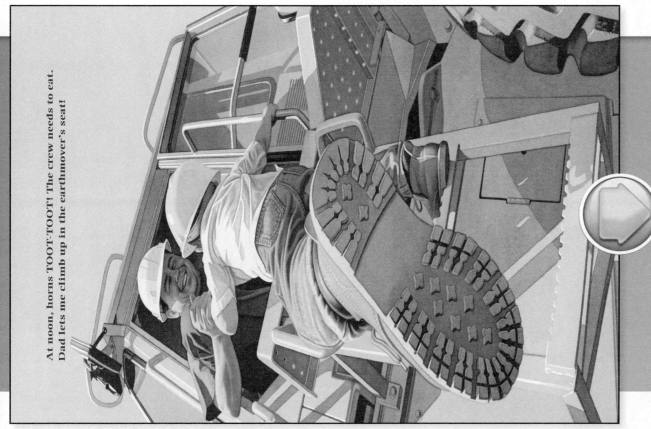

At noon, horns TOOT-TOOT! The crew needs to eat. Dad lets me climb up in the earthmover's seat!

Big Book, pp. 12–13

Inferential

What does the sound of the horn tell the crew? (It tells them that it is noon and therefore time for them to eat their lunch.)

DAY 3

Develop Vocabulary, continued

Recall
What machine is this? (a steamroller)

- This machine is a steamroller.
  What does a steamroller do?

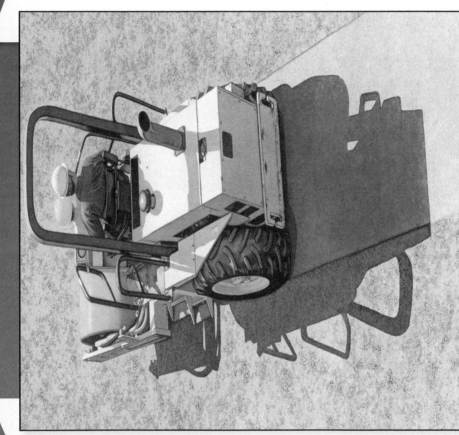

Dad's giant grader smoothes over the ground.
His steamroller follows to crush the dirt down.

Big Book, pp. 14–15

DAY 4

Guide Comprehension, continued

Compare and Contrast
How are the grader and the steamroller different? (The grader smoothes over the ground. It goes first. The steamroller crushes the dirt down. It goes second.) How are they alike? (They are both used to make the ground hard and flat.)

Wh- question

What is the cement mixer pouring out? (gray glop; cement)

- The cement mixer is pouring out gray glop called cement. What is the cement used to make?

Cement mixer turns out gray glop by the yard. The foundation forms. It sets up and dries hard.

Big Book, pp. 16–17

Recall

How is the foundation made? (A cement mixer pours out cement, which dries and hardens to make the foundation.)

Develop Vocabulary, continued

DAY 3

Open-ended

What is the boy looking up at? (a crane)

• The boy is looking up at a crane. How do you know that is what he is looking up at?

Expand Vocabulary girders, mortar

Cranes are like arms, lifting girders and brick. Crews bolt, nut, and mortar them, solid and thick.

Big Book, pp. 18–19

Guide Comprehension, continued

DAY 4

Compare and Contrast

What does the boy compare cranes to? Why? (He compares them to arms because the cranes lift things just as we lift things with our arms.)

Distancing

Where is the worker standing? (on the roof of the building)

- The worker is standing on the roof of the building. Why does a building need a roof?

Zip-zap! The power tools fasten the ply. The new roof is waterproof. School will be dry.

Big Book, pp. 20–21

Inferential

Why is it important that a roof is waterproof? (A waterproof roof will keep rain from getting inside the building and getting everything and everyone in the building wet.)

Develop Vocabulary, continued

DAY 3

Wh- question

What are the frames for the walls made of? (gray metal)

- These gray metal frames show where the walls of the rooms will be. What kinds of rooms does the boy mention?

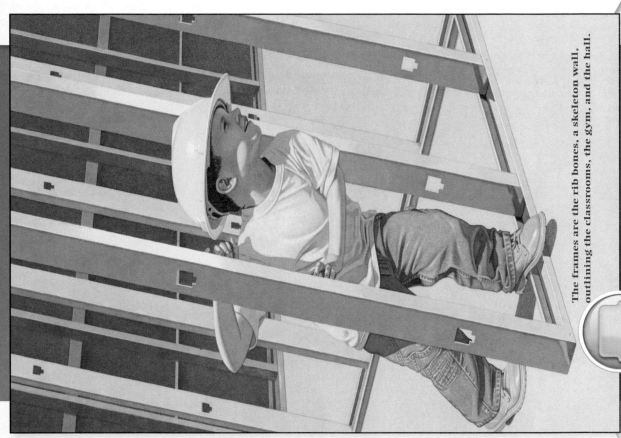

The frames are the rib bones, a skeleton wall, outlining the classrooms, the gym, and the hall.

Big Book, pp. 22–23

Guide Comprehension, continued

DAY 4

Compare and Contrast

What does the boy compare the frames to? Why? (He compares them to the rib bones of a skeleton because the frames will support the walls just as our bones support our bodies.)

Distancing

What is this worker doing? (welding pipes)

• This worker is welding two pieces of pipe together. Why is he wearing a face mask and heavy gloves?

Develop Vocabulary pipes, wire

The team works inside, welding pipes using fire, sealing windows and tile, running cables and wire.

Big Book, pp. 24–25

Inferential

Why is the worker welding the pipes? (By welding the place where the two pipes meet, the worker makes sure that the pipes won't leak there.)

Develop Vocabulary, continued

DAY 3

Wh- question
What is the boy doing to the new floor? (polishing it with a cloth)

- The boy is polishing the new floor with a cloth. What can he see in the floor?

The teachers have meetings. Dad's last workers rush. Our waxed floors are gleaming. The toilets all flush.

Big Book, pp. 26–27

Guide Comprehension, continued

DAY 4

Inferential
Why can the boy see his reflection in the new floor? (The new floor is so clean and smooth that it acts like a mirror and reflects things.)

Recall

What is the boy in now? (a bucket truck)

- The boy is in a bucket truck. What does a bucket truck do?

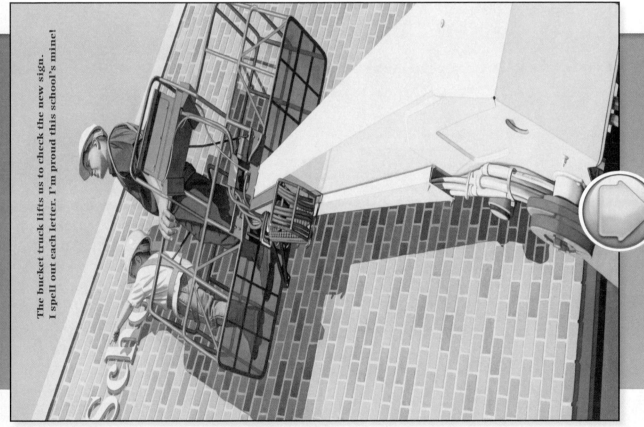

The bucket truck lifts us to check the new sign. I spell out each letter. I'm proud this school's mine!

Big Book, pp. 28–29

Recall

How does the bucket truck help the boy and his dad? (It lifts them up so they can check the sign high up on the wall of the building.)

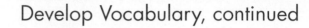
Develop Vocabulary, continued

DAY 3

Open-ended
Where are the children going? (into the new school)

• The children are going into the new school. Do you think they are happy to be going to a new school? Why or why not?

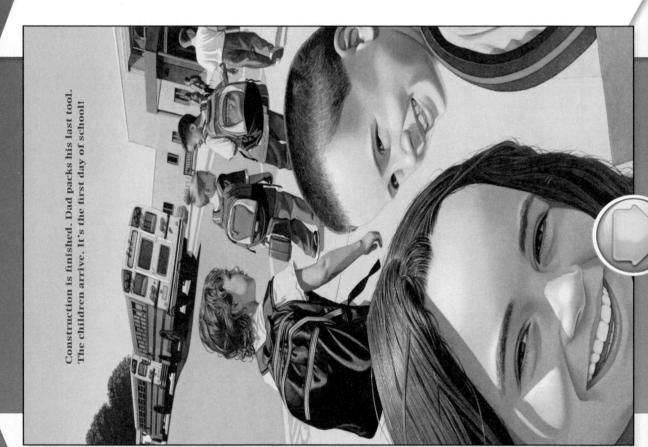

Construction is finished. Dad packs his last tool. The children arrive. It's the first day of school!

Big Book, pp. 30–31

Guide Comprehension, continued

DAY 4

Compare and Contrast
How is the way the construction site looks here different from the way it looks on pages 4–5? (The construction site on pages 4–5 is an empty piece of ground with a few bits of grass. The construction site here is covered with school buildings, sidewalks, pavement, buses, and children.)

Wh- question

What is the boy doing? (swinging on a swing by the new school)

- The boy is swinging on a swing in the new school's playground. What is he still wearing?

Continue with DAY **3**

Conventions p. 74

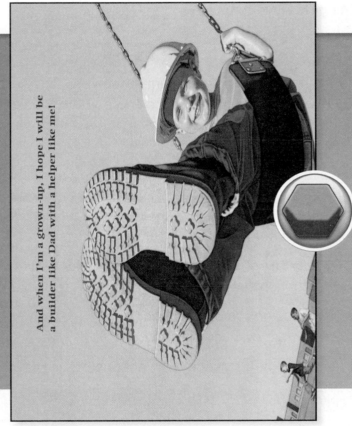

And when I'm a grown-up, I hope I will be a builder like Dad with a helper like me!

Big Book, p. 32

Inferential

Why do you think the boy is still wearing his hard hat and work boots? (I think he likes wearing them. He looks proud and happy. I think he is proud of the hard hat and boots because they show that he helped build his school.)

Skip to DAY **4**

Conventions p. 88

Conventions
Verbs

Review

Remind children of what they learned about verbs. Verbs are words that tell about things we can do. Verbs are action words. Wave your hand as if you are saying good-bye to the class. What is the verb for what I am doing? The verb is *wave*. I can use the verb *wave* in a sentence that tells about what I am doing: *I wave my hand.*

Write these sentences on the board:

> **The girls wave to us.**
>
> **Lisa waves to us.**

Read the first sentence and point to the verb. The verb in this sentence is *wave.* Read the second sentence and point to the verb. The verb in this sentence is *waves. Waves* has an *-s* at the end because it tells about what one person is doing.

Guide practice

Tell a child to do something or pretend to do something. What is the verb for what (Tarik) is doing? Use the verb in a sentence that tells about what (Tarik) is doing. Continue with the routine until all children have had a chance to act out a verb.

Team Talk Pair children and have them take turns telling what one worker at a construction site does. Then have them tell what two workers do.

On their own

Use *Reader's and Writer's Notebook,* p. 409, for more practice with verbs.

Daily Fix-It

Use the Daily Fix-It for more conventions practice.

Reader's and Writer's Notebook, p. 409

Writing
List

Teach

Write the following in a column on the board: *desk, pencils, crayons, books.* Read the list aloud. This is a list of things in the classroom. A list is a group of words, names, or numbers written one below the other. A list can help us keep track of things we need or things to do. People make lists everyday. Have children think of reasons to make a list.

Model

Discuss *Building with Dad.* We can make a list of machines in the story in order to help us remember them. Write *Machines* on the board. We will name our list *Machines.* What machine does the groundbreaking? A bulldozer does the groundbreaking. Write *bulldozer* on the board under *Machines.* What does the machine do? It pushes dirt. Write *pushes dirt* next to *bulldozer.*

Guide practice

Have children provide more names of machines from *Building with Dad* for the list. Have children tell what each machine does. Draw a simple picture for each item.

Independent writing

Have children turn to p. 410 of *Reader's and Writer's Notebook.* Have children write or dictate a list of things from *Building with Dad* they want to learn more about.

 INTERACT with TEXT

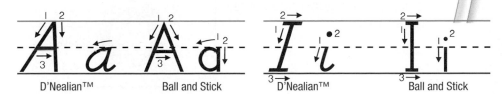

Answers will vary.

Reader's and Writer's Notebook, p. 410

Daily Handwriting

Write *Adam, Izzy, pal,* and *lid.* Review correct letter formation of uppercase *A* and *I* and lowercase *a* and *i.*

Aa — D'Nealian™   Aa — Ball and Stick   Ii — D'Nealian™   Ii — Ball and Stick

Have children write *Adam, Izzy, pal,* and *lid* on their Write-On Boards. Remind them to use proper left-to-right and top-to-bottom progression and proper spacing between letters when writing *Aa* and *Ii.*

Objectives
- Practice reciting language.
- Speak loudly and clearly.
- Take turns speaking.

Listening and Speaking
Recite Language

Review   When we recite things, we say things that we have memorized. When we memorize, we put things in our memory so that we remember them and can say them anytime we want.

Model   Hold up AlphaBuddy. AlphaBuddy has memorized a nursery rhyme that you might know too. He wants to recite this nursery rhyme.

> Little Miss Muffet
> Sat on a tuffet,
> Eating her curds and whey.
> Along came a spider,
> That sat down beside her
> And frightened Miss Muffet away.

Have children turn to p. 29 of *My Skills Buddy.* Use the Listening and Speaking bullet on p. 28 of *My Skills Buddy* to guide the discussion. Have AlphaBuddy recite the nursery rhyme several times, pausing after each line so that children can repeat the line after him. Remind children that when they recite language, they need to speak loudly and clearly to make sure that everyone can hear and understand them. Remind children that good speakers take turns.

My Skills Buddy, p. 29

Independent practice

Have children come to the front of the class to recite a favorite nursery rhyme, or share a line from AlphaBuddy's nursery rhyme. Refer children to the Rules for Speaking from p. 2 of *Reader's and Writer's Notebook.* Tell children to speak loudly and clearly when speaking. Remind listeners to take turns speaking.

Name

Speaking Rules

1. Speak clearly.
2. Tell only important ideas.
3. Choose your words carefully.
4. Take turns speaking.
5. Speak one at a time.

Reader's and Writer's Notebook, p. 2

Be a Good Speaker

1. Speak loudly and clearly.
2. Tell only important ideas.
3. Choose your words carefully.
4. Take turns speaking.
5. Speak one at a time.

Differentiated Instruction

 Strategic Intervention

Model Oral Language Play a CD of nursery rhymes to reinforce the importance of volume, clarity, and inflection in recited language.

English Language Learners

Physical Response Have children act out the rhyme and recite key words or phrases from each line, such as *Miss Muffet, sat, eating, spider, sat down,* and *frightened away.*

Objectives
- Review skills learned and practiced today.
- Recite a rhyme, speaking loudly and clearly.

Wrap Up Your Day

✔ **Concept Talk** Today we reread the story about building a new school. What kinds of machines are used to build the school?

✔ **Respond to Literature** Today we read about a gift that Jen and Max get from their mom and dad. What was in the big red box?

✔ **Conventions** Have children act out a verb while the other children guess what the verb is.

✔ **Homework Idea** Have children recite "Little Miss Muffet" or another nursery rhyme they know by heart to their family. Remind them to speak loudly and clearly so their families can hear them and understand them.

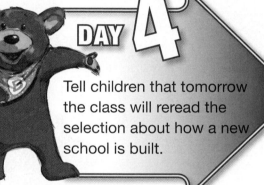

Preview DAY 4

Tell children that tomorrow the class will reread the selection about how a new school is built.

Science
How to Build a School

Materials: Big Book *Building with Dad*, white construction paper, crayons, colored markers, tape

Illustrate the Steps in a Process Display the Big Book *Building with Dad.* Help children recall that the book tells about the steps in building a school. Divide children into small groups, and give the groups paper, crayons, and markers. The members of each group are to work together to draw pictures of the steps in building the school, one step per sheet. For example, their first picture may show the bulldozer clearing the site, and the next picture may show the cement mixer pouring the foundation. Tell children they may draw many steps, but they must draw at least three.

Tell About the Sequence After the groups have finished, have them put their pictures in order and show and explain their sequence to the class. Finally, tape each group's pictures end to end to make a storyboard. Display the storyboards on a bulletin board titled *How to Build a School.*

Comprehension
Max and Jen

Materials: Kindergarten Student Reader K.6.1, *Max and Jen;* chart paper; markers

Compare and Contrast Characters Display Kindergarten Student Reader K.6.1, *Max and Jen.* Help children recall the story. Draw a T-chart on chart paper. Write *Jen and Max* above the T. Write *Alike* and *Different* as the two headings. How are Jen and Max alike and different? Have children look at the illustrations as well as the text.

Jen and Max	
Alike	Different
They are six.	Jen is a girl. Max is a boy.
They are big kids.	Jen zips on her bike. Max runs.
They have curly black hair.	
They like to zip and run.	Jen has a pink shirt and red shorts. Max has a yellow shirt and green shorts.
They like Tag.	

Conventions
Word Sort

Materials: index cards with these words written on them—(verbs) *drips, jogs, nods, rubs, sells, sits, stands, wags;* (nouns) *cat, desk, dog, gift, man, rug;* (adjectives) *best, damp, flat, hot, pink, six*

Identify Verbs, Nouns, and Adjectives Write the verbs, nouns, and adjectives on index cards. Mix the cards and lay them out in four rows of five cards each. Read the words with children. Tell them to sort the words into three groups—nouns, verbs, adjectives. After children are finished, read the words in each group together to check the sorting.

Objectives

- Discuss the concept to develop oral language.
- Build oral vocabulary.

Today at a Glance

Oral Vocabulary
waterproof, gleaming

Phonemic Awareness
/y/ and /kw/

Phonics
/y/ Spelled *Yy*
/kw/ Spelled *qu*
Spell Words

Comprehension
◉ Compare and Contrast

Conventions
Pronouns *I* and *me*

Writing
Extend the Concept

Vocabulary
Compound Words

TRUCKTOWN on Reading Street

Start your engines!

- Display "This Is the Way" and lead the group in saying the rhyme a few times.
- Next have the group clap the rhythm as they recite the rhyme.
- When children master the rhythm, have them march around the room as they say the rhyme.

Truckery Rhymes

Concept Talk

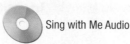
Question of the Week
How is a school built?

Build concepts

Write the question of the week on the board. Read the question as you track the print. Tell children to respond in complete sentences. Display the Sing with Me Chart 31B.

Listen for Amazing Words

We are going to sing this song again. Listen for the Amazing Words *waterproof* and *gleaming*. Sing the song several times to the tune of "Here We Go 'Round the Mulberry Bush." Tell children to sing along with you. Have them stand up and then sit down each time they hear the Amazing Word *waterproof* or *gleaming*.

Sing with Me Audio

ELL Produce Oral Language Use the Day 4 instruction on ELL Poster 31 to extend and enrich language.

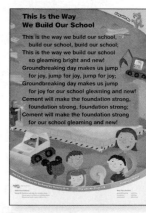

This Is the Way We Build Our School

This is the way we build our school,
   build our school, build our school;
This is the way we build our school
   so gleaming bright and new!
Groundbreaking day makes us jump
   for joy, jump for joy, jump for joy;
Groundbreaking day makes us jump
   for joy for our school gleaming and new!
Cement will make the foundation strong,
   foundation strong, foundation strong;
Cement will make the foundation strong
   for our school gleaming and new!

Talk with Me/Sing with Me Chart 31B

ELL Poster 31

Oral Vocabulary
Amazing Words

Amazing Words

ground breaking	trenches
foundation	welding
waterproof	gleaming

Teach Amazing Words

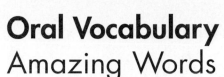 **Oral Vocabulary Routine**

1. **Introduce the Word** The school's new roof is *waterproof,* so rain can't get through it. What is our new Amazing Word for something that is able to keep water from coming through? Say it with me: *waterproof.*

2. **Demonstrate** *An umbrella is waterproof.* What are some other things you know that are *waterproof?*

   Repeat steps 1 and 2.

   Introduce the Word The school's new floors are *gleaming* because they are so clean and smooth that they reflect the light. What is our new Amazing Word for giving off a reflected light? Say it with me: *gleaming.*

   Demonstrate *The freshly washed and waxed car is gleaming in the sunshine.* What are some other things you know that are *gleaming?*

3. **Apply** Tell children to use *waterproof* and *gleaming* to describe parts of the new school.

Routines Flip Chart

Use Amazing Words

To reinforce the concept and the Amazing Words, have children supply the appropriate Amazing Word for each sentence.

The furniture was _____ after he polished it. (gleaming)

When it rained, they stayed in their _____ tent. (waterproof)

Differentiated Instruction

 Strategic Intervention

Clarify Meaning If children need help completing the sentences, say a sentence using both *waterproof* and *gleaming* one at a time and ask children to choose the sentence that makes sense.

A **Advanced**

Build Background Have children look through magazines to find pictures of things that can be described as *gleaming.*

Objectives
- Review /y/ spelled *Yy*.
- Review /kw/ spelled *qu*.

Check Phonemic Awareness
SUCCESS PREDICTOR

Phonemic Awareness
Review /y/ and /kw/

Review

Display the *yarn* Picture Card. This is *yarn. Yarn* begins with /y/. What sound does *yarn* begin with? Continue with the *yak, yellow,* and *yo-yo* Picture Cards.

Display the *quilt* Picture Card. This is a *quilt. Quilt* begins /kw/. What sound does *quilt* begin with? Continue with the *quarter* and *queen* Picture Cards.

I am going to say some words. When you hear /y/ at the beginning of the word, hold your arms up in the shape of a *y*. When you hear /kw/ at the beginning of the word, make a circle over your head with your arms. Listen carefully: *quiet.* Do you hear /y/ or /kw/ at the beginning of *quiet?* I hear /kw/ at the beginning, so I will make a circle over my head with my arms. Continue with the following words: *yawn, quote, year, yard, quest, quick, yell, quill, quart, you, yes.*

Corrective feedback

If... children cannot discriminate /y/ or /kw/, **then...** say each sound several times and have children watch you closely as you do so.

Explain that /kw/ is two sounds, /k/ and /w/, blended together. Have children practice saying /y/ and /kw/.

Picture Card

Picture Card

Phonics
/y/ Spelled *Yy* and /kw/ Spelled *qu*

Review

Display the *Qq* Alphabet Card. This is a *queen*. *Queen* begins with /kw/. What letters spell the sound /kw/? Yes, the letters *qu*. *Q* is a special letter because it is usually with its buddy *u*. When we see *q* words, they usually begin with *q* and *u*. Repeat the routine with the *Yy* Alphabet Card.

Write *yam* on the board. Help me blend this word. Listen as I say each sound, /y/ /a/ /m/. Now let's blend the sounds together to read the word: /y/ /a/ /m/, *yam.* Let's try some more. Continue the routine using the following words: *quilt, yak, quiz, yank, quack.*

Alphabet Card

Alphabet Card

Don't Wait Until Friday

MONITOR PROGRESS ⟳ **Check Phonemic Awareness**

Practice blending the following words: *pig, will, Sam, fit, can, dig, if, tap, at, gap, big, Kip, nap, in.*

If... children cannot blend the sounds to read the words,

then... use the small-group Strategic Intervention lesson, p. DI•4, to reteach blending.

Continue to monitor children's progress using other instructional opportunities so they can be successful with the Day 5 Assessment. See the Skills Trace on p. 20.

Day 1	Day 2	Day 3	**Day 4**	Day 5
Check Phonemic Awareness	Check Sound-Spelling/ Retelling	Check Word Reading	Check Phonemic Awareness	Check Oral Vocabulary

Success Predictor

Differentiated Instruction

A **Advanced**

Support Phonemic Awareness
Tell children to listen closely to the three words you will say and tell you what sound they hear that is the same in two of the words. Say these words: *yo-yo, year, queen; yes, quit, yard; quiet, quack, you; quiz, young, quarter.*

ELL

English Language Learners
Support Phonemic Awareness
Children may be confused because the letter *y* can represent both a consonant and a vowel sound. Point out that when the letter *y* appears at the beginning of the word, it represents /y/.

Phonemic Awareness

Success Predictor

Spelling
/a/ Spelled *Aa*, /i/ Spelled *Ii*

ROUTINE   Spell Words

Spell words

1 **Review Sound-Spellings** Display the *Aa* Alphabet Card. This is an *astronaut. Astronaut* begins with /a/. What is the letter for /a/? (*a*) Continue the routine with the *Ii* Alphabet Card.

2 **Model** Today we are going to spell some words. Listen to the three sounds in sat: /s/ /a/ /t/.

- What is the first sound in sat? (/s/) What is the letter for /s/? (*s*) Write *s* on the board.

- What is the middle sound you hear? (/a/) What is the letter for /a/? (*a*) Write *a* on the board.

- What is the last sound you hear? (/t/) What is the letter for /t/? (*t*) Write *t* on the board.

- Point to *sat.* Help me blend the sounds of each letter together to read this word: /s/ /a/ /t/. The word is *sat.* Repeat with the word *win.*

3 **Guide Practice** Now let's spell some words together. Listen to this word: /h/ /i/ /m/. What is the first sound in *him?* (/h/) What is the letter for /h/? (*h*) Write *h* on the board. Now you write *h* on your paper. What is the middle sound in *him?* (/i/) What is the letter for /i/? (*i*) Write *i* on the board. Now you write *i* on your paper. What is the last sound in *him?* (/m/) What is the letter for /m/? (*m*) Write *m* on the board. Now you write *m* on your paper. Now we can blend the sound of each letter together to read the word: /h/ /i/ /m/. What is the word? (*him*) Continue spell and blend practice with the following words: *hand, crib, tag, lip.*

4 **On Your Own** This time I am going to say a word. I want you to write it on your paper. Remember, first say the word slowly in your head and then write the letter for each sound. Listen carefully. Write the word trap. Give children time to write the word. How do you spell the word *trap*? Listen to the sounds: /tr/ /a/ /p/. The first sound is /tr/. What are the two letters for /tr/? Did you write *tr* on your paper? What is the letter for /a/? Did you write *a* on your paper? What is the letter for /p/? Did you write *p* on your paper? Name the letters in *trap. Trap* is spelled *t, r, a, p.* Continue the activity with the words *glass, lid, mat,* and *swim.*

Routines Flip Chart

Get Set, Roll! Reader 31
 Practice /a/ Spelled *Aa* and /i/ Spelled *Ii*

Review

Review the high-frequency words *where, was, the, see, little, she,* and *said.* Have children read each word as you point to it on the Word Wall.

Read Get Set, Roll! Reader 31

Display Get Set, Roll! Reader 31, *A Nap.* Today we will read a book about Rita. Point to the title of the book. What is the title of the book? (*A Nap*) We can read all the words in this book.

Use the routine for reading decodable books found in the Routine Flip Chart to read Get Set, Roll! Reader 31.

Get Set, Roll! Reader 31

Differentiated Instruction

SI Strategic Intervention

Medial Sound Identification Make a two-column chart on the board with the headings /a/ and /i/. Have children identify the middle sound in each of the spelling words and write the spelling word in the appropriate column.

A Advanced

Use Spelling Words Have children write sentences using the words *him, hand, crib, tag,* and *lip.*

Small Group Time

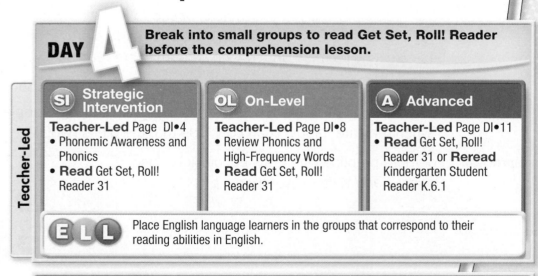

DAY 4 Break into small groups to read Get Set, Roll! Reader before the comprehension lesson.

Teacher-Led

SI Strategic Intervention	**OL** On-Level	**A** Advanced
Teacher-Led Page DI•4 • Phonemic Awareness and Phonics • **Read** Get Set, Roll! Reader 31	**Teacher-Led** Page DI•8 • Review Phonics and High-Frequency Words • **Read** Get Set, Roll! Reader 31	**Teacher-Led** Page DI•11 • **Read** Get Set, Roll! Reader 31 or **Reread** Kindergarten Student Reader K.6.1

ELL Place English language learners in the groups that correspond to their reading abilities in English.

Practice Stations
• Visit the Let's Write! Station
• Visit the Read for Meaning Station

Independent Activities
• Read independently
• Audio Text of the Big Book
• *Reader's and Writer's Notebook*

 ELL

English Language Learners

Frontload Reader Take a picture walk with children to preview the reader before starting the routine.

Objectives

◎ Practice compare and contrast.
• Review draw conclusions.

Comprehension
🎯 Compare and Contrast

Practice compare and contrast

Envision It!

Have children turn to the Compare and Contrast picture on p. 14 in *My Skills Buddy*. As you look at the pictures, remind children that when we compare things, we tell how they are alike, or similar. When we contrast things, we tell how they are different, or not similar.

My Skills Buddy, pp. 14–15

Team Talk Pair children and have them compare and contrast their classroom and the playground at their school.

Draw Conclusions

Review

Direct children to the picture on pp. 114–115 of *My Skills Buddy*.

When you use what you know, hear, or see to make up your mind about things, you are drawing conclusions. Good readers draw conclusions because it helps them understand what they are reading.

• How does the girl feel about the present? (She is happy about it.)

• How did you draw that conclusion? (The girl is smiling. People smile when they are happy. I can conclude that the girl is happy.)

More practice

For more practice with draw conclusions, use *Reader's and Writer's Notebook,* p. 411.

Reader's and Writer's Notebook, p. 411

Third Read—Big Book
Building with Dad

Guide comprehension

Display *Building with Dad.* Tell children a conclusion is based on what they know, hear, and see.

- The boy spends a lot of time at the construction site. What can you conclude about how he feels about construction work? (He likes it. He enjoys watching and helping with the work.)

- Look at how the boy and his dad are dressed at the beginning of the book. What can you conclude about the time of year when the construction started? (They are wearing jackets, and the boy is wearing a cap, so the construction must have started in late winter or early spring.)

Reread *Building with Dad.* Return to p. 59. Follow the Day 4 arrow and use the Guide Comprehension notes to give children the opportunity to gain a more complete understanding of the story.

DAY 2 — Read for enjoyment

DAY 3 — Reread using Develop Vocabulary notes

DAY 4 — Reread using Guide Comprehension notes

Differentiated Instruction

 Strategic Intervention

Draw Conclusions Reread *Max and Jen.* Use these prompts to help children draw conclusions: *Why did Mom and Dad give Max and Jen a gift? How did Max and Jen feel when they opened the gift?*

 Advanced

Access Content Tell children that good readers find story clues to help them draw conclusions. Page through *Building with Dad* and have them find clues to support their conclusions.

ELL

English Language Learners
Build Survival Vocabulary Use the Compare and Contrast picture to help children understand the expression "rain or shine." Point to the cloud and sun and say: Sometimes people will send you an invitation for a party or other event that says "rain or shine." That means the event will happen no matter what the weather is like, whether it is raining or the sun is shining.

Objectives

- Practice using pronouns *I* and *me*.
- Write or dictate sentences about building together.

Conventions
Pronouns *I* and *me*

Review   Remind children of what they learned about the pronouns *I* and *me*. Pronouns are words that can take the place of nouns. Use the pronouns *I* or *me* in place of your name in a sentence. Listen for the pronouns in these sentences: *I walked to the library. Dad made lunch for me.*

Guide practice   I am going to say a sentence. Stand up if you hear a pronoun. **Say:** *Jose makes lunch. I set the table. Jose cuts up apples and grapes. Jose gives me a bowl of fruit. I sit next to Jose. Jose goes to school with me.* As children stand, have them say the pronoun they heard in the sentence. Write the sentence on the board. Read the sentence with children, pointing to the pronoun. Then have children copy one of the sentences with *I* or *me* on their Write-on Boards.

On their own   Use *Reader's and Writer's Notebook,* p. 412, for more practice with pronouns *I* and *me*.

Daily Fix-It   Use the Daily Fix-It for more conventions practice.

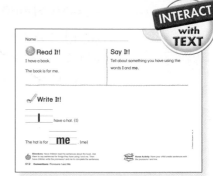

Reader's and Writer's Notebook, p. 412

Writing
Extend the Concept: Text to Self

Discuss building new things

We just read a story about building a new school. A boy and his dad watch workers build the school. They see the how the workers and machines help build the new school. Discuss how each machine has a different job in the building process. Talk about how building a new school is a team effort.

Ask children to think about how they could work together to make a classroom garden. Talk about the jobs children can do and what tools they need.

Guide practice

Use children's contributions to the discussion to write sentences.

> **We dig with a shovel.**
>
> **We water the plants with a hose.**
>
> **We use a rake to smooth out the dirt.**
>
> **We use a trowel to set the plants.**

Encourage children to help you write more sentences. Read the sentences aloud with the children.

Independent writing

Have children write or dictate their own sentence about how they can help make the classroom garden, or they may copy a sentence from the board. Have children illustrate their sentences and share them with the class.

Daily Handwriting

Write uppercase *A* and *I* and lowercase *a* and *i* on the board. Review correct letter formation with children.

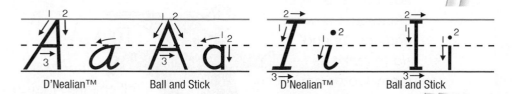

D'Nealian™   Ball and Stick   D'Nealian™   Ball and Stick

Have children write a row each of uppercase *A* and *I* and lowercase *a* and *i* on their Write-On Boards. Remind them to use proper left-to-right and top-to-bottom progression when writing *Aa* and *Ii*.

Differentiated Instruction

 A **Advanced**

Sequence Steps Have children sequence the steps in making a classroom garden.

Daily Fix-It

How do u get to school.
How do <u>you</u> get to school<u>?</u>

This week's practice sentences appear on Teacher Resources DVD-ROM.

 E L L

English Language Learners
Build Background List garden tools on the board and review how they can be used with children.

Vocabulary
Compound Words

playground   classroom   bookshelf

Teach

Write the words *playground, classroom,* and *bookshelf* on the board. Point to each word as you read it. These are compound words. Each compound word is made up of two shorter words. Have children turn to p. 28 of *My Skills Buddy.* Incorporate the second Vocabulary bullet on the page into the discussion. Direct them to the pictures of the children playing and the grassy area. If we put these two words together, what compound word do we make? Then direct them to the pictures of the teacher and students and the empty room. If we put these two words together, what compound word do we make? If we want to make the compound word *bookshelf,* what two words should I use?

My Skills Buddy, p. 28

Team Talk Pair children and have them take turns saying the compound words *playground, classroom,* and *bookshelf* in sentences.

Wrap Up Your Day

✔ **Phonemic Awareness** I am going to say some words. Tell me whether each word begins with /y/ or /kw/. Listen carefully: *quack, yawn, yes, queen, yo-yo, quick, quilt, yellow, question, yard.*

✔ **Homework Idea** Have children add consonants or blends to the word endings -*at* and -*id* to make as many words as they can. Tell children to read their words to their family.

Preview DAY 5

Tell children that tomorrow they will talk about some of the books and stories they have read this week.

Science
Describing Objects

Materials: wooden craft stick, cloth bandanna, paper envelope, ball of clay, plastic spoon, metal nail, bar magnet, bowl of water, chart paper, markers

Identify Properties of Objects Display the wooden craft stick. Have children describe it. Point out that when they described the object, they told about its color, size, and shape. These are three properties that scientists use to describe an object. Have children pass the craft stick around as you ask:

- What material is it made of?
- What color is it?
- What is its size and shape?
- Is it heavy or light?
- Is it rough or smooth?
- Is it magnetic? (Use bar magnet.)
- Does it float or sink in water? (Test it in the bowl of water.)

Record Properties of Objects List children's answers on chart paper. Continue the routine with the other objects, adding more columns to the chart paper. When children have examined all objects, model how an object can be described using the information in its column.

Comprehension
Two Seasons

Materials: weather reports from newspapers and television; copies of a Venn diagram or Graphic Organizer 28, one per child

Compare and Contrast Display weather reports about winter and summer weather. Discuss with children the characteristics of winter and summer. Write phrases about each season on the board for children to copy. Provide each child with a copy of a Venn diagram. Have children label one circle *Winter* and the other *Summer*. Remind them to write how the seasons are alike in the center section and how the seasons are different in the two circles.

Conventions
Replace Nouns with Pronouns

Materials: index cards with pronouns *I* and *me* written on them

Use *I* or *me* Write the following verbs on index cards: *hop, sit, skip, spin, snap, jump, trot, drop, stop, clap, stand.* Distribute one card to each child. Ask a child to act out the verb on his or her card. Have classmates describe the action: *Jack hops by Joy.* Have the child repeat the sentence replacing his/her name with the pronoun *I* or *me*: *Jack hops by me.*

Objectives
- Review the concepts.
- Build oral vocabulary.

Today at a Glance

Oral Vocabulary
groundbreaking, trenches, foundation, welding, waterproof, gleaming

Phonemic Awareness
◉ Initial and Medial /a/ and /i/

Phonics
◉ /a/ Spelled *Aa*
◉ /i/ Spelled *Ii*

Comprehension
◉ Compare and Contrast

Conventions
Pronouns *I* and *me*

Writing
This Week We…

Check Oral Vocabulary
SUCCESS PREDICTOR

TRUCKTOWN on Reading Street

Start your engines!

- Display "This Is the Way" and lead the group in saying the rhyme a few times.
- Have half the group recite the rhyme while the other half acts it out.
- Then have the groups change roles.

Truckery Rhymes

Concept Wrap Up

Question of the Week
How is a school built?

Listen for Amazing Words

Write the question of the week on the board. Track the print as you read it to children. Have them use Amazing Words in their responses (*groundbreaking, trenches, foundation, welding, waterproof, gleaming*). Display Sing with Me Chart 31B. Let's sing "This Is the Way We Build Our School." I want you to listen for the Amazing Words we learned this week. Answer in complete sentences. Sing the song several times to the tune of "Here We Go 'Round the Mulberry Bush." Have children listen and say "Amazing!" each time they hear an Amazing Word. Then have them discuss how a new school is built. Remind children to speak one at a time.

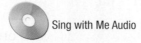 Sing with Me Audio

This Is the Way We Build Our School

This is the way we build our school,
build our school, build our school;
This is the way we build our school
so gleaming bright and new!
Groundbreaking day makes us jump
for joy, jump for joy, jump for joy;
Groundbreaking day makes us jump
for joy for our school gleaming and new!
Cement will make the foundation strong,
foundation strong, foundation strong;
Cement will make the foundation strong
for our school gleaming and new!

Talk with Me/Sing with Me Chart 31B

ELL Check Concepts and Language Use the Day 5 instruction on ELL Poster 31 to monitor children's understanding of the lesson concept.

ELL Poster 31

Oral Vocabulary
Amazing Words

Review

Let's Talk Display Talk with Me Chart 31A. We learned six new Amazing Words this week. Let's say the Amazing Words as I point to the pictures on the chart. Point to each picture and give children the chance to say the appropriate Amazing Word before offering it.

Have children supply the appropriate Amazing Word.

> **The construction workers are _____ the pipes.** (welding)
>
> **Everyone had a shovel on _____ day.** (groundbreaking)
>
> **Cement and rocks will make a strong _____.** (foundation)
>
> **The school is so new and clean that it is _____.** (gleaming)
>
> **The backhoes dig deep _____.** (trenches)
>
> **The _____ roof keeps the children dry.** (waterproof)

Amazing Words

groundbreaking   trenches
foundation   welding
waterproof   gleaming

Talk with Me/Sing with Me Chart 31A

It's Friday

MONITOR PROGRESS   **Check Oral Vocabulary**

Demonstrate Word Knowledge Monitor the Amazing Words by asking the following questions. Have children use the Amazing Word in their answer.

• **What is the part of a building do all the other parts rest on?** (foundation)

• **Which word means "won't let water through"?** (waterproof)

• **What are long, narrow ditches in the ground?** (trenches)

• **What word describes something smooth that reflects light?** (gleaming)

• **Which word describes the work that must be done before building can begin?** (groundbreaking)

• **When a worker joins two pipes by heating the ends so they melt together, what is he doing?** (welding)

If... children have difficulty using the Amazing Words,

then... reteach the words using the Oral Vocabulary Routine on the Routines Flip Chart.

Day 1	Day 2	Day 3	Day 4	Day 5
Check Phonemic Awareness	Check Sound-Spelling/ Retelling	Check Word Reading	Check Phonemic Awareness	**Check Oral Vocabulary**

Success Predictor

Oral Vocabulary   Success Predictor

Objectives

◎ Review initial and medial /a/ and /i/.
◎ Review /a/ spelled *Aa*.
◎ Review /i/ spelled *Ii*.

Phonemic Awareness Review
↻ /a/ and /i/

Isolate initial and medial /a/	Display the *cat* Picture Card. What is the middle sound in *cat*? Say the word with me: /k/ /a/ /t/, *cat*. Review medial /a/ with these Picture Cards: *fan, bag, hat*.
Isolate initial and medial /i/	Display the *brick* Picture Card. What is the middle sound in *brick*? Say the word with me: /br/ /i/ /k/, *brick*. Review medial /i/ with the Picture Cards *six* and *pig*.
Discriminate medial sounds	I am going to say two words. If the words have the same middle sound, say "Yes." If the words do not have the same middle sound, say "No." Listen carefully: *fan, did*. What sound do you hear in the middle of *fan*? (/a/) What sound do you hear in the middle of *did*? (/i/) *Fan* and *did* do not have the same middle sound, so what do we say? (no) Continue with these word pairs: *mat, slap; trip, bag; fill, lit; flap, grip; stand, cramp; skin, grit*.

Picture Card

Picture Card

Phonics Review

 /a/ Spelled *Aa* and
/i/ Spelled *Ii*

Teach /a/ *Aa* and /i/ *Ii*

Display the *Ii* Alphabet Card. This is an *igloo*. What sound do you hear at the beginning of *igloo*? What letter spells that sound? Repeat the routine with the *Aa* Alphabet Card.

High-frequency words

Write the word *do* on the board. This is the word *do*. Let's say it together. What is this word? Repeat the routine with *here, little, with,* and *what*.

Apply phonics in familiar text

Let's Reread Have children reread one of the books specific to the target sounds. You may wish to review the decodable words and high-frequency words that appear in each book prior to rereading.

Decodable Reader 31
My Skills Buddy, p. 18

Kindergarten Student
Reader K.6.1

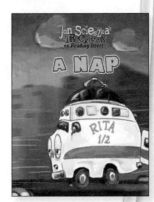

Get Set, Roll! Reader 31

Small Group Time

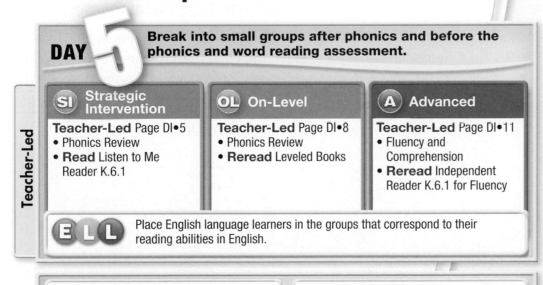

DAY 5

Break into small groups after phonics and before the phonics and word reading assessment.

Teacher-Led

SI Strategic Intervention

Teacher-Led Page DI•5
• Phonics Review
• **Read** Listen to Me Reader K.6.1

OL On-Level

Teacher-Led Page DI•8
• Phonics Review
• **Reread** Leveled Books

A Advanced

Teacher-Led Page DI•11
• Fluency and Comprehension
• **Reread** Independent Reader K.6.1 for Fluency

 Place English language learners in the groups that correspond to their reading abilities in English.

Practice Stations
• Visit the Read for Meaning Station
• Visit the Let's Make Art Station

Independent Activities
• Read independently
• Story Sort
• Concept Talk Video

Differentiated Instruction

SI Strategic Intervention

Practice Sound-Spelling
Display the Alphabet Cards *Aa, Ii, Cc, Ff, Hh, Ll, Pp, Oo, Ss,* and *Tt*. Say the sounds each letter spells and have children write the letter.

A Advanced

Sound-Spelling Say the following words and have children identify the letter that spells the initial sound: *fan, fit, fat, mat, mitt, man*. Repeat the words and have children identify the letters that spell the medial and final sounds.

E L L

English Language Learners
Support Phonics To help children learn the relationships between sounds and letters, have them spell several words from Decodable Reader 31 on their Write-On Boards. Use the words *big, fit, pass,* and *tap*.

Assess
- ◎ Read words with /a/ and /i.
- • Read high-frequency words.
- • Read sentences.

Assessment
Monitor Progress

/a/ Spelled Aa and /i/ Spelled Ii

Whole Class Divide a sheet of paper into four sections for each child. Read the words below. Say each word, sound it out phonetically, and say the word again. Have children write the letters for the sounds in the word in one of the sections of their paper.

| cat | dip | fin | ham |

MONITOR PROGRESS	**Check Word and Sentence Reading**

If... children cannot complete the group assessment,
then... use the Reteach lesson in *First Stop.*

If... you are unsure of a child's grasp of this week's skills,
then... use the assessment below to obtain a clearer evaluation of the child's progress.

/a/ Spelled Aa, /i/ Spelled Ii, and high-frequency words

One-on-One To facilitate individual progress monitoring, assess some children on Day 4 and the rest on Day 5. While individual children are being assessed, the rest of the class can reread this week's books and look for words with /a/ and /i/.

Word reading

Use the word lists on reproducible p. 97 to assess a child's ability to read short *a* and *i* words. We're going to read some words. I'll read the first word, and you read the rest. The first word is *pat*, /p/ /a/ /t/. The first word is *pat*. For each child, record any decoding problems.

Sentence reading

Use the reproducible sentences on p. 97 to assess a child's ability to read words in sentences. Have the child read two sentences aloud. Have each child read different sentences. Start over with sentence one if necessary.

Record scores

Monitor children's accuracy by recording their scores using the Word and Sentence Reading Chart for this unit in *First Stop*.

Name _____

Read the Words

pat	☐	sad	☐
hid	☐	spin	☐
my	☐	you	☐
rip	☐	snap	☐
lap	☐	see	☐
are	☐	quit	☐

Read the Sentences

1. I hid my bat from Gus.

2. We are sad that Jeff quit.

3. Can you spin the green top?

4. Did you see the red van?

5. I like my big hat.

Note to Teacher: Children read each word. Children read two sentences.

Scoring for Read the Words: Score 1 point for each correct word.

Short *a* (*pat, lap, sad, snap*) _____ /___4___
Short *i* (*hid, rip, spin, quit*) _____ /___4___
High-Frequency Words (*my, are, you, see*) _____ /___4___

MONITOR PROGRESS
• Review short *a*
• Review short *i*
• Review high-frequency words

Objectives

- Recognize expository text.
- Practice compare and contrast.

My Skills Buddy, pp. 30–31

Let's Practice It!
Expository Text

Teach

Tell children that today they will listen to an expository text. An expository text explains something. Review the features of expository text with children.

- Expository text tells about real-life people, places, or events.
- The author groups information in a way to help us understand what we read.
- Expository text includes pictures to help us understand the text.

Have children turn to pp. 30–31 of *My Skills Buddy*. I am going to read an expository text called "Two Kinds of Homes." Look at the pictures as I read. Read the text of "Two Kinds of Homes." As you read, direct children to look at the appropriate picture.

Guide practice

Discuss the features of expository text and the bulleted text on *My Skills Buddy*, p. 30

- Expository text tells about real-life people, places, or events. What is the topic of "Two Kinds of Homes"? (the kinds of homes that some Native Americans once lived in: pueblos and tipis) How do you know? (the title as well as the pictures tell about two kinds of homes)

- The author of an expository text groups information in a certain way to help us understand what we are reading. How does the author group information in this selection? (The author discusses pueblos first and then tipis so that we can learn about one kind of home at a time.) Why does the author do that? (to compare and contrast the kinds of homes)

- Expository text includes pictures to help us understand the text. Which home looks like an apartment building? (pueblo) Which home looks like a big upside-down cone? (tipi)

- Expository texts provide information, but sometimes we have more questions. What questions do you have about pueblos and tipis?

Two Kinds of Homes

Some Native Americans lived in the deserts in the south and west part of the United States. They built pueblos. Pueblos look like apartment buildings. The rooms are stacked one on top of the other. Thick walls keep the rooms cool. The walls are usually made of adobe bricks. Adobe is a kind of clay. These Native Americans were farmers. They stayed in one place. They built their pueblos to last a long time.

Other Native Americans lived in the middle part of the United States called the Great Plains. They built tipis. Tipis look like big upside-down cones. The frames of the tipis are made of long wooden poles. Animal hides are stretched over the frames and sometimes painted. The tipis can be put up and taken down quickly. These Native Americans were hunters who followed animal herds. They moved from place to place. They carried their tipis with them.

Assess
● Compare and contrast elements of a story.

Comprehension Assessment
Monitor Progress

Review

◎ **Compare and Contrast** When we compare things, we tell how they are alike, or the same. When we contrast things, we tell how they are different, or not the same. What do we do when we compare? (tell how things are alike) What do we do when we contrast? (tell how things are different)

Read "Good Morning, Digger"

Tell children that you are going to read them a story about a child who is watching machines build something in a vacant lot. Have children think about how the lot looks before and after the machines come and about what the different machines do. After I read the story, I am going to ask you to compare and contrast what the lot looks like and what the machines do. Read "Good Morning, Digger" on p. 74 of the Read Aloud Anthology.

Read Aloud Anthology

Check compare and contrast

After you read the story, have children answer the following questions.

- How does the lot look before the machines come? (The lot is vacant and full of weeds and broken glass.) How does the lot look after the machines are gone? (The lot has a new community center and garden.)
- What does Digger do? How is it different from what Dump Truck does? (Digger digs up dirt to make a hole. Dump Truck carries the dirt away.)
- What does Cement Mixer do? How is that different from what Tall Crane does? (Cement Mixer pours wet gray cement into the hole in the ground. Tall Crane lifts and swings parts of the building up to the workers.)
- What does Flat Bed do? How are Digger, Dump Truck, Cement Mixer, Tall Crane, and Flat Bed alike? (Flat Bed carries Digger and Tall Crane to and from construction sites. All the machines are used to construct a building.)

Corrective feedback

If... children cannot compare and contrast,
then... reteach compare and contrast using the Reteach lesson in *First Stop.*

Assess compare and contrast

Use the blackline master on p. 101. Make one copy for each child. After they color and cut out the pictures, have children compare and contrast the pictures. Then have them paste each picture in the correct circle.

Name _____

Compare and Contrast

Sort these pictures. Which belong at the construction site? Which do not belong there?

At the Construction Site   **Not at the Construction Site**

Note to Teacher: Have children color the pictures, cut them out, and paste each picture in the correct circle.

Objectives
- Review pronouns *I* and *me.*
- Write or dictate words to complete a poem.

Conventions
Pronouns *I* and *me*

Review | Remind children of what they learned about the pronouns *I* and *me.* Pronouns are words that can take the place of nouns. When I tell about myself, I use the pronouns *I* or *me* instead of using my name.

Model | When I tell about myself I can say my name. [*Name*] *rode a bike. Grandpa gave the bike to* [*name*]. I can use the pronouns *I* and *me* in place of my name. I *rode a bike. Grandpa gave the bike to* me.

Guide practice | Tell children to repeat each sentence using the pronoun *I* or *me* in place of the name. After children say the sentence with the pronoun *I* or *me,* write the completed sentence on the board. Read the sentence with children, pointing to the pronoun.

Tom ate a banana. (I ate a banana.)
Maria drew a picture. (I drew a picture.)

Give the book to Tess. (Give the book to me.)
The dog barked at Paul. (The dog barked at me.)

On their own | Have children draw a picture of something they like to do at school. Have them write about their picture using the pronouns *I* or *me.*

Daily Fix-It | Use the Daily Fix-It for more conventions practice.

Writing
This Week We...

Review

Display *Building with Dad, Dig Dig Digging,* Sing with Me 31B, Phonics Songs and Rhymes Chart 31, Decodable Reader 31 from *My Skills Buddy,* Kindergarten Student Reader K.6.1, and Get Set, Roll! Reader 31. This week we learned about building a new school. We read new books, and we sang new songs. Which book or song was your favorite? Let's share our ideas with each other.

Team Talk Pair children and have them take turns telling which book or song was their favorite and why.

Model writing a poem

Write the poem below on the board. Let's think about the machines that help us build. We can use the name of the machine and what it does to complete this poem. Model how to complete the poem with the name of a machine and verbs that tell what it does.

> See the _____. (cement mixer)
> **What does it do?**
>
> It _____ and it _____ (turns, pours)
> **Until it is through.**

Guide practice

Work with children to complete the poem using other machine names and verbs. Have children echo read each time the poem is completed.

On their own

Have children fill in the poem with another machine name and a verb telling what it does.

Daily Handwriting

Write uppercase *A* and *I* and lowercase *a* and *i* on the board. Review correct letter formation with children.

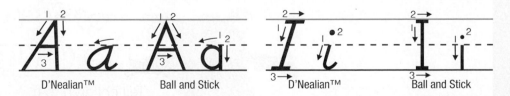

D'Nealian™   Ball and Stick   D'Nealian™   Ball and Stick

Have children write a row of uppercase *A* and *I* and lowercase *a* and *i* on their Write-On Boards. Remind them to use proper left-to-right and top-to-bottom progression.

Differentiated Instruction

SI Strategic Intervention

Support Writing Remind children to leave a space the width of their little finger between words.

Daily Fix-It

do you like me
Do you like me?

This week's practice sentences appear on Teacher Resources DVD-ROM.

ELL

English Language Learners
Poster Preview Prepare children for next week by using Week 2 ELL Poster number 32. Read the Poster Talk-Through to introduce the concept and vocabulary. Ask children to identify and describe objects and actions they see.

Objectives
- Review weekly concept.
- Review compare and contrast

Wrap Up Your Week!

Amazing Words

You've learned

0	0	6

words this week!

You've learned

1	8	6

words this year!

Illustrate compare and contrast

Question of the Week
? How is a school built?

This week we read about building a new school. The construction site looks different before and after a new building is built.

- Fold a sheet of construction paper in half for each child.
- Tell children to label the left half *Before* and the right half *After*.
- Have children draw two pictures—what the construction site looked like *before* the school was built and what it looked like *after* the school was built.
- Have children write or dictate a sentence that compares or contrasts the pictures.

Next Week's Question
? What tools do you need to build things?

Discuss next week's question. Guide children in making connections between building a school using machines and building using tools.

Preview NEXT WEEK

Tell children that next week they will read about tools you need to build things.

Science
What Is a House Made of?

Materials: home design and decorating magazines, poster board, scissors, glue, markers, pencils

Identify the Parts of the Classroom Label parts of the classroom, such as the windows, doors, floor, ceiling, chalkboard, and so on. Help children read each label, and discuss the materials each part is made of.

Identify the Parts of a House Display pictures of the interior and exterior of a house, and help children name the major parts of a house. Write these parts in the first column of a two-column chart. In the second column of the chart, identify materials that are used to make each part in the first column.

Make a Poster Have children cut pictures from magazines of the parts listed in the first column of the chart. Have them glue the pictures onto poster board and label each picture. Then tell them to use the second column to make labels identifying the materials used to make each pictured part.

Part of a House	What It Is Made From
wall	wood, nails, paint
roof	wood, tar, nails
window	wood, glass
door	wood, doorknob, glass

Conventions
Pronoun Sentences

Materials: magazines, construction paper, crayons, pencils

Use *I* or *me* Tell children to look through magazines or other printed materials to find pictures of people or animals doing things. Have children draw a picture of themselves doing the same activity. Then have them write or dictate a sentence for their picture that uses the pronoun *I* or *me*.

Phonics
Build Words

Materials: word endings worksheet, small squares of paper, glue

Make Words Using Blends Provide each child with a worksheet like this:

Give each child six small squares of paper with the initial blend *tr,*

____ip	____ap
____ip	____ap
____ip	____ap

sn, or *fl.* Have children place each blend in front of a word ending to make six words. Once they have arranged the blends correctly, have children glue the blends in place.

Weekly Assessment

Use the whole-class assessment on pages 96–97 and 100–101 in this Teacher's Edition to check:

✔ 🔊 **Short *a* Spelled *Aa***

✔ 🔊 **Short *i* Spelled *Ii***

✔ 🔊 **Comprehension Skill** *Compare and Contrast*

✔ **High-Frequency Words**

Teacher's Edition, Day 5

Managing Assessment

Use the Assessment Handbook for:

✔ **Observation Checklists**

✔ **Record-Keeping Forms**

✔ **Portfolio Assessment**

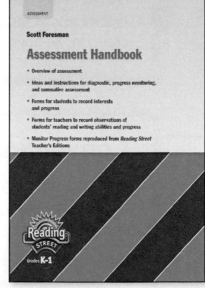

Assessment Handbook

Teacher Notes

Small Group Time

Pacing Small Group Instruction

⏱ 20–30 mins.

5 Day Plan

DAY 1	• Phonemic Awareness/ Phonics • Decodable Story 31
DAY 2	• Phonemic Awareness/ Phonics • Decodable Reader 31
DAY 3	• Phonemic Awareness/ Phonics • Concept Literacy Reader K.6.1 or Kindergarten Student Reader K.6.1
DAY 4	• Phonemic Awareness/ Phonics • Get Set, Roll! Reader 31
DAY 5	• Phonics Review • Listen to Me Reader K.6.1

3 or 4 Day Plan

DAY 1	• Phonemic Awareness/ Phonics • Decodable Story 31
DAY 2	• Phonemic Awareness/ Phonics • Decodable Reader 31
DAY 3	• Phonemic Awareness/ Phonics • Concept Literacy Reader K.6.1 or Kindergarten Student Reader K.6.1
DAY 4	• Phonemic Awareness/ Phonics • Get Set, Roll! Reader 31

3 Day Plan: Eliminate the shaded box.

SI Strategic Intervention   **DAY 1**

Phonemic Awareness•Phonics

■ **Isolate /a/ and /i/** Display the *bat* Picture Card. This is a *bat. Bat* has /a/. Say it with me: /b/ /a/ /t/, *bat*. Repeat with *cap, man,* and *pan.* What sound do you hear in the middle of all of these words? They all have /a/. Continue the routine with the following Picture Cards: *wig, six, pig.*

■ **Connect /a/ to *Aa* and /i/ to *Ii*** I am going to say three words. I want you to tell me which word has /a/. Listen carefully: *pan, pin, pen.* Which word has /a/? *Pan* has /a/. *Pin* and *pen* do not have /a/. Write the letters *Aa* on the board. The letter *a* stands for /a/. Continue discriminating medial /a/ with the following sets of words: *tip, top, tap; ban, bin, bun; flop, flap, flip.* Then use the same sets to identify the word with medial /i/.

Decodable Story 31

■ **Review** Review the previously taught high-frequency words by writing each word on the board and having children read the word with you.

a	the	is	he	one	little	go

> **If...** children have difficulty reading the words,
> **then...** say a word and have children point to the word. Repeat several times, giving assistance as needed.

■ **Read** Have children read *Vin and the Bag* orally. Then have them reread the story several times individually.

Reader's and Writer's Notebook,
pp. 403–404

Objectives
• Identify the common sounds that letters represent.
• Read at least 25 high-frequency words from a commonly used list.

 **SI** Strategic Intervention DAY **2**

Phonemic Awareness•Phonics

- **Discriminate /a/ and /i/** Display Phonics Songs and Rhymes Chart 31. Sing "Here Comes King Vip's Big Ship" to the tune of "Little Sally Saucer" with children. The word *stand* has /a/. The word *sit* has /i/. When you hear a word with /a/ like *stand,* stand up. When you hear a word with /i/ like *sit,* sit down. For words that don't have /a/ or /i/, stoop down.

- **Recognize *Aa* and *Ii*** Ask children to name words that begin with /a/ and /i/. List the words on the board as they say them. Have children echo read the list of words. Then ask children to take turns circling the *a* and *i* in the words on the board.

Decodable Reader 31

- **Review** Review the high-frequency words by writing *is* on the board. This is the word *is.* What word is this? Continue with the following words: *go, here, do, little, with, the, what.*

   If... children have difficulty reading the words,
   then... say a word and have children point to the word. Repeat several times, giving assistance as needed.

- **Read** Display the cover of *If Kip Can* on p. 18 of *My Skills Buddy.* Ask a volunteer to read the first page of the story. Have children tell the things Kip can do and the things Sam can do. Continue through the story in this manner.

My Skills Buddy

More Reading
Use Leveled Readers or other text at children's instructional level.

Small Group Time

SI Strategic Intervention

DAY 3

Phonemic Awareness•Phonics

■ **Isolate /a/ and /i/** Display the *cat* Picture Card. This is a *cat. Cat* has /a/. Say it with me: /k/ /a/ /t/, *cat.* Display the *pig* Picture Card. This is a *pig. Pig* has /i/. Say it with me: /p/ /i/ /g/, *pig.* Do *cat* and *pig* have the same sound in the middle? No, *cat* has /a/ and *pig* has /i/. Repeat with *bat* and *tip.*

■ **Connect /a/ to *Aa* and /i/ to *Ii*** Display the *Aa* Alphabet Card. These are the letters *Aa.* The letter *a* can stand for /a/. What is this a picture of? (an astronaut) Say the word with me: /a/ /a/ /a/, *astronaut.* Repeat the routine with the *Ii* Alphabet Card. Can you hear a different sound at the beginning of *astronaut* and *igloo?* The sounds are /a/ and /i/.

■ **Blend Sounds** Write *big* on the board. Have children blend the sound of each letter to read the word. Repeat the routine with the words *bag, cat,* and *slip.*

■ **Review High-Frequency Words** Write *here* on the board. Have volunteers say the word and use it in a sentence. Continue with the word *do, little, with,* and *what.*

■ **Read** To practice phonics and high-frequency words, have children read Kindergarten Student Reader K.6.1. Use the instruction on pp. 56–57.

For a complete lesson plan and additional practice, see the **Leveled Reader Teaching Guide**.

Concept Literacy Reader K.6.1

■ **Preview and Predict** Display the cover of the Concept Literacy Reader K.6.1. Point to the title of the book. The title of the book is *What Do We Need?* What is the man doing on the cover? What do you think the book is about? Have children tell about the picture and what they think the book might be about.

■ **Set a Purpose** We talked about the title of the book. Let's read the book to learn about what we need to build a building. Have children read the Concept Literacy Reader.

■ **Read** Provide corrective feedback as children read the book orally. During reading, ask them if they are able to confirm any of the predictions they made prior to reading.

If... children have difficulty reading the book individually,

then... read a sentence aloud as children point to each word. Then have the group reread the sentences as they continue pointing to the words.

■ **Retell** Have children retell the content as you page through the book. Help them identify what the book is about. Also call attention to the order of the steps to build a building.

Concept Literacy Reader K.6.1

Objectives
- Identify the common sounds that letters represent.
- Predict what might happen next based on the title.
- Retell important facts in a text, heard or read.

 **Strategic Intervention** **DAY 4**

Phonemic Awareness•Phonics

- **Play London Bridge** Play the game "London Bridge Is Falling Down" with children. Have children stand in a circle, with two children forming a "bridge". Sing the song with children as they walk around the circle. When the song ends, call out *Aa* or *Ii*. The child caught inside the bridge must then say a word that has that letter's sound. Continue the routine several times, giving many children a chance to practice words.

- **Blending** Write *yes* on the board. Help me blend this word. Listen as I say each sound: /y/ /e/ /s/. Now let's blend the sounds together to read the word: /y/ /e/ /s/, *yes.* Continue with *quit, yip, yet, kit,* and *quill.*

Get Set, Roll! Reader 31

- **Review** Review the following high-frequency words with children prior to reading the story: *where, was, the, little, see, she, said.*

- **Read** Display Get Set, Roll! Reader 31, *A Nap.* Today we will read a new story about Rita. Point to the title of the story. The title of the story is *A Nap.* What is a nap? Why do people take naps? Look at the picture and think about the title. What do you think this story will be about?

  If... children have difficulty reading the story individually, **then...** read a sentence aloud as children point to each word. Then have the group reread the sentences as they continue pointing to the words.

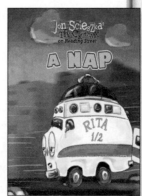

Get Set, Roll! Reader 31

- **Reread** Use echo reading of Get Set, Roll! Reader 31 to model fluent reading. Use your oral reading to model for children where to pause, when to change pitch, and which words to stress. Then have children reread orally three to four times, or until they can read with few or no mistakes.

More Reading

Use Leveled Readers or other text at children's instructional level.

Objectives
- Identify the common sounds that letters represent.
- Read at least 25 high-frequency words from a commonly used list.
- Predict what might happen next based on the cover.

Small **Group Time**

More Reading

Use Leveled Readers or other text at children's instructional level.

SI Strategic Intervention

Phonics Review

■ **Discriminate /a/ and /i/** Write *Aa* and *Ii* on the board. These are the letters *Aa* and *Ii*. Which letter stands for /a/? The letter *a* can stand for /a/. Which letter stands for /i/? The letter *i* can stand for /i/. Point to your lip. What is this? This is my lip. The word *lip* has /i/ in the middle. Say it with me: /l/ /i/ /p/, *lip*. Hold up your hand. What is this? This is my hand. The word *hand* has /a/ in the middle. Say it with me: /h/ /a/ /n/ /d/, *hand.* When I say a word that has /i/, I want you to point to your lip. When I say a word that has /a/, I want you to show your hand. Use the following words: *clap, slip, snack, sad, sing, wig, hat, pin, rat, bag, quack, win.*

Listen to Me Reader K.6.1

■ **Preview and Predict** Display the cover of the book. The title of this story is *A Stand for Tim.* It is written by Megan Albrecht. It is illustrated by Pamela Leavens. What kind of stand does Tim have? What will happen at the stand? Tell me your ideas.

Listen to Me Reader K.6.1

■ **Set a Purpose** Review children's ideas. Point out that after they read, they will know more about Tim's stand. Tell children that you will read the story with them. Follow along with your finger as I read. Then we will take turns reading this page. Repeat this routine through all of the pages. Guide children to decode words.

■ **Reread for Fluency** Use echo reading of Listen to Me Reader K.6.1 to model reading fluently. Use your oral reading to model for children when to pause, when to change pitch, and which words to stress. Then have children reread orally three to four times, or until they can read with few or no mistakes.

Objectives
• Identify the common sounds that letters represent.
• Predict what might happen next based on the cover.

OL On-Level — DAY 1

Phonemic Awareness•Phonics

- **Discriminate /a/ and /i/** Display the *cat* Picture Card. This is a cat. Say the sounds in *cat* with me: /k/ /a/ /t/, *cat*. What sound do you hear in the middle? /a/ is in the middle. Write *Aa* on the board. The letter *a* can stand for /a/. Display the *pig* Picture Card. This is a *pig*. Say the sound in *pig* with me: /p/ /i/ /g/, *pig*. What sound do you hear in the middle of *pig*? /i/ is in the middle of *pig*. Write *Ii* on the board. The letter *i* can stand for /i/. I am going to say some words. When you hear a word that has /a/, I want you to meow like a *cat*. When you hear a word that has /i/, I want you to oink like a *pig*. Use the following words: *fill, bag, six, sand, van, wig, bin, fan.*

Objectives
- Identify the common sounds that letters represent.

Pacing Small Group Instruction
20–30 mins.

5 Day Plan	
DAY 1	• Phonemic Awareness/ Phonics • Decodable Story 31
DAY 2	• Phonemic Awareness/ Phonics • High-Frequency Words • Decodable Reader 31
DAY 3	• Phonemic Awareness/ Phonics • Kindergarten Student Reader K.6.1
DAY 4	• Get Set, Roll! Reader 31
DAY 5	• Phonics Review • Reread Leveled Books

OL On-Level — DAY 2

Phonemic Awareness•Phonics

- **Discriminate /a/ and /i/** Draw four apples and four insects on the board. Collect twelve Picture Cards, including the following cards: *hammer, igloo, insect, kitten, lamp, mask, sandcastle, zipper.* Mix the cards and display them one at a time. Have a child name the picture. If the name has /a/, have the child write a lowercase *a* in one of the apples. If the name has /i/, have the child write a lowercase *i* in one of the insects.

- **High-Frequency Words** Display the following word cards: *what, with, little, do, here.* Say the word *what* and select a child to point to the word. Have children say the word and use it in a sentence. Continue with the other words.

Objectives
- Identify the common sounds that letters represent.
- Read at least 25 high-frequency words from a commonly used list.

3 or 4 Day Plan	
DAY 1	• Phonemic Awareness/ Phonics • Decodable Story 31
DAY 2	• Phonemic Awareness/ Phonics • High-Frequency Words • Decodable Reader 31
DAY 3	• Phonemic Awareness/ Phonics • Kindergarten Student Reader K.6.1
DAY 4	• Get Set, Roll! Reader 31

3 Day Plan: Eliminate the shaded box.

More Practice

For additional practice with this week's phonics skills, have children reread the Decodable Story (Day 1) and the Decodable Reader (Day 2).

Small Group Time

Phonemic Awareness•Phonics

■ **Listen for /a/ and /i/** Tell children you will tell them a story and they should listen for /a/ and /i/. When you say a word that has /a/, the children should clap and repeat the word. When you say a word that has /i/, the children should wiggle around and repeat the word. Tell a simple story, emphasizing the /a/ and /i/ words and pausing to give children a chance to clap or wiggle and repeat the word. *Kat* and *Kip* are *six*. They are *twins. Kat* and *Kip can spin.* They *dance* and *spin* for mom and *dad. Kat* and *Kip* have a *cat.* They play *with* the *cat* in the house. Read the story again and have children write *a* when they hear /a/ and *i* when they hear /i/.

Kindergarten Student Reader K.6.1

Kindergarten Student Reader K.6.1

■ **Preview and Predict** Display the cover of the book. The title of this story is *Max and Jen.* Look at the cover. What are Max and Jen holding? What do you think they are going to do in this story? Tell me your ideas.

■ **Set a Purpose** Review the list of things children think might happen in the story. Remind children they will read to find out about Max and Jen.

■ **Read** Have children follow along as they read the story with you. After reading p. 2, ask children to describe Max and Jen. Continue with each page. Ask the following questions:

- What can Max and Jen do?

- Who gives Max and Jen gift?

- What is in the big red box?

- Do Max and Jen like the gift?

■ **Summarize** Have children retell the story to a partner and tell what Max and Jen do at the end.

■ **Text to Self** Help children make personal connections to the story as they tell about a gift they were given.

Objectives
- Identify the common sounds that letters represent. • Predict what might happen next based on the cover.
- Predict what might happen next based on the title. • Make connections to own experiences.

 OL On-Level — DAY 4

Get Set, Roll! Reader 31

- **Review** Review the words *where, was, the, see, little, she,* and *said* by writing each word on the board and saying the word with children. Then give clues to a word and have children tell which word it is.

- **Activate Prior Knowledge** Remind children that a nap is when someone sleeps for a short amount of time. Why do people take naps?

- **Read** Display Get Set, Roll! Reader 31, *A Nap.* Point to the title of the story. *A Nap* is the title of the story. We can read all the words in this story. Let's read to find out who takes a nap.

Objectives
- Read at least 25 high-frequency words from a commonly used list.

More Reading

Use Leveled Readers or other text at children's instructional level to develop fluency.

OL On-Level — DAY 5

Phonics Review

- **Complete the Word** Gather ten index cards and write one of the following letter combinations on each card: *p__t, h__t, p__n, f__n, fl__p, cl__p, b__g, t__p, cr__b, b__t.* Divide the class into pairs and distribute the cards so that each pair has one or two cards. Have children read the letters on their cards, taking turns inserting /a/ and /i/ in the blanks. Have the pairs choose one of the words formed by adding *a* or *i* and write their word on the board. For example, children with *p__t* could write either *pit* or *pat.* Continue until all children choose a letter and write a word.

Objectives
- Identify the common sounds that letters represent.
- Recognize that new words are created when letters are changed.

Small Group Time

Pacing Small Group Instruction

5 Day Plan

DAY 1	• Phonemic Awareness/ Phonics • Decodable Story 31
DAY 2	• Phonics • Spelling • Decodable Reader 31
DAY 3	• Independent Reader K.6.1 or Kindergarten Student Reader K.6.1
DAY 4	• Get Set, Roll! Reader 31 or Kindergarten Student Reader K.6.1
DAY 5	• Fluency/Comprehension • Independent Reader K.6.1

3 or 4 Day Plan

DAY 1	• Phonemic Awareness/ Phonics • Decodable Story 31
DAY 2	• Phonics • Spelling • Decodable Reader 31
DAY 3	• Independent Reader K.6.1 or Kindergarten Student Reader K.6.1
DAY 4	• Get Set, Roll! Reader 31 or Kindergarten Student Reader K.6.1

3 Day Plan: Eliminate the shaded box.

More Practice

For additional practice with this week's phonics skills and to develop fluency, have children reread the Decodable Story (Day 1) and the Decodable Reader (Day 2).

A — Advanced — DAY 1

Phonemic Awareness•Phonics

■ **Play Tic-Tac-Toe** Make a tic-tac-toe board and write a different letter in each of the nine squares. Divide the class into pairs. Give each pair a copy of the tic-tac-toe board and two sets of counters (one color for each child). Then have children play tic-tac-toe with their partners. Explain to children that to put a counter on a square, they need to name the letter in that square and a word that begins with that letter. Have children play until one player covers a row across, down, or diagonally, or until the board is filled.

Objectives
• Identify the common sounds that letters represent.

A — Advanced — DAY 2

Phonics•Spelling

■ **Words with Aa** Display the following Picture Cards in random order: *bag, bat, cap, cat, fan, flag, map, van.* Have children name each picture. What is alike about all of these words? They all have /a/ in the middle. Have volunteers write the word on the board and circle *a.* Repeat the routine with these /i/ Picture Cards: *pig, six, wig.*

■ **Spell Sounds** Give each child the following letter tiles: *e, g, i, j, m, n, o, t, w.* Listen to the sounds in the word *slip:* /s/ /l/ /i/ /p/, *slip.* What are the letters for /s/ and /l/?  They are *s* and *l.* Place your *s* and *l* tiles in front of you. Continue with the remaining sounds. Then have children take away their *s* tile. Blend the sounds to read the word. What new word did we make? (lip) Then have children spell *bat, at* and *trip, rip.*

Objectives
• Identify the common sounds that letters represent.
• Recognize that new words are created when letters are deleted.
• Use letter-sound correspondences to spell consonant-vowel-consonant (CVC) words.

 **A** Advanced

DAY 3

For a complete lesson plan and additional practice, see the **Leveled Reader Teaching Guide**.

Independent Reader K.6.1

- **Practice High-Frequency Words** Write *they* on the board. Have volunteers say the word and use it in a sentence. Continue with the words *yellow, with,* and *you.*

- **Activate Prior Knowledge** Remind children that homes come in many different shapes and sizes. Picture walk through *Homes* and have children describe the homes in the illustrations.

- **Compare and Contrast** Display the cover of *Homes.* Have children tell how the homes in the selection are alike and how the homes are different.

Independent Reader K.6.1

- **Reread for Fluency** After rereading with children, model reading fluently for them. I am going to read this book aloud. I will read the words with no mistakes. I want you to read it aloud with me. Try to read the words just as I do.

  • Use echo reading of Independent Reader K.6.1 to model reading fluently. Use your oral reading to model for children where to pause, when to change pitch, and which words to stress. Then have children reread orally three to four times, or until they can read with few or no mistakes.

- **Read** For more practice with phonics and high-frequency words and to develop fluency, have children read Kindergarten Student Reader K.6.1. Use the instruction on pp. 56–57.

More Reading

Use Leveled Readers or other text at children's instructional level.

Objectives
- Read at least 25 high-frequency words from a commonly used list.
- Tell how facts or settings are the same and/or different.

Small Group Time

More Reading

Use Leveled Readers or other text at children's instructional level.

A Advanced **DAY 4**

Kindergarten Student Reader K.6.1

- **Preview and Predict** Display the cover of Kindergarten Student Reader K.6.1. This is Max and Jen. Tell me about them by looking at the picture. What are they wearing? What do you think they like to do? How old do you think they are?

- **Reread** Use Kindergarten Student Reader K.6.1 to practice reading fluently.

- **Text to Self** Ask children to think about their friends. What things do you do with your friends? Would you be friends with Max and Jen?

- **Read** Have children read Get Set, Roll! Reader 31, *A Nap.* Use the instruction on p. 85.

Kindergarten Student Reader K.6.1

Objectives
- Read at least 25 high-frequency words from a commonly used list.
- Make connections to own experiences.

A Advanced **DAY 5**

Fluency•Comprehension

- **Reread for Fluency** Use the Independent Reader K.6.1 to model reading fluently for children. I am going to read this selection aloud. I will read the words with no mistakes. I want you to read it aloud with me. Try to read the words just as I do.

- **Comprehension** After children have finished reading, have them retell what they learned in the selection. Then have children write or draw a picture that shows how their home is similar and different to the homes on p. 2.

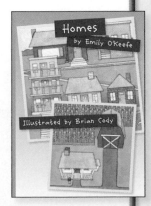

Independent Reader K.6.1

Objectives
- Read at least 25 high-frequency words from a commonly used list.

Support for English Language Learners

Concept Development

■ **Read the Concept Literacy Reader** To build background and vocabulary, read *What Do We Need?* Begin by having children look at the pictures in the book. What are the workers doing? (digging, putting in floors, etc.) What do you think they are making? (a school) Read the book aloud, pausing to discuss each page. Model sentence patterns and vocabulary that describe how the school is being built. We need walls. We need windows. We need a roof. On a second reading, have children talk about the work being done on each page.

■ **Develop Oral Language** Revisit *What Do We Need?* Then have children sing the following song with you to the tune of "Old MacDonald Had a Farm":

> What do we need to build our school? e, i, e, i, o.
> What do we need to build our school? e, i, e, i, o.
> A hole and a floor and window and door—
> What do we need to build our school? e, i, e, i, o.
> A pipe and a wall and a roof and hall—
> What do we need to build our school? e, i, e, i, o.

Phonemic Awareness/Phonics

■ **Frontload Words with Initial /a/ and /i/** Have children look at the picture on pp. 12–13 of *My Skills Buddy*. Look at this big balloon. Point to the ant balloon. Listen to its name: *ant*. What sound does *ant* begin with? *Ant* begins with /a/. Listen to these words that begin with /a/: *ax, apple, animal*. Point to the igloo and ink in the drawing, and repeat the procedure for /i/. Listen to these words that begin with /i/: *igloo, ink, is, in, it*. Then have children sing the following song with you to the tune of "The Farmer in the Dell":

> The ant is in the wood.   Hi-ho, the derry-o,
> The ant is in the wood.   The ant is in the wood.

Add verses with *The ax is in the wood* and *The animal's in the woods*.

■ **Connect /a/ to Aa and /i/ to Ii** Use letter tiles to display *ant* and *in*. Read the words aloud. This word is *ant*: /a/ /n/ /t/, *ant*. Say the word with me. Use sentences such as *The ant is in the hole*. Point to *a* in *ant* and ask: What letter is this? Yes, this is *a*. Repeat the procedure for *i*, linking it to *in*. Use the sentence *Is it in the hole?*

Content Objective

• Develop content knowledge related to the building of a school.

Language Objectives

• Understand and use grade-level content area vocabulary.

• Recognize the sounds of English.

Concept Literacy Reader K.6.1

Daily Planner

DAY 1	• Concept Development • Phonemic Awareness/ Phonics • Listening Comprehension
DAY 2	• Comprehension • Vocabulary
DAY 3	• Phonemic Awareness/ Phonics • Conventions
DAY 4	• Phonemic Awareness/ Phonics • Concepts and Oral Language
DAY 5	• Language Workshop • Writing

Support for English Language Learners

Content Objective
- Understand compare and contrast.

Language Objective
- Learn and use academic vocabulary.

Use Learning Strategies

Preview To prepare students to compare and contrast details, have them preview the illustrations on pp. 14–15 of *My Skills Buddy.* Cover part of p. 15 so only the purple bike is showing. What does this picture show? (a bike and rain) What color is the bike? (purple) How many wheels does it have? (two) Now show the whole page. Repeat the questions above to help children note contrasting details (blue bike, sun, three training wheels). Would you rather ride your bike in the rain or in the sun?

My Skills Buddy, pp. 14–15

Listening Comprehension: Compare and Contrast

■ **Provide Scaffolding** Discuss the illustrations on pp. 14–15 in *My Skills Buddy* to frontload vocabulary. Point to the illustrations on p. 15. Explain the similarities and differences in the two bikes and the weather above them. Help children understand that both scenes show bikes that are the same size, but they are different colors. One bike has training wheels and the other does not. One bike is in sunshine and the other is in rain. Support your words with gestures or simple drawings.

■ **Prepare for the Read Aloud** The modified Read Aloud below prepares children for listening to the oral reading "A House for Freckles" on p. 27.

A House for the Dog

Marie has a dog. His name is Freckles. Marie and her dad are building a doghouse for Freckles. Marie wants the doghouse to look like their big house.

Marie and her dad plan. They measure. They cut. They nail boards to make a floor and walls. They leave a hole for the door. Then they make a roof.

Marie paints the doghouse. She makes it the same color as their big house. She is happy the house looks like their big house. Freckles is happy too.

■ **First Listening** Write the title of the Read Aloud on the board. This story is about Marie and her dad. They are building a house for their dog, Freckles. After reading, ask children to recall what the story is about. What are Marie and her dad building? What does Marie want the dog's house to look like?

■ **Second Listening** Write the name *Freckles* on the board. As you listen, remember the dog's name. Think about what the dog's house will look like. After reading, point to *Freckles* on the board and ask children to tell the dog's name again (Freckles) and what the doghouse looks like (like the big house). How is the doghouse like the big house? (It has a floor, walls, a door, and a roof.)

Objectives
- Understand implicit ideas in increasingly complex spoken language commensurate with grade-level learning expectations. • Understand information in increasingly complex spoken language commensurate with grade-level learning expectations.

DAY 2

Comprehension

■ **Provide Scaffolding** Display *Building with Dad*. Lead a detailed picture walk through the story, naming what you see in the illustrations and describing what is happening. Use gestures and facial expressions to convey meaning. Focus on the following:

• **Set the Scene** Use the cover of the Big Book to help children understand that this story takes place at the building site of a school. Describe what the building site is like. A building site is a place where a new building will go up. A school will be built on this site. Have you ever seen a building go up?

• **Frontload Vocabulary** As you lead the picture walk, use the photographs to introduce unfamiliar words in the text. Include *groundbreaking* (p. 6), *trenches* (p. 10), *foundation* (p. 17), *welding* (p. 25), *waterproof* (p. 20), and *gleaming* (p. 27). Display pp. 6–7. What happens during groundbreaking? Display pp. 16–17. What do you think the foundation of the building is?

Vocabulary: Compound Words

■ **Frontload Vocabulary** Discuss the illustrations on p. 28 in *My Skills Buddy* to frontload vocabulary. Cover the bottom half of p. 28 so that only the playground pictures are showing. Point to the picture of the children. What are the children doing? (playing) Point to the picture of the ground. What does this picture show? (Elicit *ground*.) Point to the picture of the playground. What word is made from the two words *play* and *ground*? (*playground*) Discuss what a playground is. Repeat for the other pictures and compound words *bookshelf* and *classroom*.

■ **Provide Scaffolding** Write on the board: *play + ground = ____; book + shelf = ____; class + room = ____*. Read the "equations" aloud with children and have them name each compound word. This shows us that two words can be put together to make a new word. Have children think of other possible compound words.

■ **Practice** Have children work in groups. Provide each group with a card for the words *play, ground, book, shelf, class,* and *room*. Have the groups assemble the compound words and discuss.

Content Objective
• Develop background knowledge.

Language Objective
• Learn and use compound words.

Use Learning Strategies
Remind children that if they have trouble remembering the compound words, they can refer to the illustrations on p. 28.

Big Book

Support for English Language Learners

Content Objective
- Use learning strategies.

Language Objectives
- Connect /a/ with *Aa* and /i/ with *Ii*.
- Use pronouns.

Transfer Skills

Pronouncing /a/ Many languages do not have an exact equivalent to /a/ in English. Children who speak Cantonese, Farsi, Japanese, Portuguese, and Russian may tend to pronounce the sound as /e/. Explain that when making /a/, the tongue is flat, but when making /e/, it is slightly raised. Pronounce the word pairs *and/end* and *pat/pet*. Have children listen for the different sounds and then repeat after you.

Use Learning Strategies

Help children understand that when we use the pronouns *I* and *me,* we are referring to ourselves. Write these sentences on the board and read them aloud: ____ *am here. It is for* ____. Have children work together to decide which pronoun belongs in each sentence.

Phonemic Awareness/Phonics

■ **Isolate Medial /a/ and /i/** Say *hat* and emphasize medial /a/. Repeat using *sad, dad,* and *pan*. Then repeat the procedure for medial /i/, using the words *pig, Tim,* and *did*.

■ **a/ Spelled *Aa* and /i/ Spelled *Ii*** Write a few familiar words that contain the letter *a*: *sat* and *at*. Explain each with brief sentences and demonstrations: I sat down. We are at the store. Repeat for /i/, using the words *tip* and *bit*. Use the sentences: *It is the tip of my finger. The bird bit it.* As you say the words aloud, isolate the medial letter with your finger. Have children repeat the words after you and isolate the medial sounds. Then ask a volunteer to name the medial letter and sound in each word.

Conventions: Pronouns *I* and *Me*

■ **Provide Scaffolding** Point to the image on p. 6 of *Building with Dad*. I will wait for the groundbreaking to begin. It will be exciting for *me*. Write the words *I* and *me* on the board. Point to yourself as you say the pronoun. Review with children that the pronouns *I* and *me* are used to refer to themselves.

■ **Practice** Find the word *me* on page 5. Page through the Big Book and have children find *me* (p. 5) and *I* (p. 8). Have children repeat the sentence on each page and point to themselves while saying *I* or *me*.

Leveled LS Support

Beginning/Intermediate Have children use a round-robin to play the following game. Ask the first child to make up a sentence using *I* or *me* to begin a story. The next child is to repeat that first sentence and add another one, again using *I* or *me*.

Advanced/Advanced-High Say a sentence leaving out the word *I* or *me* to begin a story. Children are to decide whether *I* or *me* is needed and say the complete sentence. Allow them to help each other decide which word to use. Say sentences such as: ____ *am fine. It is for* ____.

Objectives
• Distinguish intonation patterns of English with increasing ease • Speak using a variety of grammatical structures with increasing accuracy and ease as more English is acquired. • Use visual and contextual support to develop grasp of language structures needed to comprehend increasingly challenging language.

Phonemic Awareness/Phonics

■ **Review /y/ and /kw/** To review /y/, say words that contain initial /y/: *yes, yell, yet, you*. Segment and blend each word. For example, say the sounds /y/ /e/ /s/, and blend them to pronounce *yes*. Have children repeat after you. Then call out word pairs, and ask which word contains /y/: *jet, yet; hack, yak*. Repeat the procedure for /kw/ with these words: *quick, quit, quack, quiz*. Call out these word pairs, and have children tell which word contains /kw/: *quick, kick; quit, hit*.

■ **/y/ Spelled *Yy* and /kw/ Spelled *qu*** Use letter tiles including *q, u, i, t, y, e,* and *s*. Hold up the letter tile for *y*. What is this letter? What sound does it make? Confirm that the letter is *y*, and it makes /y/ as in the word *yes*. Hold up the tiles for *q* and *u*, and ask: What are these letters? What sound they make? Confirm that *q* and *u* make /kw/ as in *quack*. Write the words *yet* and *quit* on the board. Help children read the words aloud.

Concepts and Oral Language

■ **Revisit Talk with Me Chart 31A** Have students describe what is in each picture. Help them identify pictures that go with the words *groundbreaking, foundation, waterproof, trenches, welding,* and *gleaming*.

■ **Develop Oral Language** Introduce language patterns that help describe the builders' work on Talk with Me Chart 31A. Write this sentence frame on the board: *The builders _____.* Let's use this sentence pattern to talk about building. Point to the photograph of people with shovels. *The builders will start the groundbreaking work.* Help children identify what is shown in the other photographs, using sentences such as: *The builders are putting up walls; The builders are welding; The builders will use a screw; The builders will lay a pipe in the trench.* Play a game with students in which you ask a question about the pictures, such as: Which picture shows the builders welding? Have children point to the correct picture and then answer your question with a sentence, such as *This photo shows the builders laying a pipe in a trench.*

Leveled LS Support

Beginning/Intermediate Have children repeat the question you ask. Let them take turns pointing to a photograph on the chart.

Advanced/Advanced-High Encourage children to use their prior knowledge about building to think of other words, such as *office, store,* or *skyscraper.*

Content Objectives
• Develop oral language.
• Use learning strategies.

Language Objectives
• Connect /y/ with *Yy* and /kw/ with *qu*.
• Learn English language patterns.

Use Learning Strategies
Work with children to create a list of things they would like to have in a new school being built for them. As children name things list them on the board. Have children talk about their idea of the best school building possible.

Talk with Me Chart 31A

Support for English Language Learners

Content Objectives
- Understand *Building with Dad*.
- Practice compare and contrast.

Language Objectives
- Retell a selection through speaking and writing.
- Write using grade-level vocabulary.

Monitor and Self-Correct
Have children exchange their sentences and drawings with a partner for editing before finishing their work.

Home Language Support
Invite children to share ideas in their home languages before creating their sentences and drawings.

Language Workshop: Retell

■ **Introduce and Model** Display p. 16 of *Building with Dad*. Look at the machine in this photo. Do you remember what it is called? (bulldozer) Act out driving a bulldozer. I am driving a bulldozer. First I get in. Then I turn the wheel. Then I use the shovel to scoop up dirt.

■ **Practice** Have children take turns acting out other building actions. Help them find pictures in the story that show their action. Then have them decide how to act out using the machine. (Child's name) is acting out driving a bulldozer. Repeat for the cement mixer (pp. 16–17), welding (pp. 24–25), cleaning the floors (pp. 26–27). Ask children to repeat the names of the machines and tools the builders use as they retell the selection.

Writing: Write About *Building with Dad*

■ **Prepare for Writing** We acted out using the building machines. We talked about what we would like to build in a new school. Now let's write about building our school. Have each child fold a piece of paper in half to create two sections.

■ **Create Sentences About *Building with Dad*** Have children copy the sentence starters *The old school* _____. on the left half and *The new school* _____. on the right half of the page. Have children compare and contrast their old and new school buildings by drawing something from the old school and what will replace it in the new school. For example, what did the old lunchroom look like? What will the new lunchroom look like? Then ask children to write or dictate the rest of the sentence to complete the sentence frames. When children are finished, have them trade their sentences and drawings with a partner for editing and suggestions.

Beginning Write the sentence frames for children and have them write or dictate words to complete the sentences.

Intermediate Guide children in copying the sentence frames and writing words to complete the sentences.

Advanced/Advanced-High Encourage children to write their sentences on their own. You might also have children help less-proficient partners complete their sentences.

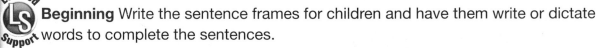

Objectives

• Edit writing for standard grammar and usage, including subject-verb agreement commensurate with grade-level expectations as more English is acquired. • Edit writing for standard grammar and usage, including appropriate verb tenses commensurate with grade-level expectations as more English is acquired.

Common Core Standards
Weekly Planning Guide

Selection: **Old MacDonald had a Woodshop**
Genre: Animal Fantasy

Alignment of the Common Core Standards with This Week's Skills and Strategies

This Week's Common Core Standards for English Language Arts	Instructional Summary
Reading Standards for Literature	
Literature 3. With prompting and support, identify characters, settings, and major events in a story.	The lesson provides instruction on the literary elements of **character.** It explains that a character is the person or animal the story is about. This week's selections help develop skills for understanding character. The lesson also provides instruction to **predict** and **set a purpose** to help children look at the selection to predict what the selection might be about. Then they learn to set a purpose to help them understand what they read.
Literature 5. Recognize common types of texts (e.g., storybooks, poems).	
Literature 7. With prompting and support, describe the relationship between illustrations and the story in which they appear (e.g., what moment in a story an illustration depicts).	
Foundational Skills Standards	
Foundational Skills 2.a. Recognize and produce rhyming words.	Children use the decoding process to segment and blend phonemes to make words and then change initial sounds to make **rhyming words.**
Foundational Skills 2.c. Blend and segment onsets and rimes of single-syllable spoken words.	
Writing Standards	
Writing 3. Use a combination of drawing, dictating, and writing to narrate a single event or several loosely linked events, tell about the events in the order in which they occurred, and provide a reaction to what happened.	Writing activities include **completing sentences** to tell about feelings. Group activities for writing include a **response** to the literature, a **song,** and writing about tools children use. The wrap-up activities ask children to write about a character and a tool that character might use.
Writing 8. With guidance and support from adults, recall information from experiences or gather information from provided sources to answer a question.	
Speaking and Listening Standards	
Speaking/Listening 2. Confirm understanding of a text read aloud or information presented orally or through other media by asking and answering questions about key details and requesting clarification if something is not understood.	This week's lessons help children understand **fact and opinion** by having them distinguish that a fact is something that is true for everyone and an opinion is something that is true for the person saying it but is not necessarily for everyone. Children use details from pictures and text to determine facts and opinions.
Speaking/Listening 4. Describe familiar people, places, things, and events and, with prompting and support, provide additional detail.	
Language Standards	
Language 1.a. Print many upper- and lowercase letters.	Language skills include **handwriting skills** in the lesson and concentrate on letter formation as well as good writing habits. Children work with **prepositional phrases,** learning that a prepositional phrase can tell *where, when, or how.*
Language 1.e. Use the most frequently occurring prepositions (e.g., *to, from, in, out, on, off, for, of, by, with*).	

Additional Support for a Common Core Standard This Week

Use the following instruction to supplement the teaching of one of this week's Common Core Standards.

Common Core Standard: Language 1.e.
Review with children that a preposition is a word that shows us how a noun is related to other parts of a sentence. Also review that a prepositional phrase uses a preposition and the words that come after it to tell us *where, when,* or *how.*

• Write this sentence frame on the board: *I rode _____ the bus.* Have children provide a word to finish the sentence *(on, in).* Then point to the prepositional phrase and help children decide whether the phrase tells *where, when,* or *how.*

• Continue with these sentence frames: *I climbed _____ the wall. I walked _____ the park. I ran _____ my friends. I got _____ the car.*

ISBN-13: 978-0-328-64361-5   ISBN-10: 0-328-64361-0

Week 6

Ants and Their Nests

Question of the Week
How do ants build their nests?

Concept Talk Guide children as they discuss questions such as:
- Where do birds build their homes?
- Why do many animals build their homes in the ground?

Writing Reread and discuss what you wrote about how a bird builds a nest, underlining key words in your draft. Have children write or dictate the group draft or copy the underlined key words on p. 474 in *Reader's and Writer's Notebook*.

Grade K • Unit 6 • Week 2
Old MacDonald had a Woodshop

Unit 6
THE BIG **What are different ways of building?**

Week 5

The House That Tony Lives In

Question of the Week
Who helps to build a house?

Concept Talk Guide children as they discuss questions such as:
- What happened to this builder? How did the builder solve the problem?

Writing Have children turn to p. 458 of *Reader's and Writer's Notebook.* Have them copy a line from the poem about the house and then draw a picture of the house.

Week 4

Alistair and Kip's Great Adventure!

Question of the Week
What can friends build together?

Concept Talk Guide children as they discuss questions such as:
- What would you and your friends build using the large box? Would it be real or make-believe?

Writing Have children turn to p. 446 of *Reader's and Writer's Notebook.* Have them copy the poem about Alistair and Kip's trip and then draw a picture to go with it.

Common Core Standards and Concept Development

- Introduce and explore this unit's weekly concepts through rich, structured conversations
- Develop complex content knowledge and vocabulary
- Expand on a single concept with engaging literature and nonfiction
- Build better readers in all content areas

 Align instruction to **Common Core Anchor Standards**

Week 3

Building Beavers

Question of the Week
How do beavers build their homes?

Concept Talk Guide children as they discuss questions such as:
- What new information did you learn about beavers?

Writing Have children turn to p. 434 of *Reader's and Writer's Notebook.* Have them copy the rhyme about beavers and draw a picture of the beaver.

Week 1

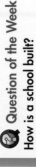

Building with Dad

Question of the Week
How is a school built?

Concept Talk Guide children as they discuss questions such as:
- What is cement used for?
- What kinds of machines are used to build the school?

Writing Have children turn to p. 410 of *Reader's and Writer's Notebook.* Have them write or dictate a list of things from *Building with Dad* they want to learn more about.

You Are Here: Week 2

Old MacDonald had a Woodshop

Question of the Week
What tools do you need to build things?

As children answer this unit's Big Question and this week's Question of the Week, they will address:

Reading 3. Analyze how and why individuals, events, and ideas develop and interact over the course of a text. **(Also Reading 7.)**

Concept Talk Guide children as they discuss questions such as:
- What kind of sounds do these tools make?

As children answer this week's Concept Talk question, they will address:

Speaking/Listening 2. Integrate and evaluate information presented in diverse media and formats, including visually, quantitatively, and orally.

Writing Have children turn to p. 422 of *Reader's and Writer's Notebook.* Have them complete the song "Old MacDonald" by copying an animal word from the list and then illustrating that animal. Sing the song with children, featuring each child's picture for a verse.

As children write about this week's prompt, they will address:

Writing 3. Write narratives to develop real or imagined experiences or events using effective technique, well-chosen details, and well-structured event sequences.

Listening and Speaking On page 49, children learn to discuss fact and opinion. By doing so, they address:

Speaking/Listening 4. Present information, findings, and supporting evidence such that listeners can follow the line of reasoning and the organization, development, and style are appropriate to task, purpose, and audience.

This Week's ELL Overview

ELL Handbook

- Maximize Literacy and Cognitive Engagement
- Research Into Practice
- Full Weekly Support for Every Selection

Old MacDonald had a Woodshop
- Routines to Support Instruction

- Transfer Activities
- Professional Development

Daily Leveled ELL Notes

ELL notes appear throughout this week's instruction and ELL Support is on the DI pages of your Teacher's Edition. The following is a sample of an ELL note from this week.

English Language Learners

Beginning Pronunciation The /o/ sound is similar to the sound of the letter *a* in Spanish, Portuguese, and Tagalog. Children may need to practice seeing and hearing word pairs such as *hat* and *hot, cat* and *cot,* and *map* and *mop* in order to pronounce /o/ words correctly.

Intermediate Build Background Clarify meanings in the song by explaining that a fix-it shop is a place people bring items for repair, or fixing. Explain that a "fix-it man" or "fix-it woman" is a person who repairs toys and small machines.

Advanced Survival Vocabulary Explain to children that they can use the word *where* to find things they need in the classroom. Write the following sentence frame on the board: *Where is the _____?* Have children think of classroom items. List the items on the board. Have them take turns practicing asking for the items using the sentence frame.

Advanced High Extend Language Explain that when talking about two similar objects, we use *this* to refer to the one that is closer to us and *that* to refer to the one that is farther away. Have children practice using the words *this* and *that* to point out objects in the classroom.

ELL by Strand

The ELL lessons on this week's Support for English Language Learners pages are organized by strand. They offer additional scaffolding for the core curriculum. Leveled support notes on these pages address the different proficiency levels in your class. See pages DI•29–DI•34.

ELL Guy
Dr. Jim Cummins

The Three Pillars of ELL Instruction

ELL Strands	Activate Prior Knowledge	Access Content	Extend Language
Vocabulary p. DI•31	Frontload Vocabulary	Provide Scaffolding	Practice
Reading Comprehension p. DI•31	Provide Scaffolding	Set the Scene	Frontload Vocabulary
Phonics, Spelling, and Word Analysis pp. DI•29, DI•32–DI•33	Frontload Words with Initial and Medial /o/	Isolate Initial and Medial /o/	Review /a/ and /i/
Listening Comprehension p. DI•30	Prepare for the Read Aloud	First Listening	Second Listening
Conventions and Writing pp. DI•32, DI•34	Provide Scaffolding/ Introduce and Model	Practice	Leveled Practice Activities/ Leveled Writing Activities
Concept Development p. DI•29	Read the Concept Literacy Reader	Read the Concept Literacy Reader	Develop Oral Language

This Week's Practice Stations Overview

Six Weekly Practice Stations with Leveled Activities can be found at the beginning of each week of instruction. For this week's Practice Stations, see pp. 114–115.

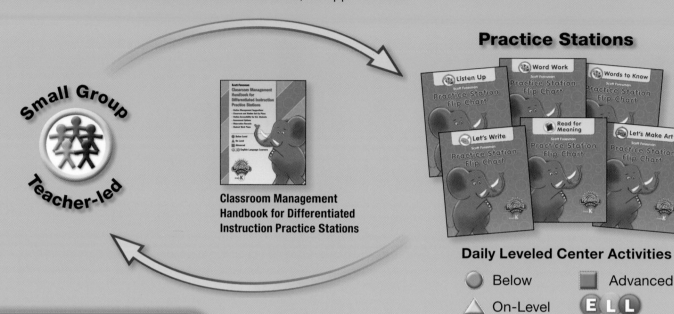

Small Group Teacher-led

Classroom Management Handbook for Differentiated Instruction Practice Stations

Practice Stations

Daily Leveled Center Activities

◯ Below ⬜ Advanced
△ On-Level **ELL**

Practice Stations Flip Charts

 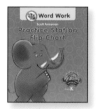   

	Listen Up	Word Work	Words to Know	Let's Write	Read for Meaning	Let's Make Art
Objectives	• Identify beginning, middle, and ending sounds of words.	• Review and build words with short *a*.	• Identify and use compound words.	• Use words to write a list.	• Compare by telling how things are alike. • Contrast by telling how things are different.	• Draw a building plan.
Materials	• *Listen Up* Flip Chart Activity 32 • Picture Cards • paper, pencils	• *Word Work* Flip Chart Activity 32 • Picture Cards: *bag, bat, black, can, cap, cat, crab, fan, flag, hat, jam, lamp, man, map, mask, pat, van, yak* • Letter Tiles • paper, pencils	• *Words to Know* Flip Chart Activity 32 • Find pictures for compound words: *playground, classroom, bookcase* • Teacher-made Word Cards for *playground, classroom, bookcase*	• *Let's Write* Flip Chart Activity 32 • Teacher-made Picture Cards: *wood, bricks, concrete, windows, doors, hammer, nails, saws, shovels, pipes, wires* • paper, pencil	• *Read for Meaning* Flip Chart Activity 32 • Little Book *Building with Dad* • pencil, crayons, paper	• *Let's Make Art* Flip Chart Activity 32 • Little Book *Building with Dad* • Teacher-made chart showing a simple flow plan • colored pencils, crayons, paper, ruler

This Week on Reading Street!

Week 2

Putting It Together

Question of the Week
What tools do you need to build things?

Daily Plan

Whole Group
- ◉ /o/ Spelled Oo
- ◉ Character
- • Vocabulary

Don't Wait Until Friday

MONITOR PROGRESS	Success Predictor			
Day 1 Check Phonemic Awareness	Day 2 Check Sound Spelling/ Retelling	Day 3 Check Word Reading	Day 4 Check Phonemic Awareness	Day 5 Check Oral Vocabulary

Small Group

Teacher-Led

- • Reading Support
- • Skill Support
- • Fluency Practice

Practice Stations

Independent Activities

Customize Literacy More support for a Balanced Literacy approach, see pp. CL•1–CL•31.

Whole Group
- • Writing
- • Conventions: Prepositional Phrases
- • Listening and Speaking

Assessment
- • Day 5 Assessment for Phonics
- • Day 5 Assessment for Comprehension

You Are Here! Unit 6 Week 2

This Week's Reading Selections

Trade Book
Genre: **Animal Fantasy**

Decodable Reader 32

Leveled Readers

Get Set, Roll! Reader 32

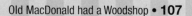

Resources on Reading Street!

	Build Concepts	Phonemic Awareness and Phonics	Vocabulary
Whole Group	Talk With Me/ Sing With Me	 Student Edition pp. 32–33 Student Edition p. 36	Student Edition p. 37 Student Edition p. 48
 Go Digital	• Concept Talk Video • Sing with Me Animations	• eReaders	
Small Group and Independent Practice	Practice Station Flip Chart Leveled Readers	Practice Station Flip Chart Decodable Reader 32 Leveled Readers Get Set, Roll! Reader 32	Practice Station Flip Chart Student Edition p. 37
Go Digital	• eReaders	• eReaders • Letter Tile Drag and Drop	
Customize Literacy	• Leveled Readers	• Decodable Reader	• High-Frequency Cards
Go Digital	• Concept Talk Video • Big Question Video • eReaders	• eReaders	• Sing with Me Animations

 Question of the Week
What tools do you need to build things?

Comprehension	Fluency	Conventions and Writing
Student Edition pp. 34–35 Trade Book	 Decodable Reader 32  Kdg. Student Reader K.6.2 Get Set, Roll! Reader 32	 Reader's and Writer's Notebook
• Envision It! Animations	• eReaders	• Grammar Jammer
Practice Station Flip Chart Leveled Readers Get Set, Roll! Reader 32	Practice Station Flip Chart Leveled Readers	Practice Station Flip Chart Reader's and Writer's Notebook
• Envision It! Animations • eReaders	• eReaders	• Grammar Jammer
• Leveled Readers	• Leveled Readers	• *Reader's and Writer's Notebook*
• Envision It! Animations • eReaders	• eReaders	• Grammar Jammer

You Are Here! Unit 6 Week 2

Week 2

My 5-Day Planner for Reading Street!

MONITOR PROGRESS — Don't Wait Until Friday

	Check Phonemic Awareness **Day 1** pages 116–131	Check Sound-Spelling Check Retelling **Day 2** pages 132–149
Get Ready to Read	**Concept Talk,** 116 **Oral Vocabulary,** 117 *saw, drill, hammer, screwdriver, file, chisel* **Phonemic Awareness,** 118–119 ◉ Initial and Medial /o/ **Phonics,** 120–121 ◉ /o/ Spelled *Oo* **Handwriting,** 122 Letters *O* and *o* **High-Frequency Words,** 123 Review *where, is, go, that, come* **READ Decodable Story 32,** 124–125	**Concept Talk,** 132 **Oral Vocabulary,** 133 *saw, drill* **Phonemic Awareness,** 134–135 ◉ Initial and Medial /o/ **Phonics,** 136–137 ◉ /o/ Spelled *Oo* **Handwriting,** 138 Words with *Oo* **High-Frequency Words,** 139 *where, is, go, that, come* **READ Decodable Reader 32,** 140–141
Read and Comprehend	**Listening Comprehension,** 126–127 ◉ Character	**Listening Comprehension,** 142 ◉ Character **READ Trade Book—First Read,** 142 *Old MacDonald had a Woodshop* **Retell,** 143 **Think, Talk, and Write,** 144
Language Arts	**Conventions,** 128 Prepositional Phrases **Writing,** 129 Wonderful, Marvelous Me! **Daily Handwriting,** 129 Letters *O* and *o* **Listening and Speaking,** 130 Discuss Fact and Opinion **Wrap Up Your Day,** 130 **Extend Your Day!,** 131	**Conventions,** 145 Prepositional Phrases **Writing,** 146 Respond to Literature **Daily Handwriting,** 146 Letters *O* and *o* **Vocabulary,** 147 Location Words **Wrap Up Your Day,** 148 **Extend Your Day!,** 149

You Are Here! Unit 6 Week 2

What tools do you need to build things?

Check Word Reading	Check Phonemic Awareness	Check Oral Vocabulary
Day 3 pages 150–177	**Day 4** pages 178–189	**Day 5** pages 190–203
Concept Talk, 150 **Oral Vocabulary,** 151 *hammer, screwdriver* **Phonemic Awareness,** 152–153 ⊙ Initial and Medial /o/ **Phonics,** 154–155 ⊙ /o/ Spelled *Oo* **READ Kindergarten Student Reader K.6.2,** 156–157	**Concept Talk,** 178 **Oral Vocabulary,** 179 *file, chisel* **Review Phonemic Awareness,** 180 /a/ and /i/ **Review Phonics,** 181 /a/ Spelled *Aa,* /i/ Spelled *Ii* **Spelling,** 182 ⊙ /o/ Spelled *Oo* **READ Get Set, Roll! Reader 32,** 183	**Concept Wrap Up,** 190 **Oral Vocabulary,** 191 *saw, drill, hammer, screwdriver, file, chisel* **Review ⊙ Phonemic Awareness,** 192 /o/ **Review ⊙ Phonics,** 193 /o/ Spelled *Oo* **Assessment,** 194–195 Monitor Progress
Comprehension, 158–159 ⊙ Character **READ Trade Book—Second Read,** 160–171 *Old MacDonald had a Woodshop*	**Comprehension,** 184 ⊙ Character **Review Plot** **READ Trade Book—Third Read,** 185 *Old MacDonald had a Woodshop*	**Let's Practice It!,** 196–197 Lullaby **Assessment,** 198–199 Monitor Progress
Conventions, 172 Pronouns *I* and *me* **Writing,** 173 Genre: Song **Daily Handwriting,** 173 Letters *O* and *o* **Listening and Speaking,** 174–175 Discuss Fact and Opinion **Wrap Up Your Day,** 176 **Extend Your Day!,** 177	**Conventions,** 186 Prepositional Phrases **Writing,** 187 Extend the Concept **Daily Handwriting,** 187 Letters *O* and *o* **Vocabulary,** 188 Location Words **Wrap Up Your Day,** 188 **Extend Your Day!,** 189	**Review Conventions,** 200 Prepositional Phrases **Writing,** 201 This Week We… **Daily Handwriting,** 201 Letters *O* and *o* **Wrap Up Your Week!,** 202 ⓠ What tools do you need to build things? **Extend Your Day!,** 203

Week 2

Grouping Options for Differentiated Instruction
Turn the page for the small group time lesson plan.

Planning Small Group Time on Reading Street!

SMALL GROUP TIME RESOURCES

DAY 1

Look for this **Small Group Time** box each day to help meet the individual needs of all your children. Differentiated instruction lessons appear on the DI pages at the end of each week.

Teacher-Led

SI Strategic Intervention	**OL** On-Level	**A** Advanced
Teacher-Led • Phonemic Awareness and Phonics **Reread** Decodable Story	**Teacher-Led** • Phonemic Awareness and Phonics **Reread** Decodable Story	**Teacher-Led** • Phonemic Awareness and Phonics **Reread** Decodable Story for Fluency

ELL Place English language learners in the groups that correspond to their reading abilities in English.

Practice Stations	**Independent Activities**
• Listen Up • Word Work	• Read Independently • *Reader's and Writer's Notebook* • Concept Talk Video

ELL Poster 32

Day 1

SI Strategic Intervention	**Phonemic Awareness and Phonics**, DI•18 **Reread** Decodable Story 32, DI•18
OL On-Level	**Phonemic Awareness and Phonics**, DI•23 **Reread** Decodable Story 32, DI•23
A Advanced	**Phonemic Awareness and Phonics**, DI•26 **Reread** Decodable Story 32 for Fluency, DI•26
 **English Language Learners**	DI•29–DI•30 Frontload Concept Phonemic Awareness and Phonics Comprehension Skill

You Are Here! Unit 6 Week 2

Reading Street Response to Intervention Kit

Reading Street Leveled Practice Stations Kit

What tools do you need to build things?

SI Strategic Intervention

Decodable Reader

Listen to Me Reader

We Build a Birdhouse
By Alison Blank

Concept Literacy Reader

Get Set, Roll! Reader

OL On-Level

Kindergarten Student Reader

Decodable Reader

Get Set, Roll! Reader

A Advanced

Independent Reader

Decodable Reader

Week 2

Small Group Weekly Plan

Day 2	Day 3	Day 4	Day 5
Phonemic Awareness and Phonics, DI•19 **Reread** Decodable Reader 32, DI•19	**Phonemic Awareness and Phonics,** DI•20 **Read** Concept Literacy Reader K.6.2, DI•20	**Phonemic Awareness and Phonics,** DI•21 **Read** Get Set, Roll! Reader 32, DI•21	**Phonics Review,** DI•22 **Read** Listen to Me Reader K.6.2, DI•22
Phonemic Awareness and Phonics, DI•23 **Reread** Decodable Reader 32, DI•23	**Phonemic Awareness and Phonics,** DI•24 **Read** Kindergarten Student Reader K.6.2, DI•24	**Review Phonics and High-Frequency Words** **Read** Get Set, Roll! Reader 32, DI•25	**Phonics Review,** DI•25 **Reread** Leveled Books, DI•25
Phonics and Spelling, DI•26 **Reread** Decodable Reader 32, DI•26	**Read** Independent Reader K.6.2 or Kindergarten Student Reader K.6.2, DI•27	**Read** Get Set, Roll! Reader 32 or **Reread** Kindergarten Student Reader K.6.2, DI•28	**Fluency and Comprehension,** DI•28 **Reread** Independent Reader for Fluency, DI•28
DI•31 Comprehension Skill Frontload Vocabulary	DI•32 Review Phonemic Awareness and Phonics Scaffold Conventions	DI•33 Review Phonemic Awareness and Phonics Revisit Concept and Oral Language	DI•34 Language Workshop Writing

Practice Stations for Everyone on Reading Street!

Listen Up!
Beginning, middle, and ending sounds

Objectives
• Identify beginning, middle, and ending sounds of words

Materials
• *Listen Up!* Flip Chart Activity 32
• Picture Cards: *bed, cap, hen, jam, mop, pen, pig, red, wig*
• paper, pencils

Differentiated Activities

🔵 Choose a Picture Card. Say the sound you hear at the beginning of the Picture Card word. Say the sound you hear in the middle, at the end.

🔺 Choose a Picture Card. Say the sound you hear at the beginning of the Picture Card word. Say the sound you hear in the middle and at the end. Find another card whose word has the same beginning, middle, or ending sound.

🟥 Choose a Picture Card. Say the sound you hear at the beginning of the Picture Card word. Say the sound you hear in the middle and at the end. Write three other words that have the same beginning, middle, or ending sound as your Picture Card word.

Word Work
/a/ spelled *Aa*

Objectives
• Review and build words with short *a*.

Materials
• *Word Work Flip* Chart Activity 32
• Picture Cards: *bag, bat, black, can, cap, cat, crab, fan, flag, hat, jam, lamp, man, map, mask, pat, van, yak*
• Letter Tiles
• paper, pencils

Differentiated Activities

🔵 Look for Picture Cards with the /a/ sound in the middle. Use the Letter Tiles to build the word *cat*.

🔺 Find Picture Cards with the /a/ sound in the middle. Use the Letter Tiles to build the word *cat*. Take away the letter *c*. Add the letter *h*. Say the new word.

🟥 Find Picture Cards with the /a/ sound in the middle. Find other Picture Cards with /a/ in the middle. Use the Letter Tiles to build the word *cat*. Take away and add letters to build three new words. Write the words on your paper.

Technology
• Letter Tiles Drag and Drop

Words To Know
Compound words

Objectives
• Identify and use compound words.

Materials
• *Words to Know* Flip Chart Activity 32
• Find pictures (or take quick digital photos and print out) for compound words: *playground, classroom, bookcase.*
• Teacher-made word cards for *playground, classroom, bookcase, play, ground, class, room, book, case*

Differentiated Activities

🔵 Find a picture card that shows a playground. Say the two shorter words that make the word *playground*. Find a picture card that shows a classroom. Say the two shorter words that make the word *classroom*. Find a picture card that shows a bookcase. Say the two shorter words that make the word *bookcase*.

🔺 Find a picture card that shows a playground. Find the word card for *playground*. Find the picture cards for classroom and bookcase. Find the word cards for *classroom* and *bookcase*.

🟥 Match the picture cards and word cards that show *playground, classroom,* and *bookcase*. Mix up the word cards *play, ground, class, room, book,* and *case*. Put the word cards back together to make compound words.

You Are Here! Unit 6 Week 2

Key

🔵 Below-Level Activities

🔺 On-Level Activities

🟥 Advanced Activities

Practice Station Flip Chart

Week 2

Let's Write!
List

Objectives
• Use words to write a list.

Materials
• *Let's Write!* Flip Chart Activity 32
• Teacher-made picture cards: *wood, bricks, concrete, windows, doors, hammer, nails, saws, shovels, pipes, wires*
• paper, pencil

Differentiated Activities

🔵 Look at the picture cards. Tell what you see in each picture. Write a list that tells the name of things you see.

🔺 Look at the picture cards. Tell how each item is used for building something. Write a list of important things needed to build a house or school.

🟥 Think about what people use to build schools, houses, and other buildings. Make a list of things that people would need.

Read For Meaning
Compare and contrast

Objectives
• Compare by telling how things are alike.
• Contrast by telling how things are different.

Materials
• *Read for Meaning* Flip Chart Activity 32
• Little Book *Building with Dad*
• pencil, crayons, paper

Differentiated Activities

When we **compare,** we tell how things are alike. When we **contrast,** we tell how things are different.

🔵 Read your book. Point to pictures in the selection that show things that are alike. Point to pictures in the selection that show things that are different.

🔺 Read your book. Point to pictures in the selection. Write a sentence that tells how they are alike. Write a sentence that tells how they are different.

🟥 Read your book. Find two things in your book that are similar. Compare them by telling how they are alike. Contrast them by telling how they are different.

Let's Make Art!

Objectives
• Draw a building plan

Materials
• *Let's Make Art!* Flip Chart Activity 32
• Little Book *Building with Dad*
• Teacher-made chart showing a simple flow plan
• colored pencils, crayons, paper, ruler

Differentiated Activities

🔵 Look at the pictures in your book. Think about the shape of the buildings. Think about the rooms inside. Make a drawing to show what a room would look like.

🔺 Look at the pictures in your book. Think about the shape of the buildings. Think about the rooms inside. Make a drawing to show a building plan. Show where the doors and windows would be.

🟥 Look at the pictures in your book. Think about the shape of the buildings. Make a drawing to show a building plan. Show where the doors and windows would be. Label each room.

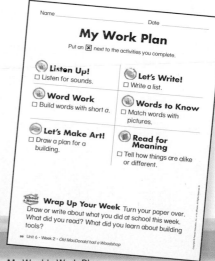

Name _____ Date _____

My Work Plan
Put an ☒ next to the activities you complete.

🎧 **Listen Up!**
☐ Listen for sounds.

✏️ **Let's Write!**
☐ Write a list.

🔤 **Word Work**
☐ Build words with short *a*.

📖 **Words to Know**
☐ Match words with pictures.

🎨 **Let's Make Art!**
☐ Draw a plan for a building.

📚 **Read for Meaning**
☐ Tell how things are alike or different.

Wrap Up Your Week Turn your paper over. Draw or write about what you did at school this week. What did you read? What did you learn about building tools?

Unit 6 • Week 2 • Old MacDonald had a Woodshop

My Weekly Work Plan

Objectives

• Share information and ideas about the concept.

Today at a Glance

Oral Vocabulary
saw, drill, hammer, screwdriver, file, chisel

Phonemic Awareness
◉ Initial and Medial /o/

Phonics
◉ /o/ Spelled *Oo*

Handwriting
O and *o*

High-Frequency Words
where, is, go, that, come

Comprehension
◉ Character

Conventions
Prepositional Phrases

Writing
Wonderful, Marvelous Me!

Listening and Speaking
Discuss Fact and Opinion

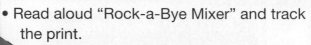

TRUCKTOWN *on Reading Street*

Start your engines! Display p. 15 of *Truckery Rhymes*.

• Read aloud "Rock-a-Bye Mixer" and track the print.

• Reread the rhyme and have children chime in as they wish.

• Ask children to identify the rhyming words. (*fall, all*)

Truckery Rhymes

Concept Talk

Question of the Week

What tools do you need to build things?

Introduce the concept

To build concepts and to focus their attention, tell children that this week they will talk, sing, read, and write about **tools and the things we build with them.** Write the question of the week and track the print as you read it.

Play the CD that features sounds heard in a workshop. What kind of sounds do these tools make?

💿 Background Building Audio

ROUTINE Activate Prior Knowledge Team Talk

1 **Think** Have children think for a minute about tools used for building.

2 **Pair** Have pairs of children discuss the question of the week. Remind them to take turns speaking. Have children use complete sentences in their discussions about how to use different tools.

3 **Share** Call on a few children to share their ideas with the group. Guide discussion and encourage elaboration with prompts such as: How do we use a hammer?

Routines Flip Chart

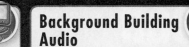
Anchored Talk

Develop oral language

Display Talk with Me Chart 32A. This week we will talk about tools. This chart shows different tools that are used to build things. Point to a tool. Who knows the name of this tool? What do we use this tool to do? Have children tell about their experiences with the tools. Remind them that they should always wear safety goggles and work with an adult when using tools.

We are going to learn six new Amazing Words this week. Listen as I say each word: *saw, drill, hammer, screwdriver, file, chisel.* Have children say each word as you point to the picture.

Display Sing with Me Chart 32B. Tell children they are going to sing a song about using tools to build things. Read the title. Have children describe the picture. Sing the song several times to the tune of "If I Had a Hammer." Listen for the Amazing Words: *saw, drill, hammer, screwdriver, file, chisel.* Have children stand up and sing with you.

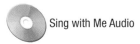 Sing with Me Audio

Talk with Me/Sing with Me Chart 32A

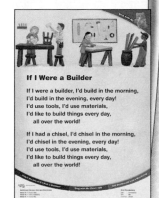

If I Were a Builder

If I were a builder, I'd build in the morning,
I'd build in the evening, every day!
I'd use tools, I'd use materials,
I'd like to build things every day,
   all over the world!

If I had a chisel, I'd chisel in the morning,
I'd chisel in the evening, every day!
I'd use tools, I'd use materials,
I'd like to build things every day,
   all over the world!

Talk with Me/Sing with Me Chart 32B

ELL Preteach Concepts Use the Day 1 instruction on ELL Poster 32 to assess and build background knowledge, develop concepts, and build oral vocabulary.

 Poster 32

Amazing Words

saw	drill
hammer	screwdriver
file	chisel

Writing on Demand

Develop Writing Fluency

Ask children to write or draw what they know about tools and building. Have them write or draw for two minutes. Children should write as much as they can. Tell them to try to do their best writing. You may want to discuss what children wrote or drew during writing conferences.

ELL

English Language Learners

Access Content Have English learners say the name of each tool in their native languages and imitate a builder using the tool.

ELL Support Additional ELL support and modified instruction is provided in the *ELL Handbook* and in the ELL Support lessons on pp. DI•29–34.

Objectives
◎ Practice initial and medial /o/.

Check Phonemic Awareness
SUCCESS PREDICTOR

My Skills Buddy, pp. 32–33

Phonemic Awareness
🔊 Initial and Medial /o/

Introduce
Today we are going to review /o/. Listen carefully: /o/ /o/ /o/. Say it with me: /o/ /o/ /o/. Display the *ox* Picture Card. *Ox* begins with /o/ /o/ /o/, *ox*. What sound does *ox* begin with? Continue this routine to practice initial and medial /o/ with the *box, otter,* and *olive* Picture Cards.

Model
Have children look at the picture on pp. 32–33 of *My Skills Buddy*. Tell them they will be listening for a familiar sound—/o/. I see an oxygen tank in the picture. What sound do you hear at the beginning of *oxygen*? I hear /o/ at the beginning of *oxygen*. The first sound in *oxygen* is /o/. What other things do you see that have /o/ at the beginning or in the middle?

Picture Card

Guide practice
As children name example words from the picture, guide them in stating that /o/ is the beginning or middle sound. Discuss with children some of the bulleted items on p. 32 of *My Skills Buddy*. Save the other bulleted items for discussion on Day 2.

Corrective feedback
If... children have difficulty naming words with /o/,
then... say *oxygen* again, emphasizing the /o/ sound—/o/ /o/ /o/, *oxygen*.

Discriminate sounds

I am going to say two words. Tell me which word begins with /o/. I will do the first one: *ostrich, lion*. I hear /o/ at the beginning of *ostrich*. *Ostrich* begins with /o/. Listen for the word that begins with /o/: *octopus, mermaid; toy, otter*.

Now listen for words that have /o/ in the middle: *cap, sock*. The middle sound in *sock* is /o/. Read the following word pairs and have children repeat the word with medial /o/: *suds, hop* (hop); *jog, jump* (jog); *lamp, dot* (dot).

Corrective feedback

If... children cannot discriminate /o/,
then... have them say /o/ /o/ /o/, *otter*.

When you say /o/, you open your mouth and drop your jaw. Say /o/ with me: /o/ /o/ /o/. Did you open your mouth and feel your jaw drop? Say *otter* with me: *otter.* Repeat the activity with *ox, olive, fox,* and *mop*.

Blend

Review blending sounds. Listen to these sounds: /t/ /o/ /p/. Say these sounds with me: /t/ /o/ /p/. Now blend the sounds with me to say a word: /t/ /o/ /p/, *top.* Continue the blending practice with *pot, bog, on,* and *hop*.

> **Don't Wait Until Friday**
>
> **MONITOR PROGRESS** ⟳ Check Phonemic Awareness   Words with /o/
>
> Say *cotton* and *silk*. Have children identify the word with /o/. Continue with *sock, sick; weird, odd; not, hum; cold, hot*.
>
> **If...** children cannot discriminate /o/ words,
>
> **then...** use the small-group Strategic Intervention lesson, p. DI•18, to reteach /o/.
>
> | **Day 1** | **Day 2** | **Day 3** | **Day 4** | **Day 5** |
> |---|---|---|---|---|
> | Check Phonemic Awareness | Check Sound-Spelling/ Retelling | Check Word Reading | Check Phonemic Awareness | Check Oral Vocabulary |
>
> *Success Predictor*

Differentiated Instruction

 Advanced

Medial /o/ Have children search the classroom for items with medial /o/, such as *box, block,* or *clock*. List these items on the board. Have each child choose a word to copy onto his or her paper. Then have children illustrate their words.

E L L

English Language Learners

Pronunciation The /o/ sound is similar to the sound of the letter *a* in Spanish, Portuguese, and Tagalog. Children may need to practice seeing and hearing word pairs such as *hat* and *hot, cat* and *cot,* and *map* and *mop* in order to pronounce /o/ words correctly.

Phonemic Awareness

Success Predictor

Objectives

◎ Associate the sound /o/ with the spelling *o*.

• Blend and read words with /o/.

Skills Trace

◉ Short *o* Spelled *Oo*

Introduce U3W5D1; U3W6D1; U6W2D1

Practice U3W5D2; U3W5D3; U3W6D2; U3W6D3; U6W2D2; U6W2D3

Reteach/Review U3W5D5; U3W6D4; U3W6D5; U4W1D4; U6W2D5; U6W3D4

Assess/Test Benchmark Assessment U3; U6

KEY:
U=Unit   W=Week   D=Day

Phonics—Teach/Model
 /o/ Spelled *Oo*

Teach

Display the *Oo* Alphabet Card. Point to the *otter* on the Alphabet Card. *Otter* begins with /o/. Say the word with me: *otter*. Write *otter* on the board and point to the *o*. *Otter* begins with /o/ spelled *o*. Now point to the letters *Oo* on the card. The sound for this letter is /o/. The names for this letter is uppercase *O* and lowercase *o*. What is the sound for this letter? What are the names for this letter?

Alphabet Card

Model

Write "The Fix-It Shop" on the board. Point to the *o* in *Shop*. When I see this letter, I think of the sound /o/. This word is *Shop*—/sh/ /o/ /p/, *Shop*. In this word, /o/ is in the middle. Listen carefully: *Shop*. What middle sound does *Shop* have? *Shop* has /o/ in the middle. The song we will sing is about a shop where things get fixed.

Guide practice

Display Phonics Songs and Rhymes Chart 32. Teach children the song "The Fix-It Shop" sung to the tune of "I've Been Working on the Railroad." Play the CD or sing the song several times. When you hear a word that has /o/ in it, I want you to hop. As you sing the song, point to words with /o/.

◉ Phonics Songs and Rhymes Audio

On their own

Have children look around the classroom for examples of uppercase *O* and lowercase *o* and keep a tally of the *Oo* words they find.

Phonics Songs and Rhymes Chart 32

Blend Words

Review

To review sound-spellings, use Alphabet Cards *Bb, Dd, Gg, Ii, Nn, Pp, Tt,* and *Ss* and the *box, inch,* and *top* Picture Cards. Then use this routine for sound-by-sound blending to have children blend new words.

ROUTINE **Sound-by-Sound Blending**

① **Connect** Write the letter *o*. What is the sound we learned for this letter? The sound is /o/. Say it with me: /o/ /o/ /o/. When you see this letter in a word, what sound will you say?

② **Model** Write *lot* on the board.

- Touch under the letter *l*. What is the sound for this letter? Say it with me: /l/ /l/ /l/. Repeat the routine for *o* and *t*.

- Let's blend the sounds together. Listen as I blend the sounds: /l/ /o/ /t/. Say it with me: /l/ /o/ /t/. Now say it without me.

- Listen as I use *lot* in a sentence: *It takes a lot of time*. Say the sentence with me. Then have children use *lot* in their own sentences.

③ **Guide Practice** Continue the routine established in step 2 with the words below:

| Bob | got | top | not | will | spin | Dad | can | get |

Children should successfully read these words before reading Decodable Story 32 on pp. 415–416 of *Reader's and Writer's Notebook*.

Corrective Feedback If children have trouble reading a word, model blending the sounds to read the word. Then have children say it with you.

Routines Flip Chart

English Language Learners
Build Background Clarify meanings in the song by explaining that a fix-it shop is a place where people bring items for repair, or fixing. Explain that a "fix-it man" or "fix-it woman" is a person who repairs toys and small machines.

Objectives
- Write *O* and *o*.
- Learn high-frequency words.

Handwriting

Introduce

Write *Oo* on the board. Words that begin with /o/ are written with an uppercase *O* or a lowercase *o*. Which letter is uppercase *O*? Which letter is lowercase *o*?

Model uppercase O

Write *October* on the board. This is the word *October*. We use uppercase letters to begin sentences and for the first letter in a name. I use an uppercase *O* at the beginning of *October* because it is the name of a month. Watch how I make an uppercase *O*. Write an *O* on the board following the stroke instructions below.

Guide practice

Have children write the uppercase *O* in the air. Use your finger to make an uppercase *O* in the air. Now write it on the palm of your hand.

Model lowercase o

Write *otter* on the board. This is the word *otter*. Watch as I trace a lowercase *o* with my finger. Write another lowercase *o* on the board following the stroke instructions. Again, have children write *o* in the air and on their hands.

Guide practice

Have children use their Write-On Boards to write a row of uppercase *O* and a row of lowercase *o*.

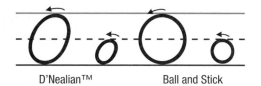

D'Nealian™   Ball and Stick

More practice

Use *Reader's and Writer's Notebook,* pp. 413, 414 for additional practice with *o*.

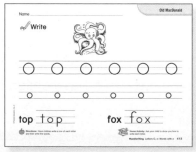

Reader's and Writer's Notebook, p. 413

Reader's and Writer's Notebook, p. 414

High-Frequency Words

Introduce

Use the routine below to teach high-frequency words *where, is, go, that,* and *come.*

Nondecodable Words

1 **Say and Spell** Some words we have to learn by remembering the letters rather than saying the sounds. We will say and spell the words to help learn them. Write *where* on the board. This is the word *where.* It has five letters. The letters in *where* are *w, h, e, r,* and *e.* Have children say and spell the word, first with you and then without you.

2 **Demonstrate Meaning** I can use the word *where* in many sentences. Here is one sentence: *Where is the pup?* Now you use the word in a sentence.

Repeat the routine with the words *is, go, that,* and *come.*

Routines Flip Chart

Academic Vocabulary

Write the following words on the board:

character	song
fact	opinion
preposition	prepositional phrase

Point to the list. This week we are going to learn these important words. They are tools for learning. As we work this week, you will hear them many times. Read the words. Preteach the Academic Vocabulary at point-of-use by providing a child-friendly description, explanation, or example that clarifies the meaning of each term. Then ask children to restate the meaning of the Academic Vocabulary in their own words.

Objectives
- Read high-frequency words.
- Decode and read words in context and isolation.

Decodable Story 32
/o/ Spelled *Oo* and High-Frequency Words

Review
Review the following high-frequency words by having children read each word as you point to it on the Word Wall.

a	the	go	me	to

Read Decodable Story 32

Distribute folded copies of Decodable Story 32, *Spin the Top.* Today we will read a story about Bob and his top. What is the title of this story? Point to the title of the story. *Spin the Top* is the title of the story. What sound do you hear in the middle of the word *top?* We will read lots of decodable words in this story. Have children read Decodable Story 32 on pp. 415–416 in *Reader's and Writer's Notebook.*

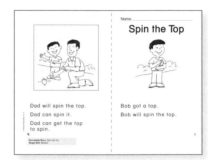

Reader's and Writer's Notebook, pp. 415–416

After children read p. 2, say Look at the cover and the title. What do you think will happen next?

Use the routine for reading decodable books to read Decodable Story 32.

ROUTINE Reading Decodable Books

1 **Read Silently** Have children whisper read the story page by page as you listen in.

2 **Model Fluent Reading** Have children finger point as you read a page. Then have children reread the page without you.

3 **Read Chorally** Have children finger point as they chorally read the page. Continue reading page by page, repeating steps 1 and 2.

4 **Read Individually** Have children take turns reading aloud a page.

5 **Reread and Monitor Progress** As you listen to individual children reread, monitor progress and provide support.

6 **Reread with a Partner** Have children reread the story page by page with a partner.

Routines Flip Chart

Small Group Time

DAY 1

Break into small groups after reading the Decodable Story and before the comprehension lesson.

Teacher-Led

SI Strategic Intervention	**OL** On-Level	**A** Advanced
Teacher-Led Page DI•18	**Teacher-Led** Page DI•23	**Teacher-Led** Page DI•26
• Phonemic Awareness and Phonics	• Phonemic Awareness and Phonics	• Phonemic Awareness and Phonics
• **Reread** Decodable Story 32	• **Reread** Decodable Story 32	• **Reread** Decodable Story 32 for Fluency

 Place English language learners in the groups that correspond to their reading abilities in English.

Practice Stations
• Visit the Listen Up! Station
• Visit the Word Work Station

Independent Activities
• Read independently
• Concept Talk Video
• *Reader's and Writer's Notebook*

Differentiated Instruction

SI Strategic Intervention

Decodable Story Before children read Decodable Story 32, *Spin the Top,* review /i/ and /o/ words with the *box, top, pig,* and *six* Picture Cards.

English Language Learners
Extra Support for ELL Write one of the following previously taught high-frequency words on the board: *a, the, go, me, to.* Read the word with children. Ask them to find examples of the word in Decodable Story 32, *Spin the Top.* Repeat the routine with the other listed high-frequency words.

Skills Trace

⊙ **Draw Conclusions**

Introduce U1W1D1; U1W5D1; U4W4D1; U6W2D1

Practice U1W1D2; U1W1D3; U1W1D4; U1W5D2; U1W5D3; U1W5D4; U4W4D2; U4W4D3; U4W4D4; U6W2D2; U6W2D3; U6W2D4

Reteach/Review U1W1D5; U1W2D4; U1W5D5; U3W4D4; U4W4D5; U5W4D4; U6W2D5

KEY:
U=Unit   W=Week   D=Day

My Skills Buddy, pp. 34–35

Listening Comprehension
⊙ Character

Introduce

Many stories are about a person or an animal. The person or animal that a story is about is called a **character**. Characters can be real or make-believe. Good readers pay attention to what characters are like and why they do things.

Envision It!

Have children turn to pp. 34–35 in *My Skills Buddy* and look at the top picture on the left side. This picture shows the characters in a story.

- Who are the two characters in the picture? (the tortoise and the hare)

- What is the tortoise like? (He is wearing a sweatband, but he doesn't look like he's fast.)

- What is the hare like? (He is wearing running shorts; he looks strong and fast.)

Model

Today I will read a story about animals that build a tree house. Read **"The Monkeys Build a Tree House"** and model how to identify and describe characters.

 Think Aloud

When I read, I find out about the people or animals in the story. "The Monkeys Build a Tree House" is about four friends who work together to build a tree house. All the characters in this story are animals.

Guide practice

After reading, ask children questions about the characters in the story.

- What kind of animals build the tree house? (monkeys)
- What are the monkeys' names? (Molly, Mitch, Megan, and Manfred)
- What are the monkeys like? (They are hard workers.)

More practice

Display the Trade Book *Goldilocks and the Three Bears*. Page through the story. Help children identify and describe the characters in the story and then tell why the characters act the way they do. Have them draw a picture of their favorite character.

Connect to everyday life

Pretend that we are writing a story about our class. Tell me about your character. What would you be like? Why would you do the things you do in our story?

Differentiated Instruction

 Advanced

Support Character Have children describe a familiar fairy tale or folk tale. Have them discuss the characters in the story. Ask children to describe the characters and tell why they do things.

Academic Vocabulary

character the person or animal that a story is about

ELL

English Language Learners
Oral Comprehension To prepare English learners for the Read Aloud, use the modified Read Aloud for the ELL Support lessons on p. DI•30.

 Read Aloud

The Monkeys Build a Tree House

The monkeys wanted to build a tree house. They got wood, nails, and tools.

"First, we cut the wood the right length," said Molly. "How do we do that?"

"I know!" yelled Megan, holding a saw.

"Wait," said Mitch. "We should measure the boards first." He measured and marked the boards. Then Megan cut them with a saw.

"Now we build!" said Manfred. He picked up the screwdriver and some nails.

"That's not right," said Molly. "Use the hammer to put in the nails."

Zip, zip. Wham! Wham! Buzz, buzz. At last, the house was finished.

"Oh no!" cried Molly, Megan, Manfred, and Mitch. "How do we get it up in the tree?"

Objectives

- Introduce prepositional phrases.
- Write and draw pictures about feelings.

Conventions
Prepositional Phrases

Review
Remind children of what they learned about prepositions. A preposition is a word that tells us how a noun is related to the other parts of a sentence. We studied these prepositions: *on, in, over, under.*

Teach prepositional phrases
A prepositional phrase is the preposition of a sentence and words that come after it that tell more about it. A prepositional phrase can tell us *where, when, or how.*

Model
Write and read this sentence: *Jill skips in the park.* The word *in* is the preposition in this sentence. Circle *in.* The words that come after *in* are *the park.* Underline *in the park.* The preposition *in* and the words that come after it make the prepositional phrase. *In the park* is the prepositional phrase. It tells us where *Jill skips.*

Guide practice
Write and read the following sentences on the board. Have children first identify the preposition and then the prepositional phrase. Circle the preposition and underline the prepositional phrase.

- Ron jogs on the path. *(on; on the path)*
- Mom looks under the sink. *(under; under the sink)*
- Ann hops over a rock. *(over; over a rock)*

Team Talk Pair children and have them illustrate one of the sentences. Have them label their drawings with the correct prepositional phrase. Then have children take turns telling partners which prepositional phrase they illustrated.

Daily Fix-It
Use the Daily Fix-It for more conventions practice.

Writing
Wonderful, Marvelous Me!
Today I Feel…

Introduce

Talk with children about feelings. Think about all the different ways we can feel at one time, in one day! We may feel worried that we won't be able to learn a new skill in class. Then, we may feel proud when we learn that new skill! Display the following list of emotion words and review it with children.

silly	tired	afraid	lonely	sad	proud	curious
happy	surprised	angry	scared	shy	nervous	excited

All of our feelings are important. Why is it important to share our feelings with others? Encourage children to share their thoughts and ideas. Remind children to speak in complete sentences.

Model

I'm going to close my eyes and look inside at my feelings. When I got to school this morning, I looked around at all your name tags and seats. I felt *happy* to know every one of you and *excited* to see everybody.

Guide practice

Ask children to think of other things that make people feel happy and excited. Have them complete the sentences *I feel happy when…* and *I feel excited when….* Write down their ideas.

Independent writing

Now you're going to share how you feel today. Close your eyes and look inside at your wonderful, marvelous feelings. What do you see? How do you feel? Why do you feel that way? Have children write or dictate how they feel and what makes them feel that way. Then have them illustrate their writing.

Daily Handwriting

D'Nealian™   Ball and Stick

Write *Oscar* and *on* on the board. Review correct letter formation of uppercase *O* and lowercase *o*.

Have children write *Oscar* and *on* on their Write-On Boards. Remind them to use proper left-to-right and top-to-bottom progression and proper spacing between letters when writing *O* and *o*.

Write Guy
Jeff Anderson

Learning to Write

Provide children with at least one reader so that they may see how writing communicates. That reader may be a partner, a family member, the teacher, or a group of classmates. Writing comes alive and has a purpose when it has an audience—young writers do as well.

Daily Fix-It

grab the box for me
Grab the box for me.

This week's practice sentences appear on Teacher Resources DVD-ROM.

Writing Routine

Day 1 Wonderful, Marvelous Me!

Day 2 Respond to Literature

Day 3 Genre Writing

Day 4 Extend the Concept

Day 5 This Week We…

Objectives
- Understand and distinguish fact and opinion.
- Face speakers.
- Ask questions to clarify information.

Listening and Speaking
Discuss Fact and Opinion

Teach

Display the *cat* Picture Card. If I say, "This is a cat," that is a fact. A fact is something that is true for everyone. No matter who you are, this is a cat.

If I say, "Cats are the best animals in the world," that is an opinion. An opinion is something that is true for the person saying it, but not necessarily for everyone. Some people might not agree that cats are the best animals in the world. That is their opinion.

Model

I am going to say one opinion and one fact about an animal. Display the *crab* Picture Card. This is a crab. That is a fact. Crabs are good to eat. That is my opinion. Does everyone think crabs are good to eat? No. My opinion is not the same as everyone else's.

Guide practice

Display the *doll* Picture Card. This is a doll. This doll is pretty. Have children identify each statement as a fact or an opinion. Remind children to face the speaker and to ask questions if they need to check information. Continue the routine with *snake* and *astronaut* Picture Cards. Refer children to the Rules for Listening and Speaking on pp. 1–2 of the *Reader's and Writer's Notebook.*

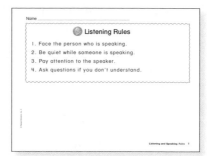

Reader's and Writer's Notebook, p. 1

Wrap Up Your Day

✔ **Oral Language** Today we talked about tools. Let's say the Amazing Words again: *saw, drill, hammer, screwdriver, file, chisel.*

✔ **Phonemic Awareness** I am going to say some words. Clap your hands when you hear a word with /o/: *rock, sheep, on, gum, doll, rob.*

✔ **Homework Idea** Send home the Family Times Newsletter on Let's Practice It! TR DVD•63–64.

Preview DAY 2

Tomorrow we will read about Old MacDonald and her woodshop.

Science
Parts of a Whole

Materials: toy vehicles

Identify Parts of Vehicles Divide the class into small groups. Distribute a toy car, truck, tractor, or other type of vehicle to each group. Ask children to look closely at the vehicles and name all the different parts that make up the vehicle. Provide help naming the different parts as necessary. List the names of the parts on chart paper. Read through the items listed in the chart when it is complete.

Vehicle	Parts	
car	tires	hood
	doors	windows
	headlights	trunk
truck	tires	hood
	doors	windows
	headlights	trailer

Draw and Label Parts of a Vehicle Ask children to draw a picture of their toy vehicle. Help them choose words from the chart to use as labels for the different parts of their vehicle.

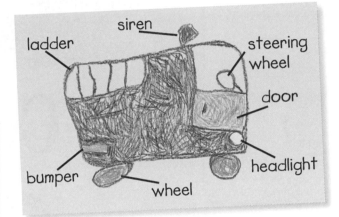

Phonemic Awareness
Matching Blends

Materials: Picture Cards—*black, block, brick, brown, clock, cloud, crab, crayon, dress, drum, flag, flashlight, grapes, green, sled, slide, snail, snake, spider, spoon, stamp, starfish, train, truck*

Identify Matching Sounds Give each child one Picture Card. Make sure that you distribute two cards for each blend. Ask a child to name the picture on his or her card. Have the child look for the person who has the Picture Card that begins with the same sound. Invite both children to the board and help them write the names of their pictures on the board. Continue until all pairs have been matched up.

Comprehension
Create a Story Character

Materials: paper, crayons, markers

Make Up a Character for a Story Help children recall some of the characters from the stories they have read in class. Review the names of the characters, whether they are people or animals, what they look like, and how they act. Then tell children to think of a story they would like to write and create one or more characters for the story. Ask them to use words or sentences to describe their character(s). Then have them draw a picture of their character(s).

DAY 2 Get Ready to Read

⏱ 20–25 mins.

Objectives

- Discuss the concepts to develop oral language.
- Build oral vocabulary.

Today at a Glance

Oral Vocabulary
saw, drill

Phonemic Awareness
◉ /o/

Phonics
◉ /o/ Spelled *Oo*

Handwriting
Words with *Oo*

Comprehension
◉ Character

Conventions
Prepositional Phrases

Writing
Respond to Literature

Vocabulary
Location Words

TRUCKTOWN on Reading Street

Start your engines! Display p. 15 of *Truckery Rhymes.* Point to "Rock-a-Bye Mixer." Who remembers which truck this rhyme is about? Yes, this rhyme is about Melvin Mixer. Let's read the rhyme together. Have a child point to the rhyming words as the class reads the rhyme again. Give additional children the opportunity to point to the rhyming words as you repeat the rhyme.

Truckery Rhymes

Concept Talk

Question of the Week

What tools do you need to build things?

Build concepts

Write the question of the week on the board and track the print as you read it aloud. Ask children to answer the question in complete sentences. To reinforce the concept and focus children's attention, display Talk with Me/Sing with Me Chart 32B. Tell children they are going to sing the song "If I Were a Builder."

💿 Sing with Me Audio

Listen for Amazing Words

The Amazing Words *saw* and *drill* are in the song "If I Were a Builder." Read the title and have children describe the tools they see in the picture. Sing the song several times to the tune of "If I Had a Hammer" until children become familiar with the words and can sing along. Have children clap when they hear the Amazing Words *saw* and *drill*.

ELL Reinforce Vocabulary Use the Day 2 instruction on ELL Poster 32 to reinforce the meanings of high-frequency words.

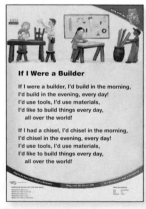

Talk with Me/Sing with Me Chart 32B

ELL Poster 32

Oral Vocabulary
Amazing Words

Amazing Words

saw	drill
hammer	screwdriver
file	chisel

Teach Amazing Words

Amazing Words — Oral Vocabulary Routine

1 Introduce the Word A *saw* is a tool that is used to cut wood. What is our new Amazing Word for a tool that is used to cut wood? Say it with me: *saw*.

2 Demonstrate Provide examples to show meaning. *A saw has a handle and a sharp blade.*

Repeat steps 1 and 2.

Introduce the Word A *drill* is a tool we use to make holes in things. It has a long sharp rod that spins around. What is our new Amazing Word for a tool that makes holes? Say it with me: *drill*.

Demonstrate *Mom used a drill to make a hole in that board.*

3 Apply Tell children to use *saw* and *drill* in complete sentences. Have pairs of children discuss how they may use a saw and drill to build a birdhouse.

Routines Flip Chart

Use Amazing Words

To reinforce the concept and the Amazing Words, have children supply the appropriate Amazing Word for each sentence.

A _____ has a sharp blade. (saw)

A _____ has a sharp rod at one end. (drill)

English Language Learners
Activate Prior Knowledge
Ask children to say the words *saw* and *drill* in their home languages.

Objectives
◎ Practice initial and medial /o/.

Phonemic Awareness
🔊 Initial and Medial /o/

Picture Card

Isolate /o/

Display the *octopus* Picture Card. This is an *octopus*. *Octopus* begins with /o/. What is this? What sound does *octopus* begin with? Continue the routine with the *otter, ox,* and *olive* Picture Cards.

Model

Display the *mop* Picture Card. This is a *mop*. Listen as I say the sounds in *mop*: /m/ /o/ /p/. I hear /o/ in the middle: /m/ /o/ /p/. Say the sounds with me: /m/ /o/ /p/. The sound /o/ is in the middle. Continue with the following words: *chop, drop, job, Mom.*

Picture Card

Guide practice

Have children look at the picture on *My Skills Buddy,* pp. 32–33. Remember that we saw an oxygen tank in the picture. *Oxygen* begins with /o/. What /o/ words did we find in the picture? Name other words with /o/, like *oxygen.* Discuss with children those bulleted items on p. 32 not discussed on Day 1.

My Skills Buddy, pp. 32–33

Corrective feedback

If... children cannot discriminate /o/,
then... have them enunciate /o/ as they segment /o/ words.

Listen as I segment a word: /d/ /o/ /t/, *dot*. What sound do you hear in the middle? I hear /o/ in the middle of *dot*. Continue with the following words: *block, fox, rock, sock.*

On their own Display Phonics Songs and Rhymes Chart 32. Remind children of the tune "I've Been Working on the Railroad." Sing the song several times. When you hear /o/ in the middle of the word, clap your hands. We can do it together the first time.

The Fix-It Shop

I've been tapping in the fix-it shop,
fixing a wooden van.
I've been sanding in the fix-it shop,
fixing it for Dan.
I tap and sand, quick as I can,
Dan wants his van.
I've been tapping in the fix-it shop,
I'm Sam the fix-it man.

Phonics Songs and
Rhymes Chart 32

Review **Blending** Listen to the sounds in this word: /f/ /o/ /ks/. Say the sounds with me: /f/ /o/ /ks/. I'm going to blend the sounds together to say the word: /f/ /o/ /ks/, *fox*. Now you try it with me: /f/ /o/ /ks/, *fox*. Continue the routine with the following words: *crab, doll, tub, jug, egg, pig.*

English Language Learners
Support Phonemic Awareness
Many languages may not have short vowel sounds or may have only approximations of short vowel sounds. If English learners have difficulty hearing the differences in these sounds, provide additional phonemic awareness activities to help them hear and pronounce words with short vowel sounds.

Objectives
- Practice /o/ spelled *Oo*.
- Blend /o/ words.

Check Sound-Spelling
SUCCESS PREDICTOR

Phonics—Teach/Model
/o/ Spelled *Oo*

Teach /o/Oo

Point to the *otter* on the *Oo* Alphabet Card. What is this? What sound does *otter* begin with? *Otter* begins with /o/. Write *otter* on the board and point to the letter *o*. The letter for /o/ is *o*.

Alphabet Card

Model

Display the *rock* Picture Card. What is this? Say the sounds in *rock* with me: /r/ /o/ /k/, *rock*. Where do you hear /o/ in *rock*? (in the middle)

Write *rock* on the board. Point to each letter as you read the sounds: /r/ /o/ /k/, *rock*. Continue the routine with the following words: *doll, fox, ox, top.*

Picture Card

Guide practice

Envision It!

Have children open *My Skills Buddy* to p. 36. Demonstrate using the blending arrows on *My Skills Buddy* p. 36 as you model blending the first word. Put your finger on the red arrow below the *s*. Say the sound that *s* stands for: /s/. Continue with letters *p, o,* and *t*. Now I run my finger along the blue arrow as I blend the letters quickly to read *spot*. Repeat with the word *got*. Have children work with a partner to blend the rest of the words on the page.

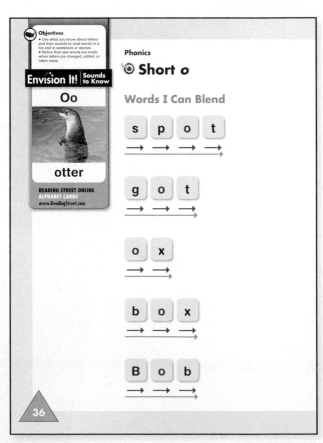

My Skills Buddy, p. 36

Blend Use the following routine to review blending *o* words.

ROUTINE **Sound-by-Sound Blending**

1. **Connect** Write the letter *o*. What is the sound for this letter? The sound is /o/. Say it with me: /o/ /o/ /o/. When you see this letter in a word, what sound will you say?

2. **Model** Write the word *spot* on the board.

   • Point to *s* and ask: What is the sound for this letter? Say it with me: /s/ /s/ /s/. Repeat the routine for *p, o,* and *t*.

   • Let's blend the sounds together. Listen as I blend the sounds: /s/ /p/ /o/ /t/. Say it with me: /s/ /p/ /o/ /t/. Say it without me.

   • Listen as I use *spot* in a sentence. *Tim can spot the top.* Say it with me. Have children use *spot* in a sentence.

3. **Guide Practice** Continue the routine established in step 2 with these words:

   Tom   Jon   got   not   hot   pot   can   sit   grin

   Have children successfully read all of the words before reading Decodable Reader 32 on pp. 38–45 of *My Skills Buddy.*

   Corrective feedback If children have difficulty blending words, model blending the sounds to read the word. Then have children say it with you.

Routines Flip Chart

A **Advanced**
Aa, Oo Display the *Aa* and *Oo* Alphabet Cards. Have children find *Aa* and *Oo* in words in *Will Cass Come?* before reading. Have them copy these words on their Write-On Boards.

SI **Strategic Intervention**
/o/ Before children read *Will Cass Come?*, review /o/ with the *octopus, olive, otter,* and *ox* Picture Cards.

MONITOR PROGRESS ⟳ **Check Sound-Spelling /o/ Spelled Oo**

Have children write the letters *Oo* on a blank card. I'm going to read some words. When you hear an /o/ word, hold your card up. Say: *ox, cart, olive, mud, fox, block, pat, put, pot.*

If... children cannot discriminate /o/ words,

then... use the small-group Strategic Intervention lesson, p. DI•19, to reteach /o/.

Continue to monitor children's progress using other instructional opportunities during the week so that children can be successful with the Day 5 Assessment.

Day 1	Day 2	Day 3	Day 4	Day 5
Check Phonemic Awareness	Check Sound-Spelling/ Retelling	Check Word Reading	Check Phonemic Awareness	Check Oral Vocabulary

Success Predictor

Sound-Spelling **Success Predictor**

Objectives
- Write *O* and *o*.
- Read high-frequency words.

Handwriting
Write Words with *Oo*

Review

Write *Otto* on the board. This is the word *Otto*. I use an uppercase *O* for the first letter in *Otto's* name. Watch me make an uppercase *O*. Write another uppercase *O* on the board using the instructional strokes indicated in the model.

Write *otter* on the board. This is the word *otter*. I use a lowercase *o* at the beginning of *otter*. Watch me make a lowercase *o*. Write another *o* on the board using the instructional strokes indicated in the model.

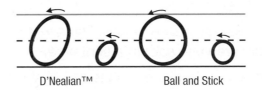

D'Nealian™   Ball and Stick

Guide practice

Have children use their Write-On Boards to make a row of uppercase *O* and a row of lowercase *o*. Circulate around the room, assisting children as necessary. Have children then write the following words: *otter, ox, on.*

High-Frequency Words

Model reading

Have children turn to p. 37 of *My Skills Buddy.* Read the high-frequency words *where, is, go, that,* and *come* together. Then have children point to each word and read it themselves. Read the sentences on *My Skills Buddy* p. 37 together to read the new high-frequency words in context.

Team Talk Pair children and have them take turns reading each of the sentences aloud.

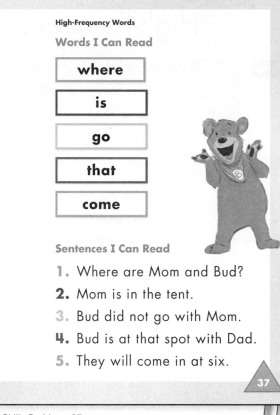

My Skills Buddy, p. 37

On their own

Use *Reader's and Writer's Notebook,* p. 417, for additional practice with this week's high-frequency words.

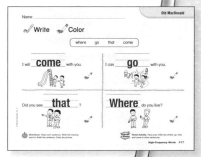

Reader's and Writer's Notebook, p. 417

Differentiated Instruction

 **Strategic Intervention**

Phonics If children have difficulty distinguishing uppercase *O* from lowercase *o,* have them practice writing the letters on paper with handwriting baselines.

E L L

English Language Learners

Extend Language Explain that when talking about two similar objects, we use *this* to refer to the one that is closer to us and *that* to refer to the one that is farther away. Have children practice using the words *this* and *that* to point out objects in the classroom.

Decodable Reader 32
🔊 /o/ Spelled *Oo* and High-Frequency Words

Review Review the previously taught high-frequency words. Have children read each word as you point to it on the Word Wall.

where	is	go	that	come

Have children turn to Decodable Reader 32, *Will Cass Come?* on p. 38 of *My Skills Buddy*. Today we will read a story about some friends who eat dinner together. Point to the title of the book. What is the title of the story? *Will Cass Come?* is the title of the story. The author's name is Tracy Hawks. *Will Cass Come?* was written by Tracy Hawks. What does an author do?

Use the routine for reading decodable books to read Decodable Reader 32.

My Skills Buddy, pp. 38–45

 Reading Decodable Books

1 **Read Silently** Have children whisper read the book page by page as you listen in.

2 **Model Fluent Reading** Have children finger point as you read a page. Then have children reread the book without you.

3 **Read Chorally** Have children finger point as they chorally read the page. Continue reading page by page, repeating steps 1 and 2.

4 **Read Individually** Have children take turns reading aloud a page.

5 **Reread and Monitor Progress** As you listen to individual children reread, monitor progress and provide support.

6 **Reread with a Partner** Have children reread the book page by page with a partner.

Routines Flip Chart

Small Group Time

DAY 2 Break into small groups after reading the Decodable Reader and before the comprehension lesson.

Teacher-Led

SI Strategic Intervention	**OL On-Level**	**A Advanced**
Teacher-Led Page DI•19	**Teacher-Led** Page DI•23	**Teacher-Led** Page DI•26
• Phonemic Awareness and Phonics	• Phonemic Awareness and Phonics	• Phonics and Spelling
• **Reread** Decodable Reader 32	• **Reread** Decodable Reader 32	• **Reread** Decodable Reader 32

ELL Place English language learners in the groups that correspond to their reading abilities in English.

Practice Stations
• Visit the Word Work Station
• Visit the Words to Know Station

Independent Activities
• Read independently
• Background Building Audio
• *Reader's and Writer's Notebook*

Differentiated Instruction

SI Strategic Intervention

Decodable Reader Before children read *Will Cass Come?*, review /a/, /i/, and /o/ with the *fan, bag, six, inch, box,* and *top* Picture Cards.

 **ELL**

English Language Learners

Support Phonics Display the *Ii, Aa,* and *Oo* Alphabet Cards. Tell children to match /a/, /i/, and /o/ to the appropriate Alphabet Card.

Objectives
- ◎ Practice character.
  - • Preview and predict.
  - • Retell a story.

Check Retelling
SUCCESS PREDICTOR

Listening Comprehension
◎ Character

Review

Envision It!

Have children turn to p. 34 of *My Skills Buddy*. Remember, a character is a person or an animal that the story is about. What do we call a person or an animal that a story is about? (a character) Good readers pay attention to characters and what they are like because it helps them understand the story.

My Skills Buddy, pp. 34–35

First Read—Trade Book
Old MacDonald had a Woodshop

Concepts of print

Display the cover of *Old MacDonald had a Woodshop*. Explain that the printed words tell us what the picture shows, Old MacDonald and her woodshop.

Preview and predict

 Think Aloud Look at the cover of the book. What do you see? I see a wood-shop. A woodshop has lots of tools in it. There is a workbench where someone can work with the tools. The title of this book is *Old MacDonald had a Woodshop*. What do you think the book will be about?

Use illustrations

Take children on a picture walk through the book. Have children tell about what they see in each picture.

Introduce genre

An animal fantasy is a story about animal characters that talk and act like people. We will read about animals building something together.

Set purpose

Remind children of the question of the week: *What tools do you need to build things?* Have them listen as you read to learn about tools we use.

Model

Read *Old MacDonald had a Woodshop* with expression for enjoyment.

Read for enjoyment

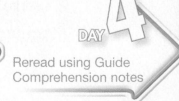

DAY 3 Reread using Develop Vocabulary notes

DAY 4 Reread using Guide Comprehension notes

Retell

Check retelling

 Envision It!

Have children turn to p. 46 of *My Skills Buddy.* Walk through the retelling boxes as children retell *Old MacDonald had a Woodshop.* Let's retell what is happening in the first box—Old MacDonald is bringing wood to her shop. Let's retell what is happening in the second box. Continue with the rest of the boxes. After children retell the story as a group, have them draw a picture to retell a favorite part of the story. Have them write or dictate a word or sentence to go with their picture.

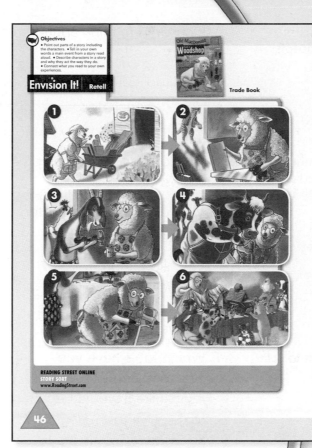

My Skills Buddy, p. 46

Top-Score Response A top-score response describes events in sequence with details.

Don't Wait Until Friday

MONITOR PROGRESS **Check Retelling**

If... children have difficulty retelling the story,

then... go through the story one page at a time, and ask children to tell what happens in their own words.

Day 1	**Day 2**	**Day 3**	**Day 4**	**Day 5**
Check Phonemic Awareness	Check Sound-Spelling/ Retelling	Check Word Reading	Check Phonemic Awareness	Check Oral Vocabulary

Success Predictor

Differentiated Instruction

A **Advanced**

Extend Concept Have children answer the question of the week by drawing pictures of as many tools as they can remember. Have them write or dictate captions to go with their pictures.

SI **Strategic Intervention**

Character Display illustrations from the story, and have children point to and name the characters. Then have them draw a picture of their favorite character using the tool with which he or she is associated.

Retelling Plan

☑ **Week 1** Assess Advanced students.

☑ **This week assess On-Level students.**

☐ **Week 3** Assess Strategic Intervention students.

☐ **Week 4** Assess Advanced students.

☐ **Week 5** Assess On-Level students.

☐ **Week 6** Assess Strategic Intervention students.

E L L

English Language Learners
Build Background Teach children or remind them of *Old MacDonald,* a nursery rhyme about farm animals. Explain that this book is another version of that nursery rhyme.

Success Predictor

Retelling

Think, Talk, and Write

Discuss concepts

Ask children to think about the animals and the tools that the animals in the story used.

• What tools did the different animals use?

• What did each animal do with the tool he or she used?

• Which tool would you like to use? Why?

Confirm predictions

Ask children to recall their predictions before you read *Old MacDonald had a Woodshop.*

• What did you think the story would be about?

• Was your prediction correct?

Have children turn to p. 47 of *My Skills Buddy.* Read the questions and directives and have children respond.

Text to self

1. Which tools have you seen someone use? Did it look like it would be fun to use that tool? Do you know how we can stay safe when we use tools?

◉ **Character**

2. Which is a character from *Old MacDonald had a Woodshop?* (the sheep, Old MacDonald) What does she do in the story? (She builds a toy farm with her friends.) What is Old MacDonald like? (She is good at building things. She is kind to build the toy farm.) Why do you think she built the toy farm? (to make other animals happy)

Look back and write

3. Let's look back at our story and write about it. We remember that each character makes a special sound with tools. Listen to hear what sound each tool makes. Display and read pp. 20–21 of *Old MacDonald had a Woodshop.* Now let's write our ideas. Discuss with children the sound each tool makes and record children's responses on chart paper. Expand the discussion by having them tell what sounds these animals make in real life.

Think, Talk, and Write

1. Which tools have you seen someone use? Text to Self

2. Which is a character from *Old MacDonald had a Woodshop?* What does she do in the story? ◉ Character

3. Look back and write.

My Skills Buddy, p. 47

Conventions
Prepositional Phrases

Review
Remind children that prepositions are words like *in, on, over,* and *under.* Prepositions tell us how words in a sentence are connected. A prepositional phrase is the preposition and words that come after it that tell more about it. A prepositional phrase can tell us *where, when,* or *how.*

Guide practice
I am going to read some sentences. Listen for the preposition and the words that come after it. Then tell me the prepositional phrase.

> **A fish lives under that dock.** *(under that dock)*
>
> **Sam travels on the train.** *(on the train)*

On their own
Use *Reader's and Writer's Notebook,* p. 418, for more practice with prepositional phrases.

Reader's and Writer's Notebook, p. 418

Daily Fix-It
Use the Daily Fix-It for more conventions practice.

Objectives
- Write complete sentences.
- Identify and use words that name locations.

Writing
Respond to Literature

Discuss
Display *Old MacDonald had a Woodshop*. Have children describe the animals they see and the tools the animals are using.

Model
The animals look like they are having fun using different tools to build the toy farm. Let's write sentences about the tools and who uses them. I am going to write:

> **The sheep has fun with a saw.**

Guide practice
Invite children to help you write more sentences about the animals having fun with tools. Remind them to use complete sentences.

> **The goat has fun with a hammer.**
>
> **The cat has fun with a drill.**

Independent writing
Have children write or dictate their own sentences about the animals and tools or copy one of the sentences the class wrote together. They may wish to use this sentence frame:

> **The _____ has fun with a _____.**

Daily Handwriting

Write *Otto* and *odd* on the board. Review correct letter formation of uppercase *O* and lowercase *o*.

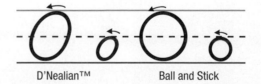

D'Nealian™   Ball and Stick

Have children write *Otto* and *odd* on their Write-On Boards. Remind them to use proper left-to-right and top-to-bottom progression and proper spacing between letters when writing *O* and *o*.

Vocabulary
Location Words

Model

Have children turn to p. 48 of *My Skills Buddy*. Use the first Vocabulary bullet on p. 48 to guide the discussion. Direct children to the picture of a train station. This is a place where people get on or get off trains. This is a *train station*. Direct them to the picture of a police station. This is a place where police officers work and keep their cars. This is a *police station*. Point to the fire station. Firefighters work and keep trucks at the *fire station*. Point to the gas station. People put gas in their cars here, at the *gas station*.

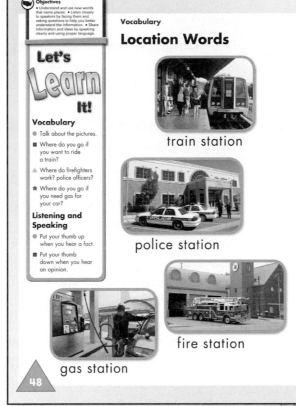

My Skills Buddy, p. 48

Guide practice

Write the words *train station, police station, fire station,* and *gas station* on the board. Point to each word as you read it.

| train station | police station | fire station | gas station |

Let's practice our new words. Have children look at the pictures on p. 48 of *My Skills Buddy*. I am going to tell you what happens at a place and make a noise that you would hear there. Point to the picture of that place and tell me its name. This is where we put gas in our cars, *pump pump!* (gas station) This is where police officers keep cars with sirens, *eeoo eeoo!* (police station) This is where people go to travel by train, *choo choo!* (train station) If you smell smoke, this place will send a big red truck, *honk honk!* (fire station)

On their own

Have children choose one of the stations and draw a picture of the vehicle they would find there. Have them tell the class which vehicle they drew and explain where to find it. Children may use the following sentence frame: *You can see my (vehicle) at a (location word).*

 Advanced

Expand Vocabulary Discuss with children other *stations,* such as a bus station, a power station, a Metro station, or even a space station. Children may also be familiar with broadcast stations, such as a radio station or television station.

E L L

English Language Learners
Cognates The word *station* may sound familiar to children whose home language is a Romance language. Though the location words studied today may have more specific translations, Romance language speakers may benefit from connecting *station* to one or more of the following cognates: *estación* (Spanish); *estação* (Portuguese); *stazione* (Italian); *station* (French).

Wrap Up Your Day

✔ **Concept Talk** Today we read about animals that use tools. What kind of tools do the animals use? Where do the animals work on their building project?

✔ **Phonemic Awareness** I am going to say a silly sentence. Clap your hands when you hear words that begin with /o/: *Ollie Octopus wore olive socks.*

✔ **Vocabulary Skill** Have some children describe the workers or vehicles found at one of the location words. Have other children guess the place that matches that description.

✔ **Homework Idea** Have children dictate a simple sentence about something they do at home using one of the following prepositions: *in, on, over, under.* Then have them draw a line under the prepositional phrase.

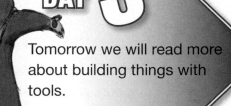

Preview

DAY 3

Tomorrow we will read more about building things with tools.

Science
Animal Cutouts

Materials: Trade Book *Old MacDonald had a Woodshop,* paper, glue, scissors, coloring tools

Cutting Tools Talk with children about the tool Old MacDonald used to cut wood. Compare the shape of the wood on pp. 6–7 to the shape of the wood pieces in the final product as shown in the illustration on pp. 26–27. Discuss how a saw, a chisel, and a file were used to change the wood into specific shapes. Ask children to name other tools that are used for cutting and tell what they are used for, such as scissors and can openers.

Change Materials Prepare several sheets with half of a face of an animal drawn along a center fold line on the paper. Photocopy these sheets to make one for each child. Show children how to fold their papers in half. Have children cut along the drawn outline on the folded paper. Then have them unfold the paper to reveal the new shape they made from a square piece of paper. Have them glue their faces on a colored background and color or glue on additional features, such as eyes, nose, mouth, and fur.

Word Work
Word Concentration

Materials: index cards

Play Concentration with Word Cards Write eight one-syllable words from *Old MacDonald had a Woodshop* on index cards. Make two sets of each card so that you have a total of 16 index cards. Read through the words with children prior to playing the game. Arrange the cards facedown in four rows of four cards each. Have children sit in a circle around the cards and take turns flipping over two cards to find matching words. Remove matching pairs from the game. When the round is over, ask each child to read the words on the cards they collected.

Social Studies
Location Stations

Materials: construction paper, scissors, glitter, glue, markers, crayons

Let's Go to Work! Divide the class into four groups. Assign each group one of the location words: *train station, police station, fire station, gas station.* Help each group brainstorm a list of people, tools, vehicles, and other things that belong in their station. Have each child in the group choose one of these things to illustrate and decorate. Draw and label four "stations" on the board and have each group tape their illustrations within the outline of the correct station. As each child tapes his or her illustration to the board, have him or her tell about the illustration and where it belongs.

Objectives
- Share information and ideas about the concept.
- Build oral vocabulary.

Today at a Glance

Oral Vocabulary
hammer, screwdriver

Phonemic Awareness
◉ Initial and Medial /o/

Phonics
◉ /o/ Spelled *Oo*

Comprehension
◉ Character

Conventions
Pronouns *I* and *me*

Writing
Song

Listening and Speaking
Discuss Fact and Opinion

TRUCKTOWN on Reading Street

Start your engines! Display p. 15 of *Truckery Rhymes.* Do you know the original "Rock-a-Bye Baby"? Recite the rhyme together:

Rock-a-bye, baby, in the treetop.
When the wind blows, the cradle will rock.
When the bough breaks,
the cradle will fall,
And down will come baby,
cradle and all.

Truckery Rhymes

Concept Talk

Question of the Week

What tools do you need to build things?

Write the question of the week on the board. Read the question as you track the print. Talk with children about tools and building. Remind children to speak in complete sentences.

Listen for Amazing Words

Let's Sing Display Sing with Me Chart 32B. Remind children that yesterday they sang "If I Were a Builder" and listened for the words *saw* and *drill*. Today we are going to listen for the words *hammer* and *screwdriver*. Sing the song several times to the tune of "If I Had a Hammer." Have children sing with you. Ask children to act out using a hammer and a screwdriver when they hear the words *hammer* and *screwdriver*.

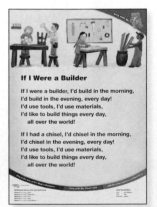

If I Were a Builder

If I were a builder, I'd build in the morning,
I'd build in the evening, every day!
I'd use tools, I'd use materials,
I'd like to build things every day,
    all over the world!

If I had a chisel, I'd chisel in the morning,
I'd chisel in the evening, every day!
I'd use tools, I'd use materials,
I'd like to build things every day,
    all over the world!

Sing with Me Audio

Talk with Me/Sing
with Me Chart 32B

Oral Vocabulary
Amazing Words

saw	drill
hammer	screwdriver
file	chisel

Teach Amazing Words

Amazing Words Oral Vocabulary Routine

1 **Introduce the Word** A *hammer* is a tool we use to pound nails into wood. A *hammer* has a long handle with a hard flat surface at the end. What is our new Amazing Word for a tool used for pounding nails into wood? Say it with me: *hammer*.

2 **Demonstrate** Provide examples to show meaning. *I like to use a hammer to nail pieces of wood together.*

Repeat steps 1 and 2.

Introduce the Word A *screwdriver* is a tool we use to loosen or tighten screws. You push a *screwdriver* into a screw and turn it around and around. What is our new Amazing Word for a tool used to screw things together? Say it with me: *screwdriver.*

Demonstrate *Sometimes it is a lot of work to turn a screwdriver.*

3 **Apply** Tell children to use *hammer* and *screwdriver* in complete sentences. Have them illustrate the words.

Routines Flip Chart

Differentiated Instruction

A **Advanced**

Support Vocabulary Have children make up a story about a new building project for Old MacDonald. Have them describe how she uses a hammer and a screwdriver. Ask children to tell the story orally or with pictures.

Use Amazing Words

To reinforce the concept and the Amazing Words, have children supply the appropriate Amazing Word for each sentence.

The builder pounded nails with a _____. (hammer)

A _____ can loosen or tighten screws. (screwdriver)

ELL Expand Vocabulary Use the Day 3 instruction on ELL Poster 32 to help children expand vocabulary.

ELL Poster 32

ELL

English Language Learners
Access Content Ask children what words in their home languages are used for *hammer* and *screwdriver*. Invite children to act out using each tool as they say the name in English.

Objectives
◎ Isolate medial /o/.
• Discriminate sounds.

Phonemic Awareness
/o/

Review | **Initial /o/** Display the *otter* Picture Card. What sound do you hear at the beginning of *otter*? Say the word with me: /o/ /o/ /o/, *otter*. What is the first sound in *otter*? (/o/) Yes, /o/ is the first sound in *otter*. Practice initial /o/ with the following words: *octopus, off.*

Picture Card

Medial /o/ | Display the *doll* Picture Card. Listen to the sounds in *doll*: /d/ /o/ /l/. How many sounds do you hear? (three) Where do you hear /o/? (in the middle) Yes, the /o/ in *doll* is in the middle. Continue the routine with the following words: *cot, not, mom, trot.*

Discriminate sounds | Listen to the sounds in *big*: /b/ /i/ /g/. How many sounds do you hear? (three) What is the middle sound in *big*? (/i/) Now listen to the sounds in *bog*: /b/ /o/ /g/. How many sounds do you hear? (three) What is the middle sound in *bog*? (/o/) I am going to say two words. I want you to tell me the middle sound in the words. Listen carefully: *block, hop.* (/o/) The middle sound in *block* and *hop* is /o/. Continue the routine with these sets of words: *pal, mat; fish, skip; pop, dot; rich, trick; plant, bath.*

Picture Card

On their own | Display the *fox, pig, duck,* and *octopus* Picture Cards. Have children choose one of the pictures to draw. Have them write *o* on their paper if the word begins with /o/.

Blend

Listen to these sounds: /m/ /o/ /p/. When I say these sounds more quickly, /m/ /o/ /p/, I make the word *mop*. Say the sounds slowly: /m/ /o/ /p/. Now say the sounds more quickly: /m/ /o/ /p/. What is the word? (*mop*) Let's blend more sounds to make words. Continue with the following words: *can, box, help, glad, fix, big, red*.

Corrective feedback

If... children cannot blend the sounds into words, **then...** use the Picture Cards to practice discriminating individual phonemes before blending.

Substitute initial sounds

Listen to this word: /p/ /o/ /t/, *pot*. Say it with me: /p/ /o/ /t/, *pot*. I can make a new word by changing the first sound in *pot* to /n/. Listen: /n/ /o/ /t/, *not*. Say it with me as I blend the new sounds: /n/ /o/ /t/, *not*. Continue substituting initial sounds with the following words: *mop, top; box, fox; rocks, socks.*

Differentiated Instruction

 Strategic Intervention

Initial /o/ Create alliterative sentences such as *Otto Ostrich offers olives* to help children discriminate initial sounds. Encourage children to help you make up the sentences. Then have them choose one to illustrate, captioning their pictures with the initial letter.

Objectives
◎ Practice /o/ spelled *Oo.*
• Substitute phonemes.
• Read /o/ words.
• Read high-frequency words.

Check Word Reading

! **SUCCESS PREDICTOR**

Phonics—Teach/Model
/o/ Spelled Oo

Review | **/o/Oo** Display the *Oo* Alphabet Card and point to the *otter.* What sound do you hear at the beginning of *otter?* What letter spells that sound? Point to the letters *Oo.* What is the sound for this letter? What are the names of these letters?

Alphabet Card

Review | **Letter Names and Sounds** Use Alphabet Cards to review the following letter names and sounds: *Aa, Bb, Dd, Ff, Hh, Oo, Xx, Yy.*

Blend sounds | Write the word *box* on the board. This word is *box.* Say the three sounds with me: /b/ /o/ /ks/. Now say the sounds with me as I point to the letters. Point to each letter as children say the sound. Let's blend the sounds together to read the word: /b/ /o/ /ks/. The word is *box.* Repeat the blending routine with *get, rag, big, bug,* and *fog.*

More practice | Use *Reader's and Writer's Notebook,* p. 419, for additional practice with /o/.

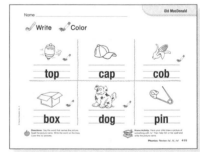

Reader's and Writer's Notebook, p. 419

Review **Sound-Spelling** Display the *olive* Picture Card. What sound do you hear at the beginning of *olive*? (/o/) What letter spells that sound? (*o*) Yes, the letter *o* spells /o/. Review the following sounds and letters with Alphabet Cards: *Aa, Bb, Ee, Ff, Mm, Rr, Tt, Ww, Yy.*

Review **High-Frequency Words** Write *you* on the board. This is the word *you*. What is this word? Continue the routine with *said, me, like, to, have, come, here,* and *look.*

Picture Card

Differentiated Instruction

A **Advanced**

Oo Provide children with grocery store ads, coupons, and safety scissors. Tell them to find and cut out foods and words that contain *Oo*. Have them write *Oo* on construction paper and paste their *Oo* pictures around the letters.

Don't Wait Until Friday

MONITOR PROGRESS ⟳ **Check Word Reading** **High-Frequency Words**

Write *where, is, go, that, come,* and *have* on the board. Have children take turns reading the words.

Practice reading these words from Kindergarten Student Reader K.6.2, *Max and Jen Fix the Big Box!*

| box | Mom | Dad | fix | tap | rap |
| big | glad | us | will | mix | red |

If... children cannot read the high-frequency words,
then... write the words on cards for them to practice at home.

If... children cannot blend sounds to read the words,
then... provide practice blending the words in chunks, /b/ -*ox.*

If... children can successfully blend sounds to read the words,
then... have them read Kindergarten Student Reader K.6.2, *Max and Jen Fix the Big Box!*

| **Day 1** | **Day 2** | **Day 3** | **Day 4** | **Day 5** |
| Check Phonemic Awareness | Check Sound-Spelling/ Retelling | Check Word Reading | Check Phonemic Awareness | Check Oral Vocabulary |

Success Predictor

ELL

English Language Learners
Support Phonics Speakers of Spanish, Tagalog, and some Asian languages may have a hard time distinguishing short vowel sounds. Have children practice pronunciation of short vowels with these word pairs: *hot, hut; cut, cot; fun, fan; bond, band.*

Word Reading

Success Predictor

Objectives
- Read /o/ words.
- Read high-frequency words.

Kindergarten Student Reader K.6.2
↺ /o/ Spelled *Oo* and High-Frequency Words

Review

Review the previously taught high-frequency words. Have children read each word as you point to it on the Word Wall.

you	said	we	to	the	have
like	come	her	look	for	my

Read Kindergarten Student Reader K.6.2

Display Kindergarten Student Reader K.6.2. Today we are going to read a new story. Point to the title. The title of this story is *Max and Jen Fix the Big Box!* The author's name is Noahlynn Duch. The pictures were drawn by Nan Brooks.

Use the reading decodable books routine to read Kindergarten Student Reader K.6.2.

ROUTINE Reading Decodable Books

Small Group

1. **Read Silently** Have children whisper read the book page by page as you listen in.

2. **Model Fluent Reading** Have children finger point as you read a page. Then have children reread the page without you.

3. **Read Chorally** Have children finger point as they chorally read the page. Continue reading page by page, repeating steps 1 and 2.

4. **Read Individually** Have children take turns reading aloud a page.

5. **Reread and Monitor Progress** As you listen to individual children reread, monitor progress and provide support.

6. **Reread with a Partner** Have children reread the book page by page with a partner.

Routines Flip Chart

Dad, can you fix Mom's big box?
"Yes, I can," said Dad.
"You can help me."

2

By Kathleen Duck • Illustrated by Hot Brooks

Kindergarten Student Reader K.6.2

Yes, we can help!
We like to help.
We can help fix the big box.

3

Dad taps. We tap.
Dad raps. We rap.
Dad is glad to have us help.

4

We will mix it.
Mom likes red.
Mom will like a big red box.

5

Mom, can you come here?
Look at the big box.
Here is the big box.

6

Look at the big box, Mom.
Dad let us help him.
The big red box is for you.

7

Yes, I like it.
I like my big box.
I like it red!

8

Small Group Time

DAY 3 Break into small groups to read the Kindergarten Student Reader before the comprehension lesson.

Teacher-Led

SI Strategic Intervention

Teacher-Led Page DI•20
• Phonemic Awareness and Phonics
• **Read** Concept Literacy Reader K.6.2 or Kindergarten Student Reader K.6.2

OL On-Level

Teacher-Led Page DI•24
• Phonemic Awareness and Phonics
• **Read** Kindergarten Student Reader K.6.2

A Advanced

Teacher-Led Page DI•27
• **Read** Independent Reader K.6.2 or Kindergarten Student Reader K.6.2

E L L Place English language learners in the groups that correspond to their reading abilities in English.

Practice Stations
• Visit the Words to Know Station
• Visit the Let's Write! Station

Independent Activities
• Read independently
• Audio Text of Trade Book
• *Reader's and Writer's Notebook*

Differentiated Instruction

A Advanced

Copy High-Frequency Words
Have children look through *Max and Jen Fix the Big Box!* for high-frequency words. Ask them to copy the high-frequency words on their Write-On Boards.

E L L

English Language Learners

Access Content Ask children to point out the naming words, such as *mom, dad,* and *box.* Have children act out the action words *tap, rap,* and *mix.*

DAY 3 Read and Comprehend

20–25 mins.

Objectives

- Recall and retell a story.
- ◎ Practice character.
- Develop and use vocabulary.
- Develop and use comprehension skills.

Comprehension

Retell the story

Have children turn to p. 46 of *My Skills Buddy* and use the retelling boxes to retell the story *Old MacDonald had a Woodshop*.

 Envision It!

Think Aloud Direct students to the first retell box. This picture is from the very beginning of the story. Old MacDonald is just bringing wood to her shop. Tell me about what she does with the wood.

Continue reviewing the retelling boxes and having children retell the story.

My Skills Buddy, p. 46

Review

Character Display *Old MacDonald had a Woodshop*. Remember, the characters in a story are the people or animals that the story is about.

- Who is this story about? (Old MacDonald)
- What is Old MacDonald like? (She is a good builder. She is kind.)
- Are there other animals in the story? Tell me about them.

More Practice

Use *Reader's and Writer's Notebook,* p. 420, for additional practice with character.

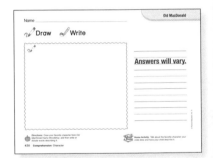

Reader's and Writer's Notebook, p. 420

158 Putting It Together • Unit 6 • Week 2

Second Read—Trade Book
Old MacDonald had a Woodshop

Develop vocabulary

Let's Reread *Old MacDonald had a Woodshop.* Follow the Day 3 arrow beginning on p. 160, and use the Develop Vocabulary notes to prompt conversations about the story.

Have children use the Amazing Words *saw, drill, hammer, screwdriver, file,* and *chisel* to talk about the story.

DAY **2**
Read for enjoyment

DAY **3**
Reread using Develop Vocabulary notes

DAY **4**
Reread using Guide Comprehension notes

Differentiated Instruction

SI **Strategic Intervention**

Build Background Provide photographs and drawings of tools for children with limited experience with them. Be sure to discuss things people do to stay safe when using tools, such as using safety goggles and masks and only building with adult supervision. Take children on a picture walk to look for similar safety precautions in the story.

English Language Learners
Frontload Story Take children on a picture walk through the story to heighten interest and draw attention to the tools and their uses. Point out clues to the final project that the animals are building with their tools. Encourage children to volunteer the names of the animals and tools in their home languages.

Develop Vocabulary

DAY 3

Wh- question

Look at the picture. Where does this story take place? (a farm)

What kind of animal is *Old MacDonald?* (sheep)

- This story takes place on a farm. How can you tell it is a farm?

Develop Vocabulary sheep

Expand Vocabulary woodshop

Trade Book, pp. 4–5

Guide Comprehension

DAY 4

Inferential

Why does the author choose a farm as a setting? (The characters in the story are a sheep, cow, rooster, and goat. These animals live on a farm.)

Wh- question
What does Old MacDonald have in her hand? (a saw)

- Old MacDonald is using the saw to cut a piece of wood. What is a saw used for?

Develop Vocabulary cat

Trade Book, pp. 6–7

Inferential
Why does Old MacDonald have to be careful when she uses a saw? (Old MacDonald has to be careful because the saw has a sharp blade.)

Develop Vocabulary, continued

DAY 3

Wh- question

What does the cat do with the drill?
(makes a hole in a piece of wood)

• The cat uses the drill to make a
  hole in a piece of wood. Who do
  you see in the doorway now?

And in her shop she had a

DRILL,

E-I-E-I-O!

With a *rurr rurr* here
and a *rurr rurr* there,

a *zztt zztt* here
and a *zztt zztt* there,

here a *zztt*, there a *zztt*, everywhere a *zztt zztt*.

Old MacDonald had a shop, E-I-E-I-O.

Trade Book, pp. 8–9

Guide Comprehension, continued

DAY 4

Open-ended

Why did the cat come into the
woodshop? (I think the cat wanted
to help Old MacDonald. I think the
cat heard Old MacDonald sawing
and wanted to see what she was
doing.)

Wh- question

What does Old MacDonald give to the goat?
(a hammer and nails)

- Old MacDonald gives the goat a hammer and nails. What does the goat do with the hammer?

Develop Vocabulary goat

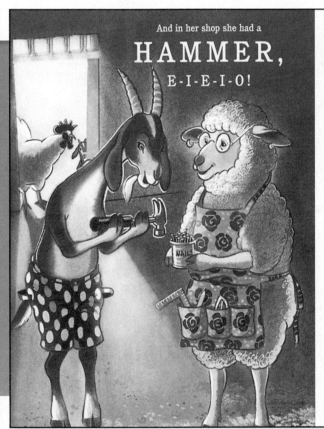

Trade Book, pp. 10–11

Recall

What sound does the hammer make?
(tap, tap)

Develop Vocabulary, continued

DAY 3

Wh- question

What kind of animal comes to the woodshop next? (a rooster)

• The rooster is the next animal to come into the woodshop. What tool does the rooster use?

Develop Vocabulary rooster

And in her shop she had a

CHISEL,

E-I-E-I-O!

With a *chip chip* here and a *chip chip* there,

a *tap tap* here and a *tap tap* there,

a *rurr rurr* here and a *rurr rurr* there,

a *zztt zztt* here and a *zztt zztt* there,

here a *zztt*, there a *zztt*, everywhere a *zztt zztt*.

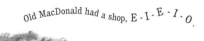
Old MacDonald had a shop, E-I-E-I-O.

Trade Book, pp. 12–13

Guide Comprehension, continued

DAY 4

Wh- question

What does the rooster do with the chisel? (The rooster chips away pieces of wood.)

Wh- question

Who is in the woodshop with Old MacDonald now? (a pig)

- A pig has come into the woodshop. What kind of tool is the pig going to use?

Develop Vocabulary pig

Trade Book, pp. 14–15

Inferential

How do you think Old MacDonald felt when the other animals came to her woodshop? (I think Old MacDonald was happy to have the other animals help with her project.)

Develop Vocabulary, continued

DAY 3

Completion
What do you think the cow is doing with the screwdriver? (putting screws in the wood)

- The cow is using the screwdriver to put screws into the wood. Let's read these pages together.

Develop Vocabulary cow

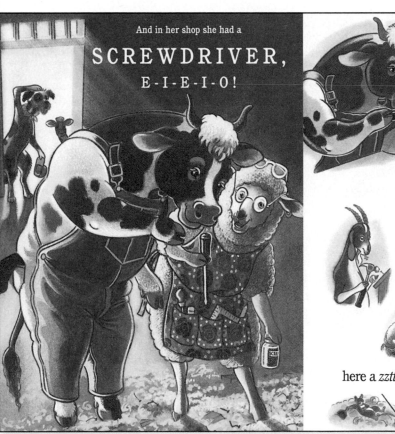

And in her shop she had a

SCREWDRIVER,
E-I-E-I-O!

With a *squeak squeak* here and a *squeak squeak* there,

a *scritch scratch* here and a *scritch scratch* there,

a *chip chip* here and a *chip chip* there,

a *tap tap* here and a *tap tap* there,

a *rurr rurr* here and a *rurr rurr* there,

a *zztt zztt* here and a *zztt zztt* there,

here a *zztt*, there a *zztt*, everywhere a *zztt zztt*.

Old MacDonald had a shop, E-I-E-I-O.

Trade Book, pp. 16–17

Guide Comprehension, continued

DAY 4

Sequence • Recall
Who is the first animal to come to the woodshop? (the cat)

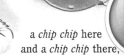

Distancing

Who is Old MacDonald giving the paintbrushes to? (a dog)

- She is giving a dog the paintbrushes. What have you done with paintbrushes?

Develop Vocabulary dog

Trade Book, pp. 18–19

Wh- question

Why is the dog wearing an apron? (The dog doesn't want to get paint on himself.)

Develop Vocabulary, continued

DAY 3

Wh- vocabulary

All the animals are busy in the woodshop. How many animals are working in the woodshop? (six)

• There are six animals working. **Point to the mouse.** What is the mouse doing?

Develop Vocabulary mouse

a *squeak squeak* here
and a *squeak squeak* there,

a *scritch scratch* here
and a *scritch scratch* there,

a *chip chip* here
and a *chip chip* there,

a *tap tap* here
and a *tap tap* there,

a *rurr rurr* here
and a *rurr rurr* there,

a *zztt zztt* here
and a *zztt zztt* there,

here a *zztt*, there a *zztt*, everywhere a *zztt zztt*.

Trade Book, pp. 20–21

Guide Comprehension, continued

DAY 4

Open-ended

What things have you worked on with your family or friends? (school projects, family party, garden, etc.)

Distancing

What do you think the animals are hiding under the blanket? (their project)

• I think the project the animals are working on is under the blanket. What else can you use a blanket for?

Trade Book, pp. 22–23

Distancing

How do you feel when you work hard and finish a project? (I feel tired. I feel proud.)

Develop Vocabulary, continued

DAY 3

Open-ended

What are all the animals doing?
(They are looking inside the
woodshop.)

• They are all trying to see
inside the woodshop. What
do you think they are trying to
see?

And in her shop she had a . . .

Trade Book, pp. 24–25

Guide Comprehension, continued

DAY 4

Distancing

When have you ever been curious
about a surprise? (Possible
responses: Christmas, Hanukkah,
birthday, vacation)

Open-ended

What do the animals build with their tools?
(a toy farm)

- They build a toy farm out of wood. What do you think the animals will do now?

Continue with **DAY 3**

Conventions p. 172

Trade Book, pp. 26–27

Compare and Contrast

How are the toy farm and a real farm alike?
(They have a barn, tractor, and animals.) How
are the toy farm and a real farm different?
(The toy farm is little and has wooden animals. The real farm is life-size and has living
animals.)

Skip to **DAY 4**

Conventions p. 186

Conventions
Pronouns *I* and *me*

Review Remind children of what they learned about pronouns *I* and *me*. The words *I* and *me* are special. You use these words when you are talking about yourself. *I* and *me* are pronouns, or words that take the place of naming words. Write these sentences on the board:

> **I can run.**
>
> **Can you run with me?**

Point to the first sentence. In this sentence, the pronoun is *I*. The word *I* is always uppercase. Point to the second sentence. In this sentence, the pronoun is *me*.

Guide practice Ask children to make up a sentence about themselves and a friend doing something they enjoy. Have children use the following sentence frame: *and My friend and _____ like to _____.* Have children illustrate their sentences and share them with the class.

Write the sentences below on the board and read them with children. Have children change the underlined word to the pronoun *me*.

- Lin hops with <u>Tom</u>. (Lin hops with <u>me</u>.)
- Can Sam skip with <u>Kim</u>? (Can Sam skip with <u>me</u>?)

Team Talk Pair children and have them take turns talking about things they do in class. Remind them to use the pronouns *I* and *me* and to speak in complete sentences.

On their own Use *Reader's and Writer's Notebook,* p. 421, for more practice with pronouns *I* and *me*.

Daily Fix-It Use the Daily Fix-It for more conventions practice.

Reader's and Writer's Notebook, p. 421

Writing
Song

Teach
The story *Old MacDonald had a Woodshop* is based on a song many of you have probably heard: "Old MacDonald Had a Farm." Do you remember how it goes? **Hum the tune, but do not sing the words.** A song is a short piece of music, or tune, with words for singing. The song we just heard had the first part, the tune. What part is missing? Yes, we are missing the words to the song!

Model
I remember the first words of "Old MacDonald Had a Farm" because they are the same as the title of the song. We start by singing: **(sing)** *Old MacDonald had a farm.* These are not the only words in this song. Do you remember what the words in this song tell us? The song tells us about the animals on the farm and the sounds they make. I'm going to draw a picture of one of these animals and write its name. **Draw a chicken on the board and label it** *chicken.* This is a chicken. *Chicken* is a word in our song. Now I can sing more words to the song. **Sing:** *Old MacDonald had a farm, E-I-E-I-O! And on that farm he had a chicken, E-I-E-I-O!* **Point to the drawing as you sing** *chicken.* Explain that the next part of the song tells what sound the animal makes. Demonstrate a chicken clucking. My picture and my song word remind me which animal sound to make: *cluck.*

Guide practice
Have children suggest other animal words for *Old MacDonald Had a Farm.* List the animals on the board and discuss what sounds they make.

Independent writing
Have children turn to p. 422 of *Reader's and Writer's Notebook.* Have them complete the song "Old MacDonald" by copying an animal word from the list and then illustrating that animal. Sing the song with children, featuring each child's picture for a verse.

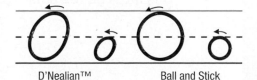

Reader's and Writer's Notebook, p. 422

Daily Handwriting

Write *Otto* and *on* on the board. Review correct letter formation of uppercase *O* and lowercase *o.*

D'Nealian™   Ball and Stick

Have children write *Otto* and *on* on their Write-On Boards. Remind children to use proper left-to-right and top-to-bottom progression and proper spacing between letters when writing *O* and *o.*

Daily Fix-It

she will get a red crab
She will get a red crab.

This week's practice sentences appear on Teacher Resources DVD-ROM.

Differentiated Instruction

A **Advanced**

Guide Writing Have children think of other locations for Old MacDonald, such as *diner, school,* or *gym.* Help them brainstorm new things Old MacDonald would have at this place, and list their responses on the board. Have each child draw an item from the list and tell what sound it would make in the song. Then sing the song with the new lyrics, for example: *Old MacDonald had a school, E-I-E-I-O! And in that school, they rang a bell, E-I-E-I-O! With a ding ding here, and a ding ding there…*

ELL

English Language Learners
Access Content Animal sounds are often similar across languages. For instance, the sound a baby chick makes is *peep peep* in English. Compare this to the French *piou piou* or the Japanese *piyo piyo.* Have English learners share animal sounds in their home languages to make this connection.

Listening and Speaking
Discuss Fact and Opinion

Review

Review fact and opinion with children. When we listen for a fact, we listen for something that is true for everyone. When we listen for an opinion, we listen for something only some people believe.

Today is Wednesday. That is a fact. It is Wednesday, no matter who you are. I think today is wonderful because I am here with you. That is my opinion. If it's raining and you have to walk home today, you might not agree that it is a wonderful day. That would be your opinion.

Model

Have children turn to p. 49 of *My Skills Buddy*. Explain to children that they can ask themselves these questions when listening for fact and opinion: *Is this true for everyone? Is this something that only some people think or believe?* Incorporate Listening and Speaking bullets on p. 48 of *My Skills Buddy.* Point to the top picture of a dog opening a door.

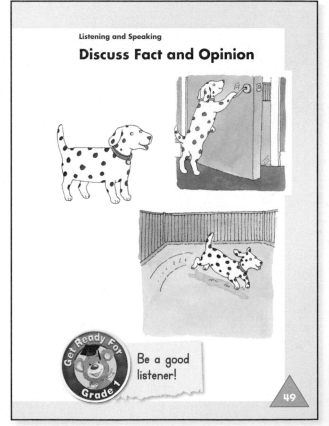

My Skills Buddy, p. 49

AlphaBuddy is going to help us think of facts and opinions about this dog. What can I say about this picture that is true for everyone? The dog is opening a door. That is a fact.

What can I say about this picture that tells what I believe?
This must be the smartest dog in the world. That is my opinion.

Independent practice

Pair children and have each partner make a statement about one of the pictures on p. 49 of *My Skills Buddy.* Tell children to listen to their partners' statements and tell if they heard a fact or an opinion. Make sure that partners take turns and that each child has the chance to state and identify a fact or opinion. Refer children to their Rules for Listening and Speaking from pp. 1–2 of *Reader's and Writer's Notebook.* Remind children that when they are the listener, they should face the speaker and ask questions to make sure they understand everything. When they are the speaker, they should speak loudly and clearly.

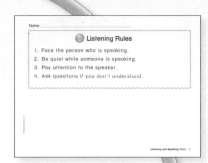

Reader's and Writer's Notebook, pp. 1–2

Be a Good Listener

1. Face the person who is speaking.
2. Be quiet while someone is speaking.
3. Pay attention to the speaker.
4. Ask questions if you don't understand.

Academic Vocabulary

fact a piece of information that can be proved to be true

opinion someone's judgment, belief, or way of thinking

Differentiated Instruction

SI Strategic Intervention

Support Listening for Fact and Opinion Show children the *carrot, grapes, jam,* and *lemon* Picture Cards. Go through the cards and state facts about each item. Identify each statement as a fact. Then go through the pictures again and state an opinion about each item. Ask children if they agree.

English Language Learners
Cognates The word *opinion* may sound familiar to speakers of Spanish, French, Italian, or Catalan, as the word originates from Latin. Make children aware of the connection between *opinion* and *opinión/opinas* (Spanish); *opinion* (French); *opinione* (Italian); and/or *opinió* (Catalan).

Objectives
- Review skills learned and practiced today.

Wrap Up Your Day

✔ **Concept Talk** Today we read about two children who fixed a box. Have you ever fixed anything?

✔ **Respond to Literature** Today we read about how Jen and Max helped their dad. How can you help your family?

✔ **Conventions** Have children write or dictate complete sentences about themselves. Have them use pronouns *I* or *me*, and remind them that the word *I* is always capitalized.

✔ **Homework Idea** Have children draw a picture of something in their home with /o/ in its name.

Preview

DAY 4

Tomorrow we will read about one of our Trucktown friends.

Science
Build a Tool Organizer

Materials: chart paper, toy tools, brown construction paper, white paper, pencils, scissors, glue

Describe Tool Uses Display p. 29 of *Old MacDonald had a Woodshop*. Use these questions to discuss the uses of the tools in the picture.

- Which tools are used to cut things?
- Which tools are used to join things together?
- Which tools are used to make holes?
- Which tools are used to paint things?

Make a chart. Put check marks on the chart to record children's responses. Compare and contrast the different uses of the tools.

	cut	join together	make holes	paint
hammer		✓		
screwdriver		✓		
chisel	✓			
drill			✓	
paintbrush				✓
saw	✓			

Make a Tool Organizer Provide children with a collection of toy tools. Have them trace the tools, cut them out, and glue them to brown construction paper. Then have them write labels for each tool on small pieces of white paper and glue them under the tools.

Music
Perform a Concert

Materials: toy instruments, various percussion instruments, blocks, whistles, bells, and other classroom items that can be made into instruments

Old MacDonald Played Some Music! We read about Old MacDonald's woodshop and sang about Old MacDonald's farm. Now let's make a band for Old MacDonald! Help children brainstorm, and then choose, instruments for the band. In Old MacDonald's woodshop and farm, we learned about the sounds tools and animals make. What sounds will our instruments make? Have each child share his or her instrument with the class and explain the sound it makes.

Drama
Dramatize the Story

Materials: toy tools

Act Out Animals Building a Toy Farm Arrange children in groups of seven. Have each child in the group choose an animal from the story to act out. Provide children with toy tools or use items in the classroom as props. Have each group act out the story. Tell children to pretend to be using their tool and to make the sound from the story. Act as the narrator to help children recall the order in which the animals entered the woodshop and to remind them of the sound for each tool.

Objectives
- Discuss the concept to develop oral language.
- Build oral vocabulary.

Today at a Glance

Oral Vocabulary
file, chisel

Phonemic Awareness
Initial /a/ and /i/

Phonics
/a/ Spelled *Aa*
/i/ Spelled *Ii*

Comprehension
◉ Character

Conventions
Prepositional Phrases

Writing
Extend the Concept

Vocabulary
Location Words

TRUCKTOWN on Reading Street

Start your engines!

- Display "Rock-a-Bye Mixer" and lead the group in saying the rhyme a few times.
- Have the group clap the rhythm as they recite the rhyme.
- When children master the rhythm, have them march around the room as they say the rhyme.

Truckery Rhymes

Concept Talk

Question of the Week

 What tools do you need to build things?

Build concepts

Write the question of the week on the board. Read the question as you track the print. Tell children to respond in complete sentences. Display Sing with Me Chart 32B.

Listen for Amazing Words

We are going to sing this song again. I want you to listen for the Amazing Words *file* and *chisel.* Sing the song several times with children to the tune of "If I Had a Hammer." Have them raise their hands when they hear *file* and *chisel*.

🔘 Sing with Me Audio

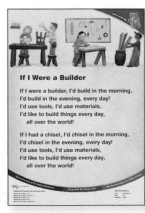

If I Were a Builder

If I were a builder, I'd build in the morning,
I'd build in the evening, every day!
I'd use tools, I'd use materials,
I'd like to build things every day,
    all over the world!

If I had a chisel, I'd chisel in the morning,
I'd chisel in the evening, every day!
I'd use tools, I'd use materials,
I'd like to build things every day,
    all over the world!

Talk with Me/Sing with Me Chart 32B

E L L **Produce Oral Language** Use the Day 4 instruction on ELL Poster 32 to extend and enrich language.

E L L Poster 32

Oral Vocabulary
Amazing Words

Amazing Words

saw	drill
hammer	screwdriver
file	chisel

Teach Amazing Words

Amazing Words Oral Vocabulary Routine

1 **Introduce the Word** A *file* is a long metal tool that is used to smooth out rough edges on wood. What is our new Amazing Word for a metal tool that smoothes out rough edges? Say it with me: *file*.

2 **Demonstrate** *I used a file to make my wooden birdhouse nice and smooth.*

Repeat steps 1 and 2.

Introduce the Word A *chisel* has a special edge to chip away small pieces of wood. What is our new Amazing Word for a tool with a special edge that chips away wood? Say it with me: *chisel*.

Demonstrate *An artist may also use a chisel to chip away small pieces of stone.*

3 **Apply** Have children describe a woodworking project using the words *file* and *chisel*. Have them point to these tools in *Old MacDonald had a Woodshop.*

Routines Flip Chart

Use Amazing Words

To reinforce the concept and the Amazing Words, have children supply the appropriate Amazing Word for each sentence.

The rough edges of the _____ smooth the wood. (file)

Dan used a _____ to carve a wooden shoe. (chisel)

Differentiated Instruction

A Advanced

Physical Response Have children act out how they would look if they were using a *file* or *chisel*. They may use *Old MacDonald had a Woodshop* for reference.

English Language Learners
Build Vocabulary If children need help completing the sentences, say a sentence using each Amazing Word and ask children to choose the sentence that makes sense.

Objectives
- Review /a/ spelled *Aa*.
- Review /i/ spelled *Ii*.

Check Phonemic Awareness
♦ SUCCESS PREDICTOR

Phonemic Awareness
Review /a/ and /i/

Review

Display the *alligator* Picture Card. This is an *alligator. Alligator* begins with /a/. What sound does *alligator* begin with? Continue with the *ant, apple,* and *astronaut* Picture Cards.

Display the *igloo* Picture Card. This is an *igloo. Igloo* begins with /i/. What sound does *igloo* begin with? Continue with the *iguana, inch,* and *insect* Picture Cards.

Corrective feedback

If... children cannot discriminate /a/,
then... have them say /a/ several times, /a/ /a/ /a/.

When you say /a/, your mouth is open and your tongue is down. Have children practice saying /a/.

If... children cannot discriminate /i/,
then... have them say /i/ several times, /i/ /i/ /i/.

When you say /i/, your mouth is straight and open and your tongue is down. Have children practice saying /i/.

Picture Card

Picture Card

Phonics
/a/ Spelled Aa and
/i/ Spelled Ii

Review

Display the *Aa* Alphabet Card. This is an *astronaut. Astronaut* begins with /a/. What letter spells the sound /a/? Yes, the letter *a.* Repeat the routine with the *Ii* Alphabet Card.

Write the word *pat* on the board. Help me blend this word. Listen as I say each sound: /p/ /a/ /t/. Now let's blend the sounds together to read the word: /p/ /a/ /t/, *pat.* What is the word? (*pat*) Let's try more. Repeat the routine with *pit, tap,* and *tip*.

Don't Wait Until Friday

MONITOR PROGRESS | **Check Phonemic Awareness**

Phoneme Segmentation Practice segmenting sounds with these words from Decodable Reader 32 after I say each word.

fix	mess	pan	big	yam
Ann	ham	Cass	grin	not

If... children cannot segment the sounds,

then... use the small-group Strategic Intervention lesson, p. DI•21, to reteach segmentation skills.

Continue to monitor children's progress using other instructional opportunities during the week so that they can be successful with the Day 5 Assessment. See the Skills Trace on p. 120.

Day 1	Day 2	Day 3	Day 4	Day 5
Check Phonemic Awareness	Check Sound-Spelling/ Retelling	Check Word Reading	Check Phonemic Awareness	Check Oral Vocabulary

Success Predictor

Differentiated Instruction

 Strategic Intervention

Support Segmentation Before asking children to segment words from the Decodable Reader, use Alphabet Cards to review initial *Ff, Mm, Pp, Bb, Yy, Hh, Cc, Gg,* and *Nn*.

Phonemic Awareness

Success Predictor

Objectives
- Spell words.
- Blend and segment words.
- Read decodable text.
- Read high-frequency words.

Spelling
↻ /o/ Spelled Oo

Spell words

ROUTINE **Spell Words**

1 **Review Sound-Spellings** Display the *Oo* Alphabet Card. This is an *otter*. *Otter* begins with /o/. What is the letter for /o/? (*o*) Continue the routine with the following Alphabet Cards: *Mm, Tt, Aa, Ss, Pp, Cc, Ii.*

2 **Model** Today we are going to spell some words. Listen to the three sounds in *got*: /g/ /o/ /t/.

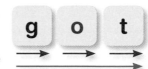

- What is the first sound in *got*? (/g/) What is the letter for /g/? (*g*) Write *g* on the board.

- What is the middle sound you hear? (/o/) What is the letter for /o/? (*o*) Write *o* on the board.

- What is the last sound you hear? (/t/) What is the letter for /t/? (*t*) Write *t* on the board.

- Point to *got*. Help me blend the sounds of each letter together to read this word: /g/ /o/ /t/. The word is *got*. Repeat with the word *mop*.

3 **Guide Practice** Now let's spell some words together. Listen to this word: /d/ /o/ /t/. What is the first sound in *dot*? (/d/) What is the letter for /d/? (*d*) Write *d* on the board. Now you write *d* on your paper. What is the middle sound in *dot*? (/o/) What is the letter for /o/? (*o*) Write *o* on the board. Now you write *o* on your paper. What is the last sound in *dot*? (/t/) What is the letter for /t/? (*t*) Write *t* on the board. Now you write *t* on your paper. Now we can blend the sound of each letter together to read the word: /d/ /o/ /t/. What is the word? (*dot*) Continue spell and blend practice with the words *on, top, nod,* and *cot*.

4 **On Your Own** This time I am going to say a word. I want you to write it on your paper. Remember, first, say the word slowly in your head and then write the letter for each sound. Listen carefully: *mob*. Give children time to write the word. How do you spell the word mob? Listen to the sounds: /m/ /o/ /b/. The first sound is /m/. What is the letter for /m/? Did you write *m* on your paper? Continue the routine with *o* and *b*. Name the letters in *mob*. *Mob* is spelled *m, o, b*. Continue the activity with the following words: *pot, cod, Don*.

Routines Flip Chart

Get Set, Roll! Reader 32
 Practice /o/ Spelled Oo

Review

Review the high-frequency words *look, of, the, you, see, a, they, he,* and *is.* Have children find each word on the Word Wall.

Teach rebus words

Write the word *tires* on the board. This is the word *tires*. Name the letters with me: *t, i, r, e, s.* Look for the word *tires* in the story we read today. Continue with the rebus word *fires*.

Read Get Set, Roll! Reader 32

Today we will read a story about a truck named Max. What is the title of the story? (*Max, the Hot Rod*) *Max, the Hot Rod* is the title of the story. We will read several words with /o/ in this story.

Use the routine for reading decodable books found in the Routines Flip Chart to read Get Set, Roll! Reader 32.

Get Set, Roll! Reader 32

Small Group Time

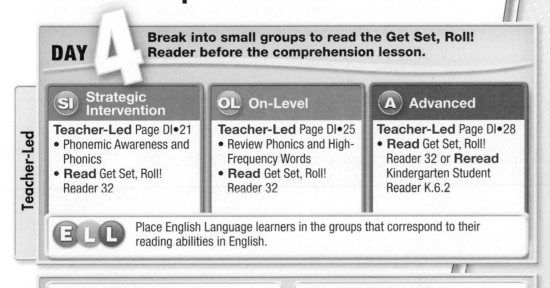

DAY 4

Break into small groups to read the Get Set, Roll! Reader before the comprehension lesson.

SI Strategic Intervention	**OL** On-Level	**A** Advanced
Teacher-Led Page DI•21 • Phonemic Awareness and Phonics • **Read** Get Set, Roll! Reader 32	**Teacher-Led** Page DI•25 • Review Phonics and High-Frequency Words • **Read** Get Set, Roll! Reader 32	**Teacher-Led** Page DI•28 • **Read** Get Set, Roll! Reader 32 or **Reread** Kindergarten Student Reader K.6.2

ELL Place English Language learners in the groups that correspond to their reading abilities in English.

Practice Stations
• Visit the Let's Write Station
• Visit the Read for Meaning Station

Independent Activities
• Read independently
• Audio Text of the Trade Book
• *Reader's and Writer's Notebook*

 ELL

English Language Learners
Frontload Reader Do a picture walk with children to preview the reader before starting the routine.

Objectives
◎ Practice character.
• Review and practice plot.

Comprehension
↻ Character

Practice character

Envision It!

Have children turn to the Literary Elements picture on pp. 34–35 of *My Skills Buddy*. As you look at the pictures, remind children that characters are the people or animals that a story is about.

Team Talk Pair children and have them take turns describing their favorite character from this week's stories.

My Skills Buddy, pp. 34–35

Plot

Review

Direct children to the Literary Elements pictures on pp. 34–35 of *My Skills Buddy*.

The plot of a story is often about solving a problem or having a goal and reaching it. A goal is something we hope to reach at the end of our hard work. Direct children to the pictures that show the beginning, the middle, and the end of the story.

• What is the goal of both characters? (to win the race)

• Look at the second picture. What is happening now? (The hare stops to take a nap. The tortoise passes him.)

• Which character reaches his goal? (the tortoise)

More practice

For more practice with plot, use *Reader's and Writer's Notebook,* p. 423.

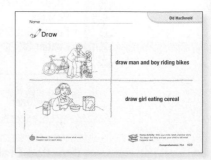

Reader's and Writer's Notebook, p. 423

Third Read—Trade Book
Old MacDonald had a Woodshop

Guide comprehension

Display *Old MacDonald had a Woodshop*. Remind children that the plot in a story tells about characters having a goal and reaching it.

- What is Old MacDonald's goal? (to build a toy farm)
- What does Old MacDonald do to reach this goal? (She has other animals help her.)
- Do Old MacDonald and the other animals reach their goal? (Yes, the animals finish building a toy farm.)

Reread *Old MacDonald had a Woodshop*. Return to p. 160. Follow the Day 4 arrow and use the Guide Comprehension notes to give children the opportunity to gain a more complete understanding of the story.

DAY **2**

Read for enjoyment

DAY **3**

Reread using Develop Vocabulary notes

Reread using Guide Comprehension notes

DAY **4**

Differentiated Instruction

 Strategic Intervention

Practice Plot Have children share a goal they would like to reach. Then have them discuss how they think they could reach this goal. Remind them that this goal could be the plot of their own story. Have them draw how their stories will "end"—each child reaching his or her goal.

English Language Learners
Professional Development
Build Background According to Dr. Jim Cummins of the University of Toronto: "It is important to *activate* students' prior knowledge because students may not realize what they know about a particular topic or issue. Their knowledge may not facilitate learning unless that knowledge is brought to consciousness."

Objectives
- Identify prepositional phrases.
- Write and draw about own experiences.

Conventions
Prepositional Phrases

Review Remind children of what they learned about prepositional phrases. A preposition is a word that tells us how the other words in a sentence are related. A prepositional phrase is made up of the preposition and any words that come after it that tell more about it.

The words *in, on, under,* and *over* are prepositions. These words may be part of prepositional phrases such as: *in the lake, on the dock, under the water,* and *over the fence.*

Guide practice Write this sentence on the board: *Ann sits.* Read the sentence with children. This sentence tells me just a little bit about what Ann is doing. If I add a prepositional phrase, I could learn more about where Ann sits. Rewrite the sentence as *Ann sits on the rug.* Now I know where Ann sits: *on the rug.* Circle *on. On* is the preposition in my sentence. Draw a line under *on the rug. On the rug* is the prepositional phrase.

Write this sentence on the board: *Tom runs over the hill.* Raise your hand when I say the preposition in this sentence. Read the sentence with children and raise your hand with them when you read *over.* Reread the sentence, having children stand during the prepositional phrase and sit down immediately after it is done. Stand with them to demonstrate. Have children stand on a rug and take turns saying the sentence *I stand on the rug.*

On their own Use *Reader's and Writer's Notebook,* p. 424, for more practice with prepositional phrases.

Daily Fix-It Use the Daily Fix-It for more conventions practice.

Reader's and Writer's Notebook, p. 424

Writing
Extend the Concept: Text to Self

Teach

We just read a story about animals that use tools to build a toy farm out of wood. Did you know there are many kinds of tools, and that not every tool is used to build things out of wood? A tool can be any object that helps us make or do something. We can use tools to help us cook, clean, draw, and write, as well as build and fix things.

Ask children to think about things they make or do at school and at home. Talk about the objects they use to help make or do these things.

Model

Draw a four-column chart on the board. Write each of the following headings at the top of a column: *Cook, Clean, Draw, Write*. Write children's contributions to the discussion in the correct columns. Write the following sentence frame on the board:

> **I use _____ to _____.**

I am going to read this sentence frame with one of our tools: *I use a mop to clean.*

Independent practice

Have children draw a tool from the list. Then have them share their drawings with the class, using the sentence frame to tell why they use their tool.

Daily Handwriting

Write uppercase *O* and lowercase *o* on the board. Review correct letter formation with children.

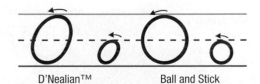

D'Nealian™   Ball and Stick

Have children write a row of uppercase *O* and a row of lowercase *o* on their Write-On Boards. Remind them to use proper left-to-right and top-to-bottom progression when writing *O* and *o*.

Daily Fix-It

can you see me.
<u>C</u>an you see me<u>?</u>

This week's practice sentences appear on Teacher Resources DVD-ROM.

Vocabulary
Location Words

train station   police station   fire station   gas station

Teach

Write the words *train station, police station, fire station,* and *gas station* on the board. Point to each word as you read it. These words tell about special locations, or places. Have children turn to p. 48 of *My Skills Buddy*. Use the remaining Vocabulary bullets in the discussion. Direct children to the picture of the train station. People get on and off trains at the *train station*. Direct children to the picture of the *police station*. Police officers park their cars at the police station. Point to the place where firefighters park their trucks. Firefighters park their fire truck at the fire station. Repeat the routine for gas station.

My Skills Buddy, p. 48

Team Talk Pair children and have them take turns telling what people do or which people work at each station.

Wrap Up Your Day

✔ **Concept Talk** Revisit the question of the week: *What tools do you need to build things?* Let's look at how we answered this question at the beginning of the lesson. Do we want to change or add to our answers?

✔ **Oral Language** Sing "If I Were a Builder" with me. When you hear an Amazing Word—*saw, drill, hammer, screwdriver, file, chisel*—act out the way a builder uses it.

✔ **Phonemic Awareness** I am going to say a sentence. Clap when you hear a word with /i/. Stand when you hear a word with /a/. Listen carefully: *Tim the fish has big black fins.*

Preview DAY 5

Tell children that tomorrow they will review some of the books and stories they have read this week.

Extend Your Day!

Science
Animal Attributes

Materials: chart paper, large sheets of light blue construction paper, fabric and paper scraps, safety scissors, crayons, glue

Contrast Animals Have children recall the characters in *Old MacDonald had a Woodshop.* Talk about the things the characters do in the story, what they wear, and how they communicate. Make a three-column chart. Have children compare the characters in the story with real animals. Write the information in the chart.

Animal Names	Animals in the Story	Real Animals
sheep	wears glasses, saws wood	eats grass and grain, says "baa"
cat	wears a vest, drills holes	purrs, drinks milk, hunts for mice

Connect to Writing Have children write a sentence about an animal in the story or a real animal. Then have them draw a picture of an animal, cut it out, and glue it to another sheet of paper. Have them draw or cut and glue fabric scraps to make their animals real or make-believe.

High-Frequency Words
High-Frequency Around the World

Materials: high-frequency word cards

Choose a Sorting Method Have children sit at tables. Ask two children seated next to each other to stand up and start the game. Show the pair a high-frequency word. The child who reads it first advances, standing next to the third child. Play continues until one child has advanced past each seat and back to his or her original spot.

Spelling
Correct Misspelled Words

Materials: list of misspelled words

Change Letters to Make Words Provide each child with a sheet of paper with these misspelled words on it: *tof, lev, dat, hig, fas, jep, het, buh, ruz.* Have children change one letter in each word to make a correctly spelled word. Tell them that some of the words can be made into more than one correctly spelled word. Have them cross out the letter they are changing and write the correctly spelled new word. Read the new words together.

dat bat
hig hit
fas fan
ruz rug

Objectives
- Review the concepts.
- Build oral vocabulary.

Today at a Glance

Oral Vocabulary
saw, drill, hammer, screwdriver, file, chisel

Phonemic Awareness
◉ Initial and Medial /o/

Phonics
◉ /o/ Spelled *Oo*

Comprehension
◉ Character

Conventions
Prepositional Phrases

Writing
This Week We…

Check Oral Vocabulary
SUCCESS PREDICTOR

TRUCKTOWN on Reading Street

Start your engines!

- Display "Rock-a-Bye Mixer" and lead the group in saying the rhyme a few times.
- Have half the group recite the rhyme while the other half acts it out.
- Then have the groups change roles.

Truckery Rhymes

Concept Wrap Up

Question of the Week
What tools do you need to build things?

Listen for Amazing Words

Write the question of the week on the board. Track the print as you read it. Have children answer the question in complete sentences using the Amazing Words *saw, drill, hammer, screwdriver, file,* and *chisel*. Display Sing with Me Chart 32B. Let's sing "If I Were a Builder." I want you to listen for the Amazing Words we learned this week. Sing the song several times to the tune of "If I Had a Hammer." Have children act out using each tool every time they hear that Amazing Word. Then discuss how the children in the picture are using the tools. Remind children to speak one at a time.

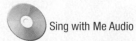 Sing with Me Audio

If I Were a Builder

If I were a builder, I'd build in the morning,
I'd build in the evening, every day!
I'd use tools, I'd use materials,
I'd like to build things every day,
all over the world!

If I had a chisel, I'd chisel in the morning,
I'd chisel in the evening, every day!
I'd use tools, I'd use materials,
I'd like to build things every day,
all over the world!

Sing with Me Chart 32B

E L L Check Concepts and Language Use the Day 5 instruction on ELL Poster 32 to monitor children's understanding of the lesson concept.

E L L Poster 32

🖥 Go Digital!   Concept Talk Video 🖥   🖥 Sing with Me Audio   Sing with Me 🖥 Animations

Whole Group

Oral Vocabulary
Amazing Words

Review

Let's Talk Display Talk with Me Chart 32A. We learned six new Amazing Words this week. Let's say the Amazing Words as I point to the pictures on the chart. Point to each picture and give children the chance to say the appropriate Amazing Word before offering it.

Have children supply the appropriate Amazing Word to complete each sentence.

The end of a _____ fits into the head of a screw. (screwdriver)

The sharp end of the _____ makes a hole in the wood. (drill)

Tim used a _____ to smooth the board. (file)

The blade is the sharp part of a _____. (saw)

Pam chipped the wood with her _____. (chisel)

I used a _____ and nails to hang the picture. (hammer)

MONITOR PROGRESS **Check Oral Vocabulary**

Demonstrate Word Knowledge Monitor the Amazing Words by asking the following questions. Have children use an Amazing Word in their answer.

• **What tool would you use to tighten screws?** (screwdriver)

• **What tool would you use to carve designs in wood?** (chisel)

• **What tool makes a tapping noise when you use it?** (hammer)

• **What tool smoothes the edges of wood?** (file)

• **What tool makes holes in wood?** (drill)

• **What tool has a handle and a blade?** (saw)

If... children have difficulty using the Amazing Words,

then... reteach the words using the Oral Vocabulary Routine on the Routines Flip Chart.

Day 1	Day 2	Day 3	Day 4	**Day 5**
Check Phonemic Awareness	Check Sound-Spelling/ Retelling	Check Word Reading	Check Phonemic Awareness	**Check Oral Vocabulary**

Success Predictor

Amazing Words

saw	drill
hammer	screwdriver
file	chisel

Talk with Me/Sing with Me Chart 32A

Differentiated Instruction

SI Strategic Intervention

Sentence Production Have children choose one Amazing Word. Ask them to say a complete sentence using that word.

Oral Vocabulary   Success Predictor

Objectives
◎ Review initial and medial /o/.
◎ Review /o/ spelled *Oo*.

Phonemic Awareness Review

/o/

Isolate initial and medial /o/

Display the *octopus* Picture Card. What is the beginning sound in *octopus*? Say the word with me: *octopus*, /o/ /o/ /o/, *octopus*. Continue to review initial /o/ with the Picture Cards *olive*, *otter*, and *ox*.

Display the *mop* Picture Card. What is the middle sound in *mop*? Say the sounds in *mop* with me: /m/ /o/ /p/. The middle sound in *mop* is /o/. Continue to review medial /o/ with the Picture Cards *box*, *dog*, and *rock*.

Discriminate medial sounds

I am going to say two words. If the words have the same sound in the middle, say "same." If the words do not have the same middle sound, say "not the same." Let's do it together first. Listen carefully: *pot, bag*. What sound do you hear in the middle of *pot*? (/o/) What sound do you hear in the middle of *bag*? (/a/) *Pot* and *bag* do not have the same middle sound, so what do we say? (not the same) Continue with these word pairs: *job, hot; cat, pod; dig, hop; lot, cod; pop, nip*.

Picture Card

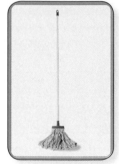

Picture Card

Phonics Review
/o/ Spelled Oo

Teach /o/Oo

Display the *Oo* Alphabet Card. This is an *otter.* What sound do you hear at the beginning of *otter?* What letter spells that sound?

High-frequency words

Write the word *go* on the board. This is the word *go.* Repeat the routine with *where, is, that,* and *come.*

Apply phonics in familiar text

Let's Reread Have children reread one of the books specific to the target letter sounds. You may wish to review the decodable words and high-frequency words that appear in each book prior to rereading.

Alphabet Card

Decodable Reader 32
My Skills Buddy, p. 38

Kindergarten
Student Reader K.6.2

Get Set, Roll! Reader 32

Differentiated Instruction

SI Strategic Intervention

Support Phonics/Handwriting Have children use Decodable Reader 32, Kindergarten Student Reader K.6.2, or Get Set, Roll! Reader 32 to find a word with initial or medial /o/. Have them copy the word on their Write-On Boards. Then have children read the word.

Small Group Time

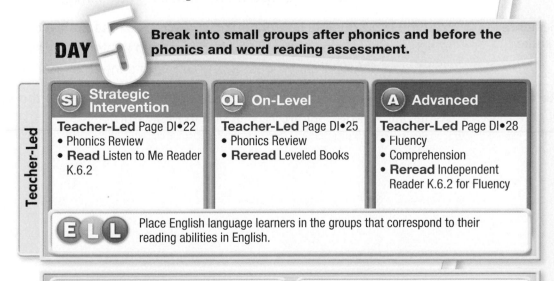

DAY 5 Break into small groups after phonics and before the phonics and word reading assessment.

Teacher-Led

SI Strategic Intervention

Teacher-Led Page DI•22
• Phonics Review
• **Read** Listen to Me Reader K.6.2

OL On-Level

Teacher-Led Page DI•25
• Phonics Review
• **Reread** Leveled Books

A Advanced

Teacher-Led Page DI•28
• Fluency
• Comprehension
• **Reread** Independent Reader K.6.2 for Fluency

E L L Place English language learners in the groups that correspond to their reading abilities in English.

Practice Stations
• Visit the Read for Meaning Station
• Visit the Let's Make Art Station

Independent Activities
• Read independently
• Story Sort
• Concept Talk Video

Assess
◎ Read words with /o/.
• Read high-frequency words.
• Read sentences.

Assessment
Monitor Progress

/o/ Spelled Oo

Whole Class Divide a paper into six sections for each child. I am going to say six words. Write the word in a box. Let's try the first one together. The word is *top*. Listen to the sounds: /t/ /o/ /p/. Write the letter for each sound. Did you write *top*? Let's try five more. Listen carefully. Continue with *pond, mom, stop, hop,* and *hot*.

MONITOR PROGRESS **Check Word and Sentence Reading**

If... children cannot complete the whole-class assessment,
then... use the Reteach lesson in *First Stop*.

If... you are unsure of a child's grasp of this week's skills,
then... use the assessment below to obtain a clearer evaluation of the child's progress.

/o/ Spelled Oo and high-frequency words

One-on-One To facilitate individual progress monitoring, assess some children on Day 4 and the rest on Day 5. While individual children are being assessed, the rest of the class can reread this week's books and look for words with /o/.

Word reading

Use the reproducible word lists on p. 195 to assess a child's ability to read words with /o/ and high-frequency words. We're going to read some words. I'll read the first word, and you read the rest. The first word is *lot,* /l/ /o/ /t/. For each child, record any decoding problems.

Sentence reading

Use the reproducible sentences on p. 195 to assess a child's ability to read words in sentences. Have each child read two sentences aloud. Have each child read different sentences. Start over with sentence one if necessary.

Record scores

Monitor children's accuracy by recording their scores using the Word and Sentence Reading Chart for this unit in *First Stop*.

Name _____

Read the Words

do	☐		jog	☐
lot	☐		frog	☐
fox	☐		stop	☐
hot	☐		like	☐
pot	☐		drop	☐
to	☐		he	☐

Read the Sentences

1. I can see the frog hop.

2. Sam will run to the shop with Don.

3. I am with my Mom and Pop.

4. We pet the dog that Tim got.

5. He will see Bob at the bus stop.

Note to Teacher: Children read each word. Children read two sentences.

Scoring for Read the Words: Score 1 point for each correct word.

Short *o* (*lot, fox, hot, pot, jog, frog, stop, drop*) _____ / __8__
High-Frequency Words (*do, to, like, he*) _____ / __4__

MONITOR PROGRESS
• Review short *o*
• Review high-frequency words

Objectives

- Recognize a lullaby.
- Identify rhythm and rhyme.
- Identify repeating words.

My Skills Buddy, pp. 50–51

Let's Practice It!
Lullaby

Teach

Today you will listen to a lullaby. A lullaby is a song, or piece of music with words for singing, that helps babies and children fall asleep. Review the features of a lullaby with children.

- A lullaby has regular beats and rhyming words like a poem.
- A lullaby has words or phrases that repeat.
- A lullaby has quiet, relaxing words to help babies and children sleep.

Have children turn to p. 50 of *My Skills Buddy*. I am going to read a lullaby called "Sleep, Baby, Sleep." Look at the pictures. What do you think this lullaby will be about? Continue to look at the pictures as I read. Read the text of "Sleep, Baby, Sleep." As you read, direct children to look at the picture.

Before reading the lullaby, explain to children the meaning of the words *green* and *vale.* We are going to hear two new words in this lullaby: *green* and *vale.* We know that *green* is a color. *Green* is also a word for a pasture or park in the middle of a town or village. A *vale* is another word for valley.

Guide practice

Discuss the features of a lullaby with children and the bulleted text on *My Skills Buddy* p. 50.

- A lullaby has regular beats and rhyming words like a poem. Does this lullaby have a regular beat? (yes) What rhyming words do you hear? *(sleep/sheep; green/clean; sleep/deep; mild/child)*

- A lullaby has words or phrases that repeat. What repeating words do you hear in this lullaby? *(sleep, baby)*

- A lullaby has quiet, relaxing words to help babies and children sleep. Which words in this lullaby make you feel quiet and relaxed? (Possible responses: *little lambs; snowy fleece; soft; clean; lambs so mild; gentle child; sleep, baby, sleep*)

Sleep, Baby, Sleep

Sleep, baby, sleep,
Your father tends the sheep.
The little lambs are on the green,
With snowy fleece so soft and clean.
Sleep, baby, sleep.

Sleep, baby, sleep,
Our cottage vale is deep.
Be always like the lambs so mild,
A kind and sweet and gentle child.
Sleep, baby, sleep.

Differentiated Instruction

 Advanced

Expand Vocabulary Write *green* and *vale* on the board. Have children copy the words onto two sheets of paper. Then have them illustrate each word as it is used in the lullaby.

Academic Vocabulary

lullaby a song that helps babies and children fall asleep

English Language Learners
Access Content Play recordings of English-language lullabies and lullabies in English learners' home language(s). Have children describe how the songs sound alike. Expand discussion by having children describe how they can tell both songs are lullabies, even though they are in different languages. Have children explain the lullaby from their home language(s).

Objectives
◎ Review character.

Assess
◉ Identify characters.

Comprehension Assessment
Monitor Progress

Review

Character Characters are the animals or people who the story is about. We learn about what the characters do when we read the story. Good readers pay attention to the characters in the story because it helps them understand and remember the story.

Read "The Elves and the Shoemaker"

Tell children that you are going to read them a story about a poor shoemaker who gets some mysterious help. Ask children to think about the characters as they listen to the story. Listen carefully as I read the story. When I am done, I am going to ask you some questions about the story's characters. Read "The Elves and the Shoemaker" on pp. 76–78 of *Read Aloud Anthology.*

Read Aloud Anthology

Check character

After you read the story, have children tell you about the story's characters.

- Who is this story about? (a shoemaker, his wife, and two elves)

- What is the shoemaker like? (He is poor, hardworking, and kind.)

- What are the elves like? (They are kind, hardworking, and helpful.)

- Why does the shoemaker's wife make clothes for the elves? (The shoemaker's wife makes clothes for the elves to show she is thankful for their help.)

Corrective feedback

If... a child cannot identify the characters,
then... reteach characters using the Reteach lesson in *First Stop.*

Assess character

Use the blackline master on p. 199. Make one copy for each child. Have children color the pictures of characters from "The Elves and the Shoemaker."

Name _____

Character

Color the characters from "The Elves and the Shoemaker."

Note to Teacher: Have children color the characters from "The Elves and the Shoemaker."

MONITOR PROGRESS

• Character

Objectives
- Review prepositional phrases.
- Help write a class song.
- Practice writing *Oo*.

Conventions
Prepositional Phrases

Review
Remind children of what they learned about prepositional phrases. A prepositional phrase is made up of two parts: the preposition and any words that come after the preposition.

Model
Write the following sentences on the board:

> **Jen jogs on the path.**
>
> **Tom swims in the lake.**

Read aloud the first sentence, pointing to each word as you say it. *On* is the preposition. *On the path* is the prepositional phrase. Underline *on the path.*

Guide practice
Read the second sentence, pointing to each word as you say it. What is the preposition in this sentence? (*in*) Remember, a prepositional phrase is the preposition and the words that come after. Which words come after *in*? (*the lake*) What is the prepositional phrase in this sentence? (*in the lake*) Underline *in the lake.*

On their own
Write the following sentences on the board: *Dan plays in a park. Ed hops over the bug. Lin sleeps on a bunk. Pam sat under that tree.* Read the sentences, tracking the print as you read. Tell children to choose a sentence. Have them copy that sentence onto their Write-On Boards. Then have children underline the prepositional phrase.

Daily Fix-It
Use the Daily Fix-It for more conventions practice.

Writing
This Week We...

Review

Display *Old MacDonald had a Woodshop,* Sing with Me Chart 32B, Phonics Songs and Rhymes Chart 32, Decodable Reader 32 from *My Skills Buddy,* Kindergarten Reader K.6.2, and Get Set Roll! Reader 32. This week we read new books and sang new songs about building. We read about many different characters. Some were animals and some were people. Which character was your favorite? My favorite was the sheep, Old MacDonald.

Team Talk Pair children and have them draw pictures of their favorite character. Then have them take turns explaining their drawings.

Model writing a song

Let's write a song about the characters and tools we read about this week. Our song can sound like another song. Do you know "The Farmer in the Dell"? Sing the first verse of "The Farmer in the Dell" for children. I will sing about the sheep, Old MacDonald, and her saw. Draw and label a sheep and a saw on the board. Point to the sheep and the saw when you sing those words. Our song starts like this: *The sheep has a saw. The sheep has a saw. Hi-ho, the derry-o, the sheep has a saw.*

Guide practice

Have children suggest a character and the tool he or she uses. Draw and label the character and the tool on the board. Sing the character or tool when I point to it. Sing: *The* (point to character) *has a* (point to tool). Continue with the remainder of the verse.

On their own

Have children draw a picture of a character and tool for the song. Have them write or dictate labels for their drawing.

Daily Handwriting

D'Nealian™   Ball and Stick

Write uppercase *O* and lowercase *o* on the board. Review correct letter formation with children

Have children write a row of uppercase *O* and a row of lowercase *o* on their Write-On Boards. Remind them to use proper left-to-right and top-to-bottom progression.

Differentiated Instruction

 Advanced

Conventions The first part of "The farmer in the dell" is not a complete sentence because it doesn't have an action part. Write and read the following sentence: *The farmer works in the dell.* Now it is a complete sentence. Have children identify the preposition and prepositional phrase in the sentence. (*in; in the dell*)

Daily Fix-It

do you like me
Do you like me?

This week's practice sentences appear on Teacher Resources DVD-ROM.

English Language Learners
Poster Preview Prepare children for next week by using Week 3 ELL Poster number 33. Read the Poster Talk-Through to introduce the concept and vocabulary. Ask children to identify and describe objects and actions in the art.

Wrap Up Your Week!

Question of the Week
What tools do you need to build things?

Illustrate character

This week we read stories with characters that build and fix things with tools. Let's think about the characters from two of these stories.

- Make a Venn diagram like the one shown below. Have children describe Old MacDonald from *Old MacDonald had a Woodshop* and Max and Jen from *Max and Jen Fix the Big Box!* Write ways they are similar in the middle.

- Have children draw one of the characters doing something listed in the diagram, such as using a tool.

- Have children explain their drawing, either by describing what it shows about the character or telling why their character is performing that action.

Amazing Words

> You've learned
> **006**
> words this week!
> You've learned
> **192**
> words this year!

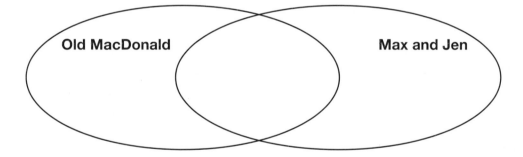

Old MacDonald   **Max and Jen**

Next Week's Question
How do beavers build their homes?

Discuss next week's question. Talk with children about where beavers live and what they build.

Preview NEXT WEEK

Tell children that next week they will read about real-life animal builders.

Social Studies
Farm Parts

Materials: Trade Book *Old MacDonald had a Woodshop,* chart paper, drawing paper, crayons

Describe the Steps to Building a Toy Farm
Talk with children about how the animals in the story *Old MacDonald had a Woodshop* built the toy farm. Discuss how they each worked on a different part of the farm and how they put the parts together to create the farm yard. Draw a web or display Graphic Organizer 17. Label the center circle *Old MacDonald's Farm.* Display pp. 26–27 in the book and ask children to identify all the different parts that make up the farm. Write their responses in the spokes of the circles. Encourage them to name other parts of a farm that might not be pictured. Add more spokes if necessary.

Connect to Writing Have children draw and color their own picture of a farm. Then have them copy words from the chart to label parts of their drawings.

Math
Counting Workers

Materials: Trade Book *Old MacDonald had a Woodshop,* counters

Counting Old MacDonald had several helpers to make the wooden farm. Six animals joined her: *1 sheep + 6 other animals = 7 animals all together.* Demonstrate with counters.

Open to p. 9. Two animals are working. How many more will come? Start with 2 and count up to 7. Keep track of how many counters it takes to reach 7. It takes five more counters to reach seven. Use the same method and count to 7 on pp. 11, 13, 15, 17, 19, 20, and 21.

Art
Drawing Faces

Materials: drawing paper, markers, crayons

Facial Proportions Show children how the eyes on an actual face are not very close to the top. Draw an oval and then lightly draw a cross in the middle. Draw the eyes on the horizontal line of the cross, with the nose and mouth below it. Then add hair or other features. Distribute predrawn ovals with dotted line crosses. Let children draw in the features. Have them add hats, rabbit ears, or other items to make the face into a character they remember from a story this week.

Weekly Assessment

Use the whole-class assessment on pages 194–195 and 198–199 in this Teacher's Edition to check:

✔  **Short _o_ Spelled _Oo_**

✔ **Comprehension Skill** _Character_

✔ **High-Frequency Words**

Teacher's Edition, Day 5

Managing Assessment

Use the Assessment Handbook for:

✔ **Observation Checklists**

✔ **Record-Keeping Forms**

✔ **Portfolio Assessment**

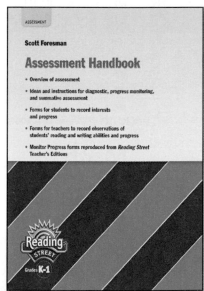

Assessment Handbook

Teacher Notes

Small Group Time

5 Day Plan

DAY 1	• Phonemic Awareness/ Phonics • Decodable Story 32
DAY 2	• Phonemic Awareness/ Phonics • Decodable Reader 32
DAY 3	• Phonemic Awareness/ Phonics • Concept Literacy Reader K.6.2 or Kindergarten Student Reader K.6.2
DAY 4	• Phonemic Awareness/ Phonics • Get Set, Roll! Reader 32
DAY 5	• Phonics Review • Listen to Me Reader K.6.2

3 or 4 Day Plan

DAY 1	• Phonemic Awareness/ Phonics • Decodable Story 32
DAY 2	• Phonemic Awareness/ Phonics • Decodable Reader 32
DAY 3	• Phonemic Awareness/ Phonics • Concept Literacy Reader K.6.2 or Kindergarten Student Reader K.6.2
DAY 4	• Phonemic Awareness/ Phonics • Get Set, Roll! Reader 32

3 Day Plan: Eliminate the shaded box.

Phonemic Awareness•Phonics

■ **Isolate /o/** Display the *octopus* Picture Card. This is an *octopus. Octopus* begins with /o/. Say it with me: /o/ /o/ /o/, *octopus.* Repeat with *otter* and *olive.*

■ **Connect /o/ to *Oo*** I am going to say three words. I want you to tell me which word has /o/. Listen carefully: *tip, tap, top.* Say the words with me: *tip, tap, top.* Which word has /o/? *Top* has /o/. Write the letters *Oo* on the board. The letter *o* stands for /o/ in words like *top.* Continue with the following sets of words: *cut, cot, cat; hot, hat, hit; pat, pet, pot.*

Decodable Story 32

■ **Review** Review the previously taught high-frequency words by writing each word on the board and having children read the word with you.

a	the	go	me	to

> **If...** children have difficulty reading the words,
> **then...** say a word and have children point to the word. Repeat several times, giving assistance as needed.

■ **Read** Have children read *Spin the Top* orally. Then have them reread the story several times individually.

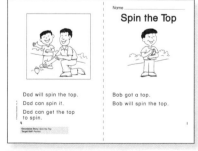

Reader's and Writer's Notebook, pp. 415–416

Objectives
• Identify the common sounds that letters represent.
• Read at least 25 high-frequency words from a commonly used list.

SI *Strategic Intervention* **DAY 2**

Phonemic Awareness•Phonics

- **Discriminate /o/** Display Phonics Songs and Rhymes Chart 32. Sing "The Fix-It Shop" to the tune of "I've Been Working on the Railroad" several times with children. Ask them to hop when they hear /o/ words.

- **Recognize** *Oo* Ask children to name words that have /o/. List the words on the board as they say them. Have children echo read the list of words. Then ask children to take turns circling *o* in the words on the board.

Decodable Reader 32

- **Review** Review the high-frequency words by writing *where* on the board. This is the word *where*. What word is this? Continue with the following words: *go, is, a, the, that, with.*

  If... children have difficulty reading the words,
  then... say a word and have children point to the word. Repeat several times, giving assistance as needed.

- **Read** Display the cover of *Will Cass Come?* on p. 38 of *My Skills Buddy.* Ask a volunteer to read the first page of the story. Have children tell the things Cass will miss while she is at the doctor's office. Continue through the story in this manner.

My Skills Buddy

More Reading

Use Leveled Readers or other text at children's instructional level.

Small Group Time

Phonemic Awareness•Phonics

■ **Isolate /o/** Display the *mop* Picture Card. This is a *mop.* Do you hear /o/? Say it with me: /m/ /o/ /p/, *mop. Mop* has /o/ in the middle. Repeat with the words *hot* and *spot.*

■ **Connect /o/ to Oo** Display the *sock* Picture Card. This is a *sock.* What is a *sock*? A *sock* is what we put on our foot. *Sock* has /o/ in the middle. Say it with me: /s/ /o/ /k/, *sock.* Display the *Oo* Alphabet Card. What is this? These are the letters *Oo.* The letter *o* can stand for /o/ in words. When you hear a word with /o/, I want you to point to your socks. Use the following words: *pond, sand, lock, swing, flop, flag, pants, hop.*

■ **Blend Sounds** Write *box* on the board. Have children blend the sound of each letter to read the word. Repeat the routine with the words *flop, got,* and *mop.*

■ **Review High-Frequency Words** Write *where* on the board. Have volunteers say the word and use it in a sentence. Continue with the word *is, go, that,* and *come.*

■ **Read** To practice phonics and high-frequency words, have children read Kindergarten Student Reader K.6.2. Use the instruction on pp. 156–157.

For a complete lesson plan and additional practice, see the **Leveled Reader Teaching Guide**.

Concept Literacy Reader K.6.2

■ **Preview and Predict** Display the cover of the Concept Literacy Reader K.6.2. Point to the title of the book. The title of the book is *We Build a Birdhouse.* What do you think the book is about? Have children tell about the cover and what they think the book might be about.

■ **Set a Purpose** We talked about the title of the book. Let's read the book to learn about how to build a birdhouse. Have children read the Concept Literacy Reader.

■ **Read** Provide corrective feedback as children read the book orally. During reading, ask them if they are able to confirm any of the predictions they made prior to reading.

If... children have difficulty reading the book individually,

then... read a sentence aloud as children point to each word. Then have the group reread the sentences as they continue pointing to the words.

■ **Retell** Have children retell the content as you page through the book. Help them identify what the book is about. Also call attention to the tools that are used in each step to build a birdhouse.

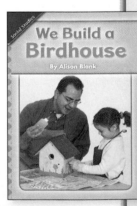

Concept Literacy Reader K.6.2

Objectives
• Identify the common sounds that letters represent. • Predict what might happen next based on the cover.
• Predict what might happen next based on the title. • Retell important facts in a text, heard or read.

 SI *Strategic Intervention* DAY **4**

More Reading

Use Leveled Readers or other text at children's instructional level.

Phonemic Awareness•Phonics

■ **Hop Till You Drop!** Gather fifteen sheets of construction paper and write one word on each sheet. Use the /o/ words *spot, hot, fox, dot, drop, box, hop, rock,* and seven other words that do not have /o/. Tape the sheets to the floor in a circle. Remind children that a circle looks like the letter *Oo.* Have children hop around the circle, hopping only on /o/ words. Have children say the word as they hop on it.

■ **Segmenting** Say *not.* I hear three sounds in *not, /n/ /o/ /t/.* How many sounds do you hear in *pod?* What are they? (three, /p/ /o/ /d/) Continue with *top, hot, spot, sock,* and *got.*

Get Set, Roll! Reader 32

■ **Review** Review the following high-frequency words with children prior to reading the story: *is, he, they, a, see, you, the, of, look.*

■ **Review Rebus Words** Write the word *tires* on the board. This is the word *tires.* Name the letters with me: *t, i, r, e, s, tires.* There are *tires* on cars and trucks. What else has *tires?* Look for the word *tires* in the story we read today. There will be a picture above the word to help us read it.

Get Set, Roll! Reader 32

■ **Read** Display Get Set, Roll! Reader 32, *Max, the Hot Rod.* Today we will read a new story about a truck named Max. Point to the title of the story. The title of the story is *Max, the Hot Rod.* Look at the picture and think about the title. What do you think this story will be about?

> **If...** children have difficulty reading the story individually, **then...** read a sentence aloud as children point to each word. Then have the group reread the sentences as they continue pointing to the words.

■ **Reread** Use echo reading of Get Set, Roll! Reader 32 to model fluent reading. Use your oral reading to model for children where to pause, when to change pitch, and which words to stress. Then have children reread orally three to four times, or until they can read with few or no mistakes.

Objectives

- Identify the common sounds that letters represent.
- Read at least 25 high-frequency words from a commonly used list.
- Predict what might happen next based on the cover.

Small Group Time

More Reading

Use Leveled Readers or other text at children's instructional level.

SI *Strategic Intervention*   DAY **5**

Phonics Review

■ **Stop and Go** Play a variation of "Red Light, Green Light." Have each child write *Oo* on a card. Then have children take the cards to the back of the room. Tell children to take a step forward and hold up the *Oo* card when you say an /o/ word. They should not move if you say a word that does not have /o/. Use the following words: *sock, rat, bin, block, flop, cub, lot, hen, pin, dot.* Continue until a child reaches the front of the room. Then have that child say the words for children and continue the game.

Listen to Me Reader K.6.2

■ **Preview and Predict** Display the cover of the book. The title of this story is *Let's Play Hopscotch.* It is written by Anita Khan. It is illustrated by Lindy Burnett. What is hopscotch? What do you think will happen in this story? Tell me your ideas.

■ **Set a Purpose** Review children's ideas. Point out that after they read, they will know more about hopscotch. Tell children that you will read the story with them. Follow along with your finger as I read. Then we will take turns reading this page. Repeat this routine through all of the pages. Guide children to decode words.

Listen to Me Reader K.6.2

■ **Reread for Fluency** Use echo reading of Listen to Me Reader K.6.2 to model reading fluently. Use your oral reading to model for children when to pause, when to change pitch, and which words to stress. Then have children reread orally three to four times, or until they can read with few or no mistakes.

Objectives
• Identify the common sounds that letters represent.
• Predict what might happen next based on the cover.

 **OL** On-Level   **DAY 1**

Phonemic Awareness•Phonics

- **Listen for /o/** Tell children you will tell them a story and they should listen for /o/. When you say a word that has /o/, children should hop and repeat the word. Tell a simple story, emphasizing /o/ words and pausing to give children a chance to hop and repeat the word. *Roxie has an otter named Tot. Tot likes to toss the ball. Roxie and Tot toss the ball. Tot flops and makes a mess. Roxie mops Tot's mess. Mop, Roxie, mop for Tot!*

- **Recognize /o/** Write uppercase *O* on the board. Name the letter as you write it several times. Then show children how to make *O* by curving their arms over their heads. *Make an o with your arms when you hear a word that has /o/. Listen carefully: got, rag, Bob, job, dust, pop, lot, fit.*

Objectives
- Identify the common sounds that letters represent.

Pacing Small Group Instruction
 20–30 mins.

5 Day Plan

DAY 1	• Phonemic Awareness/ Phonics • Decodable Story 32
DAY 2	• Phonemic Awareness/ Phonics • High-Frequency Words • Decodable Reader 32
DAY 3	• Phonemic Awareness/ Phonics • Kindergarten Student Reader K.6.2
DAY 4	• Get Set, Roll! Reader 32
DAY 5	• Phonics Review • Reread Leveled Books

 **OL** On-Level   **DAY 2**

Phonemic Awareness•Phonics

- **Discriminate /o/** Draw six socks on the board. Collect ten Picture Cards, including the following: *clock, fox, mop, ox, top, octopus.* Mix the cards and display them one at a time. Have a child name the picture. If the name has /o/, have the child write a lowercase *o* in one of the socks.

- **High-Frequency Words** Display the following word cards: *where, is, go, that, come.* Say the word *that* and select a child to point to the word. Have children say the word and use it in a sentence. Continue with the other words.

Objectives
- Identify the common sounds that letters represent.
- Read at least 25 high-frequency words from a commonly used list.

3 or 4 Day Plan

DAY 1	• Phonemic Awareness/ Phonics • Decodable Story 32
DAY 2	• Phonemic Awareness/ Phonics • High-Frequency Words • Decodable Reader 32
DAY 3	• Phonemic Awareness/ Phonics • Kindergarten Student Reader K.6.2
DAY 4	• Get Set, Roll! Reader 32

3 Day Plan: Eliminate the shaded box.

More Practice

For additional practice with this week's phonics skills, have children reread the Decodable Story (Day 1) and the Decodable Reader (Day 2).

Small Group Time

Phonemic Awareness•Phonics

■ **Illustrate the Word** Give each child a piece of paper. Have children fold the paper to create four sections. Then have them draw a picture of a word with /o/ in each box and label it with the word or the letters *Oo.*

■ **Connect /o/ to Oo** Write the letters *Oo* and the words *map* and *mop* on the board. The letter *o* can stand for /o/ in words. Which word has /o/ in the middle? Have a volunteer circle the *o* in *mop.* Then have the group read the words. Continue with these pairs of words: *jot, jet; fix, fox; top, tap; hat, hot.*

Kindergarten Student Reader K.6.2

Kindergarten Student Reader K.6.2

■ **Preview and Predict** Display the cover of the book. The title of this story is *Max and Jen Fix the Big Box.* Look at the cover. What are Max and Jen wearing? What are they doing? What do you think they are going to do in this story? Tell me your ideas.

■ **Set a Purpose** Review the list of things children think might happen in the story. Remind children they will read to find out about how Max and Jen fix the box.

■ **Read** Have children follow along as they read the story with you. After reading p. 2, ask children to tell who Max and Jen ask for help to fix the box. Continue with each page. Ask the following questions:

• What does Dad give to Max and Jen to wear while they help fix the box?

• What tools do Max and Jen use?

• Do Max and Jen like to help?

• Why do they paint the box red?

■ **Summarize** Have children retell the story to a partner and tell who Max and Jen give the fixed box to.

■ **Text to Self** Help children make personal connections to the story as they tell about something they have helped fix.

Objectives
• Identify the common sounds that letters represent. • Predict what might happen next based on the cover.
• Predict what might happen next based on the title. • Make connections to own experiences.

 **OL** On-Level

DAY **4**

Get Set, Roll! Reader 32

■ **Review** Review the words *look, of, the, you, see, a, they, he,* and *is* by writing each word on the board and saying the word with children. Then give clues to a word and have children tell which word it is. Remind children that *o* can stand for the vowel sound in sock, /o/. As they read *Max, the Hot Rod,* have them listen for words in the story that have /o/.

■ **Review Rebus Words** Write the words *tires* on the board. This is the word *tires.* Name the letters with me: *t, i, r, e, s, tires.* What has tires? Remember, when we read the story today, the word *tires* will have a picture above it to help us read the word.

■ **Read** Display Get Set, Roll! Reader 32, *Max, the Hot Rod.* Point to the title of the story. *Max, the Hot Rod* is the title of the story. Let's read to find more about Max.

Objectives
• Read at least 25 high-frequency words from a commonly used list.

OL On-Level

DAY 5

Phonics Review

■ **Isolate /o/** Display the *fox* Picture Card. This is a fox. *Fox* has /o/. Say it with me: /f/ /o/ /ks/, *fox.* Repeat with *hop, spot,* and *box.*

■ **Discriminate /o/** Display the *mop* Picture Card. This is a mop. *Mop* has /o/ in the middle. Say it with me: /m/ /o/ /p/, *mop.* What letter stands for /o/ in *mop?* Write the letters *Oo* on the board. The letter *o* can stand for /o/. Does *map* have /o/ like *mop?* No, *map* does not have /o/. Repeat the routine with the following words: *sob, sip, hit, hop, drop, fit, pot.*

Objectives
• Identify the common sounds that letters represent.

More Reading

Use Leveled Readers or other text at children's instructional level to develop fluency.

Small Group Time

5 Day Plan

DAY 1	• Phonemic Awareness/ Phonics • Decodable Story 32
DAY 2	• Phonics • Spelling • Decodable Reader 32
DAY 3	• Independent Reader K.6.2 or Kindergarten Student Reader K.6.2
DAY 4	• Get Set, Roll! Reader 32 or Kindergarten Student Reader K.6.2
DAY 5	• Fluency/Comprehension • Independent Reader K.6.2

3 or 4 Day Plan

DAY 1	• Phonemic Awareness/ Phonics • Decodable Story 32
DAY 2	• Phonics • Spelling • Decodable Reader 32
DAY 3	• Independent Reader K.6.2 or Kindergarten Student Reader K.6.2
DAY 4	• Get Set, Roll! Reader 32 or Kindergarten Student Reader K.6.2

3 Day Plan: Eliminate the shaded box.

More Practice

For additional practice with this week's phonics skills and to develop fluency, have children reread the Decodable Story (Day 1) and the Decodable Reader (Day 2).

A Advanced · DAY 1

Phonemic Awareness•Phonics

■ **Decorate with Letters** Divide the class into three groups and assign each group the letter *A, I,* or *O* and a section of a classroom bulletin board. Give each group colored streamers and tape. Have children attach the streamers in the shape of their letter on the bulletin board. Encourage children to be creative with their letters, using streamers that are twisted or scrunched up to create texture. When the groups are finished, have them present their letters to the class and name several words that begin with their letter.

Objectives
• Identify the common sounds that letters represent.

A Advanced · DAY 2

Phonics•Spelling

■ **Connect /o/ to *Oo*** Display the *ox* Picture Card. What is this word? Name the sounds with me: /o/ /ks/, *ox*. What letter spells /o/? The letter *o* can stand for /o/ in words. Display the *box* Picture Card. Name the sounds in box with me: /b/ /o/ /ks/, *box*. What sound is in the middle? What letter spells that sound? What other /o/ words do you know?

■ **Spell Sounds** Give each child the following letter tiles: *f, h, l, o, p, s, t.* Listen to the sounds in the word *hot:* /h/ /o/ /t/, *hot*. What is the letter for /h/? It is *h*. Place your *h* tile in front of you. Continue with the remaining sounds. Then have children spell *pot, stop,* and *flop*.

Objectives
• Identify the common sounds that letters represent.
• Use letter-sound correspondences to spell consonant-vowel-consonant (CVC) words.

A Advanced

More Reading

Use Leveled Readers or other text at children's instructional level.

For a complete lesson plan and additional practice, see the **Leveled Reader Teaching Guide**.

Independent Reader K.6.2

■ **Practice High-Frequency Words** Write *said* on the board. Have volunteers say the word and use it in a sentence. Continue with the words *they, we,* and *come.*

■ **Activate Prior Knowledge** Remind children that a club hut is a place where children can come meet to play games and eat snacks. In the story, Jen and Zack make a club hut out of blankets and tin cans. Encourage children to share what they know about club huts. Have you ever made a club hut?

Independent
Reader K.6.2

■ **Character** Display the cover of *The Best Club Hut.* Have children tell about each character in the book and how he or she helps to make the club hut.

■ **Reread for Fluency** After rereading with children, model reading fluently for them. I am going to read this book aloud. I will read the words with no mistakes. I want you to read it aloud with me. Try to read the words just as I do.

• Use echo reading of Independent Reader K.6.2 to model reading fluently. Use your oral reading to model for children where to pause, when to change pitch, and which words to stress. Then have children reread orally three to four times, or until they can read with few or no mistakes.

■ **Read** For more practice with phonics and high-frequency words and to develop fluency, have children read Kindergarten Student Reader K.6.2. Use the instruction on pp. 156-157.

Objectives
• Read at least 25 high-frequency words from a commonly used list.
• Identify elements of a story including character.
• Describe characters in a story.

Small Group Time

More Reading

Use Leveled Readers or other text at children's instructional level.

A Advanced

DAY 4

Kindergarten Student Reader K.6.2

■ **Review** Display the cover of Kindergarten Student Reader K.6.2. This is Max and Jen and Dad. Tell me what they are doing. What are they wearing over their eyes? Why do you think they are wearing safety glasses?

Kindergarten Student Reader K.6.2

■ **Reread** Use Kindergarten Student Reader K.6.2 to practice reading fluently.

■ **Text to World** Ask children to think about safety. Why is it important to follow safety rules and to wear safety gear?

■ **Read** Have children read Get Set, Roll! Reader 32, *Max, the Hot Rod.* Use the instruction on p. 183.

Objectives
- Read at least 25 high-frequency words from a commonly used list.
- Make connections to the larger community.

A Advanced

DAY 5

Fluency•Comprehension

■ **Reread for Fluency** Use the Independent Reader K.6.2 to model reading fluently for children. I am going to read this selection aloud. I will read the words with no mistakes. I want you to read it aloud with me. Try to read the words just as I do.

Independent Reader K.6.2

■ **Comprehension** After children have finished reading, have them retell what they learned in the selection. Then have children write or draw a picture of the most important characters in the selection.

Objectives
- Read at least 25 high-frequency words from a commonly used list.
- Identify elements of a story including character.

 **DAY 1**

Concept Development

■ **Read the Concept Literacy Reader** To build background and vocabulary, read *We Build a Birdhouse* with children. Have them look at the pictures in the book. What are the people making? (a birdhouse) Read the book aloud, pausing to discuss each page. Model sentence patterns and vocabulary that describe the work being done. You can use a ruler to measure. You can use a tape to measure. On a second reading, have children talk about the work being done on each page.

■ **Develop Oral Language** Revisit *We Build a Birdhouse.* Then have children sing the following song with you to the tune of "Skip to My Lou":

> Hammer, drill, skip to my Lou,
> Measure, saw, skip to my Lou,
> Paint and glue, skip to my Lou,
> We will build a birdhouse.

Phonemic Awareness/Phonics

■ **Frontload Words with Initial and Medial /o/** Have children look at the picture on pp. 32–33 of *My Skills Buddy.* This picture shows people at the lake. What are the children doing? Who is playing? Who is eating? Listen to the word *ox.* Point to the ox. What sound does *ox* begin with? *Ox* begins with /o/. Repeat the procedure for medial /o/, pointing to the top. Then have children sing the following song with you to the tune of "Here We Go Round the Mulberry Bush" to introduce words in the picture containing initial or medial /o/:

> This is the way we ride the ox,
> Ride the ox, ride the ox.
> This is the way we ride the ox,
> So early in the morning.

Repeat for *mop the floor, spin the top,* and *lock the box.*

■ **Connect /o/ to *Oo*** Write these words on the board: *on, mop.* Read them aloud. Say new phrases such as: Is she *on* the ox? Does he have the *mop*? Point to *o* and ask: What letter is this? Yes, this is *o.* Spell *on* with the letter tiles, and read it aloud. Segment and blend each sound pointing to the corresponding tile. /o/ /n/, *on.* Repeat for medial /o/ and *mop.*

Content Objective
• Develop content knowledge related to building a toy farm.

Language Objectives
• Understand and use grade-level content area vocabulary.

• Recognize the sounds of English.

Concept Literacy Reader K.6.2

Daily Planner

DAY 1	• Concept Development • Phonemic Awareness/ Phonics • Listening Comprehension
DAY 2	• Comprehension • Vocabulary
DAY 3	• Phonemic Awareness/ Phonics • Conventions
DAY 4	• Phonemic Awareness/ Phonics • Concepts and Oral Language
DAY 5	• Language Workshop • Writing

Support for English Language Learners

Content Objective
- Understand character.

Language Objective
- Learn and use academic vocabulary.

Use Learning Strategies

Preview Use the illustrations on pp. 34–35 of *My Skills Buddy* to build children's understanding of plot and characters. Point to the top inset picture labeled *Characters* on p. 34. What are these animals? (turtle and rabbit or tortoise and hare) Point to the inset picture labeled *plot* on p. 35. Help children understand what has happened. What are the tortoise and the hare going to do? (run a race) How do you think they feel right now? (excited)

My Skills Buddy, pp. 34–35

ELL English Language Learners

DAY 1

Listening Comprehension: Character

- **Provide Scaffolding** Discuss the illustrations on pp. 34–35 in *My Skills Buddy* to frontload vocabulary and character identification. Point to the middle inset picture on p. 35. The tortoise and the hare are having a race. What happens during the race? (Hare falls asleep; tortoise keeps going.) Point to the bottom inset picture and help children understand that the tortoise is crossing the finish line. Who wins the race? (tortoise) Which animal should be able to run faster, a tortoise or a hare? (hare) Why does the hare lose the race? (He takes a nap.) Why do you think the hare takes a nap? (He is too sure he will win the race; He thinks he has more time; and so on.)

- **Prepare for the Read Aloud** The modified Read Aloud below prepares children for listening to the oral reading of "The Monkeys Build a Tree House" on p. 127.

Read Aloud

The Monkeys' Tree House

Molly, Megan, Mitch, and Manfred are monkeys. They want to build a tree house. They get wood, nails, and tools.

Molly says they have to cut the wood. Megan holds up the saw. But Mitch knows they have to measure first. Then Megan cuts the wood.

Manfred says, "Now we build!" He holds up the screwdriver and some nails. But Molly knows that isn't right. She tells Manfred to use the hammer to put in the nails.

The monkeys hammer and build. Soon their tree house is done. But it is still on the ground… the monkeys forgot to put it in the tree!

- **First Listening:** Write the title of the Read Aloud on the board. This story is about monkeys that want to build a tree house. They are so excited that they want to start building right away. They forget to do things in the right order. After reading, ask children to recall the names of the characters and what their mistakes are. Megan tries to saw the wood before measuring it. Manfred tries to put nails in wood using a screwdriver instead of a hammer.

- **Second Listening:** Write the words *monkeys* and *tree house* on the board. As you listen to the story, think about what the monkeys did. What should the monkeys do before they saw the wood? (measure it) After reading, point to *monkeys* on the board and ask children to tell something about the monkeys. Elicit responses such as *too excited* and *not careful*.

Objectives
- Demonstrate English comprehension by employing analytical skills commensurate with content area and grade level needs. • Expand reading skills by employing analytical skills commensurate with content area and grade level needs.

 **DAY 2**

Comprehension

- **Provide Scaffolding** Display *Old MacDonald had a Woodshop.* Lead a picture walk through the story, naming what you see in the illustrations and describing what is happening. Use gestures and facial expressions to convey meaning. Focus on the following:

  - **Set the Scene** Use the cover of the Trade Book to help children understand that this story takes place in a woodshop on a farm. Describe what a farm is like and explain what a woodshop is. A farm has different animals. They live in a barn. In this story, Old MacDonald is a sheep. Point to the sheep on pp. 5 and 6. Old MacDonald has a woodshop. In her woodshop, she can build things with wood, using a saw and other tools. What do you think Old MacDonald will build?

  - **Frontload Vocabulary** As you lead the picture walk, use the illustrations to introduce unfamiliar words in the text. Include *saw, drill, hammer, screwdriver, file,* and *chisel.* Display p. 6. Old MacDonald is holding a saw. What does a saw do? (cuts wood) Repeat for drill (pp. 8–9), hammer (p. 11), chisel (p. 13), file (pp. 14–15), and screwdriver (pp. 16–17).

Vocabulary: Location Words

- **Frontload Vocabulary** Have children turn to p. 48 of *My Skills Buddy.* Talk about each picture, using the location words *train station, police station, fire station,* and *gas station.* For example, point to the picture of the train station. This is a train station. Here is the train. Here is where the people wait to get on or off the train when it stops. Point these out in the picture. Then repeat the procedure, inviting children to talk about the pictures, showing the location words *police station, fire station,* and *gas station.*

- **Provide Scaffolding** Write the word *station* on the board four times. Read the word aloud with children. Have children look at p. 48 of *My Skills Buddy.* As children identify the train, police, fire, and gas stations, write *train, police, fire,* and *gas* in front of the word *station* on the board. These words tell us the name of the station.

- **Practice** Have children work in pairs. Have each child draw a picture of the kind of station of his or her choice. Then have the child hold up the picture. Have other children identify which kind of station it is.

Content Objective
- Develop background knowledge.

Language Objective
- Learn and use location words.

Use Learning Strategies
Put up children's pictures under a label for each kind of station name they learned.

Trade Book

Support for English Language Learners

Content Objective
- Use learning strategies.

Language Objectives
- Connect /o/ and *Oo*.
- Use location words.

 Transfer Skills

Pronouncing /o/ If Spanish speakers struggle to say short *o* words, point out that /o/ is similar to the sound of the letter *a* in Spanish. For example, have children practice saying the following word pairs: *Mami, Mom; Papá, Poppa.*

Use Learning Strategies

Draw a pot on the board. Help children understand that when we use prepositional phrases, we are referring to locations. Say these sentences and point to the pot: The pot is on the stove. The pot is on top of the table.

Phonemic Awareness/Phonics

- **Isolate Initial and Medial /o/** Say *on,* and then model segmenting sounds by saying /o/ /n/. Emphasize the initial sound in the word. Repeat for medial /o/ with *mop.* Help children identify the medial sound in the word.

- **/o/ Spelled *Oo*** Write brief sentences with words that contain /o/ on the board: *The pot is hot. Tom got my socks.* Segment and blend words, such as *pot* = /p/ /o/ /t/ = *pot,* as you point to the words. Have children repeat the words.

Conventions: Prepositional Phrases

- **Provide Scaffolding** Point to the first image on pp. 4–5 of *Old MacDonald had a Woodshop.* The animals are on the farm. The words *on the farm* tell us where the animals are. Point to the wheelbarrow. The wood is in the wheelbarrow. The words *in the wheelbarrow* tell us where the wood is. Words like *on the farm* and *in the wheelbarrow* tell us where things are.

- **Practice** Let's name some other words that tell us where things are. Page through the Trade Book and have children look at the pictures and describe locations with phrases such as: *nail in the wood* (p. 11) and *board on the table* (p. 13).

  Leveled LS Support

  Beginning/Intermediate For each prepositional phrase, have a child demonstrate putting an object in the location. For example, have a child put an object *on the table* or *in the jar.* While performing the action, have the child identify where he or she is putting the object. (Child's name) puts the book *on the table.* Have children repeat the phrases after you and then think of their own prepositional phrases to show location.

  Advanced/Advanced-High Include some of the more challenging words in the story, such as *chisel on the wood* (p. 13), *paintbrush in the jar* (p. 18), or *mouse under the table* (pp. 26–27). Have children point to each picture and repeat the phrase to deepen their understanding.

Objectives
• Internalize new academic language by using and reusing it in meaningful ways in speaking activities that build concept and language attainment. • Develop repertoire of learning strategies commensurate with grade-level learning expectations.

 **English Language Learners**   **DAY** 4

Phonemic Awareness/Phonics

■ **Review /a/ and /i/** To review initial /a/ and /i/ in words, ask a question with words that contain /a/. Can an *ant* use an *ax?* Have children pronounce the words *ant* and *ax.* Then repeat the procedure for /i/ with the sentence: Will *it* be *in?* Have children take turns repeating the questions to a partner.

■ **/a/ Spelled *Aa* and /i/ Spelled *Ii*** Using letter tiles, display the words *ant* and *in.* Hold up the letter tile for *a.* What is this letter? Confirm that it is *a.* Point to the word *ant* and read it aloud. Segment and blend each sound in the word: /a/ /n/ /t/, *ant.* As you pronounce each sound, point to the corresponding tile. Repeat for /i/ and *in.*

Concepts and Oral Language

■ **Revisit Talk with Me Chart 32A** Display the chart. Have students name the tools in the photos. Where is the saw? Have a child point to it on the chart. Where is the hammer? Have a child point to it. Help children find the screwdriver, drill, file, and chisel. Have them repeat the names of the tools with you.

■ **Develop Oral Language** Introduce language patterns that help describe the tools on Talk with Me Chart 32A. Write this sentence frame on the board: *The _____ is used to _____.* Let's use this sentence pattern to talk about the tools: *The saw is used to saw wood. The hammer is used to put nails in wood.* Have children suggest other sentences using the frame for the following tools: screwdriver (drive screws into wood), drill (drill holes in wood), file (file rough spots on wood), and chisel (chip pieces off wood). Have children repeat the names of the tools and their uses. Then play a game with children in which you ask a question about the pictures, such as: What is the drill used to do? Have children point to the correct picture and then answer your question with a sentence, such as *The drill is used to drill holes in wood.*

 Leveled Support

Beginning Have children repeat the question you ask. Let them take a turn pointing to a picture on the chart.

Intermediate Ask questions to help children notice more details about the tools in the chart, such as: What does the hammer look like? What do you think it is made from?

Advanced/Advanced-High Encourage children to use their prior knowledge of tools to think of other descriptive words, such as *metal, pointed,* or *teeth.*

Content Objectives
• Develop oral language.
• Use learning strategies.

Language Objectives
• Connect /a/ with *Aa* and /i/ with *Ii*.
• Learn English language patterns.

Use Learning Strategies
Work with children to help them name things they would like to build with wood and the tools shown on the chart. List the item next to the child's name on the board. Have children talk about how they would go about building their project.

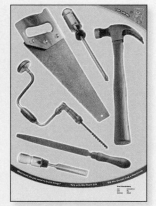

Talk with Me Chart 32A

Support for English Language Learners

Content Objectives

- Understand *Old MacDonald had a Woodshop*.

- Practice character.

Language Objectives

- Retell a selection through speaking and writing.

- Write using grade-level vocabulary.

Monitor and Self-Correct

Remind children to look at the chart if they have trouble remembering some of the tools.

Home Language Support

Invite children to share ideas in their home languages before creating their sentences.

Language Workshop: Retell

■ **Introduce and Model** Turn to pp. 4–5 of *Old MacDonald had a Woodshop.* Look at the sheep in this picture. Do you remember her name? (Old MacDonald) What is Old MacDonald doing? (carrying wood into the woodshop) Model the action. What does Old MacDonald have in her woodshop? (tools) Let's talk about the tools Old MacDonald uses and what she builds.

■ **Practice** Organize children into pairs. Assign each pair one tool used in *Old MacDonald had a Woodshop.* One child will act as though he or she is holding the wood. The other child will act as though he or she is using the tool. Let children practice and then perform their action for the class. Have the other children name the action and the tool being used. What tool is (child's name) using?

Writing: Write About *Old MacDonald had a Woodshop*

■ **Prepare for Writing** We acted out using the tools that Old MacDonald used. Let's remember what Old MacDonald is building. (toy farm) Have each child draw Old MacDonald's toy farm. Tell me about Old MacDonald. (Elicit character traits such as *busy* and *happy*.) What does she like to do? (build things from wood)

■ **Create Sentences About Old MacDonald** Have children copy the sentence starter *She makes _____.* Have children think of words for things Old MacDonald builds by looking at the picture on pp. 26–27. Elicit *pig, hen,* and *cat* and explain that these are small wooden toys. To complete the sentence frame, have children write the name of one thing Old MacDonald made. Then have them share their ideas about how Old MacDonald must feel at the beginning and end of the story.

Leveled Support

Beginning/Intermediate Write the sentence frames for children and have them write or dictate words to complete the sentences.

Advanced/Advanced-High Encourage children to write their sentences on their own. Write the sentence frame: *She is _____.* Have children complete the sentence with a word or words such as: *busy, a builder.* Remind children to help each other.

Objectives

• Monitor written language production and employ self-corrective techniques or other resources. • Learn new expressions heard during classroom instruction and interactions. • Expand and internalize initial English vocabulary by retelling simple stories and basic information represented or supported by pictures.

Common Core Standards
Weekly Planning Guide

Selection: Building Beavers
Genre: Expository Nonfiction

Alignment of the Common Core Standards with This Week's Skills and Strategies

This Week's Common Core Standards for English Language Arts	Instructional Summary
Reading Standards for Informational Text	
Informational Text 1. With prompting and support, ask and answer questions about key details in a text.	This week, children are introduced to the concept of **main idea.** Children learn that the main idea is what the story is mostly about. They also learn that details help them understand the main idea of a story. The main selection provides instruction to **predict** what the selection is about and to **set a purpose** for reading.
Informational Text 2. With prompting and support, identify the main topic and retell key details of a text.	
Informational Text 8. With prompting and support, identify the reasons an author gives to support points in a text.	
Informational Text 10. Actively engage in group reading activities with purpose and understanding.	
Foundational Skills Standards	
Foundational Skills 3.b Associate the long and short sounds with the common spellings (graphemes) for the five major vowels.	This week's lesson includes work with **blending** phonemes to make words including short vowel sounds. Children learn high-frequency words to identify words that are irregularly spelled.
Foundational Skills 3.c. Read common high-frequency words by sight. (e.g., *the, of, to, you, she, my, is, are, do, does*).	
Writing Standards	
Writing 2. Use a combination of drawing, dictating, and writing to compose informative/explanatory texts in which they name what they are writing about and supply some information about the topic.	Writing activities include learning about things to find out why things happen. Group activities for writing include a **response** to the literature, a **rhyme,** and writing **questions** about bears. The wrap-up activities ask children to write sentences in the correct order to tell how a beaver builds a lodge.
Speaking and Listening Standards	
Speaking/Listening 2. Confirm understanding of a text read aloud or information presented orally or through other media by asking and answering questions about key details and requesting clarification if something is not understood.	In the **listening** and **speaking** activities, children share their ideas and then learn to tell how to do or make something by giving oral instructions. Children restate the instruction, focusing on the order of the instructions.
Language Standards	
Language 1.b. Use frequently occurring nouns and verbs.	Children study **sentences,** learning that a sentence is a group of words that tells a complete thought. The vocabulary activity deals with words for actions (*dig, carry, eat, sleep*).
Language 1.f. Produce and expand complete sentences in shared language activities.	
Language 2. Demonstrate command of the conventions of standard English capitalization, punctuation, and spelling when writing.	

Additional Support for a Common Core Standard This Week

Use the following instruction to supplement the teaching of one of this week's Common Core Standards.

Common Core Standard: Language 1.f.
Write the following sentences on the board:
The beaver chewed on logs.
The beaver built a lodge.

- Read the first sentence and help children understand that the words are a telling sentence. Point out the capital letter at the beginning and the period at the end. Repeat the procedure for the next sentence.
- Ask children to identify the action words in the sentences. Have them circle the action words *chewed* and *built.*
- Have children work with partners to add words to one of the sentences to expand the sentence. Use this example: *The beaver built a lodge with logs.* Then have children share their work.

ISBN-13: 978-0-328-64361-5   ISBN-10: 0-328-64361-0

Unit 6

THE BIG **What are different ways of building?**

Common Core Standards and Concept Development

- Introduce and explore this unit's weekly concepts through rich, structured conversations
- Develop complex content knowledge and vocabulary
- Expand on a single concept with engaging literature and nonfiction
- Build better readers in all content areas
- Align instruction to **Common Core Anchor Standards**

Week 1

Building with Dad

Question of the Week
How is a school built?

Concept Talk Guide children as they discuss questions such as:

- What is cement used for?
- What kinds of machines are used to build the school?

Writing Have children turn to p. 410 of *Reader's and Writer's Notebook*. Have them write or dictate a list of things from *Building with Dad* they want to learn more about.

Week 2

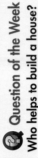

Old MacDonald had a Woodshop

Question of the Week
What tools do you need to build things?

Concept Talk Guide children as they discuss questions such as:

- What kind of sounds do these tools make?

Writing Have children turn to p. 422 of *Reader's and Writer's Notebook*. Have them complete the song "Old MacDonald" by copying an animal word from the list and then illustrating that animal. Sing the song with children, featuring each child's picture for a verse.

You Are Here: Week 3

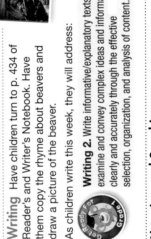

Building Beavers

Question of the Week
How do beavers build their homes?

As children answer this unit's Big Question and this week's Question of the Week, they will address:

Reading 1. Read closely to determine what the text says explicitly and to make logical inferences from it; cite specific textual evidence when writing or speaking to support conclusions drawn from the text. **(Also Reading 2.)**

Concept Talk Guide children as they discuss questions such as:

- What new information did you learn about beavers?

As children answer this week's Concept Talk question, they will address:

Speaking/Listening 2. Integrate and evaluate information presented in diverse media and formats, including visually, quantitatively, and orally.

Writing Have children turn to p. 434 of *Reader's and Writer's Notebook*. Have them copy the rhyme about beavers and draw a picture of the beaver.

As children write this week, they will address:

Writing 2. Write informative/explanatory texts to examine and convey complex ideas and information clearly and accurately through the effective selection, organization, and analysis of content.

Listening and Speaking On page 69, children learn to interpret information. By doing so, they address:

Speaking/Listening 2. Integrate and evaluate information presented in diverse media and formats, including visually, quantitatively, and orally.

Week 4

Alistair and Kip's Great Adventure!

Question of the Week
What can friends build together?

Concept Talk Guide children as they discuss questions such as:

- What would you and your friends build using the large box? Would it be real or make-believe?

Writing Have children turn to p. 446 of *Reader's and Writer's Notebook*. Have them copy the poem about Alistair and Kip's trip and then draw a picture to go with it.

Week 5

The House That Tony Lives In

Question of the Week
Who helps to build a house?

Concept Talk Guide children as they discuss questions such as:

- What happened to this builder? How did the builder solve the problem?

Have children turn to p. 458 of *Reader's and Writer's Notebook*. Have them copy a line from the poem about a house and then draw a picture of the house.

Week 6

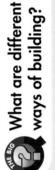

Ants and Their Nests

Question of the Week
How do ants build their nests?

Concept Talk Guide children as they discuss questions such as:

- Where do birds build their homes?
- Why do many animals build their homes in the ground?

Writing Reread and discuss what you wrote about how a bird builds a nest, underlining key words in your draft. Have children write or dictate the group draft or copy the underlined key words on p. 474 in *Reader's and Writer's Notebook*.

This Week's ELL Overview

ELL Handbook

- Maximize Literacy and Cognitive Engagement
- Research Into Practice
- Full Weekly Support for Every Selection

Building Beavers
- Routines to Support Instruction

- Transfer Activities
- Professional Development

Daily Leveled ELL Notes

ELL notes appear throughout this week's instruction and ELL Support is on the DI pages of your Teacher's Edition. The following is a sample of an ELL note from this week.

English Language Learners

Beginning Recall Vocabulary Explain to children that a beaver's home is called a *lodge.* We have learned other names for animal homes. What kind of home does a bird live in? What kind of home do bees live in?

Intermediate Support High-Frequency Words Have children choose one high-frequency word to write on their Write-On Board. Pair children and have them take turns reading the high-frequency word on their partner's Write-On Board. Then have them use the word in a sentence.

Advanced Support Writing Tell children that the first part of the rhyme is the word *pet.* Write *pet* on the board. Then have children think of words that rhyme with *pet.* Use each of the words in the rhyme to see which word makes sense.

Advanced High Physical Response Play a simple game. Have children line up. Tell them to march toward you. When you point to the Stop sign on p. 69 of *My Skills Buddy,* children should then stop walking.

ELL by Strand

The ELL lessons on this week's Support for English Language Learners pages are organized by strand. They offer additional scaffolding for the core curriculum. Leveled support notes on these pages address the different proficiency levels in your class. See pages DI•46–DI•51.

ELL Guy
Dr. Jim Cummins

The Three Pillars of ELL Instruction

ELL Strands	Activate Prior Knowledge	Access Content	Extend Language
Vocabulary p. DI•48	Frontload Vocabulary	Provide Scaffolding	Practice
Reading Comprehension p. DI•48	Provide Scaffolding	Set the Scene	Frontload Vocabulary
Phonics, Spelling, and Word Analysis pp. DI•46, DI•49–DI•50	Frontload Words with Initial and Medial /e/	Isolate Initial and Medial /e/	Review Short Vowels and Consonants
Listening Comprehension p. DI•47	Prepare for the Read Aloud	First Listening	Second Listening
Conventions and Writing pp. DI•49, DI•51	Provide Scaffolding/ Introduce and Model	Practice	Leveled Practice Activities/ Leveled Writing Activities
Concept Development p. DI•46	Read the Concept Literacy Reader	Read the Concept Literacy Reader	Develop Oral Language

This Week's Practice Stations Overview

Six Weekly Practice Stations with Leveled Activities can be found at the beginning of each week of instruction. For this week's Practice Stations, see pp. 212–213.

Small Group Teacher-led

Classroom Management Handbook for Differentiated Instruction Practice Stations

Practice Stations

Daily Leveled Center Activities

◯ Below   ▢ Advanced

△ On-Level   🄴🄻🄻

Practice Stations Flip Charts

	Listen Up	Word Work	Words to Know	Let's Write	Read for Meaning	Let's Make Art
Objectives	• Identify beginning, middle, and ending sounds of words.	• Review and build words with short *o*.	• Identify and use words for locations.	• Write a song about how people build.	• Identify and describe story characters.	• Draw a picture of tools.
Materials	• *Listen Up* Flip Chart Activity 33 • Picture Cards • Teacher-made Spinner divided into eight equal sections; with consonants you wish to review, include blends • paper, pencils, crayons	• *Word Work* Flip Chart Activity 33 • Alphabet Cards • Picture Cards: *block, box, clock, fox, mop, rock, sock, top* • Letter Tiles • paper, pencils	• *Words to Know* Flip Chart Activity 33 • Find pictures for location words: *train station, police station, fire station, gas station* • Teacher-made Word Cards • paper, pencils, crayons	• *Let's Write* Flip Chart Activity 33 • pencil, paper, crayons	• *Read for Meaning* Flip Chart Activity 33 • Trade Book *Old MacDonald had a Woodshop* • pencil, crayons, paper	• *Let's Make Art* Flip Chart Activity 33 • art paper, crayons

This Week on Reading Street!

Question of the Week
How do beavers build their homes?

Daily Plan

Don't Wait Until Friday

Whole Group
- ◉ /e/ Spelled *Ee*
- ◉ Main Idea
- • Vocabulary

MONITOR PROGRESS | **Success Predictor**

Day 1	Day 2	Day 3	Day 4	Day 5
Check Phonemic Awareness	Check Sound Spelling/ Retelling	Check Word Reading	Check Phonemic Awareness	Check Oral Vocabulary

Small Group

Teacher-Led

- • Reading Support
- • Skill Support
- • Fluency Practice

Practice Stations

Independent Activities

Customize Literacy More support for a Balanced Literacy approach, see pp. CL•1–CL•31.

Whole Group
- • Writing
- • Conventions: Telling Sentences
- • Listening and Speaking

Assessment
- • Day 5 Assessment for Phonics
- • Day 5 Assessment for Comprehension

You Are Here! Unit 6 Week 3

This Week's Reading Selections

Big Book
Genre: **Expository Nonfiction**

Decodable Reader 33

Leveled Readers

Get Set, Roll! Reader 33

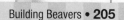

Resources on Reading Street!

	Build Concepts	Phonemic Awareness and Phonics	Vocabulary
Whole Group	 Talk With Me/ Sing With Me	 Student Edition pp. 52–53 Student Edition p. 56	 Student Edition p. 57 Student Edition p. 68
Go Digital	• Concept Talk Video • Sing with Me Animations	• eReaders	
Small Group and Independent Practice	 Practice Station Flip Chart Leveled Readers	 Practice Station Flip Chart Decodable Reader 33 Leveled Readers Get Set, Roll! Reader 33	 Practice Station Flip Chart Student Edition p. 57
Go Digital	• eReaders	• eReaders • Letter Tile Drag and Drop	
Customize Literacy	• Leveled Readers	• Decodable Reader	• High-Frequency Word Cards
Go Digital	• Concept Talk Video • Big Question Video • eReaders	• eReaders	• Sing with Me Animations

Question of the Week
How do beavers build their homes?

<table>
<tr><td>Comprehension</td><td>Fluency</td><td>Conventions and Writing</td></tr>
<tr>
<td>

Student Edition pp. 54–55   Big Book

</td>
<td>

Decodable Reader 33   Kdg. Student Reader K.6.3   Get Set, Roll! Reader 33

</td>
<td>

Reader's and Writer's Notebook

</td>
</tr>
<tr>
<td>

• Envision It! Animations
• eReaders

</td>
<td>

• eReaders

</td>
<td>

• Grammar Jammer

</td>
</tr>
<tr>
<td>

Practice Station Flip Chart   Leveled Readers   Get Set, Roll! Reader 33

</td>
<td>

Practice Station Flip Chart   Leveled Readers

</td>
<td>

Practice Station Flip Chart   Reader's and Writer's Notebook

</td>
</tr>
<tr>
<td>

• Envision It! Animations
• eReaders

</td>
<td>

• eReaders

</td>
<td>

• Grammar Jammer

</td>
</tr>
<tr>
<td>

• Leveled Readers

</td>
<td>

• Leveled Readers

</td>
<td>

• *Reader's and Writer's Notebook*

</td>
</tr>
<tr>
<td>

• Envision It! Animations
• eReaders

</td>
<td>

• eReaders

</td>
<td>

• Grammar Jammer

</td>
</tr>
</table>

You Are Here! Unit 6 Week 3

Week 3

My 5-Day Planner for Reading Street!

MONITOR PROGRESS *Don't Wait Until Friday*

	Check Phonemic Awareness **Day 1** pages 214–229	Check Sound-Spelling Check Retelling **Day 2** pages 230–247

Get Ready to Read	**Concept Talk,** 214
	Oral Vocabulary, 215 *beaver, lodge, paddle, river, stream, lake*
	Phonemic Awareness, 216–217
	  ◉ Initial and Medial /e/
	Phonics, 218–219
	  ◉ /e/ Spelled *Ee*
	Handwriting, 220 Letters *E* and *e*
	High-Frequency Words, 221
	  Review *the, was, to, like, from*
	READ Decodable Story 33, 222–223
		Concept Talk, 230
		Oral Vocabulary, 231 *beaver, lodge*
		Phonemic Awareness, 232–233
		  ◉ Initial and Medial /e/
		Phonics, 234–235
		  ◉ /e/ Spelled *Ee*
		Handwriting, 236 Words with *Ee*
		High-Frequency Words, 237 *the, was, to, like, from*
		READ Decodable Reader 33, 238–239

Read and Comprehend	**Listening Comprehension,** 224–225
	  ◉ Main Idea
		Listening Comprehension, 240
		  ◉ Main Idea
		READ Big Book—First Read, 240
		  Building Beavers
		Retell, 241
		Think, Talk, and Write, 242

Language Arts	**Conventions,** 226 Telling Sentences **Writing,** 227 Wonderful, Marvelous Me! **Daily Handwriting,** 227 Letters *E* and *e* **Listening and Speaking,** 228 Interpret Information **Wrap Up Your Day,** 228 **Extend Your Day!,** 229	**Conventions,** 243 Telling Sentences **Writing,** 244 Respond to Literature **Daily Handwriting,** 244 Letters *E* and *e* **Vocabulary,** 245 Words for Actions **Wrap Up Your Day,** 246 **Extend Your Day!,** 247

You Are Here! Unit 6 Week 3

How do beavers build their homes?

Check Word Reading	Check Phonemic Awareness	Check Oral Vocabulary
Day 3 pages 248–277	**Day 4** pages 278–289	**Day 5** pages 290–303
Concept Talk, 248 **Oral Vocabulary,** 249 *paddle, river* **Phonemic Awareness,** 250–251 ◉ Initial and Medial /e/ **Phonics,** 252–253 ◉ /e/ Spelled *Ee* **READ Kindergarten Student Reader K.6.3,** 254–255	**Concept Talk,** 278 **Oral Vocabulary,** 279 *stream, lake* Review **Phonemic Awareness,** 280 Short Vowels and Consonants Review **Phonics,** 281 Short Vowels and Consonants **Spelling,** 282 ◉ /e/ Spelled *Ee* **READ Get Set, Roll! Reader 33,** 283	**Concept Wrap Up,** 290 **Oral Vocabulary,** 291 *beaver, lodge, paddle, river, stream, lake* Review **Phonemic Awareness,** 292 ◉ /e/ Review **Phonics,** 293 ◉ /e/ Spelled *Ee* **Assessment,** 294–295 Monitor Progress
Comprehension, 256 ◉ Main Idea **READ Big Book—Second Read,** 257–271 *Building Beavers*	**Comprehension,** 284 ◉ Main Idea Review Cause and Effect **READ Big Book—Third Read,** 285 *Building Beavers*	**Let's Practice It!,** 296–297 Fable **Assessment,** 298–299 Monitor Progress
Conventions, 272 Prepositional Phrases **Writing,** 273 Genre: Rhyme **Daily Handwriting,** 273 Letters *E* and *e* **Listening and Speaking,** 274–275 Interpret Information **Wrap Up Your Day,** 276 **Extend Your Day!,** 277	**Conventions,** 286 Telling Sentences **Writing,** 287 Extend the Concept **Daily Handwriting,** 287 Letters *E* and *e* **Vocabulary,** 288 Words for Actions **Wrap Up Your Day,** 288 **Extend Your Day!,** 289	**Review Conventions,** 300 Telling Sentences **Writing,** 301 This Week We… **Daily Handwriting,** 301 Letters *E* and *e* **Wrap Up Your Week!,** 302 How do beavers build their homes? **Extend Your Day!,** 303

Grouping Options for Differentiated Instruction
Turn the page for the small group time lesson plan.

Planning Small Group Time on Reading Street!

SMALL GROUP TIME RESOURCES

DAY 1

Look for this Small Group Time box each day to help meet the individual needs of all your children. Differentiated instruction lessons appear on the DI pages at the end of each week.

Teacher-Led

SI Strategic Intervention	**OL** On-Level	**A** Advanced
Teacher-Led	**Teacher-Led**	**Teacher-Led**
• Phonemic Awareness and Phonics	• Phonemic Awareness and Phonics	• Phonemic Awareness and Phonics
Reread Decodable Story	**Reread** Decodable Story	**Reread** Decodable Story for Fluency

ELL Place English language learners in the groups that correspond to their reading abilities in English.

Practice Stations
• Listen Up
• Word Work

Independent Activities
• Read Independently
• *Reader's and Writer's Notebook*
• Concept Talk Video

ELL Poster 33

Day 1

SI Strategic Intervention		**Phonemic Awareness and Phonics,** DI•35
		Reread Decodable Story 33, DI•35
OL On-Level		**Phonemic Awareness and Phonics,** DI•40
		Reread Decodable Story 33, DI•35
A Advanced		**Phonemic Awareness and Phonics,** DI•43
		Reread Decodable Story 33 for Fluency, DI•43
 **English Language Learners**		DI•46–DI•47
		Frontload Concept
		Phonemic Awareness and Phonics
		Comprehension Skill

You Are Here! Unit 6 Week 3

Reading Street Response
to Intervention Kit

Reading Street Leveled
Practice Stations Kit

? Question of the Week
How do beavers build their homes?

 **SI** Strategic Intervention

Decodable
Reader

Listen to Me Reader

Busy Beavers
By Alison Blank

Concept Literacy Reader

A BIG DENT

Get Set, Roll! Reader

OL On-Level

Go Camping

Kindergarten
Student Reader

A BIG DENT

Get Set, Roll! Reader

The Red Egg

Decodable Reader

A Advanced

A Small Trip
By Donna Latham
Illustrated by Karen Bell

Independent
Reader

The Red Egg

Decodable Reader

Small Group Weekly Plan

Day 2	Day 3	Day 4	Day 5
Phonemic Awareness and Phonics, DI•36 **Reread** Decodable Reader 33, DI•36	**Phonemic Awareness and Phonics,** DI•37 **Read** Concept Literacy Reader K.6.3, DI•37	**Phonemic Awareness and Phonics,** DI•38 **Read** Get Set, Roll! Reader 33, DI•38	**Phonics Review,** DI•39 **Read** Listen to Me Reader K.6.3, DI•39
Phonemic Awareness and Phonics, DI•40 **Reread** Decodable Reader 33, DI•40	**Phonemic Awareness and Phonics,** DI•41 **Read** Kindergarten Student Reader K.6.3, DI•41	**Review Phonics and High-Frequency Words Read** Get Set, Roll! Reader 33, DI•42	**Phonics Review,** DI•42 **Reread** Leveled Books, DI•42
Phonics and Spelling, DI•43 **Reread** Decodable Reader 33 for Fluency, DI•43	**Read** Independent Reader K.6.3 or Kindergarten Student Reader K.6.3, DI•44	**Read** Get Set, Roll! Reader 33, or **Reread** Kindergarten Student Reader K.6.3, DI•45	**Fluency and Comprehension,** DI•45 **Reread** Independent Reader for Fluency, DI•45
DI•48 Comprehension Skill Frontload Vocabulary	DI•49 Review Phonemic Awareness and Phonics Scaffold Conventions	DI•50 Review Phonemic Awareness and Phonics Revisit Concepts and Oral Language	DI•51 Language Workshop Writing

Practice Stations for Everyone on Reading Street!

Listen Up!
Beginning, middle, and ending sounds

Objectives
• Identify beginning, middle, and ending sounds of words

Materials
• *Listen Up!* Flip Chart Activity 33
• Picture Cards
• Use a teacher-made spinner divided into eight equal sections. Write in consonants you wish to review, including blends. Make an arrow to affix in the middle.
• paper, pencils, crayons

Differentiated Activiites

⬤ Spin the spinner. Say the sound we learned for the letter the spinner lands on. Find a Picture Card for a word that has the same sound at the beginning, middle, or end. Draw a picture of something with the same sound at the beginning, middle, or end.

▲ Spin the spinner. Say the sound. Find a Picture Card that has the same sound at the beginning, middle, or end. Draw a picture of three things that have the same sound at the beginning, middle, or end.

■ Spin the spinner. Say the sound. Write five words that have the same sound at the beginning, middle, or end.

Word Work
/o/ spelled *Oo*

Objectives
• Review and build words with short *o*.

Materials
• *Word Work* Flip Chart Activity 33
• Alphabet Cards
• Picture Cards: *block, box, clock, fox, mop, rock, sock, top*
• Letter Tiles
• paper, pencils

Differentiated Activiites

⬤ Find the *Oo* Alphabet Card. Look for Picture Cards with short *o* in the middle. Use the Letter Tiles to build the word *box*.

▲ Find the *Oo* Alphabet Card. Look for Picture Cards with short *o* in the middle. Use the Letter Tiles to build the word *box*. Change a the *b* to *f*. Read the new word.

■ Find the *Oo* Alphabet Card. Look for Picture Cards with short *o* in the middle. Use the Letter Tiles to build the word on one of your cards. Take away or add letters at the beginning or the end of your word to build three new words. Write the words on your paper.

Technology
• Letter Tiles Drag and Drop

Words To Know
Location words

Objectives
• Identify and use words for locations.

Materials
• *Words to Know* Flip Chart Activity 33
• Find pictures (or take quick digital photos and print out) for location words: *train station, police station, fire station, gas station.*
• Teacher-made word cards for *train station, police station, fire station, gas station*
• paper, pencils, crayons

Differentiated Activiites

⬤ Choose a picture card and say the name for each picture.

▲ Match the picture cards and word cards that show locations. Tell what people do at each place.

■ Match the picture cards and word cards that show locations. Write a sentence that tells something people do at each place.

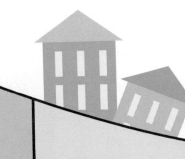

You Are Here! Unit 6 Week 3

Use this week's materials from the Reading Street Leveled Practice Stations Kit to organize this week's stations.

Key
● Below-Level Activities
▲ On-Level Activities
■ Advanced Activities

Practice Station Flip Chart

Let's Write!
Song

Objectives
• Write a song about how people build.

Materials
• *Let's Write!* Flip Chart Activity 33
• pencil, paper, crayons

Differentiated Activities

● Think of a simple song that you know. Make up new words for the song that tell about building something.

▲ Think of a simple song that you know. Make up new words for the song that tell about building something. Tell about tools builders use.

■ Think of a simple song that you know. Make up new words for the song that tell about building something. Tell what tools people use to build. Tell what sounds the tools make.

Technology
• Online Journal

Read For Meaning
Character

Objectives
• Identify and describe story characters.

Materials
• *Read for Meaning* Flip Chart Activity 33
• Trade Book *Old MacDonald had a Workshop*
• pencil, crayons, paper

Differentiated Activities

A **character** is who or what a story is about. A good way to understand a story is to think about the characters.

● Read your book. Point to the characters in the story. Draw a picture of each character.

▲ Read your book. Name the characters in the story. Draw a picture that shows what the characters do.

■ Read your book. Name the characters in the story. Draw pictures of the characters. Write sentences that tell something about each character.

Let's Make Art!

Objectives
• Draw a picture of tools.

Materials
• *Let's Make Art!* Flip Chart Activity 33
• art paper, crayons

Differentiated Activities

● What kinds of tools do people use to build things? Draw a big toolbox on your paper. Draw pictures of tools inside the toolbox.

▲ What kinds of tools do people use to build things? Draw a big toolbox on your paper. Draw pictures of tools inside the toolbox. Name each tool.

■ What kinds of tools do people use to build things? Draw a big toolbox on your paper. Draw pictures of tools inside the toolbox. Write a sentence about the tools.

Week 3

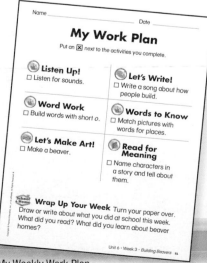

My Weekly Work Plan

Objectives

- Share information and ideas about the concept.

Today at a Glance

Oral Vocabulary
beaver, lodge, paddle, river, stream, lake

Phonemic Awareness
◉ Initial and Medial /e/

Phonics
◉ /e/ Spelled *Ee*

Handwriting
E and *e*

High-Frequency Words
the, was, to, like, from

Comprehension
◉ Main Idea

Conventions
Telling Sentences

Writing
Wonderful, Marvelous Me!

Listening and Speaking
Interpret Information

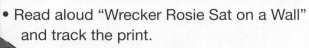

on Reading Street

Start your engines!

Display p. 16 of *Truckery Rhymes.*

- Read aloud "Wrecker Rosie Sat on a Wall" and track the print.
  - Reread the rhyme and have children chime in as they wish.
  - Ask children to identify the rhyming words. (*smashes, bashes*)

Truckery Rhymes

Concept Talk

Question of the Week

How do beavers build their homes?

Introduce the concept

To build concepts and to focus their attention, tell children that this week they will talk, sing, read, and write about **beavers and how they build their homes**. Write the question of the week and track the print as you read it.

Play the CD that features an animal expert telling about beavers. What new information did you learn about beavers?

 Background Building Audio

ROUTINE **Activate Prior Knowledge** **Team Talk**

① **Think** Have children think for a minute about beavers.

② **Pair** Have pairs of children discuss the question of the week. Remind them to take turns speaking. Have children use complete sentences in their discussions about what kind of home a beaver would build.

③ **Share** Call on a few children to share their ideas with the group. Guide discussion and encourage elaboration with prompts such as: What does a beaver look like?

Routines Flip Chart

Anchored Talk

Develop oral language

Display Talk with Me Chart 33A. What animal do you see in these pictures? This chart shows a real animal, a beaver, which makes his home in the water. Look at the pictures. What are the beavers doing in these pictures? Have children take notice of the tail and the wood the beaver is gnawing.

We will learn six new Amazing Words this week. Listen as I say each word: *beaver, lodge, paddle, river, stream, lake.* Have children say each word as you point to the picture.

Display Sing with Me Chart 33B. Today we are going to sing a song about a little beaver that does not want to sleep. Read the title and ask children to describe the picture. Sing the song several times to the tune of "Hush, Little Baby." Listen for the Amazing Words: *beaver, lodge, paddle, river, stream, lake.* Have children stand up and sing with you.

 Sing with Me Audio

Talk with Me/Sing with Me Chart 33A

Talk with Me/Sing with Me Chart 33B

ELL Preteach Concepts Use the Day 1 instruction on ELL Poster 33 to assess and build background knowledge, develop concepts, and build oral vocabulary.

 Poster 33

Amazing Words

beaver	lodge
paddle	river
stream	lake

Writing on Demand

Develop Writing Fluency

Ask children to write about what they know about beavers and the homes they build. Have children write for two minutes. Children should write as much as they can. Tell them to try to do their best writing. You may want to discuss what children wrote during writing conferences.

ELL

English Language Learners

Build Background English learners will benefit from additional visual support to understand words in the song. For example, point to the *river* and the *stream* on Talk with Me Chart 33A to scaffold meaning.

ELL Support Additional ELL support and modified instruction is provided in the *ELL Handbook* and in the ELL Support lessons on pp. DI•46–51.

Objectives

◎ Practice initial and medial /e/.
- Identify words with initial and medial /e/.
- Discriminate initial and medial /e/ words.
- Blend medial /e/ words.

Check Phonemic Awareness
! SUCCESS PREDICTOR

My Skills Buddy, pp. 52–53

Phonemic Awareness
🔊 Initial and Medial /e/

Reteach

Display the *egg* Picture Card. *Egg* begins with /e/: /e/, *egg*. What sound does *egg* begin with? Continue with the *elbow* and *elephant* Picture Cards.

Picture Card

Display the *bed* Picture Card. The middle sound in *bed* is /e/: /b/ /e/ /d/, *bed*. What is the middle sound in *bed*? (/e/) Continue with the *jet* and *pen* Picture Cards.

Have children look at the picture on pp. 52–53 of *My Skills Buddy.* Tell them that they will be listening for the sound /e/. I see an *elk* in the picture. What sound do you hear at the beginning of *elk*? I hear /e/ at the beginning of *elk*. What other things do you see that have the same beginning sound as *elk*? Repeat the routine for medial /e/ with the word *dress.*

Picture Card

Guide practice

As children name example words from the picture, guide them in stating where they hear /e/ in the word—at the beginning or in the middle. Discuss with children some of the bulleted items on p. 52 of *My Skills Buddy.* Save the other bulleted items for discussion on Day 2.

Corrective feedback

If... children have difficulty naming words with /e/,
then... say the words, emphasizing /e/.

Discriminate sounds

I am going to say some words. Listen carefully to where you hear /e/ in each word. I will do the first one: *exit*. I hear /e/ at the beginning of *exit*: /e/, *exit*.

Now let's play a sound game. I will say a word. If you hear /e/ at the beginning, reach your hands high in the air. If you hear /e/ in the middle, put your hands on your waist. Listen carefully: *elm* (hands up), *best* (hands on waist), *hen* (hands on waist), *egg* (hands up), *pet* (hands on waist), *end* (hands up).

Corrective feedback

If... children cannot discriminate /e/,
then... have them enunciate /e/ as they say *egg*.

When you say /e/, your mouth is open. Say /e/ and you'll feel a slight vibration at the back of your mouth. Your tongue is relaxed and resting. Have children say /e/ words and feel the position of their mouth and tongue. Then repeat the discrimination activity.

Review /a/, /i/, /o/

What sound do you hear in the middle of the word *pan*? Listen to the sounds: /p/ /a/ /n/. The middle sound is /a/. Have children identify the middle sound in these words: *lip, top, cap, tin, hog, fat, hip, sat, not, big, map*.

Listen to the three sounds in *pot*: /p/ /o/ /t/. I hear three sounds. We can blend the sounds to say the word. Blend the sounds with me: /p/ /o/ /t/, *pot.* Continue to blend sounds with the following words: *pop, sat, sit, fill, fast, got, flat, had, list, block, fig*.

Don't Wait Until Friday

MONITOR PROGRESS ⟳ Check Phonemic Awareness **Words with /e/**

Say *slid* and *sled*. Have children identify the word with /e/. Continue with *well, will; vet, vat; flag, yell; when, zap;* and *tent, stop*.

If... children cannot discriminate /e/,
then... use the small-group Strategic Intervention lesson, p. DI•35, to reteach /e/.

Day 1	Day 2	Day 3	Day 4	Day 5
Check Phonemic Awareness	Check Sound-Spelling/ Retelling	Check Word Reading	Check Phonemic Awareness	Check Oral Vocabulary

Success Predictor

Differentiated Instruction

 Advanced

Vowel Game Display the *Aa, Ee,* and *Ii* Alphabet Cards. Have children choose one letter and draw a picture of something that has that sound in the middle. Once children finish their drawing, have them find a partner who drew something that has the same middle sound as what they drew.

ELL

English Language Learners

Support Phonemic Awareness In many languages, short vowel sounds may not exist or may only have approximations. English learners may have a hard time hearing the differences in these sounds. Provide additional phonemic awareness activities to help children hear and pronounce words with short vowel sounds.

Phonemic Awareness

Success Predictor

Objectives
- Recognize uppercase *E* and lowercase *e*.
- Associate the sound /e/ with the spelling *e*.
- Blend and read words with /e/.

Skills Trace
Short e Spelled Ee

Introduce U4W5D1; U4W6D1; U6W3D1

Practice U4W5D2; U4W5D3; U4W6D2; U4W6D3; U6W3D2; U6W3D3

Reteach/Review U4W5D5; U4W6D5; U5W1D4; U6W3D4; U6W3D5; U6W4D4

Assess/Test Benchmark Assessment U4; U6

KEY:
U=Unit   W=Week   D=Day

Phonics—Teach/Model
 /e/ Spelled *Ee*

Introduce   Display the *Ee* Alphabet Card. Point to the *escalator* on the Alphabet Card. *Escalator* begins with /e/. Say the word with me: *escalator.* Write *escalator* on the board and point to the *e. Escalator* begins with /e/ spelled *e.* Now point to the letters *Ee* on the card. A sound for this letter is /e/. The names of these letters are uppercase *E* and lowercase *e.* What is the sound for this letter? What are the names of these letters?

Alphabet Card

Model   Write this sentence on the board: *The red hen sat at the end.* Point to the *e* in *red.* When I see this letter, I think the sound might be /e/. Let's read this word: /r/ /e/ /d/, *red.* Point to the *e* in *hen.* This word has /e/ too. I know that when I see an *e* the sound may be /e/. Let's read this word: /h/ /e/ /n/, *hen.* Repeat the routine with *end.* What does this sentence say? Point to each word as children read it.

Guide practice   Display Phonics Songs and Rhymes Chart 33. Teach children the song "Grand Sand Castle" sung to the tune of "Alouette." Play the CD and sing the song several times. When children are familiar with the song, ask them to clap when they hear the /e/ word. Ask a volunteer to come up and point to the word that contains short *e* spelled *Ee.*

Phonics Songs and Rhymes Chart 33

🔘 Phonics Songs and Rhymes Audio

On their own   Have children use imaginary *nets* to catch *Ee* in the room. When children find an *E* or *e,* have them stand next to it.

Blend Words

Review

Practice the sound-spellings of previously taught letters. Display the *Aa* Alphabet Card. What is the name of this letter? What is the sound for this letter? Continue to review the letter names and sounds with the following Alphabet Cards: *Ii, Oo,* and all consonant letters.

Differentiated Instruction

A Advanced

Connect Sound-Spelling Have children write the *Ee* words they catch in their *nets* on their Write-On Boards.

ROUTINE **Sound-by-Sound Blending**

1. **Connect** Write the letter *e* on the board. What is the sound we learned for this letter? The sound is /e/. Say it with me: /e/ /e/ /e/. When you see this letter in a word, what sound might you say?

2. **Model** Write *wet* on the board.

- Touch under the letter *w:* What is the sound for this letter? Say it with me: /w/ /w/ /w/. Repeat the routine for *e* and *t.*

- Let's blend the sounds together. Listen as I blend the sounds: /w/ /e/ /t/. Say it with me: /w/ /e/ /t/, *wet.* Now say it without me.

- Listen as I use *wet* in a sentence. *I got wet from standing in the rain.* Say the sentence with me. Then have children use *wet* in their own sentences.

3. **Guide Practice** Continue the routine established in step 2 with the words below:

pet   hen   pen   fed   nest   Jim   Kim   fun

Children should successfully read these words before reading Decodable Story 33 on pp. 427–428 of *Reader's and Writer's Notebook.*

Corrective Feedback If children have trouble reading a word, model blending the sounds to read the word. Then have children say it with you.

Routines Flip Chart

Handwriting

Introduce	Write *Ee* on the board. Words that begin with /e/ are written with an uppercase *E* or a lowercase *e*. Which letter is uppercase *E*? Which letter is lowercase *e*?
Model uppercase *E*	Write *Emma* on the board. Point to the uppercase *E*. This is the uppercase *E*. We use uppercase letters to begin sentences and for the first letter in a name. Watch as I trace the uppercase *E* with my finger. **Follow the stroke instructions pictured below.**
Guide practice	Have children write the uppercase *E* in the air. Use your finger to make an uppercase *E* in the air. Now write it on your hand.
Model lowercase *e*	Write *egg* on the board. Point to the lowercase *e*. This is a lowercase *e*. Watch as I trace the lowercase *e* with my finger. Write another lowercase *e* on the board following the stroke instructions. Again, have children write *e* in the air and on their hands.
Guide practice	Have children use their Write-On Boards to write a row of uppercase *E* and a row of lowercase *e*.

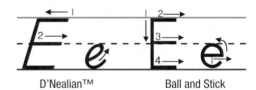

D'Nealian™   Ball and Stick

More practice   Use *Reader's and Writer's Notebook,* pp. 425, 426, for additional practice with initial *e.*

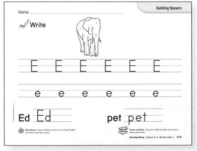

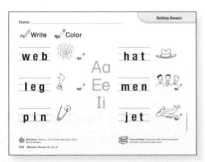

Reader's and Writer's Notebook, p. 425   Reader's and Writer's Notebook, p. 426

High-Frequency Words

Teach

Use the routine below to teach high-frequency words *the, was, to, like,* and *from.*

> ### ROUTINE — Nondecodable Words
>
> **1 Say and Spell** Some words we have to learn by remembering the letters rather than saying the sounds. We will say and spell the words to help learn them. **Write *the* on the board.** This is the word *the.* It has three letters. The letters in *the* are *t, h, e.* **Have children say and spell the word, first with you and then without you.**
>
> **2 Demonstrate Meaning** I can use the word *the* in many sentences. Here is one sentence: *The girl saw the beaver's home.* Now you use the word in a sentence.
>
> Repeat the routine with the words *was, to, like,* and *from.*

Routines Flip Chart

Academic Vocabulary

Write the following words on the board:

main idea	**informational text**
telling sentence	**rhyme**
prepositional phrase	**fable**

Point to the list. This week we are going to learn these important words. They are tools for learning. As we work this week you will hear them many times. **Read the words.** Preteach the Academic Vocabulary at point-of-use by providing a child-friendly description, explanation, or example that clarifies the meaning of each term. Then ask children to restate the meaning of the Academic Vocabulary in their own words.

Differentiated Instruction

SI Strategic Intervention

Handwriting Remind children that have learned to write all the letters of the alphabet. Have children practice writing their names on their Write-On Boards.

English Language Learners

Support High-Frequency Words Have children choose one high-frequency word to write on their Write-On Board. Pair children and have them take turns reading the high-frequency on their partner's Write-On Board. Then have them use the word in a sentence.

Objectives

- Read high-frequency words.
- Decode and read words in context and isolation.

Decodable Story 33
/e/ Spelled *Ee* and High-Frequency Words

Review

Review the previously taught high-frequency words by having children read each word as you point to it on the Word Wall.

a	they	the	was	with	for	ones	have	of	little

Read Decodable Story 33

Display Decodable Story 33. Today we will read a story about a boy, Jim, and a girl, Kim, and their pet hen. Point to the title of the story. What is the title of the story? The title of the story is *Jim and Kim.* We can read all the words in this story. Have children read Decodable Story 33 on pp. 427–428 in *Reader's and Writer's Notebook.*

Use the routine for reading decodable books to read Decodable Story 33.

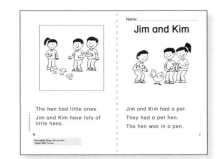

Reader's and Writer's Notebook, p. 427

ROUTINE **Reading Decodable Books**

1 **Read Silently** Have children whisper read the story page by page as you listen in.

2 **Model Fluent Reading** Have children finger point as you read a page. Then have children reread the page without you.

3 **Read Chorally** Have children finger point as they chorally read the page. Continue reading page by page, repeating steps 1 and 2.

4 **Read Individually** Have children take turns reading aloud a page.

5 **Reread and Monitor Progress** As you listen to individual children reread, monitor progress and provide support.

6 **Reread with a Partner** Have children reread the story page by page with a partner.

Routines Flip Chart

Differentiated Instruction

 Strategic Intervention

Read Short Vowel Words
Before children read *Jim and Kim,* review /a/, /i/, and /o/ words with the following Picture Cards: *ant, bag, brick, igloo, box, clock.*

Small Group Time

DAY 1 Break into small groups after reading the Decodable Story and before the comprehension lesson.

Teacher-Led

SI Strategic Intervention	**OL** On-Level	**A** Advanced
Teacher-Led Page DI•35 • Phonemic Awareness and Phonics • **Reread** Decodable Story 33	**Teacher-Led** Page DI•40 • Phonemic Awareness and Phonics • **Reread** Decodable Story 33	**Teacher-Led** Page DI•43 • Phonemic Awareness and Phonics • **Reread** Decodable Story 33 for Fluency

 Place English language learners in the groups that correspond to their reading abilities in English.

Practice Stations
• Visit the Listen Up! Station
• Visit the Word Work Station

Independent Activities
• Read independently
• Concept Talk Video
• *Reader's and Writer's Notebook*

Objectives

◎ Identify main idea.

Skills Trace

◉ **Main Idea**

Introduce U2W3D1; U3W6D1; U5W5D1; U6W3D1

Practice U2W3D2; U2W3D3; U2W3D4; U3W6D2; U3W6D3; U3W6D4; U5W5D2; U5W5D3; U5W5D4; U6W3D2; U6W3D3; U6W3D4

Reteach/Review U2W3D5; U3W1D4; U3W6D5; U4W5D4; U5W5D5; U5W6D4; U6W3D5

Assess/Test Benchmark Assessment U3

KEY:
U=Unit   W=Week   D=Day

My Skills Buddy, pp. 54–55

Listening Comprehension
 Main Idea

Introduce

All stories are about one big idea. This idea is the most important thing the author wants to talk about. This idea is the main idea of the selection. Good readers look for the main idea of a selection. It helps them understand better what the selection is about.

Have children turn to pp. 54–55 in *My Skills Buddy* and look at the picture. Help me understand the most important thing about these pictures.

- What is one way children arrive at school? (by car, by bike, by bus, or by foot)

- What is another way children arrive at school? (by car, by bike, by bus, or by foot)

- What is the main idea of this picture? (The main idea is that children come to school in different ways.)

Model

Today I will read aloud a story about how robins prepare a nest for baby birds. Read **"The Best Nest"** and model how to find the main idea.

Think Aloud When I read, I look for the most important idea in a story. I pay attention to what the words are telling me. I look for the most important thing the author is telling about. In "The Best Nest" the author tells how robin parents build a nest. This is the main idea of the story.

Guide practice

Have children tell what they think is the most important idea in "The Best Nest." Have them tell why they think this idea is the most important idea.

More practice

Display the Trade Book *This Is the Way We Go to School*. Recall with children that this story tells about the ways children around the world travel to school. Page through the story. What is the main idea of this story? What is this story all about? In this story, we learn about ways children travel to school. The book is all about how children around the world get to school.

Connect to everyday life

What story would you write about your family? What would be the main idea of your story? What would be the title of your story?

Academic Vocabulary

main idea the most important idea an author wants to talk about

The Best Nest

In spring, Mama and Papa Robin look for a safe, high spot to build their nest. Often they choose a tree. Then they start to gather building materials.

First, Mama and Papa Robin make a bed of strong materials. They fly back and forth, carrying twigs, leaves, and grass in their beaks. They may also bring string, paper, or plastic. They weave the materials to make a small cup. They may use mud to glue things together.

The inside lining of the nest must be warm and cozy for the babies. The robins use soft grasses, thistledown, feathers, spiderwebs, or sheep's wool. Mama Robin lays pale blue eggs in the finished nest. This will be home for the babies until they fly away.

English Language Learners
Oral Comprehension To prepare English learners for the Read Aloud, use the modified Read Aloud in the ELL Support lesson p. DI•47.

Objectives
- Introduce telling sentences.
- Write or dictate about something you wonder about.

Conventions
Telling Sentences

Teach sentences
Remind children that a sentence tells a complete idea. A telling sentence is a kind of sentence that tells what something or someone is or does. A telling sentence begins with an uppercase letter and ends with a period.

Model
Listen to these telling sentences:

Today is Monday.
The girl jumps up and down.

Both sentences are telling sentences. The first sentence tells us what day of the week it is. The second sentence tells us what the girl does. Write the sentences on the board. Point to the uppercase letter in each sentence. A telling sentence begins with an uppercase letter. Point to the period at the end of each sentence. A telling sentence ends with a period.

Guide practice
Write theses sentences on the board and read them one at a time:

> **What is your name?**
>
> **A lion roars loudly.**

Which of these sentences is a telling sentence? The telling sentence is *A lion roars loudly.* It tells what the lion does. It begins with an uppercase letter and ends with a period. Write more sentences on the board and have children identify the telling sentences.

Team Talk Pair children and have them take turns saying telling sentences about the classroom. Have children pretend they are going to write their telling sentence. Have them tell how they would begin the sentence and end the sentence.

Daily Fix-It
Use the Daily Fix-It for more conventions practice.

Writing
Wonderful, Marvelous Me!
I Wonder About...

Introduce

Talk with children about curiosity. Have you ever wanted to know more about something or why something happens? When we want to know more, we are curious about it. It's good to be curious about anything. What are ways we can find out more about the things we are curious about? Encourage children to share their thoughts and ideas about how to find out more.

Model

Today we're going to share our curiosity. I'm going to close my eyes and think about something I wonder about. I have three pet fish. They swim underwater all day. I know that fish breathe underwater, but I have always wondered how they do that. Draw three fish in a fishbowl on the board and write *How do fish breathe underwater?*

Guide practice

Encourage children to help you come up with possible ways fish can breathe underwater.

Write down their ideas and draw pictures when appropriate. Then read from a reference source about how fish breathe underwater. (Fish have gills. Gills are a part of fish that take the air out of the water to help fish breathe. When people and animals breathe, they need air.)

Independent writing

Now you're going to share something you wonder about. Close your eyes and use your wonderful, marvelous curiosity. What do you wonder about? Why do you wonder about that? Have children write or dictate their ideas and then illustrate them.

Daily Handwriting

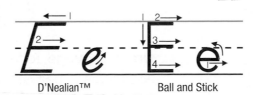

D'Nealian™   Ball and Stick

Write *Eric* and *egg* on the board. Review correct letter formation of uppercase *E* and lowercase *e*.

Have children write *Eric* and *egg* on their Write-On Boards. Remind them to use proper left-to-right and top-to-bottom progression and proper spacing between letters when writing *E* and *e*.

 Write Guy
Jeff Anderson

Writing to Learn

When children write a sentence, they are writing to learn. Provide them with a reader so that they can learn how their language communicates. The reader can be one or more peers, the teacher, or a family member. Writing has purpose when it has an audience.

Academic Vocabulary

telling sentence a sentence that tells what something or someone is or does. It begins with an uppercase letter and ends with a period.

Daily Fix-It

let's get on the jet
Let's get on the jet.

This week's practice sentences appear on Teacher Resources DVD-ROM.

Writing Routine

Day 1 Wonderful, Marvelous Me!

Day 2 Respond to Literature

Day 3 Genre Writing

Day 4 Extend the Concept

Day 5 This Week We...

Objectives
- Understand the purpose of interpreting information.
- Face the speaker when listening.

Listening and Speaking
Interpret Information

Teach

We get information lots of different ways. We can get information from words and things we read and from things we see and hear. It's important to think about the information we get and to understand what it means.

Model

I am going to tell you some information. Draw a stoplight with red, yellow, and green lights. When we want to cross a busy street, there is a stoplight. Point to the red light. When the light is red, we know not to go across the street. Point to the green light. When the light is green, it tells us we can cross the street. Remind children how to be good listeners by facing the speaker.

Guide practice

You see and hear things at school that give you information. When you are at recess and you hear the bell ring, what does that tell you? When the bell rings, you understand that recess is over. What does a ringing telephone mean? (It means someone is calling.) Continue in this way with children, noting everyday things that give information that they must interpret. Refer children to the Rules for Listening and Speaking on pp. 1–2 of *Reader's and Writer's Notebook*. Remind them to face the speaker when listening.

Name _____

Listening Rules

1. Face the person who is speaking.
2. Be quiet while someone is speaking.
3. Pay attention to the speaker.
4. Ask questions if you don't understand.

Listening and Speaking Rules 1

Reader's and Writer's Notebook, p. 1

Wrap Up Your Day

✔ **Oral Language** Today we talked about beavers and looked at pictures of beavers. Say the Amazing Words with me: *beaver, lodge, paddle, stream, river, lake.*

✔ **Homework Idea** Send home the Family Times Newsletter Let's Practice It! TR DVD•65–66.

Preview DAY 2

Tomorrow we will read about beavers making a home.

Social Studies
Comparing Homes

Materials: chart paper, large light-colored construction paper, writing and drawing tools

Identify Characteristics of Homes Talk with children about different animal homes they have read about this year. Make a two-column chart and label the columns *Animal Homes* and *People Homes*. Have children identify characteristics of each kind of home. Prompt them with questions such as: What is a bird's home made of? How does a prairie dog make a home? Where do bears live in the winter? Write children's responses in the chart. Use the completed chart to compare and contrast animal and human homes.

Animal Homes	People Homes
made of wood, leaves, twigs, mud	made of wood or brick
keeps them safe	keeps them safe
built on water, in trees, underground, on land	built on land
use teeth as tool to cut down trees, use paws to dig, use beaks to build	use human-made tools to build

Phonemic Awareness
Word Sort

Materials: short vowel Picture Cards

Just My Job Provide small groups of children with a set of short vowel Picture Cards. Have groups sort the cards by their short vowel sound. Have groups read the names of the pictures in each group aloud.

Conventions
Use Telling Sentences

Materials: Picture Cards

Tell About Picture Cards Randomly distribute one Picture Card to each child. Ask children to use statements as they describe the picture on their Picture Card, but not show the picture to their classmates. Have the other children figure out what picture the child is telling about.

Objectives
- Discuss the concepts to develop oral language.
- Build oral vocabulary.

Today at a Glance

Oral Vocabulary
beaver, lodge

Phonemic Awareness
◉ Initial and Medial /e/

Phonics
◉ /e/ Spelled *Ee*

Handwriting
Words with *Ee*

Comprehension
◉ Main Idea

Conventions
Telling Sentences

Writing
Respond to Literature

Vocabulary
Words for Actions

TRUCKTOWN on Reading Street

Start your engines! Display p. 16 of *Truckery Rhymes.* Point to "Wrecker Rosie Sat on a Wall." Who remembers which truck this rhyme is about? Yes, it's about Rosie. Let's read the rhyme together. Now have a child point to the rhyming words as the class reads the rhyme again. Give additional children the opportunity to say the rhyme aloud and track the print.

Truckery Rhymes

Concept Talk

Question of the Week

How do beavers build their homes?

Build concepts

Write the question of the week and track the print as you read it aloud. Ask children to answer the question in complete sentences. Display Sing with Me Chart 33B. Tell children they are going to sing the song about a beaver that won't go to sleep.

 Sing with Me Audio

Listen for Amazing Words

The Amazing Words *beaver* and *lodge* are in "Hush, Little Beaver." Read the title and have children describe the picture. Sing the song to the tune of "Hush, Little Baby." Have children clap when they hear the words *beaver* and *lodge.*

ELL Reinforce Vocabulary Use the Day 2 instruction on ELL Poster 33 to reinforce the meanings of high-frequency words.

Hush, Little Beaver

Hush, little beaver, go to sleep,
You've built a lodge that's very deep.

If that lodge is in river or stream,
You'll be safe, while you dream.

Hush, little beaver, go to sleep,
You've built a lodge that's very deep.

If that lodge is in a lake,
You'll paddle around, when you awake.

Talk with Me/Sing with Me Chart 33B

ELL Poster 33

Oral Vocabulary
Amazing Words

Teach Amazing Words

Amazing Words — Oral Vocabulary Routine

1 **Introduce the Word** A *beaver* is a furry brown animal with strong teeth and a wide, flat tail. A *beaver* builds its home on water. What's our new Amazing Word for a brown, furry animal with strong teeth and a wide, flat tail? Say it with me: *beaver.*

2 **Demonstrate** Provide examples to show meaning. *A beaver builds a dam across the stream.*

Repeat steps 1 and 2.

Introduce the Word A beaver's home is called a *lodge.* A beaver builds its *lodge* out of sticks and mud. What's our new Amazing Word for a beaver's home? Say it with me: *lodge.*

Demonstrate *A beaver's lodge is built in the water.*

3 **Apply** Have children use *beaver* and *lodge* in complete sentences. Have them act out a beaver building a lodge.

Routines Flip Chart

Use Amazing Words

To reinforce the concept and the Amazing Words, have children supply the appropriate Amazing Word for each sentence.

A _____ is a cozy home for a beaver. (lodge)

A _____ has large teeth. (beaver)

Amazing Words

beaver	lodge
paddle	river
stream	lake

Differentiated Instruction

SI Strategic Intervention

Sentence Production If children have difficulty completing the sentences, model saying the complete sentence and have them repeat it with you.

English Language Learners
Recall Vocabulary Explain to children that a beaver's home is called a *lodge.* We have learned other names for animal homes. What kind of home does a bird live in? What kind of home do bees live in?

Objectives
◎ Practice initial and medial /e/.
• Blend sounds.

Phonemic Awareness
↻ Initial and Medial /e/

Picture Card

Isolate /e/

Display the *egg* Picture Card. This is an *egg. Egg* begins with /e/. What is this? What does it begin with? Continue the routine with the *elevator, elbow,* and *elephant* Picture Cards.

Model

Display the *sled* Picture Card. This is a *sled.* Listen as I say the sounds: /s/ /l/ /e/ /d/, *sled.* I hear /e/ in the middle of the word, /s/ /l/ /e/ /d/. Say it with me: /s/ /l/ /e/ /d/; /e/ is in the middle. Let's try some more. Continue with the following words: *bed, desk, dress.*

Picture Card

Guide practice

Have children look at the picture on *My Skills Buddy,* pp. 52–53. Remember that we saw an *elk* in the picture. *Elk* begins with /e/. What other things begin with /e/? What things have /e/ in the middle, like *bed?* Discuss with children those bulleted items on p. 52 not discussed on Day 1.

My Skills Buddy, pp. 52–53

Corrective feedback

If... children cannot discriminate /e/ in words,
then... have them enunciate /e/ as they segment the word.

Listen as I segment a word: /r/ /e/ /d/, *red.* What sound do you hear in the middle of *red?* I hear /e/ in the middle of *red.* Continue with these words: *elk, ten, elf.*

On their own Display Phonics Songs and Rhymes Chart 33. Remind children of the song "Grand Sand Castle," sung to the tune of "Alouette." Have them sing the song with you several times. As we sing today, clap your hands when you hear /e/ in a word. You may wish to have children listen for /a/, /i/, and /o/ words also.

Review **Blend** Listen to the sounds in this word: /h/ /e/ /n/. Say them with me: /h/ /e/ /n/. Now I am going to blend the sounds together to say the word: /h/ /e/ /n/, *hen.* Continue the blending routine with the following words: *yak, jet, crab, ten, van, vest, can, flag, mask, wig, flip.*

Phonics Songs and Rhymes
Chart 33

Differentiated Instruction

SI Strategic Intervention

Access Content Have children create hand gestures to go along with the words in "Grand Sand Castle." For example, they can put their hands out for "lend us all a hand" and reach their hands up high for "Kyle, make a tower tall." Discuss the hand movements and then sing the song again.

ELL

English Language Learners
Support Phonemic Awareness English learners from various backgrounds may pronounce /e/ like the long *a* sound in *lake.* Model correct pronunciation by saying a short phrase or sentence, with both the short *e* and long *a* sounds, such as *We took our sled on the lake.* Have children repeat the sentence, and call their attention to the differences in sounds.

Objectives

◎ Practice /e/ spelled *Ee*.

◎ Practice /i/ spelled *Ii*.

• Blend /e/ words.

• Identify new words when letters are deleted.

Check Sound-Spelling

⚑ **SUCCESS PREDICTOR**

Phonics — Teach/Model
↺ /e/ Spelled *Ee*

Review /e/Ee Point to the *escalator* on the *Ee* Alphabet Card. What is this? What sound does *escalator* begin with? *Escalator* begins with /e/. Write *escalator* on the board and point to the letter *e*. The letter for /e/ is *e*.

Model Display the *red* Picture Card. What is this? Say the sounds in *red* with me: /r/ /e/ /d/, *red*. Where do you hear /e/ in *red*? (in the middle) Write *red* on the board. Point to each letter as you say the sounds, /r/ /e/ /d/, *red*. Continue the routine with the following words: *jet, lend, men, egg, dress.*

Alphabet Card

Guide practice

Envision It!

Have children open *My Skills Buddy* to p. 56. Demonstrate using the blending arrows on *My Skills Buddy*, p. 56, as you model blending the first word. Put your finger on the red arrow below *m*. Say the sound that *m* stands for: /m/. Continue with letters *e* and *n*. Now I run my finger along the blue arrow as I blend the letters quickly to read *men*. Repeat with the word *red*. Have children work with a partner to blend the rest of the words on the page. Explain to children that the word *at* on the bottom of the page is created when the letter *m* is deleted from the word *mat*. Remind children that sometimes new words can be created when letters are taken away.

My Skills Buddy, p. 56

Blend Use the following routine to review blending *e* words.

ROUTINE **Sound-by-Sound Blending**

1 **Connect** Write the letter *e*. What is the sound we learned for this letter? The sound is /e/. Say it with me: /e/ /e/ /e/. When you see this letter in a word, what sound will you say?

2 **Model** Write the word *men* on the board.

- Point to *m* and ask: What is the sound for this letter? Say it with me: /m/ /m/ /m/. Repeat the routine with *e* and *n*.

- Let's blend the sounds together. Listen as I blend the sounds: /m/ /e/ /n/. Say it with me: /m/ /e/ /n/. Now say it without me.

- Listen as I use *men* in a sentence. *The men work in the street.* Say it with me. Have children use *men* in a sentence.

3 **Guide Practice** Continue the routine established in step 2 with these words:

| Ed | red | set | well | big | add | ham | hop |

Have children successfully read all of the words before reading Decodable Reader 33 on pp. 58–65 of *My Skills Buddy*.

Corrective Feedback If children have difficulty blending words, model blending the sounds to read the word. Then have children say it with you.

Routines Flip Chart

Don't Wait Until Friday

MONITOR PROGRESS ⟳ **Check Sound-Spelling** /e/ Spelled *Ee*

Have children write *Ee* on a blank card. I am going to read some words. If you hear /e/ in the word, raise your *Ee* card. Say: *dress, fan, hen, mop, nest, sock, sled, tent, top, web.*

If... children cannot discriminate /e/ words,

then... use the small-group Strategic Intervention lesson, p. DI•36, to reteach /e/.

Continue to monitor children's progress using other instructional opportunities during the week so that children can be successful with the Day 5 Assessment.

Day 1	Day 2	Day 3	Day 4	Day 5
Check Phonemic Awareness	**Check Sound-Spelling/ Retelling**	Check Word Reading	Check Phonemic Awareness	Check Oral Vocabulary

Success Predictor

235 Sound-Spelling **Success Predictor**

Objectives
- Write *E* and *e*.
- Read high-frequency words.

Handwriting
Write Words with *Ee*

Review

Write *Eva* on the board. This is the name *Eva*. I use an uppercase *E* for the first letter in *Eva's* name. Watch me make an uppercase *E*. Write another uppercase *E* on the board using the strokes indicated in the model.

Write *end* on the board. This is the word *end*. It begins with a lowercase *e*. Watch me make a lowercase *e*. Write another lowercase *e* on the board using the proper strokes.

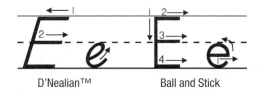

D'Nealian™   Ball and Stick

Guide practice

Have children use their Write-On Boards to make a row of uppercase *E* and a row of lowercase *e*. Circulate around the room, assisting children as necessary. Have children then write the following words: *pen, net, web, nest, fled.*

High-Frequency Words

Model reading

Have children turn to p. 57 of *My Skills Buddy*. Read the high-frequency words *the, was, to, like,* and *from* together. Then have children point to each word and read it themselves. Read the sentences on *My Skills Buddy* page together to read the new high-frequency words in context.

Team Talk Pair children and have them take turns reading each of the sentences aloud.

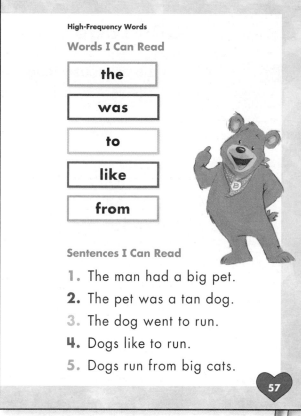

High-Frequency Words

Words I Can Read

the

was

to

like

from

Sentences I Can Read

1. The man had a big pet.
2. The pet was a tan dog.
3. The dog went to run.
4. Dogs like to run.
5. Dogs run from big cats.

57

My Skills Buddy, p. 57

On their own

Use *Reader's and Writer's Notebook*, p. 429, for additional practice with this week's high-frequency words.

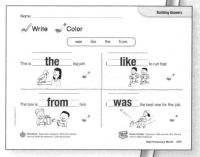

Reader's and Writer's Notebook, p. 429

Differentiated Instruction

 **Strategic Intervention**

Handwriting Have children find a word in a book or magazine that has the letter *e*. Have children write the word on their Write-On Boards. Then have them name the other letters in the word.

ELL

English Language Learners
Support Handwriting Have children practice writing their names on their Write-On Boards. What kind of letter do we begin our names with?

Objectives
- Read decodable text.
- Read high-frequency words.

Decodable Reader 33
/e/ Spelled *Ee* and High-Frequency Words

Review Review the previously taught high-frequency words. Have children read each words as you point to it on the Word Wall.

| a | the | what | do | with | to |

Have children turn to Decodable Reader 33, *The Red Egg,* on p. 58 of *My Skills Buddy.* Today we will read a story about a boy and his red egg. Point to the title. What is the title of the story? *The Red Egg* is the title of the story. Which words in the title have /e/? (*Red* and *Egg*) Point to the name of the author. The author's name is Robert Smith. What does the author of a book do? **Point to the name of the illustrator.** The illustrator's name is Perry Scott. What does the illustrator of a book do? We can read all the words in this story.

Use the routine for reading decodable books to read Decodable Reader 33.

My Skills Buddy, pp. 58–65

① **Read Silently** Have children whisper read the book page by page as you listen in.

② **Model Fluent Reading** Have children finger point as you read a page. Then have children reread the book without you.

③ **Read Chorally** Have children finger point as they chorally read the page. Continue reading page by page, repeating steps 1 and 2.

④ **Read Individually** Have children take turns reading aloud a page.

⑤ **Reread and Monitor Progress** As you listen to individual children reread, monitor progress and provide support.

⑥ **Reread with a Partner** Have children reread the book page by page with a partner.

Routines Flip Chart

Differentiated Instruction

SI Strategic Intervention

Comprehension Have children draw a picture that shows the main idea of *The Red Egg.* Tell them to show their drawing to a partner and explain the main idea.

Teacher Tip

A decodable book is a text that provides practice with targeting phonics skills by including many words using those phonics elements.

Small Group Time

DAY 2 Break into small groups after reading the Decodable Reader and before the comprehension lesson.

Teacher-Led

SI Strategic Intervention	**OL** On-Level	**A** Advanced
Teacher-Led Page DI•36	**Teacher-Led** Page DI•40	**Teacher-Led** Page DI•43
• Phonemic Awareness and Phonics	• Phonemic Awareness and Phonics	• Phonics
• **Reread** Decodable Reader 33	• **Reread** Decodable Reader 33	• Spelling
		• **Reread** Decodable Reader 33 for Fluency

ELL Place English language learners in the groups that correspond to their reading abilities in English.

Practice Stations
• Visit the Word Work Station
• Visit the Words to Know Station

Independent Activities
• Read independently
• Background Building Audio
• *Reader's and Writer's Notebook*

DAY 2 Read and Comprehend

20–25 mins.

Objectives
- ◎ Practice main idea.
- • Preview and predict.
- • Retell a selection.

Check Retelling
! **SUCCESS PREDICTOR**

Listening Comprehension
◎ Main Idea

Review

Envision It!

Have children turn to p. 54 of *My Skills Buddy.* Remind children that the most important idea in a selection is called the main idea. Good readers pay attention to the main idea because it helps them understand the selection.

My Skills Buddy, pp. 54–55

Triple Day Read!

First Read—Big Book
Building Beavers

Concepts of print

Point to the title of the selection. The title of this book is *Building Beavers.* The author of this book is Kathleen Martin-James. What does an author do? (The author writes the book.)

Preview and predict

Think Aloud

Display *Building Beavers.* Tell me what you see on the cover. I see a very wet beaver. It is in the water building something. What do you think this book will be about? Let's read to find out.

Use photographs

Take children on a walk through the book. Have children describe the photographs.

Introduce genre

Informational text teaches the reader facts about things that happen in the world. In this selection we will learn about beavers.

Set purpose

Remind children of the question of the week: *How do beavers build their homes?* Have children listen for what beavers have to do to build their homes.

Model

Read *Building Beavers* with expression for enjoyment.

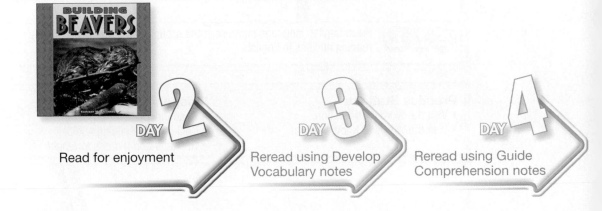

DAY 2 Read for enjoyment

DAY 3 Reread using Develop Vocabulary notes

DAY 4 Reread using Guide Comprehension notes

Retell

Check retelling

Have children turn to p. 66 of *My Skills Buddy.* Walk through the retelling boxes as children retell *Building Beavers.* Let's retell what happens in the first box— the beginning of the selection. This is a beaver. We learn about beavers in this selection. Let's retell what happens in the next box. Continue with the rest of the boxes. After children retell the story as a group, have them draw a picture to retell a favorite part of the story. Have them write or dictate a word or sentence to go with their picture.

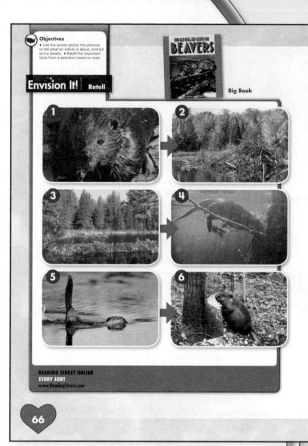

My Skills Buddy, p. 66

Top-Score Response A top-score response identifies the topic and details.

Differentiated Instruction

A **Advanced**

Retell As children retell the story, have them act out the details, such as a beaver paddling through the water or cutting down the tree with its teeth.

Academic Vocabulary

author a person who writes books, stories, poems, or plays

informational text that gives a reader facts about things in the real world

Retelling Plan

☑ **Week 1** Assess Advanced students.

☑ **Week 2** Assess On-Level students.

☑ **This week assess Strategic Intervention students.**

☐ **Week 4** Assess Advanced students.

☐ **Week 5** Assess On-Level students.

☐ **Week 6** Assess Strategic Intervention students.

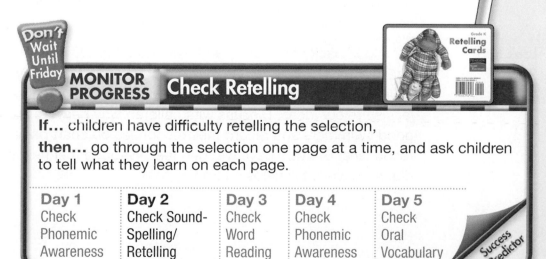

Don't Wait Until Friday

MONITOR PROGRESS **Check Retelling**

If... children have difficulty retelling the selection,

then... go through the selection one page at a time, and ask children to tell what they learn on each page.

Day 1	Day 2	Day 3	Day 4	Day 5
Check Phonemic Awareness	Check Sound-Spelling/ Retelling	Check Word Reading	Check Phonemic Awareness	Check Oral Vocabulary

Success Predictor

Think, Talk, and Write

Discuss concept

We're learning about beavers and how they build their homes. Think about how you would build a home if you were a beaver.

• What would you need to start building your home?

• Where would you put your lodge?

• Why would you put it there?

Confirm predictions

Ask children to recall their predictions before you read *Building Beavers.*

• What did you think the selection would be about?

• Was your prediction correct?

Have children turn to p. 67 of *My Skills Buddy.* Read the questions and directives and have children respond.

My Skills Buddy, p. 67

Text to world

1. What does a beaver use to cut down trees and build its house?

◉ **Main Idea**

2. What is the story *Building Beavers* mostly about? What does the first picture show? (a beaver cutting a tree with its teeth) What does the second picture show? (a beaver's lodge)

Look back and write

3. Let's look back at our story and write about it. We remember that beavers are good swimmers. Listen for what special body parts beavers have that help them swim. Read pp. 12–15 of *Building Beavers.* Now let's write our ideas. Discuss with children why beavers are such good swimmers and record their responses on chart paper. (Possible responses: Beavers have webbed feet. Webbed feet help beavers paddle. A beaver's tail helps it turn.)

Conventions
Telling Sentences

Review
Remind children that telling sentences tell what a person or thing is or does. A telling sentence begins with an uppercase letter and ends with a period.

Guide practice
We can put words together to make sentences that tell things. Listen to this sentence: *It is two o'clock in the afternoon.* What does this sentence tell us? It tells us what time it is.

Review the date with children. Have them make sentences telling something about the date. Have other children identify what the sentences tell them.

On their own
Use *Reader's and Writer's Notebook,* p. 430, for more practice with telling sentences.

Daily Fix-It
Use the Daily Fix-It exercise for more conventions practice.

INTERACT with TEXT

Reader's and Writer's Notebook, p. 430

Differentiated Instruction

SI Strategic Intervention
Discuss Concept To help children discuss the selection, allow them to use p. 66 of *My Skills Buddy* to recall important facts from *Building Beavers.*

A Advanced
Look Back and Write Allow children to write their own responses to the question.

Daily Fix-It

i ran on the red rug
I ran on the red rug.

This week's practice sentences appear on Teacher Resources DVD-ROM.

English Language Learners
Academic Vocabulary Remind children that when they predict, they think about what might happen in the book before they read it.

Objectives
- Write or dictate sentences about beavers.
- Write *E* and *e*.
- Identify and use words for actions.

Writing
Respond to Literature

Discuss concept

Display *Building Beavers*. Discuss with children the things they learned about beavers.

Model

In this selection, we learned many facts about beavers. A fact is information that is true. Let's write sentences about what we learned. I am going to write:

> **Beavers are brown and furry.**

Guide practice

Have children help you write more sentences about beavers. What kind of letter should I use at the beginning of the sentence? What should I put at the end of the sentence?

> **Beavers have long, sharp front teeth.**
> **Beavers swim well.**

Independent writing

Have children write or dictate a sentence about beavers. Some children may wish to use this sentence frame:

> **Beavers _____.**

Then have children illustrate their sentences.

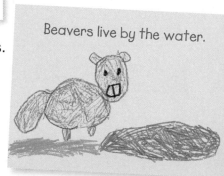

Beavers live by the water.

Daily Handwriting

Write *Ella* and *den* on the board. Review correct letter formation of upper-case *E* and lowercase *e*.

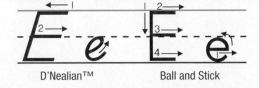

D'Nealian™   Ball and Stick

Have children write *Ella* and *den* on their Write-On Boards. Remind children to use proper left-to-right and top-to-bottom progressions when writing *E* and *e*.

Vocabulary
Words for Actions

Model

Have children turn to p. 68 of *My Skills Buddy.* Use the first Vocabulary bullet on the page to guide the discussion. Direct children to the picture of the man digging. This man can dig. He is using a shovel to make a hole in the ground. Pick up a book and carry it to the other side of the room. I carry this book. When we carry something we hold it in our hands. Direct children to the picture of the man eating. This man can eat his lunch. Put the palms of your hands together and rest your cheek on your hands, as though you are sleeping. At night, we sleep. We close our eyes and relax.

My Skills Buddy p. 68

Guide practice

Write the words *dig, carry, eat,* and *sleep* on the board. Point to each word as you read it.

dig	carry	eat	sleep

Let's practice our new words. Find an object and *carry* it to the table. Pretend you have a shovel. Show me how you would *dig* a hole in the ground. Have children look at the pictures on p. 68 of *My Skills Buddy.* Point to the man with the toolbox. What is he doing with the toolbox? Yes, he can *carry* a toolbox. Point to the man in the bed. What can this man do? Yes, he can sleep. The words *dig, carry, eat,* and *sleep* are action words.

On their own

Have children take turns acting out the action words. Have them narrate their actions by using the action word in a sentence.

Differentiated Instruction

SI Strategic Intervention

Develop Vocabulary Have children draw a picture of themselves doing each of the action words. Tell them to keep their drawings to help them understand the meanings of the words as they come up in reading, writing, and speaking.

English Language Learners
Physical Response Have children say the action words in English as they do the action.

Objectives
- Review skills learned and practiced today.
- Say telling sentences.

Wrap Up Your Day

✔ **Concept Talk** Today we heard a story about beavers and the homes they make. What else did you learn about beavers?

✔ **Phonemic Awareness** We reviewed words that have /e/. Listen to these words. Clap when you hear /e/ in a word: *shell, bug, went, escalator, vest, visit, fish, web.*

✔ **Conventions** Have children say telling sentences about themselves.

✔ **Homework Idea** Have children show their families the action words they learned. (*dig, carry, eat, sleep*)

Preview DAY 3

Tomorrow we will read about beavers again.

Science
Tree Sources

Materials: chart paper or Graphic Organizer 18, drawing paper, writing and coloring tools

Identify Resources from Trees Help children recall how beavers use trees to build their homes and to build dams. Talk about all the things trees provide for people. Draw an idea web or use Graphic Organizer 18. Label the

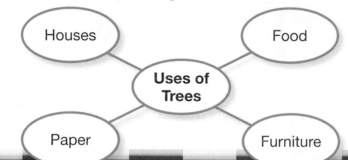

center circle *Uses of Trees.* Write children's ideas about the resources trees provide for animals and people in the surrounding circles.

Write a Sentence Give each child a piece of drawing paper. Have children choose one resource trees provide to illustrate. Then ask children to write or dictate a word or sentence to describe the resource. Gather the papers to create a class book of tree resources.

Phonics
Picture Hunt

Materials: paper bags; old magazines; scissors

Which Word Is It? Label four paper bags each with one of these letters: *e, a, i, o.* Have children find pictures in magazines or newspapers that have the short vowel sound one of these letters represents. You may want to assign one letter to a small group of three or four children. After children have exhausted their letters, have them tell what pictures they added to their paper bags.

Conventions
Telling or Not?

Play "Simon Tells" Play a revised version of Simon Says with children called Simon Tells. Tell children that "Simon" will say either a verb (action word), such as *hop,* or a statement, such as *A rabbit hops.* When children hear a statement, they should act out the sentence. If they do not hear a statement, they are to remain still. Say a variety of verbs, such as *skip, jump, talk, walk,* and *run,* and statements, such as the following: *Beavers chew on wood. Kangaroos hop along the road. Cats drink milk. Birds fly through the sky.*

Objectives

- Share information and ideas about the concept.
- Build oral vocabulary.

Today at a Glance

Oral Vocabulary
paddle, river

Phonemic Awareness
◉ Initial and Medial /e/

Phonics
◉ /e/ Spelled *Ee*

Comprehension
◉ Main Idea

Conventions
Telling Sentences

Writing
Rhyme

Listening and Speaking
Interpret Information

TRUCKTOWN on Reading Street

Start your engines! Display p. 16 of *Truckery Rhymes*. Do you know the original "Humpty Dumpty"? Recite it first, and then have children repeat it with you:

Humpty Dumpty sat on the wall,
Humpty Dumpty had a great fall.
All the kings horses,
and all the kings men
Couldn't put Humpty back together again!

Truckery Rhymes

Concept Talk

Question of the Week

How do beavers build their homes?

Write and read the question of the week as you track the print. Talk with children about beavers and how they build their homes. Remind children to speak loudly and clearly and to take turns.

Listen for Amazing Words

Let's Sing Display Sing with Me Chart 33B. Remind children that yesterday they sang "Hush, Little Beaver." Today we are going to listen for the Amazing Words *paddle* and *stream*. Sing the song several times to the tune "Hush, Little Baby." Have children sing with you. Ask children to imitate a beaver paddling in a stream when they hear the words.

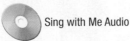 Sing with Me Audio

Hush, Little Beaver

Hush, little beaver, go to sleep,
You've built a lodge that's very deep.

If that lodge is in river or stream,
You'll be safe, while you dream.

Hush, little beaver, go to sleep,
You've built a lodge that's very deep.

If that lodge is in a lake,
You'll paddle around, when you awake.

Talk with Me/Sing with Me Chart 33B

Oral Vocabulary
Amazing Words

Teach Amazing Words

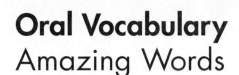 **Oral Vocabulary Routine**

1. **Introduce the Word** When beavers *paddle* through the water, they move their webbed feet back and forth. What's our new Amazing Word for what a beaver does with its feet to pull itself through the water? Say it with me: *paddle.*

2. **Demonstrate** *Other animals besides beavers paddle in the water.* What kinds of birds *paddle* in the water?

   Repeat steps 1 and 2.

   Introduce the Word A *river* is a body of water that is always flowing. A *river* can be very wide and deep and can move very fast. What's our new Amazing Word for a body of water that is always flowing? Say it with me: *river.*

   Demonstrate *It is fun to float down a river on a raft.* Have you ever been to a *river*?

3. **Apply** Have children use *paddle* and *river* in complete sentences.

Routines Flip Chart

Use Amazing Words

To reinforce the concept and the Amazing Words, have children supply the appropriate Amazing Word in each sentence.

Ducks can _____ through water too. (paddle)

A lot of boats go down this _____. (river)

 Expand Vocabulary
Use the Day 3 instruction on ELL poster 33 to help children expand vocabulary.

 Poster 33

Differentiated Instruction

A Advanced

Access Content Have children show how an animal would *paddle* through the water. Then have them discuss the other animal they have read about that can *paddle.*

ELL

English Language Learners
Use Cognates Ask children what words in their home languages are used for *paddle* and *stream*. For example, the Spanish word for *river* is *río.*

Objectives
◎ Isolate /e/.
- Discriminate sounds.
- Blend words.

Phonemic Awareness
⟳ Initial and Medial /e/

Review | **Initial /e/** Display the *elephant* Picture Card. Listen to the first sound in *elephant.* What sound does the word *elephant* begin with? Listen carefully: /e/ /e/, *elephant.* What is the first sound? Continue with *egg* and *elevator* Picture Cards.

Picture Card

Review | **Medial /e/** Display the *hen* Picture Card. Listen to the sounds in *hen:* /h/ /e/ /n/. How many sounds do you hear? (three) What is the middle sound in *hen?* Say the sound with me: /e/ /e/ /e/. Continue with the *jet, pen,* and *ten* Picture Cards.

Discriminate sounds | Display the *egg* and *jet* Picture Cards on the chalk ledge. I am going to say some words. Decide if you hear /e/ at the beginning of the word, like *egg,* or in middle of the word, like *jet.* Stand by the picture card that has the same beginning sound or middle sound. Use the following words: *let, end, red, yes, elk, web, pet, leg, elm.*

Alphabet Card

On their own | Have children draw a picture of something that begins with /e/ or has /e/ in the middle. Remind them to think about all the words they have used this week.

Blend

Listen to the sounds in this word: /j/ /e/ /t/. Say them with me: /j/ /e/ /t/. Now I am going to blend the sounds together to say the word: /j/ /e/ /t/, *jet.* Continue the blending routine with the following words: *will, Jed, hat, tent, van, vest, Val, Bev, mask, flick, clip.*

Corrective feedback

If... children cannot blend words,
then... provide practice segmenting words and then blending the sounds, such as *rock, /r/ /o/ /k/, rock.*

Review /a/, /i/, /o/

Listen for the sounds in this word: /k/ /a/ /t/. What sound do you hear in the middle of this word? I will say the sounds again /k/ /a/ /t/. The sound you hear is /a/. Say it with me: /a/ /a/ /a/. Repeat the procedure with the words *block, wig, crab, desk, jam, sled, stamp, lid, flip, flop,* and *clock.*

Phonics—Teach/Model
/e/ Spelled *Ee*

Review   **/e/Ee** Display the *Ee* Alphabet Card and point to the *escalator*. What sound do you hear at the beginning of *escalator?* What letter spells that sound? **Point to the letters *Ee*.** What is the sound for these letters? What are the names of these letters?

Alphabet Card

Review   **Letter Names and Sounds** Use Alphabet Cards to review the following letter names and sounds: *Bb, Ff, Ii, Ll, Mm, Nn, Oo, Pp, Ss, Tt, Zz.*

Blend sounds   Write *Ben* on the board. Point to each letter as you say the sound: /b/ /e/ /n/. When I blend these sounds together, I make the name *Ben.* Say the sounds with me: /b/ /e/ /n/. **Change the *B* to *t*.** Now we have a new word. Let's blend the sounds to read the word. Say them with me: /t/ /e/ /n/. What is the new word? The word is *ten.* **Continue with the following words:** *fill, fell; zip, zap; limp, lamp; sled, slid; not, net.*

More practice   Use *Reader's and Writer's Notebook,* p. 431, for additional practice with /e/.

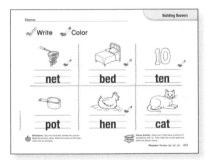

Reader's and Writer's Notebook, p. 431

Review **Sound-Spelling** Display the *Aa* Alphabet Card. What sound do you hear at the beginning of *astronaut?* What letter spells that sound? Yes, the letters *a* spells /a/. Review the following letters: *Ii, Oo,* and all consonants.

Review **High-Frequency Words** Write *from* on the board. This is the word *from.* What is this word? Continue the routine with *the, was, to,* and *like.*

Alphabet Card

Differentiated Instruction

 Advanced

High-Frequency Words
Have children practice other high-frequency words on the Word Wall. Tell them to choose one word and use it in a complete sentence.

Don't Wait Until Friday

MONITOR PROGRESS | **Check Word Reading** **High-Frequency Words**

Write *the, was, to, like,* and *from* on the board. Have children take turns reading the words.

Practice reading these words from Kindergarten Student Reader K.6.3, *Max and Jen Go Camping.*

set	get	trip	tent	van	camp	help	hill
nest	pond	jump	can	Jen	Max	fun	bump

If... children cannot read the high-frequency words,
then... write the words on cards for them to practice at home.

If... children cannot blend sounds to read the words,
then... provide practice blending the words in chunks, /s/ -*et.*

If... children can successfully blend sounds to read the words,
then... have them read Kindergarten Student Reader K.6.3, *Jen and Max Go Camping.*

Day 1	**Day 2**	**Day 3**	**Day 4**	**Day 5**
Check Phonemic Awareness	Check Sound-Spelling/ Retelling	Check Word Reading	Check Phonemic Awareness	Check Oral Vocabulary

Success Predictor

Objectives
- Read /e/ words.
- Read high-frequency words.

Kindergarten Student Reader K.6.3
/e/ Spelled *Ee* and High-Frequency Words

Review

Review the previously taught high-frequency words. Have children read each word as you point to it on the Word Wall.

they	to	go	a	the	are
see	three	look	what	green	have

Read Kindergarten Student Reader K.6.3

Display Kindergarten Student Reader K.6.3. Today we are going to read a new book. Point to the title of the book. The title of the book is *Max and Jen Go Camping.* The author's name is Mikael Wesley. This story was illustrated by Nan Brooks. We can read all the words in this story.

Use the reading decodable books routine to read the Kindergarten Student Reader.

ROUTINE **Reading Decodable Books** *Small Group*

1. **Read Silently** Have children whisper read the book page by page as you listen in.

2. **Model Fluent Reading** Have children finger point as you read a page. Then have children reread the page without you.

3. **Read Chorally** Have children finger point as they chorally read the page. Continue reading page by page, repeating steps 1 and 2.

4. **Read Individually** Have children take turns reading aloud a page.

5. **Reread and Monitor Progress** As you listen to individual children reread, monitor progress and provide support.

6. **Reread with a Partner** Have children reread the book page by page with a partner.

Routines Flip Chart

Mom and Dad get set.
Max and Jen get set.
They get set to go on a trip.

2

The red tent will go in the van.
The pots will go in the van.
Max and Jen are in the red van.

3

They will set up camp.
Dad sets up the tent.
Max and Jen help Dad.

4

Kindergarten Student Reader K.6.3

They go up a big hill.
Jen and Max see a nest.
Jen can see three eggs.

5

Look at the pond, Max.
Max can see a big bump.
What is it, Dad?

6

Mom sees a green frog.
Look at it jump.
It can jump a lot.

7

Jen and Max have fun.
It is fun to camp!

8

Differentiated Instruction

A Advanced

Access Content Review the term *camping trip* and have children tell what they know about going on a camping trip.

Small Group Time

DAY 3

Break into small groups to read the Kindergarten Student Reader before the comprehension lesson.

Teacher-Led

SI Strategic Intervention	**OL** On-Level	**A** Advanced
Teacher-Led Page DI•37 • Phonemic Awareness and Phonics • **Read** Concept Literacy Reader K.6.3 or Kindergarten Student Reader K.6.3	**Teacher-Led** Page DI•41 • Phonemic Awareness and Phonics • **Read** Kindergarten Student Reader K.6.3	**Teacher-Led** Page DI•44 • **Read** Independent Reader K.6.3 or Kindergarten Student Reader K.6.3

ELL Place English language learners in the groups that correspond to their reading abilities in English.

Practice Stations
• Visit the Words to Know Station
• Visit the Let's Write! Station

Independent Activities
• Read independently
• Audio Text of Big Book
• *Reader's and Writer's Notebook*

English Language Learners
Access Content Explain to children the term *setting up camp*. Ask children to identify other things they can set up, such as a table or a scene for a play.

Objectives
- Recall and retell a selection.
- ◎ Practice main idea.
- Develop and use vocabulary.
- Develop and use comprehension skills.

Comprehension

Retell the story

Have children turn to p. 66 of *My Skills Buddy* and use the retelling boxes to retell the selection *Building Beavers*.

 Envision It!

Think Aloud Direct children to the first retell box. This is a beaver. It has brown fur. Tell me what else we learned about beavers.

Continue reviewing the retelling boxes and having children retell the story.

My Skills Buddy, p. 66

Review

Main Idea Remind children the main idea of a book tells the most important idea of the book. Every book they read will have one important idea. Display different pages in the book. Prompt children to identify details that support the main idea. Use questions such as the following:

- What information is on these pages?
- What is the beaver doing in these pictures?

Point out that all the pages contain pictures and information about beavers. What is this book all about? This book is all about beavers.

More practice

Use *Reader's and Writer's Notebook,* p. 432, for additional practice with main idea.

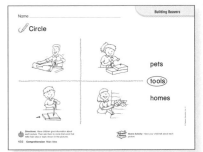

Reader's and Writer's Notebook, p. 432

 Triple Day Read!

Second Read—Big Book
Building Beavers

Let's Reread *Building Beavers*. Follow the Day 3 arrow beginning on p. 257, and use the Develop Vocabulary notes to prompt conversations about the selection.

Have children use the Amazing Words *beaver, lodge, paddle, stream, river,* and *lake* to talk about the selection.

DAY 2 Read for enjoyment

DAY 3 Reread using Develop Vocabulary notes

DAY 4 Reread using Guide Comprehension notes

Develop Vocabulary

Open-ended

What kind of animal is this? (a beaver)

• This is a beaver. Why is this beaver all wet?

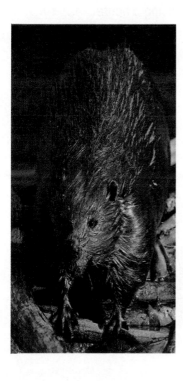

This wet, furry animal is a beaver.

What is it doing with all of these sticks?

3

Big Book, p. 3

Guide Comprehension

What other animal does the beaver remind you of? (The beaver looks like a groundhog or porcupine.)

Develop Vocabulary, continued

DAY 3

Wh- question

What is the beaver doing in the picture? (building a house)

- The beaver is building its house, called a lodge. What is the lodge made out of?

Develop Vocabulary mud

This beaver is building a house.
A beaver house is called a *lodge*.

A lodge is made of
tree branches and mud.

How do beavers build a lodge?

4

5

Big Book, pp. 4–5

Guide Comprehension, continued

DAY 4

Wh- question

Does this selection tell about real or make-believe beavers? (It tells about real beavers.) How do you know? (The pictures show real beavers and the words tell facts about beavers.)

Recall

What do beavers do with their long, sharp front teeth? (cut down trees)

- Beavers use their teeth to cut down trees. How does a beaver balance itself when it stands on its back legs?

Develop Vocabulary teeth, trees

Expand Vocabulary balance

First, beavers cut down trees with their long, sharp front teeth.

What color are this beaver's teeth?

This beaver is standing up on its back legs to chew a branch.

Its wide, flat tail helps it balance.

6

7

Big Book, pp. 6–7

Wh- **question**

Why do beavers cut down the trees? (They will use the trees to make their lodges.)

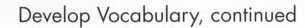
Develop Vocabulary, continued

DAY 3

Wh- question

Where do beavers build their lodges? (in the water)

- Beavers may build their lodges in streams, rivers, or small lakes. What else do beavers build?

Next, beavers carry branches and mud with their small front feet.

Beavers may build a lodge in a stream, river, or small lake.

8

Sometimes beavers build a *dam* in the water.

Water cannot flow past a dam.

9

Big Book, pp. 8–9

Guide Comprehension, continued

DAY 4

Wh- question

Why can't the water flow past the dam? (The dam is higher than the water. It holds back the water.)

Wh- question

What happens when a beaver builds a dam?
(The water on one side gets deeper.)

- The water gets deeper on one side and a
  pond is formed. Beavers build their lodges
  in the pond. What do their lodges look like?

Develop Vocabulary pond

Water gets deeper on one side
of a dam, making a *beaver pond*.

Beavers build their lodge
in the pond.

10

Most of the lodge is above water.

How do beavers get inside?

11

Big Book, pp. 10–11

Inferential

Why do you think a beaver needs a pond to
build its lodge? (A pond does not flow like a
river or stream. The pond is still so the lodge
will not move.)

DAY 3

Develop Vocabulary, continued

Distancing
What can beavers do in the water?
(swim)

• Beavers are good swimmers. Do you know how to swim?

Expand Vocabulary webbed

The way into the lodge is underwater.

Beavers are good swimmers. Their back feet are *webbed*.

Animals with webbed feet have skin joining their toes.

12

13

Big Book, pp. 12–13

DAY 4

Guide Comprehension, continued

Wh- **question**
What animals can you name that also have webbed feet? (Ducks have webbed feet, and lizards and frogs have webbed feet.)

Wh- question
What helps a beaver swim? (webbed feet)

- Webbed feet help beavers paddle through the water. What else does a beaver use to help it swim?

Webbed feet help beavers paddle in the water and swim quickly.

When it swims, a beaver uses its tail to help it turn.

How else do beavers use their tails?

14

15

Big Book, pp. 14–15

Distancing
Would you like to paddle underwater like a beaver? Why or why not? (I would like to paddle and swim underwater like a beaver because I like being in the water.)

Develop Vocabulary, continued

DAY 3

Wh- question

A beaver uses its tail to swim. What else does a beaver use its tail for? (to protect itself)

- A beaver uses its tail to protect itself from predators. What is the beaver doing with its tail?

Expand Vocabulary predators

Beavers use their tails to stay safe from *predators*.

Predators are animals that hunt and eat other animals.

16

If a swimming beaver sees or smells a predator,

it lifts its tail up high. What do you think the beaver will do next?

17

Big Book, pp. 16–17

Guide Comprehension, continued

DAY 4

Wh- question

A predator kills or eats other animals. What predator do you think this beaver sees? (The beaver might see a bear or a wolf.)

Recall

What makes the water splash? (The beaver)

• The beaver hits the water with its tail to tell other beavers that a predator is near. Where does the beaver go?

Expand Vocabulary herbivores

SLAP! The beaver hits
the water with its tail.

The loud noise tells other beavers
that a predator is near.

18

Beavers are not predators.
They are *herbivores*.

Herbivores are animals
that eat only plants.

19

Big Book, pp. 18–19

Wh- **question**

What kinds of plants do you think a beaver would eat? (I think a beaver would eat any plants that were near its lodge. A beaver might eat leaves from trees or grass.)

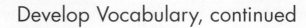
Develop Vocabulary, continued

Distancing

What are the baby beavers doing? (swimming, eating)

- Baby beavers are called kits and can swim when they are one week old. What other animal baby names we have read about?

Develop Vocabulary kits

These baby beavers are eating twigs and leaves.

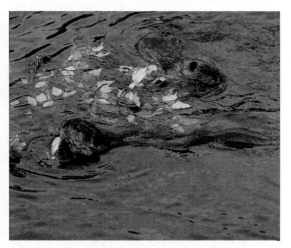

Babies drink milk from their mother when they are very young.

20

Baby beavers are called *kits*.

Kits can swim out of their lodge when they are a week old.

21

Big Book, pp. 20–21

Guide Comprehension, continued

Wh- question

Why wouldn't a baby beaver make a good pet? (Beavers are wild animals and would not make good pets. They can't be kept in a cage.)

Distancing

What does the baby beaver do with its eyes when it swims underwater? (keeps them open)

• A baby beaver keeps its eyes open because clear eyelids cover its eyes. Do you keep your eyes open underwater?

Like all beavers, this kit can keep its eyes open underwater.

Clear eyelids cover its eyes when it swims.

22

This kit is tired of swimming. It rides on its mother's tail.

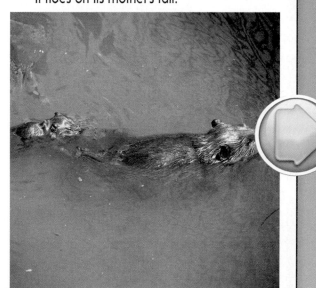

23

Big Book, pp. 22–23

Wh- question

Why is a baby beaver riding its mother's tail like a human mother carrying a baby in her arms? (Sometimes mothers carry babies when they are tired or when they cannot walk.)

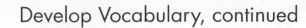
Develop Vocabulary, continued

DAY 3

Wh- question
What are this mother and kit doing?
(grooming each other)

Expand Vocabulary grooming

- They are grooming each other. Grooming keeps their fur neat and clean. Why do beavers comb their fur?

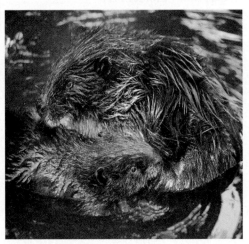

This mother and kit are *grooming*. Grooming keeps fur neat and clean.

Beavers comb their fur with their back feet.

24

Beavers smooth their fur with oil from their bodies.

This oil makes their fur water-proof.

25

Big Book, pp. 24–25

Guide Comprehension, continued

DAY 4

Distancing
Would it be fun to comb yourself with your feet? Why? (It would be fun and funny to comb myself with you feet because feet don't normally hold things.)

Open-ended

What is the beaver doing in the picture on p. 27? (chewing on a tree)

- The beaver is chewing on a tree. Do you think the beaver has strong teeth or weak teeth? Why?

As a kit grows older,
it learns to fix leaks in a dam.

26

Soon the kit will be a super builder like its parents.

27

Big Book, pp. 26–27

Distancing

The beaver is doing what its parents do. Would you like to grow up and do what your parents do? (I would like to be like my parents and do what they do because my parents are fun.)

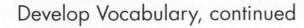
Develop Vocabulary, continued

DAY 3

Completion

This is a drawing of a beaver. What do the lines point to? (parts of the beaver)

- Let's read the labels for the different parts of the beaver together.

KEY:
▨ shows where beavers live

Find your state or province on this map. Do beavers live near you?

28

Parts of a Beaver's Body

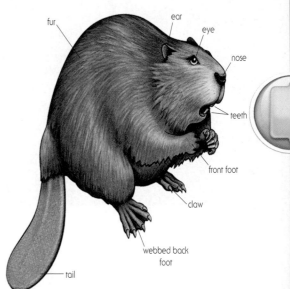

fur
ear
eye
nose
teeth
front foot
claw
webbed back foot
tail

29

Big Book, pp. 28–29

Guide Comprehension, continued

DAY 4

Wh- question

What parts of a beaver's body are the same as parts of your body? (We both have a nose, ears, eyes, and teeth.)

Wh- question

This page is called Hunt and Find. What do you see at the end of each line? (numbers)

- Each line tells us on which pages to find different pieces of information about beavers. Can you find the word *dams* in a yellow box? On what page numbers can I read about beaver dams?

Continue with DAY **3**

Conventions p. 272

Glossary

beaver pond: the deep water on one side of a beaver dam

dam: a wall built to hold back water. Beaver dams are made of sticks and mud.

grooming: keeping fur neat and clean

herbivores: animals that eat only plants

kits: baby beavers

lodge: a beaver house

predators: animals that hunt and eat other animals

webbed: having toes that are joined by skin

Hunt and Find

- beavers cutting down trees on pages 6, 27
- beaver dams on pages 9–10, 26
- beavers grooming on pages 24–25
- beaver lodges on pages 4–5, 8–9, 11
- a beaver slapping its tail on page 18
- kits swimming on pages 20–22

30

31

Big Book, pp. 30–31

Inferential

Why do you think the author included this information in this book? (The author wants to help the reader find information in the book. This is an easy way for readers to find exactly the information they need.)

Skip to DAY **4**

Conventions p. 286

Objectives
- Review prepositional phrases.
- Dictate or write a rhyme.

Conventions
Prepositional Phrases

Review

Display *Building Beavers* and pictures from the book to illustrate these sentences:

> **The pictures in this book show beavers.**
>
> **A kit rides on its mother's tail.**

Remind children about what they learned about prepositional phrases. A prepositional phrase is a group of words that tells how a noun or pronoun is related to the other words in a sentence. A prepositional phrase begins with a preposition. We learned that *on, in, over,* and *under* are prepositions. Say the sentences again. The prepositional phrase in the first sentence is *in this book*. It tells us where the pictures of beavers are. The prepositional phrase in the second sentence tells where the kit rides, *on its mother's tail.*

Guide practice

Write the following sentence frames on the board:

> **Birds fly _____.** (over the school)
>
> **Beavers build lodges _____.** (in the water)
>
> **Beavers keep their eyes open _____.** (under the water)

Read each sentence frame one at a time. Have children use prepositional phrases to complete each sentence. Write each response on the line one at a time. Read each sentence with children.

Team Talk Write *on, in, over,* and *under* on the board. Pair children and have them take turns using one of the prepositions on the board to create a prepositional phrase in a complete sentence. Then have them identify the prepositional phrase.

On their own

Use *Reader's and Writer's Notebook,* p. 433, for more practice with prepositional phrases.

Daily Fix-It

Use the Daily Fix-It to practice conventions.

Reader's and Writer's Notebook, p. 433

Writing
Rhyme

Teach

A rhyme is like a short poem. It is a few words or a sentence that sounds like a song. The words at the ends of the lines rhyme with each other. Rhyming words have the same middle and ending sound. Like a poem, a rhyme has rhythm, like clapping to a beat.

Model

Write the following rhyme on the board:

> **A kit knows how to ____.** (swim)
>
> **He is so fast! Look at ____!** (him)

Have children help you complete the rhyme using the words *swim* and *him*. Have volunteers write the words to fill in the blanks. Then read the rhyme together, clapping the rhythm as you say the rhyme. Have children identify the rhyming words *swim* and *him*.

Guide practice

Have children complete this rhyme about a beaver:

> **A beaver is not a good _____.** (pet)
>
> **He swims in a pond and gets _____.** (wet)

Have children use rhyming words to complete the last two lines.

Independent writing

Have children turn to p. 434 of *Reader's and Writer's Notebook.* Have them copy the rhyme about beavers and draw a picture of the beaver.

Reader's and Writer's Notebook, p. 434

Daily Handwriting

Write *Eli* and *set* on the board. Review correct letter formation of uppercase *E* and lowercase *e*.

Have children write *Eli* and *set* on their Write-On Boards. Remind children to use proper left-to-right and top-to-bottom progression and proper spacing between letters when writing *E* and *e*.

Daily Fix-It

i have a big sled
I have a big sled.

This week's practice sentences appear on Teacher Resources DVD-ROM.

Listening and Speaking
Interpret Information

Review

Remind children that when they interpret information, they think about what they read, see, and know and make a conclusion about the information. Remind children to face the speaker when listening.

Model

When I am crossing the street or driving and I see a red traffic light, I know to stop. The traffic light gives me information. I need to know what the red light means to be safe when I cross a street.

Guide practice

Have children turn to p. 69 of *My Skills Buddy.* Incorporate the Listening and Speaking bullets on p. 68 into the discussion. This page shows three different signs. Each one tells us different information. When you see these signs, you know what to do. Direct children to sign 1. What should you do when you see this sign? (stop) Repeat with the other signs on the page.

My Skills Buddy, p. 69

Independent practice

Have children demonstrate how to interpret information. Tell them you will play the "Silent Game." They need to watch your movements or signs and do the action you indicate. Do the following movements: gesture to a child; put up a hand to signal stop; put your finger to your lips to indicate quiet; sweep your hands in an upward motion for the class to rise and a downward motion for them to sit. Discuss with them the actions you did and how they interpreted the information. Refer children to their Rules for Listening and Speaking from pp. 1–2 of *Reader's and Writer's Notebook.* Remind children to face the speaker when listening and ask questions if they don't understand.

Reader's and Writer's Notebook, pp. 1–2

Be a Good Listener

1. Face the person who is speaking.
2. Be quiet while someone is speaking.
3. Pay attention to the speaker.
4. Ask questions if you don't understand.

Differentiated Instruction

 Advanced

Access Content Have children discuss other signs they have seen. Have them tell where they have seen the signs and what the signs look like. If children don't know what the signs mean, draw the sign on the board and explain what information it tells.

English Language Learners
Physical Response Play a simple game. Have children line up. Tell them to march toward you. When you point to the Stop sign on p. 69 of *My Skills Buddy,* children should then stop walking.

Objectives

- Review skills learned and practiced today.
- Use prepositional phrases in complete sentences.

Wrap Up Your Day

✔ **Concept Talk** Today we read about beavers and how they build their lodges. What do beavers use to build their lodges?

✔ **Respond to Literature** Today we read about a camping trip. What things did Max and Jen do on the trip?

✔ **Conventions** Have children make up a sentence that uses one of these prepositions in a prepositional phrase: *on, in, over, under*. Then have them illustrate their sentence and write the prepositional phrase on the page.

✔ **Homework Idea** Have children tell their families one thing they learned about beavers.

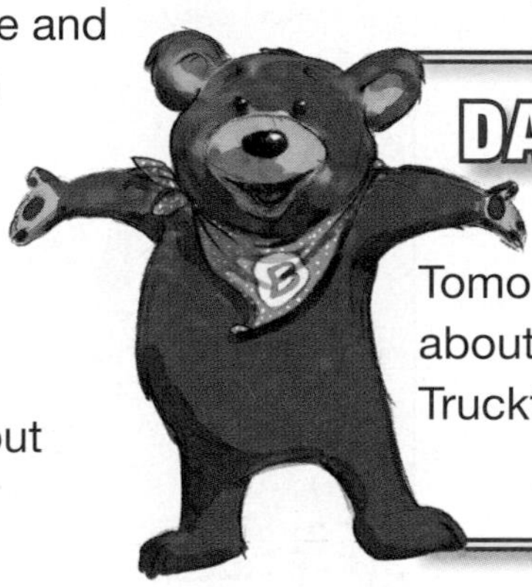

Preview DAY 4

Tomorrow we will read about one of our Trucktown friends.

Science
Compare and Contrast

Materials: Trade Book *Old MacDonald had a Woodshop,* Big Book *Building Beavers*

Real and Make-Believe Have children recall what they read in the story *Old MacDonald had a Woodshop* and in *Building Beavers.* Make a T-chart with one side labeled *Real* and the other side labeled *Make-Believe.* Let's decide if the things the animals do in these stories are what real animals do or what make-believe animals do. What do the animals do in *Old MacDonald had a Woodshop?* (They use tools.) Do real or make-believe animals use tools? (make-believe)

Write *use tools* in the *Make-Believe* column. What do the beavers do in *Building Beavers?* (They cut down trees with their teeth.) Do real or make-believe beavers cut down trees with their teeth? (real) Write *cut down trees* in the *Real* column. Have children name other things to add to the chart.

Real	Make-Believe
cut down trees	use tools
hibernate	go to school
make nests	have a party

Comprehension
What It's All About

Materials: Trade Book *Mayday! Mayday!,* paper

Recall the Main Idea Give each child a sheet of paper. Display the book and briefly review the major events in the story. Give children three possible main ideas for the story and tell them to choose what the book is all about. Then have them draw a picture of the main idea in one half of the paper. Use the following choices:

Mayday! Mayday!

a helicopter, a storm, <u>a rescue</u>

Phonics
Vowel Substitution

Substitute Vowels to Make New Words
Write these words on the board: *red, bed, ten, hit, pot, pod.* Tell children to substitute the vowel in each word with either *a, e, i,* or *o* to make as many new words from each word as they can. Have children write the new words on a sheet of paper. Ask children to read their new words aloud.

red	rod
bed	bad, bid
ten	tan, tin
hit	hot, hat
pot	pit, pat, pet
pod	pad

Objectives

- Discuss the concept to develop oral language.
- Build oral vocabulary.

Today at a Glance

Oral Vocabulary
stream, lake

Phonemic Awareness
Review /e/, /a/, /i/, /o/

Phonics
◉ Reteach /e/ Spelled *Ee*
Spell Words

Comprehension
◉ Main Idea

Conventions
Telling Sentences

Writing
Extend the Concept

Vocabulary
Words for Actions

TRUCKTOWN on Reading Street

Start your engines!

- Display "Wrecker Rosie Sat on a Wall" and lead the group in saying the rhyme a few times.
- Next, have the group clap the rhythm as they recite the rhyme.
- When children master the rhythm, have them march around the room as they say the rhyme.

Truckery Rhymes

Concept Talk

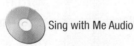
Question of the Week

How do beavers build their homes?

Build concepts

Write and read the question of the week as you track the print. Tell children to respond in complete sentences. Display Sing with Me Chart 33B.

Listen for Amazing Words

Today we are going to sing "Hush, Little Beaver." I want you to listen for the words *stream* and *lake*. Read the title and have children describe the picture. Sing the song several times to the tune "Hush, Little Baby." Tell children to sing with you. Have them clap when they hear *stream* and *lake*.

Hush, Little Beaver

Hush, little beaver, go to sleep,
You've built a lodge that's very deep.

If that lodge is in river or stream,
You'll be safe, while you dream.

Hush, little beaver, go to sleep,
You've built a lodge that's very deep.

If that lodge is in a lake,
You'll paddle around, when you awake.

Talk with Me/Sing with Me Chart 33B

🔘 Sing with Me Audio

ELL **Produce Oral Language** Use the Day 4 instruction on ELL Poster 33 to extend and enrich language.

Oral Vocabulary
Amazing Words

Amazing Words

beaver	lodge
paddle	river
stream	lake

Teach Amazing Words

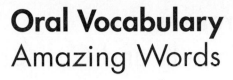 **Amazing Words** **Oral Vocabulary Routine**

1. **Introduce the Word** A *stream* is a small river. A *stream* is not very wide or very deep. What's our new Amazing Word for a small river? Say it with me: *stream*.

2. **Demonstrate** *You can walk across a stream.* What else can you do in a *stream*?

   Repeat steps 1 and 2.

   Introduce the Word A *lake* is a body of water surrounded by land. A *lake* can be small or very big. What's our new Amazing Word for a body of water surround by land? Say it with me: lake.

   Demonstrate *You can take a boat out on a lake.* What else can you do in a *lake*?

3. **Apply** Have children use *stream* and *lake* in complete sentences to tell how they are alike and how they are different.

Routines Flip Chart

Use Amazing Words

To reinforce the concept and the Amazing Words, have children supply the appropriate Amazing Word for each sentence.

A _____ **can be very deep.** (lake)

A small _____ **flows past our house.** (stream)

Differentiated Instruction

 Strategic Intervention

Visual Support Allow children to draw pictures of a *stream, lake,* and *river* to help distinguish between the three words. Tell them to label their drawings and to keep the pictures to refer to when they hear the words in stories.

Objectives
- Review /e/, /a/, /i/, /o/, and all consonants.
- Review /e/*Ee*, /a/*Aa*, /i/*Ii*, /o/*Oo*, and all consonants.

Check Phonemic Awareness
! SUCCESS PREDICTOR

Phonemic Awareness
Review Short Vowels and Consonants

Review   Display the *egg* Picture Card. This is an *egg. Egg* begins with /e/. What is the picture name? What sound does it begin with? Continue the routine with Picture Cards for the vowels *a, i, o,* and consonants.

Blend sounds   Listen to the sounds in this word: /m/ /e/ /t/. Say them with me: /m/ /e/ /t/. Now I am going to blend the sounds together to say the word: /m/ /e/ /t/, *met.* Continue the blending routine with the following words: *zap, brick, clock, past, Dan, Fred, get, hint, jazz, quick, vat, yak, went.*

Corrective feedback   **If...** children have difficulty with specific sounds, **then...** use the sound routines for saying specific sounds, and have them repeat the sounds with you.

Picture Card

Phonics
Short Vowels and Consonants

Review

Display the *Ee* Alphabet Card. *This is an escalator. Escalator begins with /e/. What letter spells this sound /e/? Yes, the letter e.* Continue the routine with *Aa, Ii, Oo,* and all consonant Alphabet Cards. Have children name each letter and tell the sound for the letter.

Alphabet Card

Differentiated Instruction

SI Strategic Intervention

Connect Sound-Spelling Tell children to use their Write-On Boards to write letters they have difficulty connecting to sounds. Have them review the sound-spellings with a partner.

Don't Wait Until Friday

MONITOR PROGRESS | **Check Phonemic Awareness**

Write *red* on the board. Have children blend the sound of each letter to read the words. Continue with the other words.

| red | mat | hen | tin | big |
| hop | pot | set | can | net |

If... children cannot blend the sounds to read the words,

then... use the small-group Strategic Intervention lesson, p. DI•38, to reteach decoding words.

Continue to monitor children's progress using other instructional opportunities during the week so that they an be successful with the Day 5 Assessment. See the Skills Trace on p. 218.

Day 1	Day 2	Day 3	**Day 4**	Day 5
Check Phonemic Awareness	Check Sound-Spelling/ Retelling	Check Word Reading	**Check Phonemic Awareness**	Check Oral Vocabulary

Success Predictor

Objectives
- Spell words.
- Blend and segment words.
- Read decodable text.
- Read high-frequency words.

Spelling
/e/ Spelled *Ee*

ROUTINE Spell Words

Spell words

1 Review Sound-Spellings Display the *Ee* Alphabet Card. This is an *escalator*. *Escalator* begins with /e/. What is the letter for /e/? (*e*) Continue the routine with the following letters: *Aa, Ii, Oo* and all consonants.

2 Model Today we are going to spell some words. Listen to the three sounds in *set*: /s/ /e/ /t/.

- What is the first sound in *set*? (/s/) What is the letter for /s/? (*s*) Write *s* on the board.

- What is the middle sound you hear? (/e/) What is the letter for /e/? (*e*) Write *e* on the board.

- What is the last sound you hear? (/t/) What is the letter for /t/? (*t*) Write *t* on the board.

- Point to *set*. Help me blend the sound of each letter together to read the word: /s/ /e/ /t/. The word is *set*. Repeat with the word *bet*.

3 Guide Practice Now let's spell some words together. Listen to this word: /b/ /e/ /t/. What is the first sound in *bet*? (/b/) What is the letter for /b/? (*b*) Write *b* on the board. Now you write *b* on your paper. What is the middle sound in *bet*? (/e/) What is the letter for /e/? (*e*) Write *e* on the board. Now you write *e* on your paper. What is the last sound in *bet*? (/t/) What is the letter for /t/? (*t*) Write *t* on the board. Now you write *t* on your paper. Now we can blend the sound of each letter together to read the word: /b/ /e/ /t/. What is the word? (*bet*) Continue spell and blend practice with the following words: *hat, bit, got, bed, sad, sod, grin, grab, step.*

4 On Your Own This time I am going to say a word. I want you to write it on your paper. Remember, first, say the word slowly in your head, and then write the letter for each sound. Listen carefully. Write the word *best*. Give children time to write the word.

How do you spell the word *best*? Listen to the sounds: /b/ /e/ /st/. The first sound is /b/. What is the letter for /b/? Did you write *b* on your paper? What is the letter for /e/? Did you write *e* on your paper? What are the letters for /st/? Did you write *st* on your paper? Name the letters in *best*. *Best* is spelled *b, e, s, t.* Continue the activity with the following words: *rest, lamp, band, bit, on, ant, red, not.*

Get Set, Roll! Reader 33
 Practice /e/ Spelled *Ee*

Review Review the high-frequency words *look, that, is, a, what, the, blue,* and *was*. Have children read each word as you point to it on the Word Wall.

Teach rebus words Write the word *truck* on the board. This is the word *truck.* Name the letters with me: *t, r, u, c, k.* Look for the word *truck* in the story we read today. A picture above the word will help you read it.

Read Get Set, Roll! Reader 33 Today we will read a book about a dent in a wall. Point to the title of the book. What is the title of the book? (*A Big Dent*) We will read /e/ words in this book.

Use the routine for reading decodable books found in the Routines Flip Chart to read Get Set, Roll! Reader 33.

Get Set, Roll! Reader 33

Differentiated Instruction

SI Strategic Intervention

Support Spelling Have children copy the correct spellings of words they misspell on their Write-On Boards.

Small Group Time

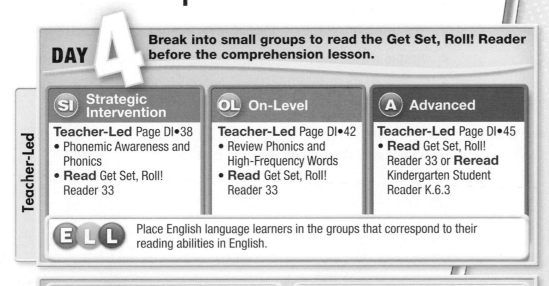

DAY 4 Break into small groups to read the Get Set, Roll! Reader before the comprehension lesson.

SI Strategic Intervention
Teacher-Led Page DI•38
• Phonemic Awareness and Phonics
• **Read** Get Set, Roll! Reader 33

OL On-Level
Teacher-Led Page DI•42
• Review Phonics and High-Frequency Words
• **Read** Get Set, Roll! Reader 33

A Advanced
Teacher-Led Page DI•45
• **Read** Get Set, Roll! Reader 33 or **Reread** Kindergarten Student Reader K.6.3

ELL Place English language learners in the groups that correspond to their reading abilities in English.

Practice Stations
• Visit the Let's Write Station
• Visit the Read for Meaning Station

Independent Activities
• Read independently
• Audio Text of the Big Book
• *Reader's and Writer's Notebook*

Objectives
◎ Practice main idea.
• Review cause and effect.

Comprehension
Main Idea

Practice main idea

Envision It!

Have children turn to the Main Idea picture on p. 54 of *My Skills Buddy*. As you look at the pictures, remind children that the details help determine the main idea of the selection. The main idea is the most important idea.

Team Talk Pair children and have them discuss the main idea of *Max and Jen Go Camping*. What is *Max and Jen Go Camping* all about?

My Skills Buddy, pp. 54–55

Cause and Effect

Review

When we think about cause and effect, we think about what happens and why it happens. Good readers look for causes and effects as they read to help them understand a selection.

Push a book off of a table. What happened? The book fell off the table. Why did the book fall off the table? I pushed the book off the table.

• What is the effect? (The book falling off the table is the effect.)

• What is the cause of the book falling off the table? (me pushing the book off the table)

More practice

For more practice with cause and effect, use *Reader's and Writer's Notebook,* p. 435.

Reader's and Writer's Notebook, p. 435

Third Read—Big Book
Building Beavers

Guide comprehension

Display *Building Beavers*. Remind children that beavers cut down trees and can change a river or stream by building a lodge or dam.

- When the beavers build a dam, they stop the river or stream from flowing. Why do they build a dam? (so they can make a lodge)

- What happens to the water on the other side of the dam? (The water cannot flow through. A pond is made behind the dam.)

Reread *Building Beavers*. Return to p. 257. Follow the Day 4 arrow and use the Guide Comprehension notes to give children the opportunity to gain a more complete understanding of the selection.

DAY **2**

Read for enjoyment

DAY **3**

Reread using Develop Vocabulary notes

DAY **4**

Reread using Guide Comprehension notes

Differentiated Instruction

 SI Strategic Intervention

Support Comprehension Have children think about how they woke up this morning. What happens in the morning? You wake up. What causes you to wake up? Some children may say a parent, an alarm clock, or the sun. Have children identify what action is the cause and what action is the effect.

Objectives
- Identify telling sentences.
- Practice telling sentences.

Conventions
Telling Sentences

Review

Remind children of what they learned about telling sentences. A telling sentence is a sentence that tells what someone or something is or does. It begins with an uppercase letter and ends with a period. I will say some telling sentences about myself. *I am a teacher. I play the piano.* These sentences are telling sentences. They tell what I am and tell something that I do.

Guide practice

Display a page from *Building Beavers*. Have the children make telling sentences about the picture. Have them tell what the beaver or beavers are doing in the picture. Write children's sentences on the board. What kind of letter should your sentence begin with? What should I put at the end of the sentence?

On their own

Use *Reader's and Writer's Notebook,* p. 436, for more practice with telling sentences.

Daily Fix-It

Use the Daily Fix-It exercise for more conventions practice.

Reader's and Writer's Notebook, p. 436

Writing

Extend the Concept: Text to World

Discuss beavers

We just read a selection about beavers. We saw pictures about what they look like, and we read about how they move and how they build their homes.

Ask children to think about all the things they learned about beavers. Talk with children about more things they want to know about beavers that they did not read about in the selection.

Guide practice

Use children's contributions to the discussion to write questions.

> **How big can a beaver get?**
>
> **What do beavers eat?**
>
> **How long can a beaver hold its breath underwater?**

Encourage children to help you write more questions. Have them read the questions with you. Discuss how the class can find answers to the questions.

Independent writing

Have children write or dictate their own question about beavers or they may copy a question from the board. Invite children to read their questions to the class.

Daily Handwriting

Write uppercase *E* and lowercase *e* on the board. Review correct letter formation with children.

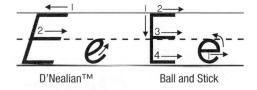

D'Nealian™   Ball and Stick

Have children write a row of uppercase *E* and lowercase *e* on their Write-On Boards. Remind them to use proper left-to-right and top-to-bottom progression when writing *E* and *e*.

Differentiated Instruction

 **Strategic Intervention**

Support Writing Remind children that questions begin with uppercase letters and end with question marks.

Daily Fix-It

will you sit with me
<u>W</u>ill you sit with me<u>?</u>

This week's practice sentences appear on Teacher Resources DVD-ROM.

English Language Learners
Build Background List garden tools on the board and review how they can be used with children.

Objectives
- Practice using words for actions in sentences.
- Produce rhyming words.

Vocabulary
Words for Actions

Teach

Write the words *dig, carry, eat,* and *sleep* on the board. Point to each word as you read it. These words tell actions. Have children turn to p. 68 of *My Skills Buddy*. Use the second Vocabulary bullet in the discussion. Direct them to the picture of the man digging. What can this man do? He can *dig.* Direct them to the man with the toolbox. What can this man do with the toolbox? He can *carry* it. Repeat with the *eat* and *sleep* pictures.

Pair children and have them take turns using the action words *dig, carry, eat,* and *sleep* in complete sentences.

My Skills Buddy, p. 68

Wrap Up Your Day

✔ **Oral Language** Sing again with children "Hush, Little Beaver." Have them clap when they hear the Amazing Words *beaver, lodge, paddle, river, stream,* and *lake.*

✔ **Phonemic Awareness** I will say a word with /e/. You say a word that rhymes with my word. Say the following words: *get, red, speck, well, beg, rest, tent, pen.*

✔ **Homework Idea** Have children find pictures in old magazines of things with the /e/ sound, and then cut them out and paste them on a sheet of paper.

Preview DAY 5

Tell children that tomorrow they will review some of the books and stories they have read this week.

Extend Your Day!

Science
Using the Earth

Materials: Big Books *Animal Babies in Grasslands, A Bed for the Winter, One Little Mouse, Building Beavers;* chart paper, drawing paper, writing and drawing utensils

Nature's Homes Review the Big Books children have read so far this year in which they have seen animal homes. Include these books: *Animal Babies in Grasslands, A Bed for the Winter, One Little Mouse,* and *Building Beavers.* Let's recall some stories we have read this year about animals and their homes. What did we learn about where these animals live and the homes they make? As you discuss the selections, make a six-column chart on the board or on chart paper. Head each column as follows: *Name; mud; grass; sticks; leaves; other.* Write the name of the selection in the *Name* column. Make a check in each column where the use of that material applies to the animals in that book. Use the other column to write materials that are not listed.

Connect to Writing Have children draw a picture of one of the animal homes listed on the chart. Have them dictate or write a statement for their picture.

Beavers live by the water.

Phonics
Match It!

Materials: Picture Cards—*ant, bed, box, desk, jet, lamp, mop, pig, six, sled, wig, yak; index cards*

Match Words with Pictures Write the word for each Picture Card on an index card. Give children a set of Picture Cards and a set of index cards. Have them match each index card with the correct Picture Card.

ant
desk
lamp

Spelling
Changeable Words

Materials: Alphabet Cards

Word Wise Distribute one Alphabet Card to each child. Display the cards *Hh, Aa,* and *Tt* to form the word *hat.* This is the word *hat.* Let's try to make a new word. Who has a letter that can be traded for one of these letters to make a new word? Continue having children exchange cards to make a new word from the current word. Write each word that is made on the board. When finished with the activity, have children read the list of words on the board together.

Objectives
- Review the concepts.
- Build oral vocabulary.

Today at a Glance

Oral Vocabulary
beaver, lodge, paddle, river, stream, lake

Phonemic Awareness
◉ Initial and Medial /e/

Phonics
◉ /e/ Spelled *Ee*

Comprehension
◉ Main Idea

Conventions
Statements

Writing
This Week We...

Check Oral Vocabulary
SUCCESS PREDICTOR

TRUCKTOWN on Reading Street

Start your engines!

- Display "Wrecker Rosie Sat on a Wall" and lead the group in saying the rhyme a few times.
- Have half the group recite the rhyme while the other half acts it out.
- Then have the groups change roles.

Truckery Rhymes

Concept Wrap Up

Question of the Week

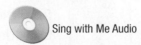 **How do beavers build their homes?**

Listen for Amazing Words

Write the question of the week on the board. Track the print as you read it to children. Have them use the Amazing Words in their responses (*beaver, lodge, paddle, river, stream, lake*). Display Sing with Me Chart 33B. Let's sing "Hush, Little Beaver" together. I want you to listen for the Amazing Words we learned this week. Say them with me: *beaver, lodge, paddle, river, stream, lake.* Sing the song several times to the tune of "Hush, Little Baby." Then discuss how beavers build their homes. Remind children to speak one at a time.

Hush, Little Beaver

Hush, little beaver, go to sleep,
You've built a lodge that's very deep.

If that lodge is in river or stream,
You'll be safe, while you dream.

Hush, little beaver, go to sleep,
You've built a lodge that's very deep.

If that lodge is in a lake,
You'll paddle around, when you awake.

Sing with Me Chart 33B

🔘 Sing with Me Audio

ELL Use the Day 5 instruction on ELL Poster 33 to monitor children's understanding of the lesson concept.

ELL Poster 33

Oral Vocabulary
Amazing Words

beaver	lodge
paddle	river
stream	lake

Review **Let's Talk** Display Talk with Me Chart 33A. We learned six new Amazing Words this week. Let's say the Amazing Words as I point to the pictures on the chart. Point to each picture and give children the chance to say the appropriate Amazing Word before offering it.

Have children supply the appropriate Amazing Word to complete each sentence.

A _____ builds a home in water. (beaver)

Beavers live in a _____. (lodge)

A beaver uses its webbed feet to _____ in the water. (paddle)

A _____ is a flowing body of water. (river)

We can cross the _____ without using a bridge. (stream)

A _____ is surrounded on all sides by land. (lake)

Talk with Me/Sing with Me Chart 33A

Differentiated Instruction

 Advanced

Amazing Words Have children choose one Amazing Word they feel as though they don't know very well. Have them say the definition in their own words, and then use that word in a sentence.

It's Friday

MONITOR PROGRESS **Check Oral Vocabulary**

Demonstrate Word Knowledge Monitor the Amazing Words by asking the following questions. Have children use the Amazing Word in their answer.

• **What body of water is surrounded by land?** (lake)

• **What animal builds a home in water?** (beaver)

• **What is the name for a beaver's home?** (lodge)

• **What flowing water is smaller than a river?** (stream)

• **How do beavers use their webbed feet?** (paddle)

• **What kind of water flows fast and is bigger than a stream?** (river)

If... children have difficulty using the Amazing Words,

then... reteach the words using the Oral Vocabulary Routine on the Routines Flip Chart.

Day 1	Day 2	Day 3	Day 4	Day 5
Check Phonemic Awareness	Check Sound-Spelling/ Retelling	Check Word Reading	Check Phonemic Awareness	**Check Oral Vocabulary**

Success Predictor

Oral Vocabulary **Success Predictor**

Objectives

◎ Review /e/ spelled *Ee.*

Phonemic Awareness Review

/e/

Isolate initial and medial /e/

Display the *elephant* Picture Card. What is the first sound in *elephant?* Say the word with me: *elephant,* /e/ /e/ /e/. Review initial /e/ in these words: *egg, elbow, elevator, elm.*

Display the *web* Picture Card. What is the middle sound in *web?* Say the sounds with me: /w/ /e/ /b/, *web.* The middle sound is /e/. Continue with these words *pet, jet,* and *men.*

Picture Card

Discriminate medial sounds

Have available the *egg, ant, igloo, and octopus* Picture Cards. Have children say the name of the picture on each card and the beginning sound. Hold up the *egg* and *ant* Picture Cards. I will say a word. Listen to the middle sound. Point to the Picture Card that has the same beginning sound as the middle sound you hear: *bed.* Do you hear /e/ or /a/ in *bed?* Hold up the *egg* Picture Card. I hear /e/ in the middle of *bed.* Continue with the other Picture Cards and the following words: *net, not, Tim, Val, rat, step, left, got, box, lift, hit, sit, jet.*

Picture Card

Phonics Review
↻ /e/ Spelled *Ee*

Teach /e/*Ee*

Display the *Ee* Alphabet Card. This is an *escalator.* What sound do you hear at the beginning of *escalator?* What letter spells that sound?

High-frequency words

Write the word *the* on the board. This is the word *the.* Let's say it together. What is this word? Repeat with *was, to, like,* and *from.*

Apply phonics in familiar text

Let's Reread Have children reread one of the books specific to the target letter sound. You may wish to review the ecodable words and high-frequency words that appear in each book prior to rereading.

Alphabet Card

Decodable Reader 33
My Skills Buddy, p. 58

Kindergarten
Student Reader K.6.3

Get Set, Roll!
Reader 33

Small Group Time

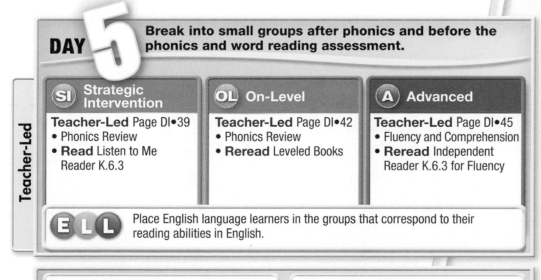

DAY 5 Break into small groups after phonics and before the phonics and word reading assessment.

Teacher-Led

SI Strategic Intervention
Teacher-Led Page DI•39
• Phonics Review
• **Read** Listen to Me Reader K.6.3

OL On-Level
Teacher-Led Page DI•42
• Phonics Review
• **Reread** Leveled Books

A Advanced
Teacher-Led Page DI•45
• Fluency and Comprehension
• **Reread** Independent Reader K.6.3 for Fluency

ELL Place English language learners in the groups that correspond to their reading abilities in English.

Practice Stations
• Visit the Read for Meaning Station
• Visit the Let's Make Art Station

Independent Activities
• Read independently
• Story Sort
• Concept Talk Video

English Language Learners
Reading Remind children that the words in the book go from left to right and top to bottom. Have them use their finger to follow along in the book.

Assess

◎ Read words with /e/.
- Read high-frequency words.
- Read sentences.

Assessment
Monitor Progress

/e/ Spelled Ee

Whole Class Divide a paper into four equal sections for each child. Have children draw and label four pictures of words with /e/.

MONITOR PROGRESS | **Check Word and Sentence Reading**

If... children cannot complete the whole-class assessment,
then... use the Reteach lesson in *First Stop.*

If... you are unsure of a child's grasp of this week's skills,
then... use the assessment below to obtain a clearer evaluation of the child's progress.

/e/ Spelled Ee and high-frequency words

One-on-One To facilitate individual progress monitoring, assess some children on Day 4 and the rest on Day 5. While individual children are being assessed, the rest of the class can reread this week's books and look for words with /e/.

Word reading

Use the word list on reproducible p. 295 to assess a child's ability to read words with short *e* and high-frequency words. We're going to read some words. I'll read the first word, and you read the rest. The first word is *pet*, /p/ /e/ /t/. For each child, record any decoding problems. Have children read the words aloud to you.

Sentence reading

Use the sentences on reproducible p. 295 to assess a child's ability to read words in sentences. Have each child read two sentences aloud. Have each child read different sentences. Start over with sentence one if necessary.

Record scores

Monitor children's accuracy by recording their scores using the Word and Sentence Reading Chart for this unit in *First Stop.*

Name _____

Read the Words

have ☐   kept ☐

pet ☐   for ☐

nest ☐   step ☐

little ☐   next ☐

hen ☐   two ☐

bend ☐   rest ☐

Read the Sentences

1. We have a pet hen.

2. A little rest will help you.

3. Mom kept one pen for Dad and me.

4. Where are two red jets?

5. Fred sat next to the little pup.

Note to Teacher: Children read each word. Children read two sentences.

Scoring for Read the Words: Score 1 point for each correct word.

Short *e* (*pet, nest, hen, bend, kept, step, next, rest*) _____ / ___8___

High-Frequency Words (*have, little, for, two*) _____ / ___4___

MONITOR PROGRESS
- Review short *e*
- Review high-frequency words

Objectives

- Recognize a fable.
- Identify the theme of fable.
- Discuss the purpose of listening to a fable.

My Skills Buddy, pp. 70–71

Let's Practice It!
Fable

Teach

Tell children that today they will listen to a fable. A fable is a kind of story. Review the features of a fable with children.

- A fable has a big idea, or theme.
- The theme of a fable tells a lesson.
- Fables are stories that are told over and over.

Have children turn to pp. 70 of *My Skills Buddy.* I am going to read a fable called "The Milkmaid and Her Pail." Based on the title, what do you predict might happen next? (Children might predict that a milkmaid will carry milk in a pail.) Look at the first picture. What do you predict might happen next based on this illustration? (Children might predict that the milkmaid will carry her milk to town.) I am going to read this fable. Look at the pictures as I read. Read the story. As you read, ask children to look at the illustrations and predict what might happen next in the text.

Guide practice

Discuss the features of a fable with children and the bulleted text on *My Skills Buddy,* p. 70.

- A fable has a big idea, or theme. What is the main idea of this fable? (Don't count your chickens before they are hatched.)

- The theme of a fable tells a lesson. What does the lesson "don't count your chickens before they are hatched" mean? (Sometimes if you plan too far ahead, things don't work out. It is best to wait until things work out.) Have you ever planned too far ahead?

- How does the milkmaid learn her lesson? (While she is thinking about the dress she will buy with the money she will make after selling her milk, she spills the milk.)

- Fables are stories that are told over and over. Why do people listen to fables? (People understand the lesson in fables. They can relate to it.)

Differentiated Instruction

SI Strategic Intervention

Academic Vocabulary Children may recall that they have learned that a fable has animal characters. Explain that fables often have animal characters but not always. This story is still considered a fable because the milkmaid learns a lesson.

Academic Vocabulary

fable a story that teaches a moral, or lesson

The Milkmaid and Her Pail

One day, a milkmaid was walking to town, carrying a pail of milk on her head.

As she walked, she thought to herself, "When I get to town, I will sell this milk. I will use the money to buy a fine hen. The hen will lay many eggs. I will let the eggs hatch into chicks. When the chicks are grown, I will take them to town and sell them. I will use the money to buy a new dress and ribbons to wear in my hair. How everyone will admire me!"

As the milkmaid imagined how beautiful she would look in her new dress and ribbons, she smiled and tilted her head back, forgetting about the pail of milk. The pail fell to the ground, and all the milk spilled out.

Moral: Don't count your chickens before they hatch.

Objectives
⊚ Review main idea.

Assess
◉ Identify main idea.

Comprehension Assessment
Monitor Progress

Review   **Main Idea** Remind children that the main idea is the most important idea in a story. What do we call the most important idea in a story? (main idea) Good readers listen to find the main idea to help them understand what they are reading.

Read "Robin's Nest"   Tell children that you are going to read them a story about a boy and a robin. Ask them to listen for the main idea of the story. Listen carefully as I read you a story. When I am done, I will ask you to tell me the main idea of the story. Read "Robin's Nest" on p. 79 of the *Read Aloud Anthology*.

Read Aloud Anthology

Check main idea   After you read the story, ask what the boy watched the robin doing.

- What animal is the story about? (a robin)
- Who is watching the robin? (Thomas)
- What is the robin doing? (building a nest for its eggs)
- What does the robin use to build the nest? (string, twigs, grass, mud)
- What is this story all about? (building a nest)

Corrective feedback   If... children cannot identify the main idea,
then... reteach main idea using the Reteach lesson in *First Stop*.

Assess main idea   Use the blackline master on p. 299. Make one copy for each child. Have children look at the pictures on the page and color the picture that shows the main idea of "Robin's Nest."

Name _____

Main Idea

Color the picture that shows what "Robin's Nest" is all about.

Note to Teacher: Have children color the picture that shows the main idea of the story.

MONITOR PROGRESS

• Main Idea

Objectives

- Review telling sentences.
- Write or dictate sentences about beavers.

Conventions
Telling Sentences

Review Remind children what they have learned about telling sentences. A telling sentence is a sentence that tells what someone or something is or does. A telling sentence begins with an uppercase letter and ends with a period.

Model I am going to say a sentence to tell you about our class: *There are [number] children in our class.* My sentence is a telling sentence. What does my sentence tell you? It tells how many children are in our class.

Guide practice Display illustrations in previously read books. Invite children to make telling sentences about the pictures. Ask other children to identify what each telling sentences tells.

On their own Have children draw a picture to tell about one of the pictures they saw in the books. Have them write or dictate a telling sentence to accompany the picture.

Daily Fix-It Use the Daily Fix-It exercise for more conventions practice.

Writing
This Week We...

Review

Display *Building Beavers,* Sing with Me Chart 33B, Phonics Songs and Rhymes Chart 33, Decodable Reader 33 from *My Skills Buddy,* Kindergarten Student Reader K.6.3, and Get Set, Roll! Reader 33. This week we learned about beavers. We read new books, and we sang new songs. Which book or song was your favorite? Let's share our ideas with each other.

Team Talk Pair children and have them take turns telling which book or song was their favorite and why.

Model writing sentences

Today we will write sentences about how beavers build their homes. What do beavers build their lodges out of? I will write the first sentence:

> **Beavers build a lodge with sticks and mud.**

What do they do with their teeth? I will write this sentence:

> **They cut down trees with their teeth.**

Guide practice

Continue writing sentences about other things beavers do as they build their lodges. Then read the sentences with children.

> **Beavers build lodges in the water.**
>
> **They swim underwater to get in the lodge.**

On their own

Have children write or dictate sentences about beavers or they may copy one from the board. Tell them to illustrate their sentence.

Daily Handwriting

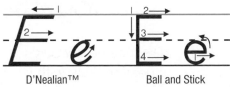

D'Nealian™   Ball and Stick

Write uppercase *E* and lowercase *e* on the board. Review correct letter formation with children.

Have children write a row of uppercase *E* and lowercase *e* on the Write-On Boards. Remind them to use proper left-to-right and top-to-bottom progression.

Differentiated Instruction

 A **Advanced**

Support Writing Encourage children to write three things beavers do when they build their lodges. Tell them to write the sentences in the order the beaver would do them. Remind them they can use sequence words *first, next, last* to put their sentences in order.

Daily Fix-It

do the dogs bark a lot
<u>Do</u> the dogs bark a lot<u>?</u>

This week's practice sentences appear on Teacher Resources DVD-ROM.

English Language Learners
Poster Preview Prepare children for next week by using Week 4 ELL Poster number 34. Read the Poster Talk-Through to introduce the concept and vocabulary. Ask children to identify and describe objects and actions they see.

Objectives
• Review weekly concept.

Wrap Up Your Week!

 Question of the Week

How do beavers build their homes?

Illustrate main idea

This week we talked about beavers building their homes.

• Make a word web like the one shown.

• Write children's responses about things they learned about beavers building their homes on the lines.

• Have children choose the most interesting thing they learned about beavers and draw a picture of it.

• Have them write a sentence about their picture.

Building Beavers

Next Week's Question

What can friends build together?

Discuss next week's question. Talk with children about how beavers build their homes by themselves and friends can build things together.

Preview
NEXT WEEK

Tell children that next week they will read about two friends who build something together.

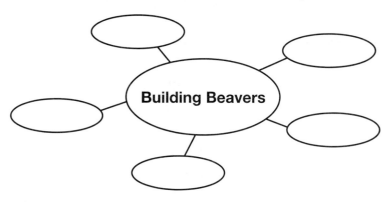

Extend Your Day!

Science
Earth's Resources

Materials: chart paper, writing and drawing tools

Resources Talk about some of the resources provided by the Earth, such as water, plants, and soil. Write each resource as a label in a three-column chart. Ask children what we do with each of these resources and record their responses in the chart.

water	plants	soil
drink	eat	grow plants
grow things	use to build shelter	use minerals in soil

Illustrate How We Use Resources Have children draw and label pictures of people using one of the three resources in the chart.

Phonics
E's in the Bag

Materials: paper bags, items that begin with the letter *e*

What Is It? Have children take a paper bag and write an uppercase *E* and a lowercase *e* on it. Have them look around the classroom for an item or a picture of an item that starts with *e*. Then have children play a guessing game of what *Ee* item is in each bag.

Social Studies
Who Lives Here?

Materials: chart paper, drawing tools, Big Books *Animal Babies in Grasslands, Building Beavers, One Little Mouse, A Bed for the Winter*

Where Animals Live Display Big Books *Animal Babies in Grasslands, Building Beavers, One Little Mouse,* and *A Bed for the Winter.* Discuss with children where all the animals live and why it suits them. Then divide chart paper into three sections for *grasslands, forest,* and *water.* Have children use the books to draw one of the scenes and the animals that live there and the homes they build.

Weekly Assessment

Use the whole-class assessment on pages 294–295 and 298–299 in this Teacher's Edition to check:

- ✔ 🔊 **Short e Spelled** *Ee*
- ✔ 🔊 **Comprehension Skill** *Main Idea*
- ✔ **High-Frequency Words**

Teacher's Edition, Day 5

Managing Assessment

Use the Assessment Handbook for:

- ✔ **Observation Checklists**
- ✔ **Record-Keeping Forms**
- ✔ **Portfolio Assessment**

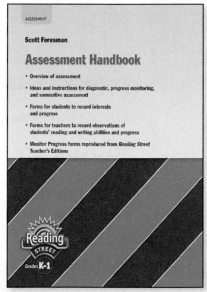

Assessment Handbook

Teacher Notes

Small Group Time

Pacing Small Group Instruction

20~30 mins.

5 Day Plan

DAY 1
- Phonemic Awareness/Phonics
- Decodable Story 33

DAY 2
- Phonemic Awareness/Phonics
- Decodable Reader 33

DAY 3
- Phonemic Awareness/Phonics
- Concept Literacy Reader K.6.3 or Kindergarten Student Reader K.6.3

DAY 4
- Phonemic Awareness/Phonics
- Get Set, Roll! Reader 33

DAY 5
- Phonics Review
- Listen to Me Reader K.6.3

3 or 4 Day Plan

DAY 1
- Phonemic Awareness/Phonics
- Decodable Story 33

DAY 2
- Phonemic Awareness/Phonics
- Decodable Reader 33

DAY 3
- Phonemic Awareness/Phonics
- Concept Literacy Reader K.6.3 or Kindergarten Student Reader K.6.3

DAY 4
- Phonemic Awareness/Phonics
- Get Set, Roll! Reader 33

3 Day Plan: Eliminate the shaded box.

SI Strategic Intervention — DAY 1

Phonemic Awareness•Phonics

- **Isolate /e/** Display the *egg* Picture Card. This is an *egg*. What sound does *egg* begin with? *Egg* begins with /e/. Say it with me: /e/ /e/ /e/, *egg.* Repeat with the *elbow* and *elephant* Picture Cards.

- **Connect /e/ to Ee** I am going to say three words. Listen for /e/ in one of the words: *pet, pit, pat.* Say the words with me: *pet, pit, pat.* Which word has /e/? *Pet* has /e/. What sound do you hear in the middle of *pit*? (/i/) What sound do you hear in the middle of *pat*? (/a/) Write the letters *Ee* on the board. The letter e can stand for /e/ in words. Continue with the following sets of words: *not, nut, net; tin, ten, tan; bug, beg, bag.*

Decodable Story 33

- **Review** Review the previously taught high-frequency words by writing each word on the board and having children read the word with you.

a	they	was	the	with	for	little	one	have

If... children have difficulty reading the words,
then... say a word and have children point to the word. Repeat several times, giving assistance as needed.

- **Read** Have children read *Jim and Kim* orally. Then have them reread the story several times individually.

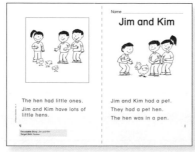

Reader's and Writer's Notebook, pp. 427–428

Objectives
- Identify the common sounds that letters represent.
- Read at least 25 high-frequency words from a commonly used list.

SI Strategic Intervention DAY 2

Phonemic Awareness•Phonics

■ **Discriminate /e/** Display Phonics Songs and Rhymes Chart 33. *Leg* has /e/ in the middle. When you hear a word in the song that has /e/ like *leg,* shake your leg. Sing "Grand Sand Castle" to the tune of "Alouette" several times with children.

■ **Recognize *Ee*** Ask children to name words with /e/. List the words on the board as they say them. Have children echo read the list of words. Then ask children to take turns circling *e* in the words on the board.

Decodable Reader 33

■ **Review** Review the high-frequency words by writing *with* on the board. This is the word *with.* What word is this? Continue with the following words: *a, what, the, do, to.*

> **If...** children have difficulty reading the words,
> **then...** say a word and have children point to the word. Repeat several times, giving assistance as needed.

■ **Read** Display the cover of *The Red Egg* on p. 58 of *My Skills Buddy.* Ask a volunteer to read the first page of the story. Have children tell what Ed does with the red egg. Continue through the story in this manner.

My Skills Buddy

More Reading

Use Leveled Readers or other text at children's instructional level.

Objectives
• Identify the common sounds that letters represent.
• Read at least 25 high-frequency words from a commonly used list.
• Retell a main event from a story read aloud.

SI *Strategic Intervention*   DAY **3**

Phonemic Awareness•Phonics

- **Isolate /e/** Display the *ten* Picture Card. This is *ten.* Do you hear /e/ in *ten?* Say it with me: /t/ /e/ /n/, *ten. Ten* has /e/ in the middle. Repeat with *hen* and *net.*

- **Connect /e/ to Ee** Display the *jet* Picture Card. This is a *jet.* Say it with me: /j/ /e/ /t/, *jet. Jet* has /e/ in the middle. Write the letters *Ee* on the board. The letter *e* can stand for /e/ in words. Say the sound with me: /e/ /e/ /e/. When you hear a word that has /e/, I want you to pretend to be a jet flying through the air. Use the following words: *nap, net, clap, tent, rest, sand, bend, can, fan, hen.*

- **Blend Sounds** Write *set* on the board. Have children blend the sound of each letter to read the word. Repeat the routine with the words *nest, bed,* and *den.*

- **Review High-Frequency Words** Write *the* on the board. Have volunteers say the word and use it in a sentence. Continue with the words *was, to, like,* and *from.*

- **Read** To practice phonics and high-frequency words, have children read Kindergarten Student Reader K.6.3. Use the instruction on pp. 254–255.

For a complete lesson plan and additional practice, see the **Leveled Reader Teaching Guide**.

Concept Literacy Reader K.6.3

- **Preview and Predict** Display the cover of the Concept Literacy Reader K.6.3. Point to the title of the book. The title of the book is *Busy Beavers.* What do you think the book is about? Have children tell about the picture and what they think the book might be about.

- **Set a Purpose** We talked about the title of the book. Let's read the book to learn what beavers can do. Have children read the Concept Literacy Reader.

- **Read** Provide corrective feedback as children read the book orally. During reading, ask them if they are able to confirm any of the predictions they made prior to reading.

If... children have difficulty reading the book individually,
then... read a sentence aloud as children point to each word. Then have the group reread the sentences as they continue pointing to the words.

- **Retell** Have children retell the content as you page through the book. Help them identify what the book is about. Also call attention to what body parts beavers use to cut, chew, swim, and build.

Concept Literacy Reader K.6.3

Objectives
- Identify the common sounds that letters represent.
- Predict what might happen next based on the title.
- Retell important facts in a text, heard or read.

 **SI** Strategic Intervention **DAY 4**

More Reading

Use Leveled Readers or other text at children's instructional level.

Phonemic Awareness•Phonics

■ **Listen for /e/** Tell children you will tell them a story and they should listen for /e/. When you say a word with /e/, children should write the letter in the air and repeat the word. Tell a simple story, emphasizing /e/ words and pausing to give children a chance to respond. *Jen* and *Ted set* up the *red tent.* Stay, *tent,* stay! The *red tent fell* in *ten* minutes. No, *tent,* no! *Jen* and *Ted set* up the *red tent* again. *Ted* used a *peg* to *set* up the *tent.* Go, *Ted,* go!

■ **Blending** Write *men* on the board. Help me blend this word. Listen as I say each sound: /m/ /e/ /n/. Now let's blend the sounds together to read the word: /m/ /e/ /n/, *men.* Continue with *den, end, hen, ten,* and *dent.*

Get Set, Roll! Reader 33

■ **Review** Review the following high-frequency words with children prior to reading the story: *look, that, is, a, what, the, blue, was.*

■ **Read** Display Get Set, Roll! Reader 33, *A Big Dent.* Today we will read a new story about a dent in a wall. Point to the title of the story. The title of the story is *A Big Dent.* Look at the cover and think about the title. What do you think this story will be about?

Get Set, Roll! Reader 33

> **If...** children have difficulty reading the story individually, **then...** read a sentence aloud as children point to each word. Then have the group reread the sentences as they continue pointing to the words.

■ **Reread** Use echo reading of Get Set, Roll! Reader 33 to model fluent reading. Use your oral reading to model for children where to pause, when to change pitch, and which words to stress. Then have children reread orally three to four times, or until they can read with few or no mistakes.

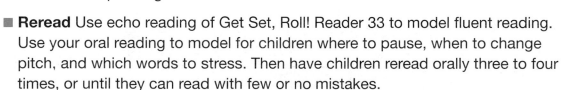

Objectives
• Read at least 25 high-frequency words from a commonly used list.
• Predict what might happen next based on the cover.

Small Group Time

More Reading

Use Leveled Readers or other text at children's instructional level.

SI Strategic Intervention   DAY **5**

Phonics Review

■ **Discriminate /e/** Draw six nests on the board. Collect twelve Picture Cards, including the following cards: *jet, red, egg, elbow, elevator, dress.* Mix the cards and display them one at a time. Have a child name the picture. If the word has /e/, have the child write a lowercase *e* in one of the nests.

Listen to Me Reader K.6.3

■ **Preview and Predict** Display the cover of the book. The title of this story is *Gus Will Stop.* It is written by Ann Witkowski. It is illustrated by Robin Boyer. What kind of animal is Gus? What kind of job do you think he has? Tell me what you think this story will be about.

Listen to Me Reader K.6.3

■ **Set a Purpose** Review children's ideas. Point out that after they read, they will know more about Gus and the bus. Tell children that you will read the story with them. Follow along with your finger as I read. Then we will take turns reading this page. Repeat this routine through all of the pages. Guide children to decode words.

■ **Reread for Fluency** Use echo reading of Listen to Me Reader K.6.3 to model reading fluently. Use your oral reading to model for children when to pause, when to change pitch, and which words to stress. Then have children reread orally three to four times, or until they can read with few or no mistakes.

Objectives

• Identify the common sounds that letters represent.
• Predict what might happen next based on the cover.

 **DAY 1**

Phonemic Awareness•Phonics

■ **Isolate /e/** Display the *pen* Picture Card. This is a pen. *Pen* has /e/. Say it with me: /p/ /e/ /n/, *pen.* Repeat with *sled, tent,* and *vest.*

■ **Discriminate /e/** Display the *Ee* Alphabet Card and the *web* Picture Card. These are the letters *Ee* and a picture of a *web.* The letter *e* can stand for /e/ in words. Does *web* have /e/? Say it with me: /w/ /e/ /b/, *web.* Yes, *web* has /e/. Show children how to make a spider with your hands. Put your thumbs together and wiggle your other fingers like spider legs. I will say some words. When you hear a word with /e/, I want you to make a spider with your hands. Use the following words: *hand, bend, pen, pin, hot, pet, let, lot, wet.*

Objectives
• Identify the common sounds that letters represent.

Pacing Small Group Instruction

20–30 mins.

5 Day Plan	
DAY 1	• Phonemic Awareness/ Phonics • Decodable Story 33
DAY 2	• Phonemic Awareness/ Phonics • High-Frequency Words • Decodable Reader 33
DAY 3	• Phonemic Awareness/ Phonics • Kindergarten Student Reader K.6.3
DAY 4	• Get Set, Roll! Reader 33
DAY 5	• Phonics Review • Reread Leveled Books

 **DAY 2**

Phonemic Awareness•Phonics

■ **Simon Says** Play a version of "Simon Says" by identifying the sounds in words. Give a simple direction, such as *Simon says hop on one foot if the word has /o/.* Then say a series of words with and without /o/. After several words, give children a new direction, such as:

Simon says clap if the word has /a/.
Simon says move your leg if the word has /e/.
Simon says wiggle your fingers if the word has /i/.

■ **High-Frequency Words** Display the following word cards: *the, was, to, like, from.* Say the word *from* and select a child to point to the word. Have children say the word and use it in a sentence. Continue with the other words.

Objectives
• Identify the common sounds that letters represent.
• Read at least 25 high-frequency words from a commonly used list.

3 or 4 Day Plan	
DAY 1	• Phonemic Awareness/ Phonics • Decodable Story 33
DAY 2	• Phonemic Awareness/ Phonics • High-Frequency Words • Decodable Reader 33
DAY 3	• Phonemic Awareness/ Phonics • Kindergarten Student Reader K.6.3
DAY 4	• Get Set, Roll! Reader 33

3 Day Plan: Eliminate the shaded box.

More Practice

For additional practice with this week's phonics skills, have children reread the Decodable Story (Day 1) and the Decodable Reader (Day 2).

Small Group Time

Phonemic Awareness•Phonics

■ **Draw and Label /e/ Words** Divide a piece of paper into four sections for each child. Ask children to draw four /e/ words. Then have them label their pictures. Encourage children to listen to the sounds in the word and write the letter for each sound.

■ **Connect /e/ to Ee** Write the letters *Ee* and the words *big* and *beg* on the board. The letter *e* can stand for /e/ in words. Which words has /e/ in the middle? Have a volunteer circle the *e* in *beg.* Then have the group read the words. Continue with these pairs of words: *bed, bid; red, rid; hem, ham.*

Kindergarten Student Reader K.6.3

■ **Preview and Predict** Display the cover of the book. The title of this story is *Max and Jen Go Camping.* Look at the cover. What do you think will happen on their camping trip? Tell me your ideas.

Kindergarten Student Reader K.6.3

■ **Set a Purpose** Review the list of things children think might happen in the story. Remind children they will read to find out about Max and Jen's camping trip.

■ **Read** Have children follow along as they read the story with you. After reading p. 3, ask children to tell what goes in the van. Continue with each page. Ask the following questions:

• Who is going on the camping trip?
• Who sets up the camp? How do you set up a camp?
• What do Max and Jen see when they go up a hill?
• What do they see at the pond?

■ **Summarize** Have children retell the story to a partner and tell whether Max and Jen have fun camping.

■ **Text to Self** Help children make personal connections to the story as they tell about their experiences camping.

Objectives
• Identify the common sounds that letters represent.
• Predict what might happen next based on the cover.
• Make connections to own experiences.

OL On-Level | DAY 4

Get Set, Roll! Reader 33

■ **Review** Review the words *look, that, is, a, what, the, blue,* and *was* by writing each word on the board and saying the word with children. Then give clues to a word and have children tell which word it is.

■ **Read** Display Get Set, Roll! Reader 33, *A Big Dent.* Point to the title of the story. *A Big Dent* is the title of the story. We can read all the words in this story. Look at the cover of the story. What do you think this story is about? Let's read to find out. Write *Ee* on the board and remind children that *e* can stand for /e/: *set, red, men, send.* Have them listen for words with /e/ as they read *A Big Dent.*

Objectives
• Read at least 25 high-frequency words from a commonly used list.
• Predict what might happen next based on the cover.

OL On-Level | DAY 5

Phonics Review

■ **Identify Medial Sounds** Have children form a line behind you. Lead the class around the room, pointing to classroom objects. Have the first child in line name the object, identify the sound in the middle of the word, and say another word with that sound. Then have the child name the letter that spells that sound. After the child's turn, have him or her move to the end of the line so that another child can have a turn. Use simple classroom objects, such as a *pen, bag, can, clock, fan, flag, hat, map, mug, cup, rock, clip,* or *desk.*

Objectives
• Identify the common sounds that letters represent.

More Reading

Use Leveled Readers or other text at children's instructional level to develop fluency.

Small Group Time

Pacing Small Group Instruction

20–30 mins.

5 Day Plan

DAY 1	• Phonemic Awareness/ Phonics • Decodable Story 33
DAY 2	• Phonics • Spelling • Decodable Reader 33
DAY 3	• Independent Reader K.6.3 or Kindergarten Student Reader K.6.3
DAY 4	• Get Set, Roll! Reader 33 or Kindergarten Student Reader K.6.3
DAY 5	• Fluency/ Comprehension • Independent Reader K.6.3

3 or 4 Day Plan

DAY 1	• Phonemic Awareness/ Phonics • Decodable Story 33
DAY 2	• Phonics • Spelling • Decodable Reader 33
DAY 3	• Independent Reader K.6.3 or Kindergarten Student Reader K.6.3
DAY 4	• Get Set, Roll! Reader 33 or Kindergarten Student Reader K.6.3

3 Day Plan: Eliminate the shaded box.

More Practice

For additional practice with this week's phonics skills and to develop fluency, have children reread the Decodable Story (Day 1) and the Decodable Reader (Day 2).

A Advanced — DAY 1

Phonemic Awareness•Phonics

■ **Spell the Letters** Divide the class into small groups. We are going to play a word game in which you get to be the letters. I will say a sound. I want you to listen to the sound and then tell me the letter that stands for that sound. Then I want you to pretend to be that letter. Work together to use your bodies to make the shape of the letter. Use a variety of letter sounds, encouraging the children to be creative and work together to form the letters.

Objectives
• Identify the common sounds that letters represent.

A Advanced — DAY 2

Phonics•Spelling

■ **Connect /e/ to Ee** Display the *egg* Picture Card. What is this word? What is the first sound in *egg*? What letter spells /e/? The letter *e* stands for /e/ in words. Display the *bed* Picture Card. Name the sounds in bed with me: /b/ /e/ /d/, *bed*. What sound is in the middle? What letter spells that sound? What other /e/ words do you know?

■ **Spell Sounds** Give each child the following letter tiles: *b, d, e, g, h, i, n, r, t.* Listen to the sounds in the word *bed:* /b/ /e/ /d/, *bed.* What is the letter for /b/? It is *b.* Place your *b* tile in front of you. Continue with the remaining sounds. Then have children blend the sounds to read the word. Then have children spell *red, hen, net,* and *grin.*

Objectives
• Identify the common sounds that letters represent.
• Use letter-sound correspondences to spell consonant-vowel-consonant (CVC) words.

 **A** Advanced

DAY 3

For a complete lesson plan and additional practice, see the **Leveled Reader Teaching Guide**.

Independent Reader K.6.3

■ **Practice High-Frequency Words** Write the previously taught high-frequency words on the board. Have volunteers say the word and use it in a sentence.

here	you	with	see	the	look

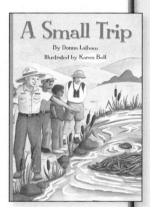

Independent
Reader K.6.3

■ **Activate Prior Knowledge** Explain to children that some people take hikes to look at things in nature. Encourage children to discuss what types of wildlife they might see if they were to take a hike through the forest.

■ **Main Idea** Display the cover of *A Small Trip.* Have children tell what the story was about.

■ **Reread for Fluency** After rereading with children, model reading fluently for them. I am going to read this book aloud. I will read the words with no mistakes. I want you to read it aloud with me. Try to read the words just as I do.

• Use echo reading of Independent Reader K.6.3 to model reading fluently. Use your oral reading to model for children where to pause, when to change pitch, and which words to stress. Then have children reread orally three to four times, or until they can read with few or no mistakes.

■ **Read** For more practice with phonics and high-frequency words and to develop fluency, have children read the Kindergarten Student Reader K.6.3. Use the instruction on pp. 254–255.

More Reading

Use Leveled Readers or other text at children's instructional level.

Objectives
• Read at least 25 high-frequency words from a commonly used list.
• Identify the topic in expository text heard or read, referring to the words.
• Identify the topic in expository text heard or read, referring to the illustrations.

Small Group Time

More Reading

Use Leveled Readers or other text at children's instructional level.

Kindergarten Student Reader K.6.3

- **Preview** Display the cover of Kindergarten Student Reader K.6.3. What is happening in this picture?

- **Reread** Use Kindergarten Student Reader K.6.3 to practice reading fluently.

- **Text to World** Ask children to think about being outdoors. What kinds of things can we see in nature?

- **Read** Have children read Get Set, Roll! Reader 33, *A Big Dent.* Use the instruction on p. 283.

Kindergarten Student Reader K.6.3

Objectives
- Read at least 25 high-frequency words from a commonly used list.
- Make connections to the larger community.

Fluency•Comprehension

- **Reread for Fluency** Use the Independent Reader K.6.3 to model reading fluently for children. I am going to read this selection aloud. I will read the words with no mistakes. I want you to read it aloud with me. Try to read the words just as I do.

- **Comprehension** After children have finished reading, have them retell what they learned in the selection. Then have children look at the cover. How can the cover of *A Small Trip* help us know what the main idea is of this selection?

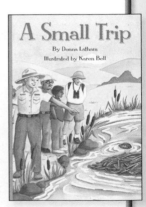

Independent Reader K.6.3

Objectives
- Read at least 25 high-frequency words from a commonly used list.
- Identify the topic in expository text heard or read, referring to the illustrations.

Concept Development

■ **Read the Concept Literacy Reader** To build background and vocabulary, read *Busy Beavers* with children. Read the title and author's name. Have children look at the cover and the pictures in the book. What are the beavers doing in the pictures? Read the book aloud, pausing to discuss each page. Model sentence patterns and vocabulary that describe the objects on the page. The beaver cuts the tree. Why is the beaver trying to cut down the tree? (to make a dam) On a second reading, have children talk about the pictures on each page.

■ **Develop Oral Language** Revisit *Busy Beavers,* pointing out that *busy* means "always working." Then have them sing the following song with you to the tune of "I'm a Little Teapot":

> I'm a busy beaver, check me out.
> I have sharp teeth and a furry little snout.
> I swim in the river, I go all about.
> When a tree falls down, you may hear me shout!

Phonemic Awareness/Phonics

■ **Frontload Words with Initial and Medial /e/** Have children look at the illustration on pp. 52–53 of *My Skills Buddy.* This is an elf village. Elves there live in trees. How do you use trees? Do you climb them? Do you swing in them? Do you sit under them? Now, listen to the word *elf.* What sound does *elf* begin with? *Elf* begins with /e/; /e/, *elf.* Then use this routine to introduce picture words beginning with /e/: In the elf village there are some eggs. *Eggs* start with *e.* (Have children point to the eggs.) In the elf village there is an elephant. *Elephant* starts with *e.* (Have children point to the elephant.) Make up a chant for other words in the picture that begin with /e/, including *elevator, elk,* and *elbow.* Then include words with /e/ in the middle, including *bed, net, bell, pen,* and *pet.*

■ **Connect /e/ to *Ee*** Use letter tiles to display the word *leg* or write it on the board. This word is *leg: /l/ /e/ /g/, leg.* Say the word with me. Have children write the word *leg* and circle the letter that makes /e/. Write and read aloud the following sentence: *Ed is not wet yet.* Point to the letter *E* in *Ed* and ask: What letter is this? Yes, this is uppercase *E.* Repeat with the *e* in *wet* and *yet.*

Content Objective
• Develop content knowledge related to building.

Language Objectives
• Understand and use grade-level content area vocabulary.

• Recognize the sounds of English.

Concept Literacy Reader K.6.3

Daily Planner	
DAY 1	• Concept Development • Phonemic Awareness/ Phonics • Listening Comprehension
DAY 2	• Comprehension • Vocabulary
DAY 3	• Phonemic Awareness/ Phonics • Conventions
DAY 4	• Phonemic Awareness/ Phonics • Concepts and Oral Language
DAY 5	• Language Workshop • Writing

Support for English Language Learners

Content Objective
• Understand main idea.

Language Objective
• Learn and use academic vocabulary.

My Skills Buddy, pp. 54–55

Listening Comprehension: Main Idea

■ **Provide Scaffolding** Point to the illustrations on pp. 54–55 in *My Skills Buddy*. Help children understand main idea. The main idea of a story tells the most important idea. Point to the main picture. Look at this picture. Where is everyone going? (school) How are children getting to school? (They are getting there by bicycle, car, bus, and by walking.) Explain that they are getting to school in different ways. The main idea of this story is that people get to school in different ways. Support your words with gestures or simple drawings.

■ **Prepare for the Read Aloud** The modified Read Aloud below prepares children for listening to the oral reading "The Best Nest" on p. 151.

The Best Nest

Mama and Papa Robin need to build a nest. It has to be in a safe place. They choose a tree. Then they get things they need to make it.

The materials need to be strong. They make a bed using twigs, leaves, and grass. They can use string, paper, or plastic too. They use mud to glue things together.

The inside of the nest has to be warm and cozy. That is because the baby birds will live there. The Robins use soft grass, feathers, spider webs, or wool to make the inside soft.

When the nest is finished, Mama Robin lays her eggs. The nest will be the baby birds' home until they fly away.

■ **First Listening** Write the title of the Read Aloud on the board. This is about Mama and Papa Robin making a nest. They have to use different materials to make the nest perfect. Ask children if they know what a nest is for. Have children name some places they have seen nests. Listen to find out how they build the nest. After reading, ask children to recall the events. What do the Robins use for the outside of the nest? What do they use for the inside of the nest? Why do they use different materials?

■ **Second Listening** Who is building a nest? (Mama and Papa Robin) Why are they building a nest? (They are building it for their babies.) What is the most important idea from this story? (It takes many different materials to build a good nest.) What is another name for the most important idea in a story? (the main idea)

Objectives
• Understand the main points of spoken language ranging from situations in which contexts are familiar to unfamiliar. • Demonstrate English comprehension by employing inferential skills commensurate with content area needs.

 DAY **2**

Comprehension

■ **Provide Scaffolding** Display *Building Beavers.* Lead a detailed picture walk through the story, naming what you see in the illustrations and describing what is happening. Use gestures and facial expressions to convey meaning. Focus on the following:

• **Set the Scene** Use the cover of the Big Book to help children understand that this story takes place in a forest near water. Remind children that a forest is an area with many trees. A lot of wild animals live in forests. What are some animals that live in the forest? (bears, birds, deer, butterflies) Have you ever been in a forest? What was it like?

• **Frontload Vocabulary** As you lead the picture walk, use the illustrations to introduce unfamiliar words in the text. Look at the picture on page 4. A beaver house is called a *lodge.* What does a *lodge* look like? (It looks like a bunch of sticks. It looks like a tee-pee.) Why do beavers need a *lodge?* (to protect them from other animals; to keep them out of the weather) Include some of the following words from the story: *balance* (p. 7); *dam* (p. 9); *paddle* (p. 14); *predator* (p. 16).

Vocabulary: Words for Actions

■ **Frontload Vocabulary** Have children turn to p. 68 of *My Skills Buddy.* Action words tell about things we do. Talk about each picture, using the action words *dig, carry, eat,* and *sleep.* For example, point to man carrying the toolbox. This is a toolbox. The man carries the toolbox. What are some things you carry to school. (backpack, lunch box, books) Have children talk about the other pictures using the action words.

■ **Provide Scaffolding** Write the words *dig, carry, eat,* and *sleep* on the board and on self-stick notes. Read the words aloud with children. These are words for actions. Hold up the self-stick note with the word *dig.* What can you dig? Then say a sentence using the action word and have children repeat the sentence: I *dig* dirt. Repeat with the other action words.

■ **Practice** Point to the words on the board. These action words tell about things we do. Let's act them out. Have a child stand up and carry something across the room. Then model the following sentence. (Child's name) carries a pencil. Have the rest of the class repeat the sentence. Continue this exercise with the other action words.

Content Objective
• Develop background knowledge.

Language Objective
• Learn and use words for actions.

Use Learning Strategies
Remind children that if they have trouble with action words, they can ask the teacher for help.

Big Book

Support for English Language Learners

Content Objective
- Use learning strategies.

Language Objectives
- Connect /e/ and *Ee*.
- Use telling sentences.

 Transfer Skills

Pronouncing /e/ In many languages, short vowel sounds may not exist or may not be like those in the English language. English language learners may have a hard time hearing the differences in these sounds. Provide additional phonemic awareness activities to help children hear and pronounce words with short vowel sounds.

Use Learning Strategies

In *Building Beavers,* the kit gets "tired of swimming" and rides on its mother's tail. Explain to children that "tired of..." is an expression. To be "tired of" something does not mean you are actually sleepy. It means that you do not feel like doing that activity anymore.

Phonemic Awareness/Phonics

- **Isolate Initial and Medial /e/** Say *end,* and then model segmenting sounds by saying /e/ /n/ /d/. Emphasize the initial sound in the word. Repeat with *egg* and *elk.* Help children identify the initial sound in each word. Then say *red,* and model segmenting sounds by saying /r/ /e/ /d/. Emphasize the medial sound in the word. Repeat with *pet* and *glen.* Help children identify the medial sound in each word.

- **/e/ Spelled *Ee*** Write the words *elf, pen,* and *beg* on the board. As you read them aloud, track the sounds and letters with your finger. Help children recognize that these words all begin with /e/ or have /e/ in the middle.

Conventions: Telling Sentences

- **Provide Scaffolding** Point to the image on p. 3 of *Building Beavers.* Read the following sentence from the story: *This wet, furry animal is a beaver.* This is a sentence. It tells us something. What does it tell us? (It tells us that the animal in the picture is a beaver.) A sentence that tells us something is called a *telling sentence.* A telling sentence ends with a period.

- **Practice** Write the following sentences on the board: *What do beavers build? Beavers are good builders.* Read the sentences aloud to the class. Which sentence is a telling sentence? (the second one) The second sentence tells us something. It ends in a period. That is a telling sentence. The first sentence asks us something. It ends with a question mark. That is not a telling sentence.

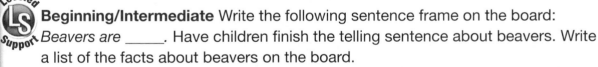 **Beginning/Intermediate** Write the following sentence frame on the board: *Beavers are _____.* Have children finish the telling sentence about beavers. Write a list of the facts about beavers on the board.

Advanced/Advanced-High Have children copy the sentence frame on a piece of paper. Have them make a telling sentence.

Objectives
- Ask [for] information ranging from using a very limited bank of high-frequency, high-need, concrete vocabulary, including key words and expressions needed for basic communication in academic and social contexts, to using abstract and content-based vocabulary during extended speaking assignments.

Support for English Language Learners

Content Objectives

- Understand *Building Beavers*.
- Understand main idea.

Language Objectives

- Tell a story through speaking and writing.
- Write using grade-level vocabulary.

Monitor and Self-Correct

Remind children that if they don't know how to say a word, they can ask the teacher for help.

Home Language Support

Invite children to share ideas in their home languages before creating their sentences.

Language Workshop: Retell *Building Beavers*

- **Introduce and Model** Turn to p. 6 of *Building Beavers*. Look at the beaver in this picture. Do you remember what it is doing? Act out the beaver's motions as you say: *The beaver cuts down a tree. It cuts the tree with its sharp teeth.* I am acting out what the beaver does. I am also telling what it does. Let's act out and tell what the beaver does.

- **Practice** Organize children into pairs. Assign each pair two pages from *Building Beaver.* Explain that one child will act like the beaver, and the other child will narrate, or tell about, what his or her partner is doing. Have children retell and summarize the directions you have just given them to make sure they understand what they are expected to do. Then review the actions on each page, and allow time for children to plan what they will do and say. Then have pairs take turns acting out and narrating their pages in the order of the book. Help children by supplying and clarifying English words as needed.

Writing: Write About *Building Beavers*

- **Prepare for Writing** We acted out what the beavers do. We talked about what the beavers do. Now let's write about what the beavers do. Have each child fold a piece of paper in half to create two sections.

- **Create Sentences About Beavers** Have children copy the sentence starters *Beavers live* _____ on the left half and *Beavers* _____ on the right half of the page. Have children draw where a beaver lives on the left half. Tell children to write or dictate the name of that place to complete the first sentence. Have children draw an action that beavers make on the right half. Then ask children to write or dictate the action to complete the second sentence. When children are finished, have them share their sentences and drawings with a partner.

Leveled Support

Beginning Write the sentence frames for children and have them write or dictate words to complete the sentences.

Intermediate Guide children in copying the sentence frames and writing words to complete the sentences.

Advanced/Advanced-High Encourage children to write their sentences on their own. You might also have children help less-proficient partners complete their sentences.

Objectives
- Expand and internalize initial English vocabulary by retelling simple stories and basic information represented or supported by pictures. • Narrate with increasing specificity and detail as more English is acquired. • Write using newly acquired basic vocabulary.

 **DAY 4**

Phonemic Awareness/Phonics

■ **Review Short Vowels and Consonants** To review short vowels and consonants read the following sentence aloud: Tim hid a box of star stickers. Have children repeat the sentence after you. Then have them pronounce just the words with short vowels and consonants: /t/ /i/ /m/. What short vowel sound does this word make? Yes, it makes the short vowel sound /i/. Repeat with all the words with short vowels and consonants.

■ **Spelling Words with Short Vowels and Consonants** Write the words *red, cat,* and *dog* on the board. Model reading each word, isolating the short vowel. Show all the sound-letter correspondences (for example, /r/ /e/ /d/ = *red*). As you read the words aloud, track the sounds and letters with your finger.

Concepts and Oral Language

■ **Revisit Talk with Me Chart 33A** Have children describe the animal, places, and things in the photos. Then say a sentence for each picture. Make sure each sentence is a telling sentence, such as *The beaver swims in the water.*

■ **Develop Oral Language** Introduce language patterns that help describe the pictures on Talk with Me Chart 33A. Write this sentence frame on the board: *The beaver lives _____.* Let's use this sentence pattern to talk about where beavers live. *The beaver lives in a lake.* Have children point to the picture of a lake. *The beaver lives in a lodge.* Have children point to the picture of a lodge. Suggest other sentences using the frame. Then play a game. Point to one of the beavers on the chart. Ask a volunteer to make up a sentence that describes the beaver. When he or she is finished, the volunteer can pick another child to make up a sentence. Encourage children to come up with a new sentence each time.

 Beginning Have children point to each picture on the chart and use the Amazing Word to describe the picture.

Intermediate Ask questions to help children notice more details about the pictures, such as What is the difference between a stream and a river? How does a beaver swim? What is a lodge made of?

Advanced/Advanced-High Encourage children to use their prior knowledge about the Amazing Words to think of descriptive words for each.

Content Objectives
• Develop oral language.
• Use learning strategies.

Language Objectives
• Spell consonant blends.
• Learn English language patterns.

Use Learning Strategies
Work with children to create a concept map titled *How Beavers Build a Dam.* Include the categories *Locations* and *Actions.*

Talk with Me Chart 33A

Customize Literacy
in Your Classroom

Table of Contents
for Customize Literacy

Customize Literacy is organized into different sections, each one designed to help you organize and carry out an effective literacy program. Each section contains strategies and support for teaching comprehension skills and strategies. *Customize Literacy* also shows how to use weekly text sets of readers in your literacy program.

Section 1: **Planning**.....................................2–7

Section 2: **Instruction** 8–15

Section 3: **Matching Books and Readers**.................16–25

Section 4: **Building Community** 26–31

Weekly Text Sets
to Customize Literacy

The following readers can be used to enhance your literacy instruction.

	Decodable Reader	Concept Literacy Reader	Below-Level Reader	On-Level Reader	Advanced Reader
Unit 6 WEEK 1	*If Kip Can*	*What Do We Need?*	*A Stand for Tim*	*Max and Jen*	*Homes*
Unit 6 WEEK 2	*Will Cass Come?*	*We Build a Birdhouse*	*Let's Play Hopscotch!*	*Max and Jen Fix the Big Box!*	*The Best Club Hut*
Unit 6 WEEK 3	*The Red Egg*	*Busy Beavers*	*Gus Will Stop*	*Max and Jen Go Camping*	*A Small Trip*

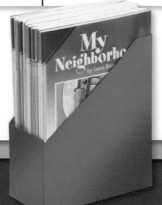

Customize Literacy in Your Classroom

Instruction in comprehension skills and strategies provides readers with avenues to understanding a text. Through teacher modeling and guided, collaborative, and independent practice, children become independent thinkers who employ a variety of skills and strategies to help them make meaning as they read.

Mini-Lessons for Comprehension Skills and Strategies

Envision It!

A Comprehension Handbook

Unit 1	Character, Setting, Sequence, Classify and Categorize, Predict and Set Purpose, Recall and Retell
Unit 2	Compare and Contrast, Setting, Main Idea, Realism and Fantasy, Sequence, Predict and Set Purpose, Recall and Retell
Unit 3	Compare and Contrast, Plot, Cause and Effect, Draw Conclusions, Main Idea, Predict and Set Purpose, Recall and Retell
Unit 4	Sequence, Cause and Effect, Character, Classify and Categorize, Setting, Predict and Set Purpose, Recall and Retell
Unit 5	Realism and Fantasy, Cause and Effect, Compare and Contrast, Plot, Main Idea, Draw Conclusions, Predict and Set Purpose, Recall and Retell
Unit 6	Compare and Contrast, Character, Main Idea, Plot, Setting, Draw Conclusions, Predict and Set Purpose, Recall and Retell

Envision It! | Visual Skills Handbook

Author's Purpose
Categorize and Classify
Cause and Effect
Compare and Contrast
Draw Conclusions
Fact and Opinion
Generalize
Graphic Sources
Literary Elements
Main Idea and Details
Sequence

Envision It! | Visual Strategies Handbook

Background Knowledge
Important Ideas
Inferring
Monitor and Clarify
Predict and Set Purpose
Questioning
Story Structure
Summarize
Text Structure
Visualize

Anchor Chart Anchor charts are provided with each strategy lesson. These charts incorporate the language of strategic thinkers. They help students make their thinking visible and permanent and provide students with a means to clarify their thinking about how and when to use each strategy. As children gain more experience with a strategy, the chart may undergo revision.

See pages 97–113 in the *First Stop on Reading Street* Teacher's Edition for additional support as you customize literacy in your classroom.

Good Readers DRA2 users will find additional resources in the *First Stop on Reading Street* Teacher's Edition on pages 100–102.

Contents

Section 1 Planning — 2

Pacing Guide

Teaching Record Chart

Section 2 Instruction — 8

Comprehension Mini-Lessons
- Compare and Contrast
- Character
- Main Idea
- Predict and Set Purpose

Glossary of Literacy Terms

Section 3 Matching Books and Readers — 16

Leveled Readers Skills Chart

What Good Readers Do

Conversation Starters: Asking Good Questions

Connecting Science and Social Studies

Section 4 Building Community — 26

Planning Teacher Study Groups

Trial Lessons

Books for Teachers

Pacing Guide

This chart shows the instructional sequence from *Scott Foresman Reading Street* for Grade K. You can use this pacing guide as is to ensure you are following a comprehensive scope and sequence. Or, you can adjust the sequence to match your calendar, curriculum map, or testing schedule.

Grade K — LANGUAGE ARTS

UNIT 1

	Week 1	Week 2	Week 3	Week 4	Week 5	Week 6
Phonological/ Phonemic Awareness	Rhyming Words	Syllables Sound Discrimination	Discriminate Sounds Segment Syllables	Discriminate Sounds	Isolate /m/ Discriminate Sounds	Isolate /t/ Discriminate Sounds Rhyme
Phonics	Letter Recognition: *Aa, Bb, Cc, Dd, Ee*	Letter Recognition: *Ff, Gg, Hh, Ii, Jj, Kk, Ll, Mm, Nn*	Letter Recognition: *Oo, Pp, Qq, Rr, Ss*	Letter Recognition: *Tt, Uu, Vv, Ww, Xx, Yy, Zz*	/m/ Spelled *Mm*	/t/ Spelled *Tt*
High-Frequency Words	*I, am*	*I, am*	*the, little*	*the, little*	*a, to*	*a, to*
Listening Comprehension	Character	Setting	Sequence	Classify and Categorize	Character	Classify and Categorize
Comprehension Strategies	Preview and Predict, Retell					

UNIT 2

	Week 1	Week 2
Phonological/ Phonemic Awareness	Isolate /a/ Oral Blending	Isolate /s/ Oral Blending
Phonics	/a/ Spelled *Aa*	/s/ Spelled *Ss*
High-Frequency Words	*have, is*	*have, is*
Listening Comprehension	Compare and Contrast	Setting

UNIT 4

	Week 1	Week 2	Week 3	Week 4	Week 5	Week 6
Phonemic Awareness	Isolate /h/ Oral Blending Segment Phonemes	Isolate /l/ Oral Blending Segment Phonemes		Isolate /g/ Segment Phonemes	Isolate /e/ Segment Phonemes Discriminate Phonemes	Isolate /e/ Segment Phonemes Discriminate Phonemes
Phonics	/h/ Spelled *Hh*	/l/ Spelled *Ll*	Consonant Blends	/g/ Spelled *Gg*	/e/ Spelled *Ee*	/e/ Spelled *Ee*
High-Frequency Words	*are, that, do*	*are, that, do*	*one, two, three, four, five*	*one, two, three, four, five*	*here, go, from*	*here, go, from*
Listening Comprehension	Sequence	Cause and Effect	Sequence	Character	Classify and Categorize	Setting
Comprehension Strategies	Preview and Predict, Retell					

UNIT 5

	Week 1	Week 2
Phonemic Awareness	Isolate /j/, /w/ Oral Blending Segment Phonemes	Isolate /ks/ Oral Blending Segment Phonemes
Phonics	/j/ Spelled *Jj* and /w/ Spelled *Ww*	/ks/ Spelled *Xx*
High-Frequency Words	*yellow, blue, green*	*yellow, blue, green*
Listening Comprehension	Realism and Fantasy	Cause and Effect

Are you the adventurous type? Want to use some of your own ideas and materials in your teaching? But you worry you might be leaving out some critical instruction kids need? **Customize Literacy** *can help.* "

	Week 3	Week 4	Week 5	Week 6
	Isolate /p/ Oral Blending	Isolate /k/ Oral Blending	Isolate /i/ Discriminate Sounds Oral Blending	Isolate /i/ Discriminate Sounds Oral Blending
	/p/ Spelled *Pp*	/k/ Spelled *Cc*	/i/ Spelled *Ii*	/i/ Spelled *Ii*
	we, my, like	*we, my, like*	*he, for*	*he, for*
	Main Idea	Realism and Fantasy	Sequence	Realism and Fantasy
	Preview and Predict, Retell			

UNIT 3

Week 1	Week 2	Week 3	Week 4	Week 5	Week 6
Isolate /n/, /b/ Oral Blending Segment Phonemes	Isolate /r/ Oral Blending Segment Phonemes	Isolate /d/, /k/ Oral Blending Segment Phonemes	Isolate /f/ Oral Blending Segment Phonemes	Isolate /o/ Oral Blending Segment Phonemes	Isolate /o/ Oral Blending Segment Phonemes
/n/ Spelled *Nn* and /b/ Spelled *Bb*	/r/ Spelled *Rr*	/d/ Spelled *Dd* and /k/ Spelled *Kk*	/f/ Spelled *Ff*	/o/ Spelled *Oo*	/o/ Spelled *Oo*
me, with, she	*me, with, she*	*see, look*	*see, look*	*they, you, of*	*they, you, of*
Compare and Contrast	Plot	Cause and Effect	Plot	Draw Conclusions	Main Idea
Preview and Predict, Retell					

	Week 3	Week 4	Week 5	Week 6
	Isolate /u/ Oral Blending Segment Phonemes	Isolate /u/ Oral Blending Segment Phonemes	Isolate /v/, /z/ Oral Blending Segment Phonemes	Isolate /y/, /kw/ Oral Blending Segment Phonemes
	/u/ Spelled *Uu*	/u/ Spelled *Uu*	/v/ Spelled *Vv* and /z/ Spelled *Zz*	/y/ Spelled *Yy* and /kw/ Spelled *qu*
	what, said, was	*what, said, was*	*where, come*	*where, come*
	Compare and Contrast	Plot	Main Idea	Draw Conclusions
	Preview and Predict, Retell			

UNIT 6

Week 1	Week 2	Week 3	Week 4	Week 5	Week 6
Isolate /a/ and /i/ Blend Phonemes Segment Phonemes	Isolate /o/ Blend Phonemes Segment Phonemes	Isolate /e/ Blend Phonemes Segment Phonemes	Isolate /u/ Blend Phonemes Segment Phonemes	Consonant and Vowel Sounds	Consonant and Vowel Sounds
/a/ Spelled *Aa* and /i/ Spelled *Ii*	/o/ Spelled *Oo*	/e/ Spelled *Ee*	/u/ Spelled *Uu*	Consonants and Short Vowels	Consonants and Short Vowels
Review: *here, do, little, with, what*	Review: *where, is, go, that, come*	Review: *the, was, to, like, from*	Review: *for, of, my, we, yellow*	Review: *have, they, four, two, blue*	Review: *you, said, see, look, three*
Compare and Contrast	Character	Main Idea	Plot	Setting	Draw Conclusions
Preview and Predict, Retell					

Pacing Guide

Grade K

LANGUAGE ARTS

UNIT 1

	Week 1	Week 2	Week 3	Week 4	Week 5	Week 6
Speaking and Listening	Follow Directions	Drama—Respond to Literature	Listen for Rhyme and Rhythm	Talk About Me	Announcements and Messages	Drama—Respond to Literature
Grammar/ Conventions	Say Our Names	Write Our Names	What We Look Like	What We Can Do	Nouns for People and Animals	Nouns for Places and Things
Writing	Song	Invitation	Poem	Instructions	Caption	Personal Narrative

UNIT 2

	Week 1	Week 2
Speaking and Listening	Listen for Sequence	Listen for Directions
Grammar/ Conventions	Nouns for More Than One	Proper Nouns
Writing	Label	List

UNIT 4

	Week 1	Week 2	Week 3	Week 4	Week 5	Week 6
Speaking and Listening	Give Directions	Compare and Contrast	Listen for Sequence	Discuss Authors and Illustrators	Listen for Story Elements: Character	Listen to Poems
Grammar/ Conventions	Subjects (Naming Parts)	Predicates (Action Parts)	Complete Sentences	Telling Sentences	Capital Letters and Periods	Pronouns *I* and *me*
Writing	Directions	Poem	Description	List	Informal Letter	List

UNIT 5

	Week 1	Week 2
Speaking and Listening	Ask and Answer Questions	Drama—Respond to Literature
Grammar/ Conventions	Questions	Question Marks and Capital Letters
Writing	Caption	Rhyme

Week 3	Week 4	Week 5	Week 6
Discussions	Listen for Setting	Give a Description	Listen for Plot
Adjectives: Colors and Shapes	Adjectives: Sizes and Numbers	Adjectives: Opposites	Adjectives
Notes	Poem	Caption	Story

UNIT 3

Week 1	Week 2	Week 3	Week 4	Week 5	Week 6
Respond to Literature	Sequence	Recite Rhymes	Oral Presentation	Messages and Letters	Ask and Answer Questions
Verbs	Verbs for Now and the Past	Verbs That Add -s	Verbs for Now and the Future	Meaningful Word Groups	Sentences
Summary	Invitation	Persuasive Statement	Caption	List	Poem

Week 3	Week 4	Week 5	Week 6
Discuss Literature	Sequence	Oral Presentation —Description	Discuss Literary Elements: Plot
Prepositions	Nouns	Nouns in Sentences	Verbs
Poem	Formal Letter	Invitation	How-to Report

UNIT 6

Week 1	Week 2	Week 3	Week 4	Week 5	Week 6
Recite Language	Discuss Fact and Opinion	Interpret Information	Discuss Literary Elements: Character	Oral Presentation —Book Report	Discuss Literary Elements: Setting
Pronouns I and me	Prepositional Phrases	Telling Sentences	Questions	Exclamations	Complete Sentences
List	Song	Rhyme	Rhyme	Poem	Report

Teaching Record Chart

This chart shows the critical comprehension skills and strategies you need to cover. Check off each one as you provide instruction.

Reading/Comprehension	DATES OF INSTRUCTION		
Predict what might happen next in text based on the cover, title, and illustrations.			
Ask and respond to questions about texts read aloud.			
Identify elements of a story including setting, character, and key events.			
Discuss the big idea (theme) of a well-known folk tale or fable and connect it to personal experience.			
Recognize sensory details.			
Recognize recurring phrases and characters in traditional fairy tales, lullabies, and folk tales from various cultures.			
Respond to rhythm and rhyme in poetry through identifying a regular beat and similarities in word sounds.			
Retell a main event from a story read aloud.			
Describe characters in a story and the reasons for their actions.			
Identify the topic of an informational text heard.			

Tired of using slips of paper or stickies to make sure you teach everything you need to? Need an easier way to keep track of what you have taught, and what you still need to cover? Customize Literacy can help. 99

Reading/Comprehension	DATES OF INSTRUCTION		
Identify the topic and details in expository text heard or read, referring to the words and/or illustrations.			
Retell important facts in a text, heard or read.			
Discuss the ways authors group information in text.			
Use titles and illustrations to make predictions about text.			
Follow pictorial directions (e.g., recipes, science experiments).			
Identify the meaning of specific signs (e.g., traffic signs, warning signs).			
Discuss the purposes for reading and listening to various texts (e.g., to become involved in real and imagined events, settings, actions, and to enjoy language).			
Ask and respond to questions about text.			
Monitor and adjust comprehension (e.g., using background knowledge, creating sensory images, re-reading a portion aloud).			
Make inferences based on the cover, title, illustrations, and plot.			
Retell or act out important events in stories.			
Make connections to own experiences, to ideas in other texts, and to the larger community and discuss textual evidence.			

Objectives:

- Children tell how things in a group are alike.
- Children tell how things are different.
- Children make groups by identifying likenesses and differences.

Texts for Teaching

- *Flowers*
- *Little Panda*
- *Trucks Roll!*
- *Building with Dad*

Leveled Readers

- See pages CL16–CL17 for a list of Leveled Readers.

Compare and Contrast

Mini-Lesson

Understand the Skill

My Skills Buddy K.6, pp. 14–15

Compare and contrast means to find the likenesses and/or differences between two or more people, places, things, or ideas. Children use the terms *alike* and *different* to talk about stories, characters in stories, their experiences, objects, and so on.

Teach

Use the Envision It! on My Skills Buddy K.6, pages 14–15 to visually teach compare and contrast. Have children point out ways the bikes and the weather are alike and different.

Tell children that two books can be the alike or different. Model using two familiar books by the same author with the same characters. Recall the books with children. Talk about the two books using *alike* and *different*. Show which parts are alike and different using the pictures, author's name, and titles.

Practice

Show children two familiar books. Recall each book with children. After talking about each book ask questions to help children think about ways the books are alike and different. Ask: Do the books have the same characters? Do the books happen in the same place? Do different things happen in each book? Draw a Venn diagram (two overlapping circles) on the board. Record similarities in the center where the circles overlap. List differences in the outer circles. As children answer the questions and talk about the books, use these sentence frames: The books are alike because _____. *The books are different because* _____. Write down what children say.

If... children have difficulty finding likenesses,

then... ask leading questions, such as: *Is there a bear in both books? Do they look different? Is it the same bear?*

Apply

Tell children that sometimes books have the same characters, happen in the same place, or are about the same things. After you read a book with children, compare it to another familiar book. Help children talk about what is alike and different in the books.

Writing

Children can write their own sentence about how the books are the same or different. Supply sentence frames if needed. Post the sentences in the appropriate place on the Venn diagram.

Character

Objectives:
- Children identify characters as the people or animals in stories.
- Children tell about what characters do in a story.
- Children tell about characters' feelings in a story.

Texts for Teaching
- *The Little School Bus*
- *Smash! Crash!*
- *Goldilocks and the Three Bears*
- *Old MacDonald had a Woodshop*

Leveled Readers
- See pages CL16–CL17 for a list of Leveled Readers.

Understand the Skill

Characters are the people or animals in a story. They can be fantastic or just like real people. Characters often solve a problem in a story. Illustrations and sentences can help you understand what characters look like, what they feel, and what they do.

My Skills Buddy K.6, pp. 34–35

Teach

Use the **Envision It!** lesson on My Skills Buddy K.6, pages 34–35 to visually teach character. Together, retell the story.

Tell children that that the characters are the people and animals that you read about in a story. Stories are about what happens to a character or what a character does. Choose a familiar story and think aloud as you model identifying characters: This book is about Peter. He is a character in the story. Peter does something in the story. He gives his chair to his little sister. At the end, he paints the chair with his dad. He feels happy in the end. Characters do things in stories. Explain that talking about what characters do is another way to describe characters.

Practice

Remind children that characters do things in stories. Find a familiar story and show it to children. Page through the story and have children name each character. Ask: What does this character do in the story? Do other characters help? How does the character feel at the beginning? at the end?

If... children have difficulty identifying what happens to characters in the story, **then...** have them select from choices.

Apply

Tell children to listen carefully as you read to figure out what the characters in the story do. They can use the pictures to help them. Have them describe each character. Ask questions to help children think about the actions of characters.

Writing

Children can think of a character they would like to write a story about. The character can be someone from a book they have read, or one they think of themselves. Have them write about what the character does in their story. They can illustrate their sentences with a picture of their character. Post the characters in the classroom on a Character Wall.

Objectives:

- Children tell the one big idea in a story or a selection.
- Children tell what they used to identify what a story or article is about.

Texts for Teaching

- *Animal Babies in Grasslands*
- *The Lion and the Mouse*
- *On the Move!*
- *Building Beavers*

Leveled Readers

- See pages CL16–CL17 for a list of Leveled Readers.

Main Idea

Mini-Lesson

My Skills Buddy K.6, pp. 54–55

Understand the Skill

The **main idea** is what a story or nonfiction article is about. Children tell what the big idea in a story or article is after hearing it read aloud. They retell the story or are able to say in a word or two what the big idea of an article is.

Teach

Use the **Envision It!** lesson on My Skills Buddy K.6, pages 54–55 to visually review main idea.

Tell children that every story tells about a big idea. They will know what the big idea is because most of the sentences will tell about it. Most of the pictures will also be about the big idea. Think aloud as you model finding the big idea. This story is all about a jungle. I see pictures of different kinds of baby animals and their mothers. The sentences tell me the names of all the baby animals. The big idea of this story is that lots of different animals live in the jungle.

Practice

Read or retell a familiar tale or selection to children and have them listen and think about what the story is mostly about. (For example, *Goldilocks* is mostly about a girl who causes trouble in a bears' house.) When you are finished, talk about what the story is mostly about and ask: What helps us figure out what the story is mostly about? Help them understand that what happens in a story helps us figure this out. In *Goldilocks*, the little girl causes trouble by eating the porridge, breaking a chair, and by sleeping in a bed. We put these events together to see what the story is mostly about.

If... children have difficulty telling what a story is mostly about,
then...retell the story with them and then ask: *What is this story mostly about?*

Apply

Ask children to listen carefully to the stories you read to hear the big ideas. Have them ask questions: *What is this story about? What are all the sentences about? Do the pictures help me think about what the big idea is? What do the pictures show?* Talk with children about the big ideas in the story.

Writing

Have children write a story and give it a title that tells what their story is mostly about. Children can illustrate their stories.

Objectives:
- Children tell what they think will happen in a story and what will happen next in a story.
- Children preview a book and set a purpose for reading.

Texts for Teaching
- *Predicting and setting purposes is a strategy that can be applied to any selection. Encourage children to make predictions and set a purpose before they read.*

Predict and Set Purpose

Mini-Lesson

Understand the Strategy
To predict means to tell what you think might happen next in a story or what the author may tell you next. Predicting goes hand-in-hand with previewing, which involves looking at text features and language to get an overview of a piece of writing. Before reading, previewing and predicting helps readers access what they already know about the topic and so **set a purpose** to guide reading.

Teach
Tell children that readers do things before they listen to or read a book. We look at the book inside and out. We think about what it might be about. Then we think about what we would like to find out as we read. Model predicting and setting purpose using the tips below.

Before We Listen or Read
• Look at the cover. What do you see?
• Look inside. What do you see?
• Think. What will this story will be about?

As We Listen or Read
• Listen or read carefully.
• Did you predict what would happen?
• Think. What will happen next?

After We Listen or Read
• Look back. Did you predict what would happen?
• Think. Do you like this story? Why or why not?

Practice and Apply
Use the strategy on a new story. Record some purposes children have. Record some predictions they make. After reading, return to them and talk about whether their purposes were met. How close were their predictions?
If... children have difficulty making predictions,
then... model the process using text clues and personal experience.

Anchor Chart
Anchor charts help children make their thinking visible and permanent. With an anchor chart, the group can clarify their thinking about how to use a strategy. You might make a chart of the strategy Predict and Set Purpose to hang in the classroom.

Glossary of Literacy Terms

This glossary lists academic language terms that are related to literacy.
They are provided for your information and professional use.

A

alliteration	the repetition of a consonant sound in a group of words, especially in poetry
animal fantasy	a story about animals that talk and act like people
antonym	a word that means the opposite of another word
author's purpose	the reason the author wrote the text
autobiography	the story of a real person's life written by that person

B

background knowledge	the information and experience that a reader brings to a text
biography	the story of a real person's life written by another person

C

cause	why something happens
character	a person, an animal, or a personified object in a story
classify and categorize	put things, such as pictures or words, into groups
compare and contrast	tell how things are the same and different
comprehension	understanding of text being read—the ultimate goal of reading
comprehension strategy	a conscious plan used by a reader to gain understanding of text. Comprehension strategies may be used before, during, or after reading.
context clue	the words, phrases, or sentences near an unknown word that give the reader clues to the word's meaning

D

details	small pieces of information
dialogue	written conversation
draw conclusions	arrive at decisions or opinions after thinking about facts and details and using prior knowledge

E

effect	what happens as the result of a cause
expository text	text that contains facts and information. Also called *informational text.*

F

fable	a story, usually with animal characters, that is written to teach a moral, or lesson
fact	piece of information that can be proved to be true
fairy tale	a folk story with magical characters and events
fantasy	a story that could not really happen
fiction	writing that tells about imaginary people, things, and events
folk tale	a story that has been passed down by word of mouth
foreshadowing	the use of hints or clues about what will happen later in a story

generalize make a broad statement or rule after examining particular facts

graphic organizer a drawing, chart, or web that illustrates concepts or shows how ideas relate to each other. Readers use graphic organizers to help them keep track of and understand important information and ideas as they read. Story maps, word webs, Venn diagrams, and KWL charts are graphic organizers.

graphic source a chart, diagram, or map within a text that adds to readers' understanding of the text

G

historical fiction realistic fiction that takes place in the past. It is an imaginary story based on historical events and characters.

humor writing or speech that has a funny or amusing quality

H

idiom a phrase whose meaning differs from the ordinary meaning of the words. *A stone's throw* is an idiom meaning "a short distance."

imagery the use of language to create beautiful or forceful pictures in the reader's mind

inference conclusion reached on the basis of evidence and reasoning

inform give knowledge, facts, or news to someone

informational text writing that contains facts and information. Also called *expository text*.

interview a face-to-face conversation in which someone responds to questions

I

legend a story coming down from the past about the great deeds of a hero. Although a legend may be based on historical people and events, it is not regarded as historically true.

literary elements the characters, setting, plot, and theme of a narrative text

L

main idea the big idea that tells what a paragraph or a selection is mainly about; the most important idea of a text

metacognition an awareness of one's own thinking processes and the ability to monitor and direct them to a desired goal. Good readers use metacognition to monitor their reading and adjust their reading strategies.

monitor and clarify a comprehension strategy by which readers actively think about understanding their reading and know when they understand and when they do not. Readers use appropriate strategies to make sense of difficult words, ideas, or passages.

M

Instruction

M

moral	the lesson or teaching of a fable or story
mystery	a story about mysterious events that are not explained until the end, so as to keep the reader in suspense
myth	a story that attempts to explain something in nature

N

narrative	a story, made up or true, that someone tells or narrates
narrator	a character in a selection or someone outside the story who tells the story
nonfiction	writing that tells about real things, real people, and real events

O

onomatopoeia	the use of words that sound like their meanings, such as *buzz* and *hum*
opinion	someone's judgment, belief, or way of thinking
oral vocabulary	the words needed for speaking and listening

P

personification	a figure of speech in which human traits or actions are given to animals or inanimate objects, as in *The sunbeam danced on the waves.*
persuade	convince someone to do or to believe something
play	a story that is written to be acted out for an audience
plot	a series of related events at the beginning, middle, and end of a story; the action of a story
poem	an expressive, imaginative piece of writing often arranged in lines having rhythm and rhyme. In a poem, the patterns made by the sounds of the words have special importance.
pourquoi tale	a type of folk story that explains why things in nature came to be. *Pourquoi* is a French word meaning "why."
predict	tell what a selection might be about or what might happen in a text. Readers use text features and information to predict. They confirm or revise their predictions as they read.
preview	look over a text before reading it

Q

questioning	a reading strategy in which readers ask and answer questions to help make sense of what they read

R

reading vocabulary	the words we recognize or use in print
realistic fiction	a story about imaginary people and events that could happen in real life

Instruction

repetition	the repeated use of some aspect of language
rhyme	to end in the same sound(s)
rhythm	a pattern of strong beats in speech or writing, especially poetry

R

science fiction	a story based on science that often tells what life in the future might be like
semantic map	a graphic organizer, often a web, used to display words or concepts that are meaningfully related
sequence	the order of events in a selection or the order of the steps in which something is completed
sequence words	clue words such as *first*, *next*, *then*, and *finally* that signal the order of events in a selection
setting	where and when a story takes place
stanza	a group of lines in a poem
steps in a process	the order of the steps in which something is completed
story map	a graphic organizer used to record the literary elements and the sequence of events in a narrative text
story structure	how the characters, setting, and events of a story are organized into a plot
summarize	give the most important ideas of what was read. Readers summarize important information in the selection to keep track of what they are reading.
supporting detail	piece of information that tells about the main idea

S

tall tale	a humorous story that uses exaggeration to describe impossible happenings
text structure	the organization of a piece of nonfiction writing. Text structures of informational text include cause/effect, chronological, compare/contrast, description, problem/solution, proposition/support, and ask/answer questions.
theme	the big idea or author's message in a story
think aloud	an instructional strategy in which a teacher verbalizes his or her thinking to model the process of comprehension or the application of a skill
topic	the subject of a discussion, conversation, or piece of text

T

visualize	picture in one's mind what is happening in the text. Visualizing helps readers imagine the things they read about.

V

Leveled Readers Skills Chart

Scott Foresman Reading Street provides more than six hundred leveled readers. Each one is designed to:

- Practice critical skills and strategies
- Build vocabulary and concepts
- Build fluency
- Develop a lifelong love of reading

Grade K

Title	Level*	DRA Level	Genre	
Max the Duck	A	1	Fantasy	
Fun for Us	B	2	Informational Text	
Nick the Fix-It Man	B	2	Informational Text	
Red and Blue	B	2	Realistic Fiction	
We Have Fun Together	B	2	Fantasy	
Two or Three?	B	2	Realistic Fiction	
Buds for Mom	B	2	Realistic Fiction	
A Walk in the Forest	B	2	Realistic Fiction	
Looking for Animals	B	2	Realistic Fiction	
Skip and Run	C	3	Fantasy	
A Winter Home	C	3	Informational Text	
A Yard for All	C	3	Fantasy	
The Fawn	C	3	Realistic Fiction	
We Can Do It!	C	3	Realistic Fiction	
Fun with Gram	C	3	Realistic Fiction	
They Will Grow	C	3	Realistic Fiction	
What Can You Do?	C	3	Informational Text	
Sad and Glad	C	3	Realistic Fiction	
The Trip	C	3	Informational Text	
Pigs	C	3	Informational Text	
Frog's New Home	C	3	Informational Text	
Five Bears	C	3	Fantasy	
My Walk in Antarctica	C	3	Realistic Fiction	
A Trip to Washington, D.C.	C	3	Informational Text	
The Bus Ride	C	3	Realistic Fiction	
The Boat Ride	C	3	Realistic Fiction	
Ming on the Job	C	3	Realistic Fiction	
The Big Train	D	4	Realistic Fiction	
Get On the Bus!	D	4	Realistic Fiction	
Catch the Ball!	D	4	Realistic Fiction	
Homes	D	4	Informational Text	
The Best Club Hut	D	4	Realistic Fiction	
A Small Trip	D	4	Informational Text	
The Box	D	4	Informational Text	
Our Camping Trip	D	4	Realistic Fiction	
Safe Places for Animals	D	4	Informational Text	

* Suggested Guided Reading Level. Use your knowledge of children's abilities to adjust levels as needed.

This chart lists titles of leveled readers appropriate for students in Kindergarten. Use the chart to find titles that meet your students' interest and instructional needs. The books in this list were leveled using the criteria suggested in *Matching Books to Readers: Using Leveled Books in Guided Reading, Grades K–3* by Irene C. Fountas and Gay Su Pinnell. For more on leveling, see the *Reading Street Leveled Readers Leveling Guide.*

Comprehension Strategy	Target Comprehension Skill	Additional Comprehension Instruction	Vocabulary
Recall/Retell	Character	N/A	N/A
Recall/Retell	Setting	N/A	N/A
Recall/Retell	Sequence	N/A	N/A
Recall/Retell	Classify and Categorize	N/A	N/A
Recall/Retell	Character	N/A	N/A
Recall/Retell	Classify and Categorize	N/A	N/A
Recall/Retell	Compare and Contrast	N/A	N/A
Recall/Retell	Setting	N/A	N/A
Recall/Retell	Main Idea	N/A	N/A
Recall/Retell	Realism and Fantasy	N/A	N/A
Recall/Retell	Sequence	N/A	N/A
Recall/Retell	Realism and Fantasy	N/A	N/A
Recall/Retell	Compare and Contrast	N/A	N/A
Recall/Retell	Plot	N/A	N/A
Recall/Retell	Cause and Effect	N/A	N/A
Recall/Retell	Plot	N/A	N/A
Recall/Retell	Draw Conclusions	N/A	N/A
Recall/Retell	Main Idea	N/A	N/A
Recall/Retell	Sequence	N/A	N/A
Recall/Retell	Cause and Effect	N/A	N/A
Recall/Retell	Sequence	N/A	N/A
Recall/Retell	Character	N/A	N/A
Recall/Retell	Classify and Categorize	N/A	N/A
Recall/Retell	Setting	N/A	N/A
Recall/Retell	Realism and Fantasy	N/A	N/A
Recall/Retell	Cause and Effect	N/A	N/A
Recall/Retell	Compare and Contrast	N/A	N/A
Recall/Retell	Plot	N/A	N/A
Recall/Retell	Main Idea	N/A	N/A
Recall/Retell	Draw Conclusions	N/A	N/A
Recall/Retell	Compare and Contrast	N/A	N/A
Recall/Retell	Character	N/A	N/A
Recall/Retell	Main Idea	N/A	N/A
Recall/Retell	Plot	N/A	N/A
Recall/Retell	Setting	N/A	N/A
Recall/Retell	Draw Conclusions	N/A	N/A

Matching Books & Readers

What Good Readers Do

You can use the characteristics and behaviors of good readers to help all your children read better. But what are these characteristics and behaviors? And how can you use them to foster good reading behaviors for all your children? Here are some helpful tips.

Good Readers enjoy reading! They have favorite books, authors, and genres. Good readers often have a preference about where and when they read. They talk about books and recommend their favorites.

Develop this behavior by giving children opportunities to respond in different ways to what they read. Get them talking about what they read, and why they like or dislike it.

This behavior is important because book sharing alerts you to children who are somewhat passive about reading or have limited literacy experiences. Book sharing also helps you when you select books for the class.

Good Readers select books they can read.

Develop this behavior by providing a range of three or four texts appropriate for the child and then letting the child choose.

This behavior is important because children gain control over reading when they can choose from books they can read. This helps them become more independent in the classroom.

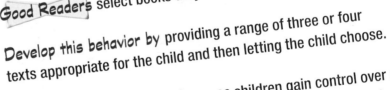

Good Readers use text features to help them preview and set purposes.

Develop this behavior by having children use the title and illustrations in fiction texts or the title, contents, headings, and other graphic features in nonfiction texts to make predictions about what they will be reading.

This behavior is important because previewing actually makes reading easier! Looking at features and sampling the text enables readers to predict and set expectations for reading.

Good Readers predict and ask questions before and while they read.

Develop this behavior by asking questions. After reading a passage, ask children what they think will happen next in a fiction text. Have them ask a question they think will be answered in a nonfiction text and read on to see if it is.

This behavior is important because when children predict and ask questions as they read, they are engaged. They have a purpose for reading and a basis for monitoring their comprehension.

66 **Want to improve your children's performance by fostering good reading behaviors? Customize Literacy can help. 99**

Good Readers use effective strategies and sources of information to figure out unknown words.

Develop this behavior by teaching specific strategies for figuring out unknown words, such as sounding out clusters of letters, using context, reading on, and using references.

This behavior is important because when readers have a variety of strategies to use, they are more able to decode and self-correct quickly. Readers who do these things view themselves as good readers.

**CH-
QU-
ST-**

Good Readers construct meaning as they read and then share or demonstrate their understanding.

Develop this behavior by having children retell what they read or write a summary of what they read in their own words.

This behavior is important because the ability to retell or write a summary is essential for success in reading. It shows how well a child has constructed meaning.

Good Readers make connections.

Develop this behavior by asking questions to help children make connections: *What does this remind you of? Have you ever read or experienced anything like this?*

This behavior is important because making connections helps readers understand and appreciate a text. Making connections to self, the world, and other texts supports high-level thinking.

Matching Books & Readers

Conversation Starters

Asking Good Questions Children want to read and listen to interesting and thought-provoking books! You can help them talk about these books. Use questions such as the following to assess listening comprehension and help children think about books. As you read longer books, pause often to ask questions about past and future events.

Cause and Effect

- What happens in this story?

- Why does it happen?

Character

- Who is in this story?

- What does this character like to do?

- How did the character feel in this part of the book?

- What does this character think about what happens in the book?

- Does this character seem real or made-up? What makes you think so?

- What character would you like to be? Why?

Classify and Categorize

- How are these things alike?

- Do these things belong in the same group?

- Is this thing like the others? Does it belong in the group?

- How do you know that it is like/not like the others?

- How would you group these things?

Compare and Contrast

- How are these things/characters/stories alike?

- How are these things/characters/stories different?

Draw Conclusions

- What happens in the story?

- What did the characters do to show you that they are kind/mean/strong?

- Which character do you like best? Why?

- Do you like this story? What makes you like it or dislike it?

Main Idea

- What is this story all about?

- What is the big idea of this story?

- What clues help you know what the story is about?

Plot

- In the story, what happens at the beginning? in the middle? at the end?

- What are other important things that happen in the story?

- What do you think is the most exciting/ important thing that happens?

- What is the problem that the character must solve/fix?

- How is that problem solved or fixed?

Realism and Fantasy

- Could this story happen in real life? Why do you think as you do?

- What things in the story could happen in real life?

- Do the people in this story act like people you know?

- How do you know if a story is make-believe or could really happen?

Sequence

- In this story, what happened first? next? last?

Setting

- What do the pictures tell you about when and where this story happened?

- What is this place like? What do you think it would be like?

- Does the place seem real or made-up? How can you tell?

- Do you want to visit this place? Why?

Matching Books & Readers

Connecting Science and Social Studies

Scott Foresman Reading Street Leveled Readers are perfect for covering, supporting, or enriching science and social studies content. Using these books ensures that all students can access important concepts.

Grade K Leveled Readers

Science

Earth and Space Science

Fiction Books
- *We Can Do It!*

Life Science

Nonfiction Books
- *A Winter Home*
- *What Can You Do?*
- *The Trip*
- *Pigs*
- *Frog's New Home*
- *A Small Trip*
- *Safe Places for Animals*

Fiction Books
- *A Walk in the Forest*
- *Looking for Animals*
- *Skip and Run*
- *A Yard for All*
- *The Fawn*
- *Fun with Gram*
- *They Will Grow*
- *Sad and Glad*

Physical Science

Fiction Books
- *Catch the Ball!*
- *The Best Club Hut*

Grade K Leveled Readers

Social Studies

Citizenship

Nonfiction Books

• *Fun for Us*
• *Nick the Fix-It Man*
• *The Box*

Fiction Books

• *Red and Blue*
• *We Have Fun Together*
• *Two or Three?*
• *Buds for Mom*
• *Ming on the Job*

Culture

Nonfiction Books

• *Homes*

Fiction Books

• *Max the Duck*
• *Five Bears*
• *My Walk in Antarctica*
• *The Bus Ride*
• *The Boat Ride*
• *Get On the Bus!*
• *Our Camping Trip*

History

Fiction Books

• *The Big Train*

Geography

Nonfiction Books

• *A Trip to Washington, D.C.*

Matching Books & Readers

Connecting Science and Social Studies

Grade 1 Leveled Readers

Science

Earth and Space Science

Nonfiction Books
- All About the Weather
- The Communication Story
- Over the Years
- Ready for Winter?
- Using the Telephone

Fiction Books
- Cody's Adventure
- Marla's Good Idea
- What a Detective Does

Life Science

Nonfiction Books
- All About Food Chains
- Animals Change and Grow
- Around the Forest
- Around the World
- Baby Animals in the Rain Forest
- Bees and Beekeepers
- The Dinosaur Detectives
- The Dinosaur Herds
- Fun in the Sun
- Honey
- In My Room
- Learn About Butterflies
- Learn About Worker Bees
- Let's Go to the Zoo
- Let's Visit a Butterfly Greenhouse
- Look at Dinosaurs
- A Mighty Oak Tree
- Monarchs Migrate South
- People Help the Forest
- The Seasons Change
- Seasons Come and Go
- What Animals Can You See?

Life Science

Fiction Books
- Bix the Dog
- Britton Finds a Kitten
- Carlos Picks a Pet
- Cary and the Wildlife Shelter
- Mac Can Do It!
- Mack and Zack
- Plans Change
- Sam
- The Sick Pets
- Time for Dinner
- What Brown Saw
- Which Animals Will We See?
- Which Fox?

Physical Science

Nonfiction Books
- The Inclined Plane
- Simple Machines at Work
- Simple Machines in Compound Machines

Grade 1 Leveled Readers

Social Studies

Citizenship

Nonfiction Books

- *A Class*
- *A Garden for All*
- *Great Scientists: Detectives at Work*
- *Here in My Neighborhood*
- *A New Library*
- *Puppy Raiser*
- *The Story of the Kids Care Club*
- *Ways to Be a Good Citizen*

Fiction Books

- *The Art Show*
- *At Your Vet*
- *Big Wishes and Her Baby*
- *Double Trouble Twins*
- *Fly Away Owl!*
- *Grasshopper and Ant*
- *Hank's Song*
- *Let's Build a Park!*
- *Look at My Neighborhood*
- *My Little Brother Drew*
- *On the Farm*
- *Paul's Bed*
- *A Play*
- *Rules at School*
- *Space Star*
- *Squirrel and Bear*
- *That Cat Needs Help!*

Culture

Nonfiction Books

- *Cascarones Are for Fun*
- *My Babysitter*
- *Special Days, Special Food*
- *We Are a Family*
- *What Makes Buildings Special?*

Fiction Books

- *Go West!*
- *Grandma's Farm*
- *Gus the Pup*
- *Jamie's Jumble of Junk*
- *A New Baby Brother*
- *A Party for Pedro*
- *A Visit to the Ranch*
- *Where They Live*

History

Nonfiction Books

- *School: Then and Now*
- *Treasures of Our Country*

Fiction Books

- *Loni's Town*

Government

Nonfiction Books

- *America's Home*
- *Our Leaders*

Fiction Books

- *Mom the Mayor*

Matching Books & Readers

Planning Teacher Study Groups

Adventurous teachers often have good ideas for lessons. A teacher study group is a great way to share ideas and get feedback on the best way to connect content and students. Working with other teachers can provide you with the support and motivation you need to implement new teaching strategies. A teacher study group offers many opportunities to collaborate, support each other's work, share insights, and get feedback.

Think About It

A weekly or monthly teacher study group can help support you in developing your expertise in the classroom. You and a group of like-minded teachers can form your own study group. What can this group accomplish?

- Read and discuss professional articles by researchers in the field of education.

- Meet to share teaching tips, collaborate on multi-grade lessons, and share resources.

- Develop lessons to try out new teaching strategies. Meet to share experiences and discuss how to further improve your teaching approach.

Let's Meet!

Forming a study group is easy. Just follow these four steps:

1. **Decide on the size of the group.** A small group has the advantage of making each member feel accountable, but make sure that all people can make the same commitment!

2. **Choose teachers to invite to join your group.** Think about whom you want to invite. Should they all teach the same grade? Can you invite teachers from other schools? Remember that the more diverse the group, the more it benefits from new perspectives.

3. **Set goals for the group.** In order to succeed, know what you want the group to do. Meet to set goals. Rank goals in order of importance and refer often to the goals to keep the group on track.

4. **Make logistical decisions.** This is often the most difficult. Decide where and when you will meet. Consider an online meeting place where group members can post discussion questions and replies if people are not able to meet.

What Will We Study?

Use the goals you set to help determine what your group will study. Consider what materials are needed to reach your goals, and how long you think you will need to prepare for each meeting.

How Will It Work?

Think about how you structure groups in your classroom. Use some of the same strategies.

- **Assign a group facilitator.** This person is responsible for guiding the meeting. This person comes prepared with discussion questions and leads the meeting. This could be a rotating responsibility dependent on experience with various topics. This person might be responsible for providing the materials.

- **Assign a recorder.** Have someone take notes during the meeting and record group decisions.

- **Use the jigsaw method.** Not everyone has time to be a facilitator. In this case, divide the text and assign each portion to a different person. Each person is responsible for leading the discussion on that particular part.

Meet Again

Make a commitment to meet for a minimum number of times. After that, the group can reevaluate and decide whether or not to continue.

" Have some great teaching tips to share? Want to exchange ideas with your colleagues? Build your own professional community of teachers. **Customize Literacy** gets you started. "

Trial Lessons

Use your colleagues' experiences to help as you think about new ways to connect content and students. Use the following plan to create a mini-lesson. It should last twenty minutes. Get the support of your colleagues as you try something new, and then reflect on what happened.

Be Creative! As you develop a plan for a mini-lesson, use these four words to guide planning: *purpose*, *text*, *resources*, and *routine*.

- **Purpose:** Decide on a skill or strategy to cover. Define your purpose for teaching the lesson.

- **Text:** Develop a list of the materials you could use. Ask your colleagues for suggestions.

- **Resources:** Make a list of the available resources, and consider how to use those resources most effectively. Consider using the leveled readers listed on pages CL16–CL17 and CL22–CL25 of Customize Literacy.

- **Routine:** Choose an instructional routine to structure your mini-lesson. See the mini-lessons in Customize Literacy for suggestions.

Try It! Try out your lesson! Consider audio- or videotaping the lesson for later review. You may wish to invite a colleague to sit in as you teach. Make notes on how the lesson went.

How Did It Go? Use the self-evaluation checklist on page CL29 as you reflect on your trial lesson. This provides a framework for later discussion.

Discuss, Reflect, Repeat Solicit feedback from your teacher study group. Explain the lesson and share your reflections. Ask for suggestions on ways to improve the lesson. Take some time to reflect on the feedback. Modify your lesson to reflect what you have learned. Then try teaching the lesson again.

Checklist for Teacher Self-Evaluation

How Well Did I ...

How Well Did I ...	Very Well	Satisfactory	Not Very Well
Plan the lesson?			
Select the appropriate level of text?			
Introduce the lesson and explain its objectives?			
Review previously taught skills?			
Directly explain the new skills being taught?			
Model the new skills?			
Break the material down into small steps?			
Integrate guided practice into the lesson?			
Monitor guided practice for student understanding?			
Provide feedback on independent practice?			
Maintain an appropriate pace?			
Assess student understanding of the material?			
Stress the importance of applying the skill as they read?			
Maintain students' interest?			
Ask questions?			
Handle student questions and responses?			
Respond to the range of abilities?			

Building Community

Books for Teachers

Children aren't the only ones who need to read to grow. Here is a brief list of books that you may find useful to fill your reading teacher basket and learn new things.

A Professional Bibliography

Adams, M. J. "Alphabetic Anxiety and Explicit, Systematic Phonics Instruction: A Cognitive Science Perspective." *Handbook of Early Literacy Research.* The Guilford Press, 2001.

Adams, M. J. *Beginning to Read: Thinking and Learning About Print.* The MIT Press, 1990.

Afflerbach, P. "The Influence of Prior Knowledge and Text Genre on Readers' Prediction Strategies." *Journal of Reading Behavior,* vol. XXII, no. 2 (1990).

Armbruster, B. B., F. Lehr, and J. Osborn. *Put Reading First: The Research Building Blocks for Teaching Children to Read.* Partnership for Reading, Washington, D.C., 2001.

Bear, D. R., M. Invernizzi, S. Templeton, and F. Johnston. *Words Their Way.* Merrill Prentice Hall, 2004.

Beck, I., M. G. McKeown, and L. Kucan. *Bringing Words to Life: Robust Vocabulary Instruction.* The Guilford Press, 2002.

Biemiller, A. "Teaching Vocabulary in the Primary Grades: Vocabulary Instruction Needed." *Vocabulary Instruction Research to Practice.* The Guilford Press, 2004.

Blachowicz, C. and P. Fisher. "Vocabulary Instruction." *Handbook of Reading Research,* vol. III. Lawrence Erlbaum Associates, 2000.

Cunningham, P. M. and J. W. Cunningham. "What We Know About How to Teach Phonics." *What Research Says About Reading Instruction,* 3rd ed. International Reading Association, 2002.

Daniels, H. *Literature Circles.* 2nd ed. Stenhouse Publishers, 2002.

Dickson, S. V., D. C. Simmons, and E. J. Kame'enui. "Text Organization: Instructional and Curricular Basics and Implications." *What Reading Research Tells Us About Children with Diverse Learning Needs: Bases and Basics.* Lawrence Erlbaum Associates, 1998.

Diller, D. *Making the Most of Small Groups: Differentiation for All.* Stenhouse Publishers, 2007.

Duke, N. K., V. S. Bennett-Armistead, and E. M. Roberts. "Bridging the Gap Between Learning to Read and Reading to Learn." *Literacy and Young Children: Research-Based Practices.* The Guilford Press, 2003.

Duke, N. K. and C. Tower. "Nonfiction Texts for Young Readers." *The Texts in Elementary Classrooms.* Lawrence Erlbaum Associates, 2004.

Ehri, L. C. and S. R. Nunes. "The Role of Phonemic Awareness in Learning to Read." *What Research Has to Say About Reading Instruction.* 3rd ed. International Reading Association, 2002.

Fountas, I. C. and G. S. Pinnell. *Guided Reading: Good First Teaching for All Children.* Heinemann, 1996.

Fountas, I. C. and G. S. Pinnell. *Matching Books to Readers: Using Leveled Books in Guided Reading, K-3.* Heinemann, 1999.

Harvey, S. and A. Goudvis. *Strategies That Work: Teaching Comprehension to Enhance Understanding.* 2nd ed. Stenhouse Publishers, 2007.

Hiebert, E. H. and L. A. Martin. "The Texts of Beginning Reading Instruction." *Handbook of Early Literacy Research.* The Guilford Press, 2001.

Indrisano, R. and J. R. Paratore. *Learning to Write, Writing to Learn. Theory and Research in Practice.* International Reading Association, 2005.

Juel, C., G. Biancarosa, D. Coker, and R. Deffes. "Walking with Rosie: A Cautionary Tale of Early Reading Instruction." *Educational Leadership* (April 2003).

National Reading Panel. *Teaching Children to Read.* National Institute of Child Health and Human Development, 1999.

Pressley, M. *Reading Instruction That Works: The Case for Balanced Teaching,* 3rd ed. The Guilford Press, 2005.

Smith, S., D. C. Simmons, and E. J. Kame'enui. "Word Recognition: Research Bases." *What Reading Research Tells Us About Children with Diverse Learning Needs: Bases and Basics.* Lawrence Erlbaum Associates, 1998.

Snow, C., S. Burns, and P. Griffin, eds. *Preventing Reading Difficulties in Young Children.* National Academy Press, 1998.

Vaughn, S., P. G. Mathes, S. Linan-Thompson, and D. J. Francis. "Teaching English Language Learners at Risk for Reading Disabilities to Read: Putting Research into Practice." *Learning Disabilities Research & Practice,* vol. 20, issue 1 (February 2006).

Acknowledgments

Acknowledgments

Illustrations
Cover: Rob Hefferan
12 Amanda Haley
28–29, 49, 68, 108, 112 Anthony Lewis
32 Jannie Ho
39–45 Natalia Vasquez
50 Karen Stormer Brooks
52 Ron Lieser
59–65 Maria Mola
70–71 Martha Aviles
72 Stephen Lewis
79–85 Cale Atkinson
90 Ivanke & Lola
92 Jamie Smith
99–105 Dani Jones
110–111 Constanza Basaluzzo
119–125 Robbie Short
130–151 Cecilia Rebora

Photographs
Every effort has been made to secure permission and provide appropriate credit for photographic material. The publisher deeply regrets any omission and pledges to correct errors called to its attention in subsequent editions.

Unless otherwise acknowledged, all photographs are the property of Pearson Education, Inc.

Photo locators denoted as follows: Top (T), Center (C), Bottom (B), Left (L), Right (R), Background (Bkgd)

10 (B) ©Ralf Gerard/Getty Images
30 (T) ©Digital Focus/Alamy
31 (T) ©Royalty-Free/Corbis
45 ©David R. Frazier PhotoLibrary, Inc./Alamy Images, ©Enigma/Alamy Images, ©Visions of America, LLC/Alamy Images
88 ©David Young-Wolff/PhotoEdit, Inc., ©Jeff Greenberg/Alamy Images, ©Tim Mantoani/Masterfile Corporation, ©Blend Images/Jupiter Images
128 Frank Greenaway/©DK Images, Geoff Brightling/©DK Images, Tim Ridley/©DK Images.

144

Teacher Editions

KWL Strategy: The KWL Interactive Reading Strategy was developed and is used by permission of Donna Ogle, National-Louis University, Skokie, Illinois, co-author of *Reading Today and Tomorrow*, Holt, Rinehart & Winston Publishers, 1988. (See also the *Reading Teacher*, February 1986, pp. 564–570.)

Understanding by Design quotes: Wiggins, G. & McTighe, J. (2005). *Understanding by Design.* Alexandria, VA: Association for Supervision and Curriculum Development.

Illustrations

Cover Rob Hefferan

Running Header Steven Mach

Photos

Every effort has been made to secure permission and provide appropriate credit for photographic material. The publisher deeply regrets any omission and pledges to correct errors called to its attention in subsequent editions.

Unless otherwise acknowledged, all photographs are the property of Pearson Education, Inc.

Teacher Resources

Looking for Teacher Resources and other important information?

In the **First Stop** on Reading Street

- Dear Kindergarten Teacher

- Research into Practice on Reading Street

- Guide to Reading Street

- Assessment on Reading Street

- Writing on Reading Street

- Differentiate Instruction on Reading Street

- ELL on Reading Street

- Customize Literacy on Reading Street

- Digital Products on Reading Street

- Teacher Resources for Kindergarten

- Index

Teacher Resources

Looking for Teacher Resources and other important information?

In the **First Stop** on Reading Street

- Dear Kindergarten Teacher

- Research into Practice on Reading Street

- Guide to Reading Street

- Assessment on Reading Street

- Writing on Reading Street

- Differentiate Instruction on Reading Street

- ELL on Reading Street

- Customize Literacy on Reading Street

- Digital Products on Reading Street

- Teacher Resources for Kindergarten

- Index